MUSICAL PRODIGIES

Glenn Gould at thirteen, with his dog, Nicky (Sir Nickolson of Garelocheed), Toronto, 1946. Photograph by Gordon W. Powley. By permission of the Estate of Glenn Gould.

MUSICAL PRODIGIES

Perilous Journeys, Remarkable Lives

BY

CLAUDE KENNESON

Amadeus Press
Reinhard G. Pauly, General Editor
Portland, Oregon

AMADEUS PRESS
The Haseltine Building
133 SW Second Avenue, Suite 450
Portland, Oregon 97204 USA

Printed in Hong Kong

Library of Congress Cataloging-in-Publication Data

Kenneson, Claude.
Musical prodigies : perilous journeys, remarkable lives / by Claude
Kenneson
    p.   cm.
Includes bibliographical references (p.   ) and index.
ISBN 1-57467-046-8
1. Child musicians. 2. Gifted children. 3. Musicians—Biography. I. Title.
ML81.K46   1999
780′.87′9—dc21   98-28636
                                                                        CIP
                                                                        MN

To Horace Britt (1881–1971)

Genial and dimpling, looking for all the world like an instrumental Peter Pan who would never consent to grow up, Horace Britt played the Saint-Saëns concerto, played it with a masterly urbanity and an irreproachable technique.

Redfern Mason
San Francisco Examiner
17 March 1928

Contents

Part Two: The Innovators

Foreword

THE twentieth century has produced many startling scientific observations of children and their creative aptitudes. When asked about their future goals and ambitions, many small children will offer answers exhibiting extraordinary vision, remarkable intuition, and unusual prescience. Such children are old in the most wonderful sense. They are amazingly aware of the world at an early age. In addition to their incredible thirst for knowledge, they often have the ability to discern the difference between truth and façade. The possible peril that exceptional children face is that their natural wonder and oldness are in danger of being dashed by time and improper guardianship.

So much depends on their good fortune to be properly nurtured. And yet, it is a very thought-provoking and difficult responsibility to educate the child who is mature in a way unrelated to chronological age. It is no accident that so much of today's young talent blossoms in countries where the educational system imposes the study of music and gives emphasis to that delicate balance between matter and spirit.

To be sure, the conservatories whose names weave through these stories were ruled with an iron discipline that gave their students strength, and in today's world we need to offer children the guidelines for structuring their own inner architecture—hence, connecting with what Bejun Mehta calls our Muse world.

We should not aspire to create the virtuoso. Every artist fortunate enough to have a career undergoes the strengthening experiences of self-motivation and self-discipline. As Claude Kenneson understands so well, we are not training a prodigy; instead, we are nurturing a soul who in turn will inspire us all.

—VAN CLIBURN

Preface

I WAS A gifted child but certainly not a prodigy. There is a vast difference between the two. One is sometimes remarkable, the other always phenomenal, startling to witness. I was only ten years old when I first met a genuine prodigy—a child capable of extraordinary, early achievement—but I knew intuitively upon hearing Abraham Chavez play that the great violinist he was to become had already been forged. Of course I had no idea how this had come about, and even after a lifetime of intimate friendship I do not completely understand the unfolding of his childhood as a prodigy. Yet I never cease to be amazed when I hear in his playing the trace elements of the radiant child he once was. Even as he enters his sixth decade as a violinist, he retains his gamin quality.

I recall waiting to hear Yehudi Menuhin in a recital in Mexico—I was an excited youngster; he must have been in his thirties. Knowing that this famous violinist had been a prodigy, I was eager to see a similarity between Yehudi and Abraham, but when Menuhin began playing Tartini's sonata, "Devil's Trill," I realized instantly that these two violinists stood far apart from each other even though life had dealt each a fateful, precocious childhood. Each was unique. They played the violin in completely different ways, each making music according to his own physical prowess, intellect, and sensibility. It was also true that one was famous while the other was not-so-famous, but this distinction held no great significance for me then or now.

During that recital so long ago I was in no way disappointed in Menuhin's artistry; however, I was more than surprised that he got off to a troubled start before an exuberant, unusually noisy audience. When the stage lights flashed unexpectedly during the Tartini sonata, Menuhin was startled but continued playing. Although he was obviously unsettled, he quickly hit his stride and astounded everyone with his performance. In my naiveté I had assumed that all such Promethean violinists invariably played to perfection regardless of unexpected circumstances. To me it was a valuable lesson to learn that grownup prodigies are subject to human foibles. It made Yehudi Menuhin seem all the more significant for being entirely believable.

In 1972 when Menuhin listened to his own vintage performance of Elgar's Violin Concerto, captured on disc in London in 1932 when he was barely sixteen, he commented on his wonder years:

> Two separate sensations are evoked in me: one, the memory of a child grappling with an intransigent violin and finding an enormous sense of fulfillment and self expression, of a totality of purpose, challenge, and idea; the other of a continuum such a vocation brings, of being in a certain measure still that same child only with added dimensions—as a sapling which can only grow into a tree, a plant that cannot alter its basic organism.[1]

The phenomenon of the musical prodigy is endlessly fascinating, and fortunately articulate musicians often feel compelled to talk about their wonder years, which they may do with eloquent candor. For me, the opportunity to ponder their stories and those of prodigies past continues a lifelong interest. As I set out to write this book I revisited the formative thoughts and experiences of my own life as a cellist and teacher blessed with gifted students, among them several prodigies. What is my firsthand experience, my experiential knowledge as a teacher? What can these stories tell us? I hope that readers of all ages will find in these accounts something useful and inspiring, as I have. At the very least I would celebrate the perilous, glorious journeys of prodigies in music.

Acknowledgments

I thank Nadia Koutzen, Evelyn Glennie, Kató Havas, Gary Karr, Bejun Mehta, Zara Nelsova, Aldo Parisot, and Shauna Rolston for speaking to me so generously about their childhoods.

I express my gratitude to David Henry Feldman, author of *Nature's Gambit*, whose research in developmental psychology offers everyone the possibility of a deeper understanding of the phenomenon of the child prodigy.

Acknowledgment with appreciation is also made to the scholars and biographers Emily Anderson, Herbert R. Axelrod, David Blum, Margaret Campbell, Joan Chissell, G. I. C. de Courcy, Robin Daniel, Carol Easton, David Ewen, Renee Fisher, Otto Friedrich, Barbara B. Heyman, Seymour W. Itzkoff, H. L. Kirk, Robert Magidoff, Helen Matheopoulos, Geoffrey Payzant, Howard Reich, Nancy B. Reich, Claude Samuel, Maynard Solomon, Yakov Soroker, and Artur Weschler-Vered, and to the late Nathan Broder, Lev Ginsburg, and Boris Schwarz.

I am grateful to Lorand Fenyves, Seymour W. Itzkoff, Yo-Yo Ma, Ruggiero Ricci, Mstislav Rostropovich, and János Starker for their contributions; to Patrick Gallois for his remarks on the legacy of Georges Barrère; to Deborah Thackery-Tyers for reading the story of Evelyn Glennie's childhood; and to Todd Jones and Thomas von Stackelberg for the restoration of photographs.

Acknowledgment of permission to republish documentary materials is made to the following among many contributors: Harper Collins for Iris du Pré's essay "Born for the Cello"; Doubleday, a division of Bantam Doubleday Dell Publishing Group, Inc., for permission to reprint a photograph of Gregor Piatigorsky; SYM Music Company, Ltd., for permission to reprint a photograph of Lord Menuhin; the Estate of Glenn Gould; the Primrose International Viola Archive; and Scala/Art Resource, New York.

CLAUDE KENNESON
Edmonton

PROLOGUE

"It was all fun when I was little!" Shauna Rolston at an early cello lesson.

A Personal View

Although I felt grownup inside, I was still a child when I came under the influence of my greatest teacher, the Belgian cellist Horace Britt, who like his friend Pablo Casals had been a celebrated nineteenth-century prodigy. When I began my work with him I was a teenager; he was by then seventy-two, a wise, loving, and optimistic mentor. I was desperate to learn but often frustrated that I couldn't fathom the subtlety of his unique cello playing by the sheer power of my adolescent will. Until I studied with him I had mistakenly imagined that the right teacher could just tell me what to do, that great teaching was based entirely on rational knowledge freely shared. His teaching proved otherwise, for he proceeded intuitively, believing that the transfer of knowledge would result from an indirect process of intellectual absorption, "a kind of musical osmosis." Like Leopold Auer, the violin teacher of Heifetz, Elman, and Zimbalist, Britt often seemed to know more than he could tell. Later I learned from Michael Polanyi that knowing more than one can tell is a natural state when the ideas to be conveyed are simply beyond words.

As I developed my own approach to teaching music to children, I had no intention of abandoning the traditional values of such masters as Horace Britt, Pierre Fournier, and Pablo Casals, but I wanted to investigate new trends and other models that might be helpful. I wanted to know more about Shinichi Suzuki's bold advance in Japan that by 1965 had set more than 150,000 modern Asian children in motion playing the violin at age three. I was also drawn to the astounding teaching of violinist Kató Havas, whose pedagogical ideas, so well conveyed in her early book, *A New Approach to Violin Playing*, were helping redirect the learning of a legion of violinists of all ages and abilities in the western world.

I crossed disciplinary lines to investigate thinkers outside the circle of great musicians, including Carl Jung ("If we stick to one field of experience only, it is not really possible to see clearly what is happening. It is not a matter of a single thrust aimed at one definite spot") and Maria Montessori ("The child who lives in an environment created by adults often lives in a world ill-adapted to his own needs . . . repressed by a more powerful adult who undercuts his will and constrains him"). I sought evaluation of my work from Dr. Frances Hellebrandt, a forward-looking behavioral scientist who always delivered new ideas but sometimes answered my question with a question ("Is it the teaching that is uninspired, or is it the approach that is self-defeating because it overrides the laws which regulate the machinery of the living body?").

In 1974 while writing my book, *A Cellist's Guide to the New Approach*, I attempted to express obscure pedagogical concepts simply—to reveal a unified approach to cello playing and music-making that was open, questing, spontaneous, and joyful. I was encouraged by Yehudi Menuhin, who wrote to me: "I feel certain that it is a most valuable contribution to the cellist's development and no doubt also the solution to any problems that beset older children."[1]

I had looked beyond the picture of a fuzzy tennis ball on the cover of athlete Tim Gallwey's sensational new book, *The Inner Game of Tennis*, to discover a treasure of imaginative innovations. As we became familiar with each other's work, Tim later wrote to me, "It was exciting and helpful to see in your book the same realizations expressed in another style for another kind of performance."

> It strengthened my convictions that a new understanding of self—of who we really are—can be helped along by the way various skills are taught. It is easy in this culture to be involved in cello, tennis, business, housework, without ever recognizing the purpose of human life. If that question is confronted, and answered, and then pursued, all else really fits into place. I feel that musical potential suffers greatly at the tongues of those childhood teachers who tell "how to" and "how not to" do everything. Furthermore, music is such a natural medium for exploring the inner game that it could lead many to the music within from which all music comes.[2]

When I was studying to become a teacher, Horace Britt's former student and brilliant colleague, Phyllis Young, had admonished us to be vigilant, explaining that a young pupil might enter our lives whose intelligence, talent, and amazing early achievement could well exceed our own and demand that we accept a staggering responsibility. Of course, she spoke of the child prodigy—tomorrow's great performer as yet undiscovered.

In 1960, after I had taught cello for almost a decade, just such a child entered my life. He was the eleven-year-old prodigy Eric Wilson. For the next six years Eric and I reveled in each other's company as we underwent a metamorphosis, he growing rapidly into a young artist and I becoming the empathetic teacher of a musical genius. By way of introduction to the stories of other musical prodigies who have captured my imagination, I would first share two personal accounts: that of Eric, my first prodigy student, and the story of Shauna Rolston, whose life I have had the privilege and joy of watching at close range to this day.

ERIC

Teaching Eric Wilson was a time of exquisite sharing that soon expanded beyond the two of us and Eric's family to other teachers and audiences. His childhood triumphs in Winnipeg, for fifty years the cradle such Canadian cello prodigies as Zara Nelsova and Lorne Munroe, generated excitement in ever-widening circles. When at fourteen Eric won the Aikens Memorial Trophy at the Manitoba Music Festival, the English adjudicator James Gibbs remarked: "His mastery is quite extraordinary considering his tender years. He is a natural cellist with an all-around grasp of style and feeling. There was real grandeur in his playing of Bach and Davidov. His cello playing spoke straight to the heart."[3]

Eric's early recitals and his debut as soloist with orchestra playing the Saint-Saëns concerto intensified my enthusiasm for his cello playing, and soon I arranged interviews for him with Pablo Casals and Leonard Rose. Such pivotal meetings were always followed by exciting long-distance telephone calls from the young cellist informing me of his successful playing for these supreme cellists.

"I am glad that I am a cellist because it has provided a remarkable life adventure for me," Eric once said, but he added:

When I was a child in Winnipeg, I attended the first through the ninth grade in a public school where there was absolutely no facility for a musical education. Fortunately, I was a member of a musical family. My case was exceptional. I did receive a musical education.

If I had the opportunity to relive the period of my early training in some different way than it actually happened, I would like to have had less isolation from my peers, from those children who shared so many things about my school life, but did not share the music-making simply because they were offered no opportunity to do so.[4]

Eric's mother frequently found him sitting on a curb near the school grounds daydreaming of being elsewhere, perhaps in a place where he would have friends his own age but who, like him, would be caught up in music's magic. This place he eventually found when he was sixteen and became a pupil of Leonard Rose at the Juilliard School.

After 1966 Eric was absent from my everyday life, absorbed in his great adventure in New York City. Leonard Rose wrote, "Eric is a brilliant cello talent. He is very advanced technically and is extremely musical and sensitive and should become one of our great cellists."[5] I followed Eric's success at every turn as he won Juilliard's Morris Loeb Prize for outstanding achievement in cello, gave the New York premieres of Peter Maxwell Davies' *Icons* and the cello concerto of György Ligeti, an avant-garde work he had pursued on his own and first performed in Europe with the Jeunesses Musicales World Orchestra. Assisted by his mother, the chamber music pianist Thelma Wilson, Eric distinguished himself in Geneva as a bronze medalist at the 1971 Concours International d'Exécution Musicale. He was the only North American out of sixty-three performers to be recognized at this international competition.

Eric crossed a new threshold in 1972. He was studying chamber music at Juilliard with Robert Mann when he cofounded the Emerson String Quartet. A new string quartet of such promise is a thing of wonder; only six years later in New York, the Emerson Quartet won the coveted Naumburg Award and immediately captured the interest of composers.

In 1979 at a concert in Berkeley I sat beside composer Gunther Schuller to hear the Emerson Quartet perform his Quartet No. 2. At the climax of the finale we both gasped when Eric turned to his last page and found it missing, accidentally left behind in his hotel room. Sensing disaster, Schuller and I gripped our chairs white knuckled, but we need not have worried. With complete assurance, the young cellist surged onward to the final chords, playing easily from memory. He was a musician!

His successful weathering of the process notwithstanding, I had vowed that the gifted young musicians around me would no longer embark on their journeys without the peers they needed. By the summer of 1979, young cellists from across Canada gathered at The Banff Center's School of Fine Arts for its new program, Special Studies for Gifted Youth. When these precocious children, many of them prodigies, came together for a few weeks of study under my direction, they established what would become long-lasting friendships, returning to Banff year after year during the summers of their childhoods. Now, almost twenty years later, when the young artists meet on the concert circuit, their conversations often turn to recollections of their wonder years and the joy of being together, then and now.

SHAUNA

As I left Hertz Hall at the University of California that night of Eric's concert, my thoughts turned homeward to a child who would be awaiting my return to Canada. By then, Eric was not the only amazing prodigy in my life: I was preparing eleven-year-old Shauna Rolston for her first audition with Leonard Rose. Recently I went back to a loop of videotape that portrays a very special moment years earlier: a lovely little girl playing her cello, filmed by the University of Alberta's Department of Radio and Television during Cello Symposium 71. I was glad to see that in the film I don't tower with my own cello over the winsome four-year-old but sit comfortably beside her on a cushion as we talk and play. The extraordinary child was Shauna appearing in her first television production.

This is the story of her precocious childhood.

On a blustery winter's day in Canada in 1967, Shauna entered the world blessed with perfect health. She was born in Edmonton on 31 January that year, the only child of my trio partners, the outstanding musicians Isobel and Thomas Rolston. Shortly after Tom called to tell me the good news, I met the exuberant new father at the maternity ward. We celebrated the miracle of this new life with Isobel, a high-spirited Scottish lass blissful in motherhood; then he and I went to the hospital nursery where we excitedly pressed against the wall of glass to see Shauna.

As I stared awe-struck at the infant, Tom spoke wistfully of her future. "I immediately thought of two things," he recalled. "She should have a musical discipline and she should learn to speak French." On hearing this my spirits soared. "Let me teach her the cello!" I said without a moment's hesitation.[6] In that moment of profound trust, the first thought of Shauna's life as a cellist emerged as her father and I watched her slumber.

Earlier in 1965, Tom had traveled to Matsumoto, Japan, to consult with Shinichi Suzuki. He returned home convinced that he would introduce Suzuki's new movement to Canada in an effort to bolster our country's dwindling number of young violin pupils. This he did, and soon a cello class was created as well, the youngsters taught by my university cello students.

When Shauna began playing the cello at two-and-a-half years old in 1969, there was already in place a social framework for her peer support since a primary objective was to prevent any isolation of these youngsters from each other and from the culture in which they thrived. "It was a very happy, secure sort of beginning," Shauna has recalled. "All my friends who were three or four were playing cello, too—so for me it was very normal." From that beginning, Shauna's life as a cellist developed in a positive, unpressured atmosphere of childhood music-making. We ensured that the initial focus was not necessarily on her being able to play a nice tune, but rather that cello playing become an integrated and reliable aspect of her life.

When tiny Shauna arrived at my studio for her first lesson on Saturday morning, 20 September 1969, it appeared to me that she had come to stay. With her was her father, a little camp stool, a new music book, her favorite blue blanket, and a perfect miniature cello made especially for her by Henry Stroppel, a kindly Swiss-Canadian furniture maker who had turned to violin making during his retirement in Edmonton. This first cello was pivotal in Shauna's early, rapid achievement. It was an instrument that would have been a godsend in earlier times when gifted young pupils struggled with huge instruments, cellos far too large for their physical capabilities.

She began the first lesson by tracing an outline of her left hand as I had done at my own first lesson. The little art work is treasured still. The tracing is a touching reminder of that toddler's dexterous left hand that was soon acting out musical ideas on the cello with great agility. Shauna was marvelously coordinated. Her right hand, with its deft sense of touch, showed the promise of an unusual talent for bowing. Not one word passed between us as I molded her pliable little bowing hand into an acceptable shape. She quickly and efficiently refined that shape as the music began to make its inevitable demands, guiding her cello bow with a light, elegant touch. Within a year she drew a tone pure as crystal from her little cello whose strings were tuned to viola pitch. Watching Shauna perform today in the world's great concert halls, I recognize that signature bow hold, essentially unaltered since her early lessons.

With her gentle child's voice Shauna began to express herself in song, an indication of the growth of her musicianship. Perhaps Shauna's lyrical gift, which continues to characterize her performances of works like the Schumann concerto, came from her mother, who often sang old folk songs beautifully while accompanying herself on the Irish harp at the conclusion of duo recitals with Tom. The little cellist quickly developed her inner voice as well, rhythmically projecting her musical ideas into agile cello playing. Although she was especially delighted when moving with considerable speed ("Song of

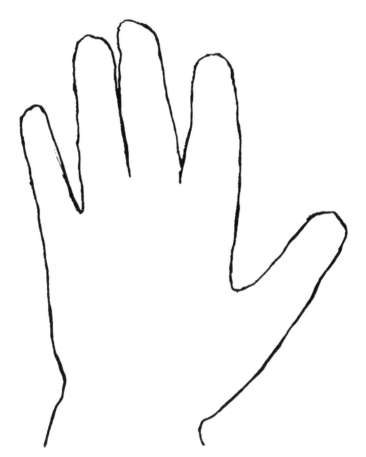

A tracing of Shauna's left hand from her first lesson in 1969. Courtesy the Rolston family.

the Wind" later gave way to the fleet scherzo of Elgar's concerto), we kept in balance the delicate equilibrium between her embryonic virtuosity and her emerging musicianship. A thoughtful learner, she had an astounding power of concentration and was never one to go far beyond even a slight musical misjudgment without a bold attempt at correction.

As her first year of study swept past, we continued in the studio to learn the great traditions of the past with a steady application of scales and arpeggios and daily studies. Favorite pieces were played in ensemble with other young cellists on weekends. This activity always included the element of play. "We would clap rhythms and play games with the bow," Shauna recalled. "I was just getting the feel of the instrument. And I remember winning cookies and gold stars!"

Commitment and obsession in the life of a wonder child are sometimes separated by a very thin line. Knowing this, Isobel and Tom assured Shauna a normal home life generously filled with love, but thoroughly disciplined. She would not end up like the Hungarian prodigy pianist Erwin Nyiregyházi, who at eighteen was still unable to tie his own shoes, feed or dress himself, let alone make career decisions on his own. Shauna learned to look after her own possessions. She took care of her cat Susie, an intrepid feline determined to demonstrate her possession of nine lives. While Shauna learned the alphabet at home, she simultaneously learned to read music. "My Mom took a Kleenex box and filled it with cards. On the cards were notes and on the back were the names. I quickly learned these things as a matter of course."

Wise decisions were made daily about Shauna's welfare and happiness. She was allowed to wear her new patent leather shoes to kindergarten one day simply because she found them beautiful and they were after all meant to be enjoyed. When the time came for her to be picked up, she walked stiff-legged toward the car, placing one step carefully after the other. "Shauna, why are you walking so strangely?" Isobel asked. "I'm saving my new shoes!" came her confident answer; then they both laughed.

During the early years, Isobel, like all the mothers involved in Edmonton's Society for Talent Education, supervised Shauna's daily cello practice, and in a most natural way: "I made sure that she was holding the bow properly, sitting upright, that sort of thing. You know what children are like. You have to teach them how to use a knife and fork. You always have to remind them to put the cap back on the toothpaste." As engaging as Isobel's supervision was, the time came when it was necessary for Shauna to take charge of her own learning—to practice on her own. We gathered at the Rolston home on a sunny spring day, and after a good visit Isobel said, "Shauna, it's time for you to practice now. And today I think you should work by yourself." A rather subdued Shauna withdrew to her bedroom, a cheerful room peopled with stuffed animals, where the cello waited. To see the outcome of this important rite of passage, we sat quietly in the living room as the music began in the distance. Suddenly silence descended on the house, broken only by a plaintive voice that called out, "Somebody better come help me!" As difficult as it was, we all remained seated as Isobel reassured her. "You're doing well, Shauna. Just continue working for a while longer!" When the music began again, we knew that Shauna had embarked on one of the most difficult experiences any musician encounters: facing oneself in privacy each day for a period of serious problem-solving.

The better to take her place in Canada with its two official languages, she began to learn French at three, first at Le Colibri, a French-language kindergarten in Edmonton, then the following year at the Lycée Français in London where the family lived during her father's busy sabbatical year. A seasoned trooper at five, she went on tour with our string quartet in the summer of 1972, carrying her cello and her favorite blue blanket from London to the Island of Sark in the English Channel. At the Purbeck Festival in Dorset, she gave an impromptu performance at Langton Matravers as a guest of Kató Havas' Summer School. "Although my father had bought me a fancy dress," Shauna remembers,

I refused to wear it because I had a favorite yellow nightgown with long sleeves to which I was rather partial and considered perfectly suitable concert attire. Seated on an upturned waste paper basket, I suddenly realized that my nightgown was not cut wide enough for concert giving. There was no room for my cello. With a five-year-old's characteristic lack of inhibition—Whoosh!—and the nightgown was over my head and the problem solved.

As George Willey reported in *The Strad*, "One of the delights of the Purbeck Festival was the cello playing of five-year-old Shauna Rolston, daughter of one of Canada's foremost violinists, Thomas Rolston. Shauna's playing so enchanted her audience that she may well one day reach the same rare quality of artistry that Thomas Rolston brought to his performances."[7]

At five she began the first grade at Edmonton's l'École Grandin and continued to study in French at that fine elementary school until she was twelve.

As an adult she returned there to play for the enthusiastic bilingual students, many of whom study music. "My father and I played for my classmates at this school when I was in grade five. It was great to again be in that very special place where I grew up, where there is real interest in the lives of children. There they are nurtured."

An avid concertgoer, Shauna pursued her musical education not only in the studio and at home, but in the concert hall where she listened, watched, and learned. Although she was an ardent performer by six, her unusual talent, startling intelligence, and great sensibility to music was never exploited. We assured her ample time to serve her apprenticeship, and any presumed responsibility to the talent she may have inherited from her performing parents went undiscussed. It was only later when she easily learned Locatelli's sonata with its quixotic staccato bowing—a bugaboo for most adult cellists—that my amazement must have shown itself. "I guess it is in my genes," Shauna explained to me. "My Dad can *really* do this!" she said, unleashing a torrent of brilliant, short notes.

Upon the family's return to Canada from London in 1972, her parents wisely limited her public performances and she never regarded herself as a child prodigy in the usual sense. "The plot thickened when she became six and seven," her father said, "because we began playing as a trio. The whole point was to have her play with us so that she was talking and thinking in professional terms even though her cello parts were always simpler." The television studios of the Canadian Broadcasting Corporation held no fear for Shauna, who seemed always to understand systems, whether they were the basis of cello fingerings or academic achievement or somehow explained human nature. Once she experienced the bright lights and the incessant delays of television production, she was at home with the medium. She has remained so as an international recording artist.

Throughout her life as a cellist, Shauna has respected order and approached learning music in a responsible way. While young and totally occupied with her own development, Shauna's real task was to discover herself as a unique, separate, worthwhile individual in her own environment. Mastering the control of her own will and feelings, achieving a timely separation from her parents, and succeeding in early social relationships with peers were all appropriate and healthy preoccupations. A prodigy like Shauna may develop quite naturally as she plays music in her own way, unconcerned with destiny and protected from the stress of having constantly to achieve adult goals.

She conservatively built her repertoire over an extended period, moving gracefully from such traditional genre pieces as Squire's "Tarantella" and the sonatas of Breval and Vivaldi to ever more elaborate works, many written for her. As a mature artist she performs a vast repertoire according to the demands of her career, including a full spectrum of solo works and the complete ensemble music of Brahms, Mendelssohn, and others. "The music she learned as a child was treated as a gift," her father explained. "We called her new pieces 'presents' as we did a doll or a toy at Christmas. We would sit down for about four days and work through the new piece with great care for detail, and that would be her gift of that Schubert or Brahms trio *for life*."

Unlike many prodigies who seek recognition in the arena of performance competitions, Shauna never felt driven to compete in this way:

> When my friends from Banff who were Olympic athletes won gold medals in competition, I shared in their excitement and understood the significance, but as a young child I didn't feel the need to compare myself to other young cellists, and later it never even occurred to me that I would want to compete in an event like the Tchaikovsky Competition in Moscow. Music never meant that to me. Competition was not something I valued nor felt could define who I was as a musician.
>
> When I was six I played my first trio concert with my parents. At nine I gave my first full recital. When I reached eleven, all my friends were excited by the prospect of competitions and their enthusiasm made me curious. That year I did take part in my only competition.

Shauna entered and won in her class, emerging from the national Canadian Music Competition with the second highest marks in the nation, but having satisfied the urge to take part, she pursued competitions no further. Her musical life was by then richly designed. Not only did she study the cello, but from musicologist Brian Harris she learned music history and with composer Violet Archer she studied theory.

On 4 May 1978 Leonard Rose gave an unforgettable performance in Edmonton of Richard Strauss' *Don Quixote*, his first appearance following a serious bout with cancer, which robbed him of his life in 1984. The following morning before taking his plane to New York, he relaxed at the Rolston home to hear Shauna play. One of the world's revered teachers, Rose was responsible for the unfolding musical lives of prodigies Yo-Yo Ma, Lynn Harrell, and, somewhat later, Matt Heimovitz. Since he would never falsely encourage a young player, his opinion was greatly valued. After hearing Shauna play several works, he was deeply moved by the child's performance of "Reigen," the round dance from David Popper's "Im Walde" Suite. Throughout the rest of his life he continued to follow Shauna's artistic achievements with the happy prospect of someday teaching her. Later he compared my abiding commitment to her talent with his own great concern for Yo-Yo Ma and wrote, "Shauna is so remarkable in every way. I do hope to have the pleasure of working with this wonderful child."[8] In the intervening years, he often took time from his rigorous schedule to hear Shauna play, and while he was too ill by 1983 to hear her Town Hall debut in New York, he later listened with great pleasure to a taped recording of that recital.

On 25 November 1978, a few months after playing the first time for Leonard Rose, eleven-year-old Shauna made her hometown debut as soloist with orchestra, perhaps one of the most difficult feats for a prodigy no matter where it takes place, Paris or San Diego or Halifax. She performed *Symphonic Variations* by Léon Boëlmann with the Edmonton Symphony Orchestra. Her father conducted. The next day the press reported: "Her phrasing was elegant and graceful, then sonorous and sustained . . . expertly contrasted and articulated. She was sensitive and sympathetic at every turn."[9] While her technical prowess and masterful interpretation belied her age, on center stage of Edmonton's Jubilee Auditorium there perched a little golden-haired girl still in knee-length stockings. Playing on Eric Wilson's three-quarter-sized cello, the hardy instrument on which he himself had made his debut years earlier, she successfully projected her already sonorous, romantic tone above the orchestra, filling the cavernous concert hall. The deed was done. Shauna had become a concerto player and only a few years later was hailed by the Canadian press as "a national sensation . . . probably the finest young cellist Canada has produced since Zara Nelsova."

Soon after her debut, Shauna and her family moved to Banff in the Canadian Rockies, where her parents had become artistic directors of the School of Fine Arts at The Banff Centre. Shauna loved the mountains and her new-found friends, and her work continued seriously in the idyllic mountain retreat. During her first year in Banff, she refined the Saint-Saëns concerto we had begun studying earlier, working with The Banff Centre's distinguished guest teacher, Zara Nelsova, who soon became her loving mentor. As she finished her first master-class performance of the concerto with a sudden, strong flourish, an intense silence fell over the room, then a crash of applause as Nelsova rose from her chair, reached for Shauna, and touched her hand. "Beautiful," she uttered as they held hands for a moment, apprentice and master. Shauna participated regularly in The Banff Centre's cello master classes with Zara Nelsova, as well as with Aldo Parisot, János Starker, Tsuyoshi Tsutsumi, and Gabriel Magyar. At the Britten-Pears School at Aldeburgh in England she enjoyed a summer's work with William Pleeth, the teacher of English prodigy Jacqueline du Pré.

By fourteen Shauna had gained the approbation of many great cellists. As a final gesture to her childhood, I arranged for her to play for the French master Pierre Fournier. After hearing her perform the Concerto in C Major by Haydn and Fauré's *Élégie*, Fournier turned to me and said poignantly, "I've worked all my life on bow control. Just see what she can do already at fourteen!" The next summer she studied with him in Geneva, and in September he said, "Shauna deserves every success in the world by her exquisite personality as a cellist and great interpreter of every kind of music!"[10] Fournier's son, the celebrated pianist Jean Fonda, recalled: "In September 1982, listening to my father's master class in Geneva, a young, *very* young Canadian girl played, making a true impact on the listeners. There was a quality of tone and phrasing so natural, something not teachable, through everything she played."

> After the class I spoke to my father about this attractive-looking young girl: He smiled and said to me, "I knew you would fall for that kind of talent—she has it, don't you think?" Hearing so many young cellists, most of them brilliant instrumentalists, I cannot help thinking of her deeply committed playing, with a sonority straight from the heart, never forced, letting the music speak for and by itself. Without mentioning any names among her male or female colleagues, from the past or alive, she has this rare gem: projecting through a natural intensity without excessive vibrato or tonal histrionic approach![11]

> There was no perilous voyage for Shauna as she approached maturity. "I sailed through the potentially difficult transition from gifted child to adult musician because I was never marketed as a prodigy. I never felt like a wind-up toy," she said.

> It was disturbing to me that many people who didn't understand the prodigy phenomenon wanted to explain it in terms other than its

Shauna Rolston at fourteen, performing with the Calgary Philharmonic, 1981. Courtesy the Rolston family.

reality. By ten I was taking my responsibilities of being a musician totally seriously. How could I possibly be anything other than what I was at that moment? Why try to justify my reality at ten by wondering what I would be like if I were only eight or already fifteen? Nathan Milstein has recognized this syndrome, remarking that when he was very young reviewers pondered "what if" he were older and when he was eighty "what if" he were again twenty-five. In this they seem to have come full circle with their exercise in futility. At fourteen, I was told that I should "go to New York and *suffer* for my art." How absurd! Every life has its full share of suffering. Why seek out more?

One often wonders what becomes of a prodigy grown up. Shauna made her successful New York debut at Town Hall in 1983 assisted by her mother, the high-spirited Scottish lass *still* blissful in motherhood. In 1986 Shauna was the youngest recipient of a major award from Pro Musicis, an American foundation established by the Franciscan friar Eugene Merlet in 1965. In this role she was presented in glamorous, high-profile recitals in Boston, Los Angeles, Chicago, Washington, DC, New York, Paris, and Rome, but also in the unorthodox venues of addiction rehabilitation centers, psychiatric wards, jails, and juvenile detention centers where her ability to communicate herself and her music was always put to the test. "This was an important part of my life," she has explained.

It's an honest, grounding sort of experience to play for people who have no reason not to be themselves. They'll tell you if they hate it or if they love it. As the tough barriers are broken down, this audience often responds with genuine respect and enthusiasm.

I have always pretended that everyone in the audience is my friend. I find that for my concerts this kind of make-believe is comforting and bonds me to the audience. Carrying out the Pro Musicis projects in Europe where there was sometimes a language barrier proved to be even more challenging than those situations where English is spoken. In a psychiatric hospital in Rome we couldn't speak together easily, but this proved less important than the exchange in music. That very special audience was thrilled by the communication of the music itself.

At Yale University Shauna earned a distinguished Bachelor of Arts degree in art history and a Master of Music degree in performance all the while studying with Aldo Parisot and fulfilling concert engagements on four continents. For two years she was Parisot's much-admired teaching assistant on the New Haven campus and in New York the artistic director of a concert series she established at the Yale Club. At twenty-seven in the fall of 1994, she returned to Canada and like an extraordinary musical magnet attracted the largest cello class in Canada to the University of Toronto where she had become the new professor of cello. Whether in concerts, recordings, or broadcasts, she continues to perform with great authority. "An Elgarian for our time," media critic Joanne Talbot has called her. "Shauna Rolston is a name to watch for—her recording of Elgar's cello concerto is worthy to stand alongside Jacqueline du Pré's classic account. It could be the most remarkable performance of the last twenty years."[12]

Although Canada is home, Shauna is a cellist of international stature: the distinctive voice of her cello reverberates from New York to Tokyo.

In an ancient fresco in the cupola of the church of Santa Maria dei Miracoli in Saronno, twenty miles north of Milan, an angel dressed in a luminous blue robe plays a cello for all to see. Not all of the instrument's pegs are visible, and consequently the exact number of its strings cannot be determined, but that it is a cello there is no doubt. This earliest known portrayal of an authentic cello suggests that such instruments and their players were known in everyday life in northern Italy early in the sixteenth century.[13]

When Gaudenzio Ferrari painted the Saronno fresco in 1535, he may have known a little girl from this Italian village who played the cello almost five centuries ago. With down-turned eyes and pensive expression, noble high brow crowned with luxurious ringlets, the blue angel is evocative. Imagine the child in motion—her pudgy left hand moving along the strings, her deft bow strokes conjuring the voice of her primitive cello. One can almost hear her playing a Renaissance bass line. Was she a supernatural creation of Ferrari's imagination or the artist's model merely holding the cello as an angelic prop? Was she a genuine cellist? Perhaps she was the village prodigy. We will never know. The blue angel in Ferrari's fresco is enigmatic. She represents yet another beginning of a human endeavor shrouded in mystery.

Since the time of Ferrari's blue angel, at least twenty-five generations of cellists—many of them prodigies—have contributed their countless performances to the development of music. Not only have they played for the pleasure and enlightenment of millions, but each in his or her own way has inspired others—cello makers, cello teachers, and living composers—to ever greater achievement. Will music lovers in centuries to come remain curious about Ferrari's blue angel or, for that matter, the cello prodigies of our day? Perhaps those who come after the wonder children that currently enchant us will teach us even more. The ancient blue angel captured in a fresco still life may offer only a faint, rudimentary indication of the potential of such children. Yet certainly her legacy is theirs.

The blue angel. A detail from the Italian fresco A Choir of Angels (1535–36) by Gaudenzio Ferrari in the cupola of Saronno Cathedral. Courtesy Scala/Art Resource, New York.

Reader's Guide

The prodigy is an individual child with the gift of an extraordinary talent. But I think that the prodigy is also much more. The very existence of the prodigy is itself a gift of immense importance, for the phenomenon offers insights into the workings of the human mind. The prodigy teaches us about the expression and development of potential and about something deeper as well—something about how humanity has gotten where it is, why it has gotten there, and perhaps how we might better choreograph our uniquely human dance.

David Henry Feldman, *Nature's Gambit*

WHAT IS a musical prodigy? Derived from the Latin *prodigium*, the word *prodigy* appeared in print as early as 1653 when Thomas Gataker wrote, "What is a prodigie, but some thing that comes to passe besides, beyond, above, or against the cours of nature?"[1] *Webster's Third International Dictionary* confirms the archaic definition: "a monstrosity, something out of the usual course of nature, like a comet or a meteor." The traditional mythologies—the curious legends of Paganini and Liszt, for example—portrayed musical prodigies as unexplained and somehow unnatural occurrences, as the German term *Wunderkind* (literally, wonder child) would suggest.

Prodigy is what we have come to call a child who displays extraordinary talents. Without reference to anything outside the natural order of things, Barbara Jepson in a *New York Times* article described today's prodigies in music simply as those who "display a level of poise, technical prowess, and musicality well beyond their years."[2]

From childhood to old age, Niccolò Paganini, the legendary eighteenth-century Italian violinist, made people wary because he was perceived as a mysterious, unexplainable human creation. His avid followers believed that he drew his inspiration from the realm of the supernatural. About Paganini a Leipzig critic wrote in 1829:

> This man with the long black hair and the pale countenance opens to us with his violin a world which we had never imagined, except perhaps in dreams. There is in his appearance something so supernatural that one looks for a glimpse of a cloven hoof or an angel's wing.[3]

While Paganini himself encouraged his bizarre, mystical legend as he achieved super stardom across Europe, he eventually paid the price when his artistic accomplishments were attributed not to his genuine human abilities, but to the prevailing superstition that he, like Faust, had struck a fateful bargain for his unparalleled success. This Faustian myth held full sway even after Paganini's death. During an unbelievable postmortem saga, both church and state conspired against his burial in consecrated ground, his remains periodically disturbed for eighty-six years until his ultimate interment in 1926 in the Camposanto di Genoa.

Paganini's legend, provocative as it is, tells us little about the reality of his precocious childhood, many details of which will forever remain a mystery. It was not until he was forty-five that Paganini finally spoke of his childhood to his earliest biographers, and his silence on many issues was not surprising since by middle age he was intent on establishing the idea that he was self-taught, self-made, and self-directed, that "great ideas sprang spontaneously from the inner flame that animated him."[4]

That there was a sublime match of wonder child to music that yielded the prodigy Paganini seems certain. Possessed neither by devils nor angels but endowed with unusual human potential, young Niccolò was drawn inexorably to music and prospered in its embrace. His abilities developed with awesome speed when his father began teaching him at the age of five.

Technological advances in broadcasting and recording have enabled us to observe musical prodigies with an immediacy heretofore unknown. Some day such resources may help us to understand how and why prodigies function. Even today, when violinist Sarah Chang appears on television, for example, first at age ten playing a recital in London, then later at fourteen as soloist with the New York Philharmonic, we can judge for ourselves the young musician described by Yehudi Menuhin as "the most wonderful, perfect, ideal violinist I have ever heard."[5]

Early Rapid Development

The ability to develop exceedingly quickly is the hallmark of the prodigy, whether the ability expresses itself in the prodigy-prone field of music or elsewhere. Throughout human history, exceptional children have revealed themselves as prodigies in math, chess, and other arenas. At the magical age of eleven, Blaise Pascal secretly constructed a geometry of his own, Jacques Inaudi appeared in public demonstrating his sensational computational ability, and Norbert Wiener, who would become one of the world's greatest mathematicians, neared graduation at Tufts University, determined to undertake graduate studies at Harvard. Before the public fascination with little Bobby Fisher, most people considered chess just another game.

The physical demands of performance vary within every domain, so that extremely young performing prodigies may emerge in music more readily than in such other fields as sculpture or dance. Not until they reached midadolescence could youngsters like Michelangelo Buonarroti and Marie Taglioni have met the physical challenge of their chosen artistic endeavors. The inspired Michelangelo was strong enough by fourteen to break marble with his thunderbolt strokes when he entered the court life of the Medicis. He continued this demanding physical task until the creation of his *Pietà rondanini* in Milan, a fragment he sculpted toward the end of his life as he approached ninety. Marie Taglioni, the first ballerina as we understand that term today, crossed the stage of the Paris Opéra in three bounds when she was fifteen, "leaping in time" as no dancer had before.

Encounters With Music

To release the potential in a child prodigy, music itself must fascinate and beguile, which it has always done by its very nature. An infant climbing onto the bench to strike the keys of the piano is a familiar domestic occurrence, one that is usually terminated quickly by a parent whose patience runs short under the barrage of noisy play activity. However, some exceptional children enact a quite different ritual when they spontaneously play music on some accessible instrument—often a piano or a violin—grasping an auspicious moment to express themselves. If such fortuitous play activity is frequently repeated, a musical child may soon be revealed as a genuine prodigy. Of course, many such forays into the realm of music result in unfulfilled promise, but not so with Alicia de Larrocha, the great Spanish pianist, a former prodigy and now a highly esteemed artist. "It seems to me that I was born listening to music because I was completely surrounded by it," de Larrocha has said. "My first toy was my aunt's piano, which I much preferred to dolls."[6] Not surprisingly, the one-year-old's pounding the keys soon destroyed her aunt's patience, and she locked the piano. To show her displeasure at losing her toy, Alicia started to scream and beat her head on the tile floor until it bled. To quiet her, her aunt promised that if she behaved, she would allow her to take up the piano seriously. When Alicia was two, her aunt began tutoring her, giving her a little instruction at a time.

In 1842, the prodigy composer Felix Mendelssohn wrote, "People usually complain that music is so ambiguous that it leaves them in doubt as to what they are supposed to think, whereas words can be understood by everyone. But to me it seems exactly the opposite."[7] Clearly there is something inherent in the structure of music and in the means of transferring the knowledge of that structure from composer to performer to listener that makes music accessible to the prodigy, although it may remain an unsolvable riddle to other children.

In New York in 1947, pianist Lorin Hollander demonstrated a startling level of comprehension just hours after he heard his father's string quartet rehearsing a work by Haydn. Lorin was three-and-a-half at the time.

When I came home, I wanted somehow to put down what I had heard. I found some drawing paper and began to draw spirals. My father asked me what I was doing, and I began to sing him back the piece, which I remembered perfectly, and told him I was trying to write it down.[8]

His father explained that there was already a way to write this music and brought out the Haydn score to show him. Within a few minutes Lorin knew the notes, the clefs, everything. Outside a car horn honked and his father asked him what note it was: "F-sharp!" His father clinked a glass with a spoon: "B-flat!"

Shinichi Suzuki's Talent Education movement began in 1932 when

Suzuki was teaching violin at Tokyo's Imperial Conservatory. In an inspired moment with four-year-old Toshiya Eto, Suzuki realized the potential of his "mother tongue concept"—that the secret to educating all human ability lies in the marvelous facility of children to speak their mother tongue quite effortlessly. Today Suzuki's groundbreaking mass music-education venture, which had its genesis in this notion, remains one of the world's most widely used methods of teaching the violin to youngsters.

Most Talent Education pupils begin studying the violin at age three under the supervision of a bonafide teacher and a willing parent, usually the mother. Although Japanese violinist Takako Nishizaki has some misgivings about the method, she has acknowledged that her prodigious talent was discovered when she became a pupil of Shinichi Suzuki. "Of course it is a fun way to make music and for children to enjoy it," Nishizaki has said.

> I would strongly recommend it as a first stage in teaching children, but I think such systems are cynical if they are thought to be anything other than a beginning. They offer so much yet can leave the student with no immediate future. . . . I am one of the survivors of the system, but anyone in Japan who is serious about learning to play the violin goes to a conventional teacher.[9]

"I am not trying to train professionals, but to give happiness to all children," Dr. Suzuki said.[10] His concept is sometimes forgotten by pupils and their parents in their exhilarating rush to leave apprenticeship behind and enter the next phase of development. Nishizaki returned to her father's tuition until she qualified for admission to New York's Juilliard School. After completing her training there, she went on to become one of Japan's most recorded concert violinists. While much can be said both pro and con about the Asian phenomenon of early childhood training in music, many prodigies-to-be have been caught in the great net of Suzuki's Talent Education movement.

For anyone who has experienced the slow struggle of a young, normally talented child grappling with the violin and its music, the dramatic stories of accelerated learning that characterize the genuine prodigy's early encounters with the violin seem unbelievable. Erica Morini, the great violin virtuoso who died in 1996 at the age of ninety-one, revealed this story at the zenith of her international career:

First I studied with my father. When I was three-and-a-half years old
I played Sarasate's *Gypsy Airs*, yet my father was not satisfied. He complained that it was so much trouble to teach me. I finally satisfied him
at the age of five when I learned the violin concerto by Paganini.

I took my audition for Otakar Ševčik's master class at the Vienna
Academy when I was eight years old. I remember there were many
professors seated around a table, one of them Arnold Rosé. They asked
me what I would like to play. I told them I would like to play the
Paganini concerto. There was much laughter. "And what cadenza are
you going to play for us, little one?" they jokingly inquired. The Sauret
cadenza, I replied. "The Sauret? The most difficult cadenza of all!" they
exclaimed, holding their sides with laughter. "Well, little one, we will
be satisfied if you will just play the cadenza for us." I must say I played
it like a fiend—with great fire and emotion. They were astonished!

However, at that time, I was more interested in having a good time
and going to the pastry shops to eat cookies than playing the violin.[11]

The Nurturing Influence

Nurturing a prodigy is a team effort. The protagonists include family and
friends, teachers of all sorts, and patrons and concert managers in various
guises. Because the interplay between these forces spells success or failure
for the wonder child, the great problem is to keep the power of the team in
balance. The complex group dynamics are in a constant state of flux. When
an overly ambitious parent becomes an exploiter, a self-seeking teacher over-
whelms parental control, or a greedy manager overrides all, the balance is lost
and the welfare of the child endangered.

The family remains the supporting base of the team, since both teachers
and managers are relatively transitory characters in this unfolding drama.
We know little of Erica Morini's parents, an Italian father and a Viennese
mother, other than what she has briefly told us about her father, who initially
occupied two overlapping roles on her nurturing team—he was both parent
and teacher. In the lives of musical prodigies who are born into families of
musicians, such overlapping roles on the nurturing team are not an unusual
occurrence. Until they were adults, Wolfgang Mozart and Clara Schumann
were dominated by powerful fathers. Both Leopold Mozart and Friedrich
Wieck ruled the lives of their prodigies in multiple capacities as parent,
teacher, and manager.

In the two centuries before the birth of Johann Sebastian Bach, seven generations of the Bach clan included more than fifty cantors, organists, and town musicians. Johann Sebastian was simply carrying on the family trade when he looked after the musical education of his own children of which twenty were born to his two marriages. His sons Wilhelm Friedemann (the Halle Bach), Carl Philipp Emanuel (the Berlin Bach), Johann Christoph (the Bückeburg Bach), and Johann Christian (the London Bach) all achieved fame as musicians. Perhaps the advent of any child prodigy in the Bach clan was less of a surprise than in other families, but a surprise nevertheless.

The musical prodigy exacts tremendous parental attention. The appearance of extreme talent is an unusual family event that calls for an ardent response.

Nathan Haendel said of his daughter Ida, "I was sure in her that there was a great genius and it didn't mean a thing to me what other people said." His preoccupation with his prodigious daughter began the day that three-year-old Ida took her sister's violin from the table to play her first tune, and it lasted more than sixty years. Speaking of her father as an organizing force in her life, Ida Haendel has said, "In my case I had my father which I thought (and a lot of people thought) was absolutely marvelous."[12]

Yehudi Menuhin has commented on raising a prodigy: "The exorbitant demands it makes can neither be ignored nor be reduced to normal measure, and the special concentration it attracts necessarily overturns ordinary priorities. There is no doubt that I shaped my parents' lives as much as they shaped mine."[13]

Because many different teachers may play a role in the prodigy's early learning process, questions about the teacher's role are bound to arise. David Feldman's answer is direct: "Whatever degree of confidence the child has—indeed, whatever degree of talent—it will come to fruition only under the guidance of teachers who are themselves greatly gifted in the ability to catalyze potential into durable achievement."[14]

When in 1830 Paganini established the idea with his biographers that he was self-taught, self-made, and self-directed, he did not entirely deny his training but diminished its importance, thus creating the notion that the musical prodigy needs very little musical education. The parents of modern prodigies tend to follow a different line of reasoning, knowing that today's wonder child does not easily progress from early discovery to acceptance in the highest musical echelons without systematic instrumental training. Legions of parents worldwide conceive ambitions for the musical education of their prodigious children, plans that frequently culminate at such institutions as the Vienna Academy or the Juilliard School, where precocious students from the Pacific Rim now represent large percentages of the enrollment.

Not only do many of today's prodigies receive superb musical training from childhood to maturity, but their general educations are frequently pursued with great vigor as well. While earning a degree in art history at Yale, cellist Shauna Rolston carried her academic work with her on concert tours. Her colleague, cellist Yo-Yo Ma, distinguished himself for four years studying the humanities at Harvard while continuing his musical pursuits in the summers. Conductor Simon Rattle retired to Oxford for three terms to study English and American literature.

For instrumentalists and singers alike, the twentieth century has become the age of the master teacher. Pianist Glenn Gould completed his study with Alberto Guerrero; soprano Patrice Munsel coached with William Hermann; conductor Guido Cantelli had Arturo Toscanini as his mentor. Yet the prodigy's earliest teacher often may not be a master teacher. The role is sometimes filled by a devoted parent who is a musician or by a dedicated teacher well known to the family but possessing no far-reaching reputation. Common sense tells us that many such early teachers will eventually exhaust their teaching ideas when working with musical prodigies. And some may find it difficult to relinquish their role, even when they find themselves pedagogically impoverished, no longer able to transform potential into achievement. What is essential, however, is that the early teacher has the imagination and enthusiasm to ignite the prodigy's initial learning process.

The truth is that musical prodigies begin the process of mastering music at a very early age and move forward with such astounding acceleration that they may be on their second or third teacher at an age when most children are just beginning their first lessons, peering with wonder and perhaps a little trepidation down the long road that stretches before them.

The Element of Play

The element of play is ever-present in the stories of many prodigies' childhoods, and the recognition by teachers of the universality of children playing at music-making has important implications. Many ancestral teachers probably doled out lessons that were strictly utilitarian in nature, devoid of all humor and rarely concerned with any form of make-believe. Some contemporary music teachers still give such lessons to children (perhaps among them undiscovered prodigies), lessons not designed for children but conceived for end-gaining adults engaged in the life-or-death pursuit of instrumental technique for its own sake.

While some children are more inventive than others, even the simplest play activity of most, far from being random, follows the child's own unspoken rules. While these rules may be subject to some discussion and negotiation, young children are usually well aware of the line between fantasy and reality and easily work out variations and combinations according to whim. When he was five, cellist Gregor Piatigorsky armed himself with two sticks, a long one for the cello and a short one for the bow, and pretended to play the cello, those magic sticks lifting him into an imagined world of sound where he could summon every mood at will. By realizing that make-believe and the element of play occupy a vital role in a child's mastery of a musical instrument, much as they do in the mastery of language, teachers may find greater freedom to explore and develop their youngest students' interest in musical performance.

Burden of Early Success

Unexpected, early success exacts a toll from the young prodigy who must deal with the realities of a lifestyle known to almost no other children and few adults. Aside from any artistic consideration, the success of public engagements, media appearances, and record sales may rise or plummet according to ever-changing public opinion and the whims of critics. Even when bolstered by management's well-conceived publicity and superior marketing skills, such vulnerable careers are rarely carefree. The unpredictability of professional life adds an extra dimension to the demands on the child's emotional state.

Although the mastery of music comes with awesome speed to most prodigies, life's other challenges may not be so easily met. The wonder child who performs superbly on stage at ten may not accomplish ordinary tasks equivalently off stage and may feel severely tested by sacrifices in everyday life.

By keeping the human child dependent for an unusually long period, Nature is providing the necessary time for learning and the transmission of culture to occur. In view of this, the nurturing team must be constantly vigilant when mounting personal concerns about apparently ordinary, normal processes put the prodigy's well-being at serious risk. While balancing unusually advanced abilities in one area with more ordinary abilities in another, the working prodigy may begin to feel alienated from siblings and peers. The wonder child's emotional life may become seriously hampered by veiled threats of failure when the child finds it difficult to make friends at play, assume the domestic chores of childhood, finish school homework on time, or a myriad other things taken for granted and accomplished easily by children leading a more normal life.

Most working prodigies remain tenacious in spite of the pitfalls of early professionalism, sustaining optimum personal energy and fortitude. They remain determined to do one specific thing at all costs—perform music superbly. But such determination endures only when, as Feldman has phrased it, they perceive meeting the challenge as "absolutely essential for satisfaction, expression, and well-being."[15]

Transition to Maturity

The transition from wonder child to mature artist is complex and difficult for many, a perilous journey rarely accomplished without extreme physical and emotional adjustment. It frequently entails a temporary withdrawal from the artistic pursuit and may suddenly end in emotional defeat and mental anguish or in some extreme cases the complete abandonment of music.

The tragic testimony of pianist Ruth Slenczynska[16] tells us that the life of a prodigy can be an almost unendurable traumatic experience when the child is exploited as a musical or social curiosity. In Slenczynska's case, an obsessive, abusive father was at the core of the problem. According to her account, he imposed an unnatural regimen during her childhood, waking her at six every morning to begin practicing in her nightgown, and during the eight or nine hours that followed, punishing her mistakes at the piano with slaps to the face and denial of meals. She was allowed neither friends nor toys, trapped in the unforgiving task of becoming a pianist. When the world of music took notice of her performances at age four, the media speculated that she was a Mozart reincarnated, or was playing in an hypnotic trance, under a spell. After her Berlin debut, critics mounted the platform to search the piano for a concealed mechanism; in Copenhagen, a doctor was sent to examine her to ascertain if she were a midget, but he announced to the press, "This is a genuine child." Not until Slenczynska was fifteen did she gain her independence. She broke completely with her father—and with music.[17]

More than once the Society for the Prevention of Cruelty to Children has terminated the public performances of musical prodigies in New York to prevent possible exploitation. When the prodigy pianist Joseph Hofmann first appeared there in 1887, his triumph with twenty-four concerts and forty more planned was cut short by the concerns of Alfred Corning Clark, a man who ironically was later to be his benefactor with the gift of fifty thousand dollars to finance his further study. The legal judgment that ensued brought about Joseph's withdrawal from the stage for six years, but during that period he continued to study in Europe and finally made his long-anticipated return to the concert platform as a young man of eighteen.

He performed in Russia where audiences had never heard him as a boy, so that no comparison was made except with the world of contemporary pianists. The approval restored his self-confidence, but he was a long time winning America back. About this aspect of his career, he has said, "How difficult it is to be a prodigy and then to come back later and hope to be accepted as a mature artist."

It is rather like being the son of a famous father, except that in this case it is your own self they are comparing you with, to your disadvantage. You are in the shadow of your early power, and it is a heart-breaking business to climb out of it into your own light.[18]

The time required for an artistic metamorphosis varies in the life of every prodigy. Joseph Hofmann's withdrawal began at age eleven and lasted six years, but János Starker's began late at twenty-one and fortunately only lasted seven months. Some are spared and do not withdraw at all, but perhaps they are the exception. Yehudi Menuhin has remarked, "There is no such thing as an instant biography. Maturity, in music and in life, has to be earned by living."[19]

The search for maturity is not restricted to prodigies in music; in every domain prodigies go through a stage when their conflict with the world is greater than that of most other children.

While the prodigy mathematician Norbert Wiener had suspected that adults viewed him as an oddity, he suffered terribly as an adolescent when he realized that his peers held much the same view. Reflecting on his own search for maturity, Wiener has said, "Every child, in gaining emotional security, believes in the values of the world around him. He wishes to believe that his elders are all wise and good. When he discovers that they are not, he faces the necessity of loneliness and of forming his own judgment of a world that he can no longer fully trust."[20] While Wiener realized that the prodigy shares this experience with every child, he acknowledged that the problem is compounded by the prodigy's belonging half to the adult world and half to the world of the children about him.

Two Modes of Expression

When the possibilities of performing or composing present themselves in tandem during the earliest musical experiences, prodigies seem enthralled by these two distinct acts of creativity. The urge to interpret existing music is probably the more seductive of the two modes of expression and arises quite naturally when the child hears music performed, then attempts to replicate the act. The prodigy learns by doing and learns with incredible speed, discovering the technical means to accomplish the physical act of performing as the act itself unfolds—the spontaneous violin playing of Ida Haendel and Van Cliburn's playing a just-heard piece at the piano are examples. There is a period of reflection—a time lapse—between hearing the music and then recreating it in performance, but for the prodigy the incubation of this call to action may be exceedingly brief.

The ability to bring something absolutely new into existence is not granted to every mature composer and certainly not to the prodigy composer whose early attempts may reveal a certain facility, but lack genuine originality. Indeed, such juvenilia will probably never be as original as the innocent prodigy may suppose.

Because novice composers require a medium through which to express their creative thought processes, the keyboard often serves the purpose once its functions have been explored. Little Wolfgang Mozart was giving shape and meaning to his first compositions by the age of four after he had become familiar with playing the music of other composers on the harpsichord. Mozart's juvenilia still exist in the notebook in which his father Leopold notated his little pieces. Before he created his masterpieces, even Wolfgang had to serve an apprenticeship during which he both learned the basic craft of composition (an arduous and time-consuming task for most composers) and continued to develop his musical insight.

Suzanne Langer has described composing music as an act of *"formulation and representation* of emotions, moods, mental tensions, and resolutions—a 'logical picture' of sentient, responsive life, a source of insight."[21] Prodigy composers are able to create Langer's "logical picture" only in their own due time. They can bring insight to bear on their own creativity only when such insight has sufficiently developed. Of course, prodigy composers may reach the moment when their compositions represent the hoped for "logical picture" far sooner than expected. With the period of their juvenilia far behind them, Franz Schubert, Frédéric Chopin, Felix Mendelssohn, and Georges Bizet all composed original, lasting masterpieces during their adolescence.

Charles Rosen succinctly drew the parameters of the two modes of expression:

> The act of composing is the act of fixing those limits within which the performer may move freely . . . the limits the composer sets belong to a system which in many respects is like a language: it has an order, a syntax, and a meaning. The performer's freedom is—or should be—bound in another way. The performer brings out that meaning, makes its significance not only clear but almost palpable.[22]

Composing and performing embody two very different processes. When music is composed, order is made out of chaos; when it is performed, an already ordered creation is made palpable and, as Rosen said, its symbolic text transformed into the reality of sound. In the past, these two modes of expression frequently manifested themselves as complementary activities in the lives of musicians, but the exigencies of modern careers seem to have caused prodigies to concentrate on one mode of expression to the virtual exclusion of the other. Samuel Barber, singer and pianist, was eventually known only as a composer and Jascha Heifetz, a skilled composer, is remembered solely as a performer, but the vestiges of a dualism of purpose existed in both artists.

Throughout their artistic lives, performers attempt to "bring out the meaning" of music composed by others. Their search for meaning in music is their most significant task and an aspect of the musician's vocation often instinctively recognized by the wonder child. During childhood, the performing prodigy will learn the traditional methods of this search, discovering both the instrumental and interpretive skills that make it possible to transform the notation of a musical score into the most sophisticated performance. The eventual mastery of such skills will assure the significance of such transformations.

By the very nature of an unusual endowment of talent and temperament, the wonder child is often compelled by intuition to choose between the two modes of expression, either to create new music by bringing order to his

intellectual soundscape or to convey the meaning of existing music by inter-
preting it in performance.

This book explores aspects of prodigy life by telling the amazing stories of
many musical prodigies from the eighteenth century to the present. These
stories often concern the full circle of their lives, not just what they did as
children. For some we can see how the promise of a prodigy childhood was
borne out; how the difficult passage through adolescence was weathered;
whether choices about how much, how soon, were well made; and which
influences endured.

Part One, "The Grand Tradition," deals first with the quintessential
musical prodigy, composer Wolfgang Amadeus Mozart. We continue with
stories of violinist Niccolò Paganini, pianist Clara Schumann, and cellist
Pablo Casals. Although these four prodigies, whose childhoods occurred
between 1756 and 1896, had many things in common, they arrived at maturity under vastly different circumstances.

Later chapters offer accounts of prodigies whose careers brought them
into international prominence during the twentieth century. Most of them
will be remembered by music lovers who either were privileged to hear them
on stage or who came to admire their artistry through early phonograph
recordings. Chapter 5, "A Family Portrait," is the saga of two families, the
Britts and the Koutzens. The stories of four generations of related musical
prodigies unfold in Belgium, France, Russia, and finally America. Chapter 6,
"California Crossroads" tells of four prodigies from the grand tradition—
Jascha Heifetz, Emanuel Feuermann, Gregor Piatigorsky, and Artur Rubinstein—whose accomplishments virtually assured the domination of the prodigy world by pianists, violinists, and cellists for decades to come. Chapter 7,
"Midcentury Keyboard Masters," concerns four contemporary pianists—
Glenn Gould, Martha Argerich, Daniel Barenboim, and Van Cliburn—all
born within a decade of each other between 1932 and 1942, modern artists
whose lives as prodigies present striking contrasts between their cultural
heritages, personal temperaments, and artistic accomplishments.

Chapter 8 is about discovery. It deals with the role of musical competitions and concert management in the career development of young musicians, painting a picture of competition far different from the friendly rivalry
played out in the distant past between Mozart and Clementi. Chapter 9,
"Warsaw, 1935," is a detailed account of the first International Henryk

Wieniawski Violin Competition, an event that remains for many the most memorable of modern violin competitions.

Chapter 10, "Virtuosos of the Twenties and Thirties From A to Z," is devoted to the childhood stories of seven eminent string players: Aldo Parisot, Isaac Stern, János Starker, Ruggiero Ricci, Mstislav Rostropovich, Yehudi Menuhin, and Zara Nelsova.

Part Two, "The Innovators," begins with the stories of guitarist Andrés Segovia, flutist Georges Barrère, violist William Primrose, and percussionist Evelyn Glennie, each of whom embarked on a courageous odyssey that no one had dared before them. The particular instruments they played and the creation of new music they inspired brought them to international attention "Against All Odds" and somewhat later than most traditional prodigies. Chapter 12, "Pocket Toscaninis," tells about three little boys—Pierino Gamba, Joey Alfidi, and Lorin Maazel—who became prodigy conductors in a sphere dominated by older men. Chapter 13, *The Rose Tree*, An Opera," is about the American composer Samuel Barber, who began writing music when he was two, created his first opera at ten, and emerged as a significant twentieth-century American composer.

Chapter 14, "The Spirit of the Gypsy," concerns a Transylvanian girl, Kató Havas, whose prodigy life as a violinist drew on the mystical sensibility of her gypsy friends and teachers in prewar Hungary, a sensibility that she later incorporated into her exquisite pedagogy. Gary Karr's childhood in Los Angeles in the 1940s is the subject of chapter 15, "Bass Is Beautiful." Born into a family tradition of double-bass playing, he gladly accepted his legacy, astounding the musical world with new possibilities for the double bass as a solo instrument.

Jacqueline du Pré and Yo-Yo Ma have become the standard bearers of at least twenty-five generations of cellists. Chapter 16, "Born for the Cello," tells the childhood stories of these two artists, du Pré, whose meteoric career ended after a long bout with multiple sclerosis, and Yo-Yo Ma, one of the century's supreme instrumentalists.

The book concludes with Bejun Mehta's extraordinary essay entitled "A Process of Prodigy." Mehta writes with candor and insightful authority about his childhood as a celebrated boy soprano, a remarkable story that illuminates many wondrous elements of the prodigy's experience.

THE GRAND TRADITION

In 1929 the New York Telegraph *called ten-year-old Ruggiero Ricci "the greatest genius of our time in the world of interpretive music." Courtesy Ruggiero Ricci.*

CHAPTER ONE

The Miracle From Salzburg

WOLFGANG AMADEUS MOZART

On 5 August 1764 we had to rent a country house outside London, in Chelsea, so that father could recover from a throat ailment which brought him near to death. While our father lay dangerously ill, we were forbidden to touch the piano. And so, to occupy himself, Mozart composed his first symphony [K. 16] for all the instruments of the orchestra.

Mozart's sister, Nannerl, recalling the prodigy at age eight

WOLFGANG Amadeus Mozart, the quintessential musical prodigy, was born in Salzburg on 27 January 1756 at eight in the evening. He began composing music when he was four. Like no child before him, he toured Europe as a prodigy for three years, astounding kings and commoners alike with his stellar performances before returning home at age ten. Until his untimely death in Vienna on 5 December 1791 at the age of thirty-six, Mozart continued to perform at the keyboard and conduct his operas, also completing more than six hundred musical works during three decades of highly productive labor. His most significant masterpieces have remained in the performance repertoire for two centuries.

Leopold Mozart called his son "a God-given miracle." Probably the greatest human influence in Wolfgang's brief life, Leopold described his son's childhood profusely in letters, but he did not begin the process at once, so unfortunately there is no extant information regarding the wonder child's first three years. After Wolfgang's death, his elder sister, Marianne von Berchtold (always called Nannerl), confirmed many details of their shared

childhood,[1] but regarding her brother's infancy her memory failed. He was
the seventh child of a family in which two survived. His birth brought his
mother near death.

Her name was Maria Anna Pertl. She was a Salzburg girl. When she
married Leopold Mozart, a musician descended from German weavers and
bookbinders in Augsburg, he was employed as fourth violinist in the court
orchestra at Salzburg, but he rose quickly through the ranks to become
deputy Kapellmeister in charge of the archbishop's musical establishment.

Leopold began teaching Nannerl to play the harpsichord when she was
seven. Not wanting to be excluded from his father's attention, Wolfgang,
who was about three, also began to play at the keyboard using Nannerl's
music book (*Notenbuch*). In its margins Leopold entered notations that stand
as evidence of his son's early ability to perform: "Wolfgang learned this minuet in his fourth year" or "This minuet and trio was learned by Wolfgang in
half an hour between nine and half past on 26 January 1761, one day before
his fifth birthday." Wolfgang's first compositions, two short keyboard pieces,
soon appeared in the same music book, entered there in Leopold's hand.
Before the end of the boy's seventh summer in 1763, there were eight more
little pieces.

Johann Schachtner, the Salzburg trumpeter, was a close family friend.
After Mozart's death he told a charming story to Nannerl about her brother,
who at about four had already tried his hand at composing what he inno-
cently called a "concerto." The boy had written it down in a notation he
invented for his own purpose.[2] "What are you writing?" Leopold asked his
son. "A clavier concerto, the first part is nearly finished," answered the four-
year-old. When Leopold asked to be shown the work, Wolfgang objected.
"It's not ready yet," the child insisted. At first the men laughed at the sight of
ink blotches and smudges, but on closer examination of the ragged pages,
Leopold was awestruck when he realized that it was genuine music, but far
too difficult to be played. "That's why it's a concerto," Wolfgang explained.
"You must practice it until you can get it right," he said. "Look! Here's how it
goes." The child played his music at the keyboard and managed to reveal just
enough of his idea to demonstrate what he had intended.

Determined to create an indestructible family unity that would survive
life's inevitable upheavals, Leopold found his true vocation as teacher and
impresario to his prodigies during their early travels, a concert tour to Munich
and Vienna, then a European tour that lasted more than three years.
Although opinion has always been divided about Leopold's complex manip-

ulation of his children during this period, father and son clearly had a symbiotic relationship. During the grand tour, Wolfgang's sudden acclaim as a prodigy became the source of Leopold's personal power. He carried the burden of his son's worldly success, freeing Wolfgang from the yoke of fame and adulation. Leopold's entire existence seemed justified in this role of authority. For Wolfgang, his greatest reward was his father's approval, and he reacted with excessive obedience to Leopold's constant demands. During his amazing childhood he performed his part in the family scheme willingly. He never deviated from his highly structured existence nor did he show any dissatisfaction with the unusual role Leopold created for him. Nannerl later recalled a poignant ceremony enacted every night at bedtime until Wolfgang reached the age of ten. The boy composed a melody he would sing aloud each night, while his father, sitting nearby in a chair, would add his voice in counterpoint. Once the ritual was finished, Wolfgang would kiss his father good night and fall asleep, peaceful and contented. His childhood motto was "Next to God comes Papa."

The Mozart children never attended any school, but relied entirely on Leopold as their teacher. With his father's guidance, Wolfgang pursued a study of the basic disciplines, learning the three Rs, history and geography, French and Italian (languages in which he soon became quite fluent), and some aspects of Latin. Nannerl later confirmed Wolfgang's quest for knowledge: "Even as a child he was desirous of learning everything he set eyes on; in drawing [and] adding he showed much skill but, as he was too busy with music, he could not show his talents in any other direction."[3] Schachtner, the family friend, wrote, "Whatever he was given to learn occupied him so completely that he put all else aside, even music. When he was doing sums, the tables, chairs, walls, even the floor was covered with chalked figures."[4] At six the boy stubbornly taught himself to play the violin (although his father was a distinguished violin teacher) and soon was able to join chamber music evenings at home.

During his childhood journeys, Wolfgang occasionally had a few formal, specialized music lessons from musicians other than Leopold. Giovanni Manzuoli, a castrato singer celebrated for the power and sonority of his soprano voice and for his dignified singing style, gave Wolfgang some singing lessons in London in 1764 when the boy was eight. (Later they met again in Florence when Manzuoli became interested in appearing in Wolfgang's opera.) During Wolfgang's first Italian tour six years later, he visited Bologna twice and there met Padre Giovanni Martini, who instructed him in counterpoint and fugue writing. A venerable composer, scholar, and teacher, Padre Martini had earlier taught Johann Christian Bach among his more than one hundred pupils.

Performing prodigies must often meet the demands of those who insist on long hours of practice. Indeed, some innocents have been forced to the task when they resist such labor, but not Wolfgang. He worked happily at the keyboard without any coercion. Even when he had been playing the entire day without rest, he would start again without hesitation if his father demanded he do so. The tenacious child established a work pattern to which he held fast throughout his life and even a summary review of his adulthood reveals an unimaginable discipline in all artistic pursuits.

While it was his ability as a keyboard performer that entranced Europe during the grand tour, Wolfgang began serving his apprenticeship as a serious composer at the same time. His unyielding commitment to do two specific things extraordinarily well at all costs—perform and compose—soon produced unheard-of results. At first only small keyboard pieces were entered in Nannerl's music book, but Wolfgang returned to Salzburg from the grand tour having composed a large number of keyboard sonatas with violin or flute accompaniment, several symphonies, four keyboard concertos, and a serenade for harpsichord and orchestra. His first published works appeared at this time in Paris, London, and The Hague, three of the cities the Mozarts visited on their travels. On 28 May 1764 Leopold wrote, "What he knew when we left Salzburg is a mere shadow of what he knows now. It exceeds all that one can imagine," and later on 8 June 1764, "My boy knows in this his eighth year what one would expect from a man of forty. Indeed only he who sees and hears him can believe it."[5]

The myth of Wolfgang as "favorite of the muses" or "divine child," the notion that the prodigy's inspiration came directly from God, was first conceived by Leopold, but perpetuated by poets, philosophers, and musicians for a century after the composer's death. Whatever Wolfgang's ultimate source of childhood inspiration, his early works were influenced by perhaps thirty composers, not the least of whom were Michael Haydn (brother of the famous Haydn) with whom he alternated as concertmaster of the court orchestra in Salzburg, and Johann Christian Bach. During Wolfgang's first visit to London, Johann Christian Bach, the Queen's music teacher, had taken him on his lap as they played alternately on the same keyboard for two hours while improvising for King George III and Queen Sophie Charlotte at the "Queen's House," Buckingham Palace. About this event Nannerl later reported that Herr Bach played a few bars, then Wolfgang continued, and in this way they played a whole sonata and "someone not seeing it would have thought that only one man was playing it."[6]

In London in the spring of 1764, scientist Daines Barrington examined Wolfgang's unusual ability to improvise vocal works in various affects—songs of love, of anger, of rage. After having suggested to the boy that he would be glad to hear an extemporary love song such as Manzuoli might choose in an opera, the examination proceeded and, according to the scientist, nothing could exceed the masterly manner in which Wolfgang sang:

> The boy who continued to sit at his harpsichord looked back with
> much archness, and immediately began five or six lines of a jargon
> recitative proper to introduce a love song. He then played a symphony
> which might correspond with an air composed to the single word,
> *Affetto.* . . . Finding that he was in humour, and as it were inspired,
> I then desired him to compose a song of rage such as might be proper
> for the opera stage. The boy again looked back with much archness,
> and began five or six lines of a jargon recitative proper to precede a
> song of anger . . . and in the middle of it, he had worked himself up
> to such a pitch, that he beat his harpsichord like a person possessed,
> rising sometimes in his chair.[7]

The eight-year-old also impressed the eminent historian Charles Burney when at a performance he demonstrated an incredible knowledge of the art of singing, imitating the unique styles of several opera singers as well as their songs in an extemporized opera to nonsense words. To this he added an overture in two movements, all with taste and imagination, correct harmony, melody, and modulation after which "he played at marbles, in the true childish way of one who knows nothing."[8]

Those who heard Wolfgang's keyboard performances were astonished at his ability to improvise in the varied styles of others. He once wrote to his father that he could more or less adopt or imitate any kind and any style of composition. The music of Wagenseil, Johann Christian Bach, Padre Martini, and the Haydns presented no barriers to his understanding. With agile mind and nimble fingers he drew his conclusions from the music of these contemporaries, claiming what he wished and needed in his urgent advance toward mastery. Leopold assisted his son by notating the earliest pieces in Nannerl's book in his own hand and later collaborated in the preparation of

new works by committing skeletal, technical elements to paper, the final
results to be worked out by the child. Of course, Leopold was cautious in
these matters, having no wish for the world to question their collaboration.
Even today the Mozart myth claims great compositions emerging from Wolfgang's earliest youth, but the Symphony in G Minor, K. 183, is probably his
earliest work to hold its place in the modern orchestral repertoire. It was
composed when he was seventeen.

On their tours, Wolfgang and Nannerl grew closer with each rough mile
traveled as they amused each other by sharing their daydreams. In his vivid
imagination Wolfgang created the Kingdom of Back (*das Königreich Rücken*)
and was so intrigued by his fantasy that he urged their servant, who could
draw a little, to make a map of it while he dictated the names of cities, market towns, and villages.[9] In the Kingdom of Back Nannerl was queen. Wolfgang was king and reigned supreme. All adults were excluded. This must
have been a welcome relief from their real life situation in which Leopold
dominated their every move.

Always the wily business man, Leopold prepared public notices to attract
music lovers—and the merely curious—to the grand tour's public concerts
and entertainments. During the London season where the allure of the
guinea was almost overwhelming, he showed little restraint, writing, "Our
fortune is struck and cannot be denied," undoubtedly intending to secure the
family's fortune in the course of the tours. Toward the end of their London
residence, Leopold put the children on daily public view and commented,
"God willing, I shall make in London my chief profit of some thousands of
gulden. . . . Once I leave England, I shall never see guineas again. So we
must make the most of our opportunity."[10] Leopold's notices continued to
appear in London's *Public Advertiser* in 1765 while the Mozart family was living at the home of the corset maker, Thomas Williamson, at 20 Frith Street
near Soho Square. He advised the general public that they would "find the
family at home every day in the week from twelve to two o'clock and have an
opportunity of putting Mozart's talents to a more particular proof," or they
could come to the great room in the Swan and Harp Tavern in Cornhill
where, for a small entrance fee, Leopold would supply "an opportunity to all
the curious to hear the two young prodigies perform."[11]

While of course we have no aural record of those early performances
that endeared Wolfgang forever to Europe's rapt listeners, the magnitude of
his technical accomplishments and the various settings in which he displayed his abilities have been well described. The format of his public per-

formances seems vaudevillian. It was announced that the wonder child would

> play a concerto on the violin, accompany symphonies on the clavier [the generic term for the stringed keyboard instruments], traverse the manual or keyboard of the clavier, and lay on the cloth as well, as though he had the keyboard under his eyes; he will further most accurately name from a distance any notes that may be sounded for him either singly or in chords, on the clavier or on every imaginable instrument including bells, glasses, and clocks. Lastly, he will improvise out of his head, not only on the pianoforte, but also on an organ.[12]

No doubt Wolfgang held the listeners in the palm of his little hand on these unforgettable occasions.

The noble patrons provided a reasonably artistic environment for the children's appearances, but we can only guess what they thought of Leopold's questionable taste regarding money-making. If his management of the public entertainments seems exploitative, he faithfully offered much the same celebration of talent and accomplishment on every occasion, regardless of venue or audience. There is no doubt that he rode the crest of these successes and experienced surprisingly little opposition from anyone.

Everyone was excited by the prospect of hearing Wolfgang, from the scientific examination of his expertise by Daines Barrington, Fellow of the Royal Society, to an entertainment for England's royalty at the palace. Inspired by the presence of the knowledgeable musicians at court, Wolfgang was "filled with passion and attentiveness."[13] His musical improvisations at the keyboard before the king and queen rose to unexpected heights when he was joined by Johann Christian Bach. At home or at the Swan and Harp Tavern where commoners could pay two shillings and six pence to hear the Mozart prodigies, Wolfgang may have come to resent playing for those who did not understand music and only demanded trifles to satisfy their curiosity.

In his headlong rush, Leopold sometimes put the children's health at risk, but who is to judge whether they would have been safer at home in Salzburg in a time of unchecked epidemics? Wolfgang was seriously ill on a half-dozen occasions during his childhood travels. In Paris and London he was stricken with rheumatic fever and tonsillitis. His high fever in Paris probably indicated erythema nodosum. In The Hague he suffered an attack of typhoid fever; in Munich he had a bout with rheumatic fever, an illness that returned from time to time throughout his life; in Olmütz he came down with small-pox. Later in Vienna, Wolfgang was blind for nine days, but recovered his sight. In Italy he seems to have had bronchitis and jaundice. He encountered illness and even the threat of death at every turn, and although often bedridden for extended periods, Wolfgang survived.

With their parents, Wolfgang and Nannerl traveled several thousand miles in the family coach pulled by six post horses, stopped in eighty-eight cities and towns, and performed for audiences totaling many thousands who for decades would recall the performances as astonishing feats of virtuosity.

After the grand tour, Wolfgang remained at home in Salzburg for nine months during which time he moved toward a career in the theater, a pursuit he would sustain until his death at which time he was the acknowledged master of opera. In his eleventh year he took such diverse material as a biblical text, a Latin school play, and a parody on a work by Rousseau and successfully transformed them. In every case, he not only composed a great deal of music, but set it in music notation for a cast of singers and an orchestra, and conducted the performances from the harpsichord in the tradition of his time. It is difficult to imagine any young musician meeting such demands, much less an eleven-year-old. The accomplishment confirmed Wolfgang's exceedingly rapid advance as a composer.

First came an invitation to join his two older colleagues, Michael Haydn and Anton Adlgasser, in jointly composing a Singspiel (*Die Schuldigkeit des ersten Gebots*, K. 35), an extended musical drama with a religious text written by a local merchant and based on a passage from the New Testament. Wolfgang completed his section of the work in February and March, and it was first performed after evening prayers in the Rittersaal (the Knights' Room) at the Salzburg court on 12 March 1767. Leopold had assisted his son by writing dialogues and supplying dynamic markings to the full score. (Today the parts of this sacred Singspiel, K. 35, composed by Haydn and Adlgasser, are lost.) Next came a commission from the University of Salzburg where Wolfgang had previously appeared as an "extra" at age five in a Latin school drama. Rufinus Widl, a Dominican monk teaching in Salzburg, wrote a new tragedy in Latin for a springtime school performance. He planned the inclusion of an *intermedio*, a musical interlude performed between the acts of the play, and it was eleven-year-old Wolfgang who faced the task of composing it. The child quickly understood the Latin text and set to music a drama of the ancient gods revealed through mistaken identity, murder, and banishment. The result was *Apollo et Hyacinthus*. The school records mention that Widl's play had its first performance after the midday meal on 12 May 1767 on the stage across from the theater of the Old University. The music met with general approbation; for his efforts Wolfgang received a gold medal worth twelve ducats.

Next came *Bastien and Bastienne*, Wolfgang's first opera, based on a parody of Jean-Jacques Rousseau's *intermède, Le devin du village*. Its composition was begun in Salzburg when the family friend Schachtner (who had poetic successes to his credit) versified the German translation for Wolfgang, who immediately set to work bringing the characters to life. Set in a bucolic village with a field in the distance, the plot reveals a love intrigue involving the shepherdess Bastienne, her lover Bastien, and Colas the magician. The occasion of its first performance is not known, but many think that it was produced by an amateur company in Vienna at the country house of Dr. Franz Anton Mesmer, the famous magnetist and physician.

After nine months at home in Salzburg, Leopold grew restless to travel again. He was granted another leave by the archbishop and set out with the entire family for Vienna in September 1767. There they encountered a smallpox epidemic. Unbeknownst to them, the oldest son of the goldsmith Johann Schmalecker, with whom the Mozarts were lodging, had contracted the disease. When two other children of the goldsmith came down with smallpox, Leopold took Wolfgang and moved, probably to the home of the physician Laugier,[14] leaving his wife as well as Nannerl and a servant with the Schmaleckers. In late October the Mozarts fled to Olmütz in Bohemia, but there was no escape—both children were infected. Delirious with smallpox, Wolfgang was taken to the Cathedral Deanery where his convalescence included being taught card tricks by the court chaplain, Johann Hay. Nannerl later reported that her brother learned the tricks with great rapidity. Wolfgang also practiced fencing as his health improved and by Christmas was able to play a concert with Nannerl at a tavern in Brünn. Nearly four months had elapsed since the Mozarts had left Salzburg, hoping for an audience with Emperor Joseph II. Ten days after they returned to Vienna from Bohemia, the goal was achieved. Wolfgang was received at court.

In a letter to Salzburg, Leopold soon revealed that the emperor himself had twice asked Wolfgang if he would like to compose an opera and conduct it himself. Of course the boy said yes. "What sort of a turmoil do you suppose has secretly arisen among the composers here? Today we are to see a Gluck and tomorrow a boy of twelve seated at the harpsichord and conducting his own opera," Leopold wrote, not guessing that by the end of July the tide of fortune would turn against Wolfgang.[15] To Leopold it seemed that a conspiracy of Vienna's composers had incited the singers and stirred up the orchestra against them, that everything was done to prevent the performances of this opera from going ahead. Boldly upholding the family's financial interests, Leopold handed the emperor a letter of complaint, accusing the theater's impresario of preventing a performance. The angry father complained of intrigues against Wolfgang and demanded unpaid professional fees and a reimbursement for their expenses.

Although the Mozarts returned home with assurances from the emperor, Wolfgang's comic opera in the Italian style, *La finta semplice* (The Pretended Simpleton), was never performed in Vienna. He completed the comedy in Salzburg, where it was first performed in the small court theater in 1769. It was not heard again in Mozart's lifetime.

The twelve-year-old boy, who had not yet set foot in Italy but was soon to go there with his father on three separate tours, showed a startling grasp of the Italian language in *La finta semplice*. Wolfgang's calling card was verbal prankishness, the manipulation of languages his delight. He created order out of the chaos of words and music that swarmed in his mind, composing clearly structured arias and ensemble finales supported by orchestral accompaniments that surpass the everyday achievements of other opera composers of his time. Exploiting the wide range of comedic styles at his command without compromising his musical intentions, Wolfgang triumphed in opera buffa's most severe test. The intelligibility of Marco Coltellini's libretto was never obscured. The creation of *La finta semplice* paved the way for Mozart's later contributions to the opera buffa repertoire, the popular trilogy *Le nozze di Figaro* (The Marriage of Figaro), *Don Giovanni* (Don Juan), and *Così fan tutte* (The School for Lovers).

In December 1769 Leopold and Wolfgang set out for their first tour of Italy. The trip lasted more than fifteen months and included forty cities and towns where Wolfgang, now a young teenager, gave many concerts. When they reached Milan, they lodged at the Monastery of Saint Mark where they occupied three large guest rooms. Attended by Father Alphonso, they ate their meals and entertained visitors before a comforting fireplace in the main room. Each night their beds were warmed, which pleased Wolfgang who seemed always happy to retire.

For their three Italian trips, they were made welcome at the Melzi Palace in Milan, the home of Count Carlo di Firmian, the governor-general of Lombardy. During his initial visit to Milan, Wolfgang received his first Italian commission from Count Firmian, who invited him to compose an opera to be performed over the next carnival season in Milan's Teatro Regio Ducale. This new opera seria would be based on a familiar tale from Roman history. A fee of one hundred ducats, an amount currently equal to about $30,000, was agreed upon by contract in order to avoid another financial crisis such as the one that had plagued Leopold in Vienna—there, despite his cleverness at business, he had obtained neither a written contract nor an advance payment for *La finta semplice*.

After receiving Count Firmian's commission, the Mozarts left Milan and traveled to Rome where they stayed for a month. Wolfgang soon wrote Nannerl on 21 April 1770:

> The castrato Manzuoli is negotiating with the Milanese to sing in my opera. . . . with that in view he sang four or five arias to me in Florence, including some which I had to compose in Milan, in order that the Milanese, who had heard none of my dramatic music, should see that I am capable of writing an opera. The libretto has not yet been chosen [but] I recommended a text by Metastasio.[16]

On Easter Sunday father and son were received by Pope Clement XIV, who issued an order to Cardinal Pallavicini that the Order of the Golden Spur be conferred on the boy "who since earliest youth had excelled in the sweetest sounding of the harpsichord."[17] With the knighthood secured, they continued traveling throughout southern Italy for the next three months.

On their return to Bologna in mid-July, they stayed at the Saint Mark Inn where they were visited by the composer Joseph Myslivecek who brought the contract for the Milan opera and for an oratorio in Padua. During this stay Wolfgang also received the libretto for his new opera, a text based on Jean Racine's *Mithridate*, a play that had first been staged in Paris one hundred years earlier. Over a four-month period, the Italian librettist Vittorio Cigna-Santi had turned his translation of Racine's tragedy about the King of Pontus into an effective new opera text. Wolfgang immediately studied the new libretto and quickly began composing the recitatives. Even though he was allowed only five months to write his first opera for Italy, singers would not be assigned their roles until the following October, so that he had to compose the many arias later when he knew the singers and their voices. Mozart's lengthy score contains an overture and twenty-five numbers. No other opera of Mozart has so many different versions, sketches, fragments, and variants of its individual parts.

Ten days before the first performance, the dreaded intrigues began as they had in Vienna with *La finta semplice*. It was rumored that such a young Austrian boy could not possibly write an Italian opera, but after the first orchestral rehearsal all gossip was silenced. The premiere, conducted by Wolfgang from the harpsichord, was a sensational success. Leopold wrote his wife the details of this momentous event in the artistic life of their young son: "Two things happened which have never happened before in Milan [during a premiere] . . . an aria by the prima donna was repeated and after almost all the arias there was the most tremendous applause and cries of *Evviva il Maestrino* (Long live the little master)."[18] The critic of *Gazzetta di Milano* reported that a number of arias "vividly express the passions and touch the listeners' hearts." Wolfgang wrote Nannerl:

> The opera, God be praised, is a success, for every evening the theater
> is full, much to the astonishment of everyone, for several people say
> that since they have been in Milan they have never seen such crowds
> at a first opera. . . . Yesterday the copyist called on us and said that he
> had orders to transcribe my opera for the court at Lisbon.[19]

With the triumph in Milan of *Mitridate, Ré di Ponto*, Wolfgang had assured himself an unassailable reputation as a young opera composer. It was still three weeks until his fifteenth birthday.

The travelers reached Salzburg after an absence of fifteen months to find an important commission from the Empress Maria Theresa awaiting their return. Wolfgang was invited to compose a work to celebrate the forthcoming marriage of Archduke Ferdinand of Austria and Princess Maria Ricciarda of Modena. The new work, *Ascanio in Alba* (K.111), would take the form of a theatrical serenade in two acts. Leopold and Wolfgang returned to Milan for their second Italian tour at the beginning of September and there read Giuseppe Parini's libretto for *Ascanio* for the first time. Circumstances again demanded intensive work from Wolfgang, who had until then composed only the overture. On 13 September Leopold wrote his wife: "Wolfgang will have completely finished the serenata in twelve days' time . . . the recitatives are all finished, as are the choruses, of which there are eight, and of which five are also danced. We saw the dances being rehearsed today, and marveled at the hard work of the two ballet masters. The first scene is Venus coming out of the clouds."[20]

Following the initial success of *Mitridate* in Milan, the management of the Teatro Regio Ducale commissioned a second opera from Wolfgang, this time for the 1772–73 season. *Lucio Silla*, the last of Mozart's operas written for Italy, was based on a libretto by Giovanni de Gamerra, revised and enlarged by the famous librettist Pietro Metastasio. Wolfgang's contract required that the recitatives be completed by October. He arrived in Milan in November to compose the arias for the individual singers and on 5 December wrote Nannerl, "I still have fourteen numbers to compose and then I shall have finished. It is impossible for me to write much, as I have no news. . . . I can think of nothing but my opera and I am in danger of writing down not words but a whole aria."[21] After an exhausting and confusing period of intense labor, the dress rehearsal took place on 23 December. The first performance was staged on the day after Christmas. At the premiere, the music alone lasted four hours, without the ballets. By 23 January, the new opera had been given twenty-six times and was the success of the season.

We shall never know everything about Wolfgang's personal life in Italy as a young boy quickly becoming a man, but father and son were still inseparable: they shared a room and often the bed. Leopold continued to impose a strict code of behavior on Wolfgang, frequently impressing his deep conviction that most men were untrustworthy and virtually all women ensnaring. Despite his father's pessimism, Wolfgang continued to relish life. The sources of his amusement seem almost limitless; billiards, bowling (a game he learned in Rome), fencing, horseback riding, dancing, and pantomime. Beer, wine, tobacco, and colorful clothing were among his temptations. In fleeting postscripts to his mother and sister he declared that he still loved to travel if the carriage was warm and the coachman drove the horses at high speed when the roads allowed. A note from Bologna revealed his great desire to ride on a donkey! An indefatigable sightseer, he visited art galleries and ancient ruins and the popular carnivals. And he found good friends, two boys his own age. In Bologna he met Giuseppe Pallavicini and, in Florence, Thomas Linley, the English violin prodigy who was in Italy to study with Pietro Nardini. When Wolfgang and Thomas parted, tears were shed.

In Rome Wolfgang snared a Vatican secret, thrilling Leopold by the sheer virtuosity of the musical escapade. Gregorio Allegri had composed his celebrated Miserere for the exclusive use of the papal choir of the Sistine Chapel. The music for this nine-part choral setting of a penitential psalm for the Holy Week was guarded jealously. The chapel singers were forbidden on pain of excommunication to take away a single copy. While gazing in wonder at Michelangelo's masterpiece painted on the ceiling, Wolfgang memorized the Miserere's every detail. He returned a few days later on Good Friday with his own fair copy concealed in his hat, heard the Miserere again, then made a few minor corrections. Soon all Rome and even the Pope himself knew of the boy's exploit. "The achievement has done him great credit," Leopold wrote his wife. "We shall bring it home with us. As it is one of the secrets of Rome, we do not wish to let it fall into other hands."[22]

What Leopold could not bring home was the elusive thing for which he so fervently yearned during the final Italian tour, the promise of prominent positions for Wolfgang and himself in Milan or Florence. It was his fondest dream to relocate the Mozart family in Italy where he had enjoyed such importance as an impresario. When he returned to Austria, he began to have some doubts that his son, now a teenager about to embark on his difficult transition to maturity, would still be able to capture the avid attention of an adoring public as once he had as a young child. At this time, Leopold could not have guessed that over the next two decades Wolfgang would shape a new, independent existence for himself in Vienna, where as a freelance musician in the service of no one but himself, he would secure his fame for all time. In a resolute letter to his wife, Leopold concluded that God probably had some other plan for father and son than prominent careers in Italy.

In Ludwig von Köchel's often-revised chronological catalog of Mozart's complete works, the entries run from K. 1 to K. 626, including 370 works composed during the period of Mozart's youth. An additional collection of unfinished music appears mostly in the appendix of Köchel's catalog. Ranging from a snippet to a sketch of one hundred measures, these important fragments were protected by Mozart's widow, Constanze, after his death; she considered them comparable to the literary fragments of classical authors of ancient Greece.

Can such enormous productivity be explained? Not easily! Generations have imagined music pouring from Mozart's mind and heart in a seemingly endless flow from an inspired source. That Mozart was quick and inspired as a composer, that he shaped and gave meaning to his music internally, even refined entire compositions in his mind before committing them to paper, of this there is no doubt. He once told his father that he must physically write at breakneck speed because while everything that concerned him at the moment had been composed, it was not yet written down. But this is not the whole story. Recent scholarship has shown that the creation of such masterpieces as his six string quartets dedicated to Joseph Haydn required not only inspiration, but painstakingly hard work. This is evident in the copious revisions in the composer's autograph manuscripts.

Before his departure from Italy in 1773, Wolfgang composed the motet "Exsultate, jubilate." It was written for the castrato soprano Venanzio Rauzzini, who had sung the principal role in *Lucio Silla*. Rauzzini gave the first performance of the new motet with orchestra in Milan's Theatine Church (Church of the Teati Brothers) just ten days before Wolfgang's seventeenth birthday. In the final movement of this great masterpiece (now identified as K. 165), Mozart treats the word *Alleluia* in a way that requires breathtaking virtuosity from the singer, consummate technical skill as great as that expected of a violinist or pianist performing his instrumental concertos.

With the composition of this motet, Wolfgang said goodbye to Italy and to his life as a child prodigy. When we compare his innocent Andante that appeared first in Nannerl's music book to "Exsultate, jubilate," we begin to realize that for Wolfgang Amadeus Mozart, the miracle from Salzburg, childhood had been a long voyage of self-discovery between two distant points.

CHAPTER TWO

High Venture

Niccolò Paganini

High venture sprang from this humble place. In this house on 27 October 1782 Niccolò Paganini was born to adorn Genoa and delight the world.

Anton Giulio Barrili, inscription at Paganini's birthplace

THE LEGENDARY violinist Niccolò Paganini entered the world under the sign of Scorpio in 1782 in a three-room dwelling on the seventh story of an ancient house at 38, Passo di Gattamora (Alley of the Black Cat), near the birthplace of Christopher Columbus more than three hundred years earlier. The house still stands[1] in its crooked lane on the slope of Sant' Andrea hill overlooking the docks of Porto Franco where Niccolò's father, Antonio, was a laborer.

While not all Paganini's early biographers were sufficiently superstitious to invoke the supernatural on his behalf, many started his tale with hearsay of prophetic visions and dreams visited on his mother, Teresa Bocciardo Paganini. Steeped in the Genoese folk culture of the 1780s, Teresa's prophecies add a quality of otherworldliness to the widely accepted eighteenth-century image of Paganini. These range from an angelic annunciation during the travail of his birth to an elaborate vision of the violinist playing in a burning theater in the company of a horned guitarist, a gothic dream that occurred after she had prepared the child's shroud when he was stricken with catalepsy following an attack of measles at age five. Whether caught in blinding light or adrift in swirling smoke, Teresa is forever a supplicant and angels assure her that her prayers will be answered—that Niccolò will become the world's greatest violinist.

And so he was eventually considered in his lifetime. His life story is aswarm with mystical innuendo: he was called "fallen angel," "magician of the south," "witch's brat." After an encounter with the violinist at Hotel Riesen in Weimar in 1829, the landlord remarked to writer Friedrich von Matthisson that "If I ever encountered him in the forest, I should take to my heels at once!"

It was not until he was forty-eight that Paganini finally spoke of his childhood to his earliest biographers. As a result of these conversations, two autobiographical sketches emerged in 1830, one published in Leipzig by Peter Lichtenthal, the other in Prague by Julius Schottky. Paganini remained silent on many issues, but even his scant revelations have allowed historians to piece together the events of his childhood and, at least, to speculate on important details that remain untold.

Although unsure of his exact birth date, Paganini began his first autobiographical sketch by dictating to journalist Peter Lichtenthal in Leipzig: "I was born in Genoa on the eve of St. Simeon's Day, 1784 [sic], the son of Antonio and Teresa [Bocciardo], both musical amateurs. When I was five-and-a-half, my father—a commercial broker—taught me the mandolin."[2] The temperaments of Antonio and Teresa Paganini—the pragmatic and the visionary—seem irreconcilable, but in their individual relationships to their extraordinary son, the Paganinis appear to have carried out their parental responsibilities to the best of their abilities under adverse conditions.

There is little question that the circumstances of Teresa Paganini's young life were extremely difficult. She bore a child regularly every two years until there were six, then protected them as best she could from the outside world, the squalid medieval backwash in the old quarter of Genoa where pestilence, political unrest, and revolution raged.

Young and illiterate, Teresa never took flight from such daunting adversity. She trudged endlessly up and down seven floors always to return to the primitive, cramped quarters where there were so many to nurse, to rear, and sometimes to lose to the fury of epidemics. Perhaps her desire to protect and defend her gifted son, to do what she could to help him accomplish the destiny she prayed for, was assuaged by the sound of Niccolò's violin.

When not at work on the docks, Antonio amused himself at home teaching the children to read and write, strumming his mandolin, or trying to work out winning combinations for the lottery, for he was an inveterate gambler. In a reflective moment, Antonio may have suspected the magnitude of Niccolò's precocious gift, because into the hands of his delicate and hypersen-

sitive child (who had just escaped death from measles and would soon be
stricken with scarlet fever), he placed his mandolin. One cannot overesti-
mate the importance of this parental act, nor the amount of time, energy,
commitment, and support required from Antonio once Niccolò's talent
appeared. This brief introduction to music and the subsequent instruction
were critical.

As Paganini told Lichtenthal, "Within a few months I was able to play
any music at sight,"[3] and Schottky: "Even before I was eight years old, I wrote
a sonata under the supervision of my father."[4] Thirty years later in May 1851,
Francesco Bennati wrote that Paganini's progress was so rapid that he would
be hard put to say how it all came about. There was an element of spontaneity about it that was beyond comprehension, as though his talent progressed entirely unawares. His genius developed without fatigue and without
effort.[5]

In the year-and-a-half that Antonio taught Niccolò the mandolin, the
child must have thoroughly learned the instrument's fretted fingerboard and
mastered the articulated plucking so familiar to all mandolinists. When at
seven Niccolò had his first violin—and at last a violin bow was in his hand—
his learning accelerated. Not only did he learn to play this violin,[6] he began
to compose his own music.

Niccolò's uncanny ability to perform violinistic feats usually considered
the province of adults, and his tenacity about accomplishing his specific
goals at all costs, probably left Antonio reeling after a few years of improvised teaching, for this child's violin lessons were surely an ordeal for a musical amateur, a simple man who did not even play the violin.

If Paganini's musical genius sometimes seemed obstinate and perverse,
if first one gift would have its way with him, then another, there is also evidence that his various childhood mentors cast him about from one musical
arena to the next as he alternately studied violin playing and composing.
Because adolescent boys often found employment in Genoa's theater orchestras, the prospect of Niccolò's earning a salary probably prompted Antonio to
withdraw from his role as teacher in 1792, choosing the theater violinist Giovanni Cervetto to teach the boy.[7] During the few months that Cervetto
taught him, this modest violinist may have done little more than finally
demonstrate the traditional art of bowing to the almost untutored child, but
he also introduced him to the lyric theater, a medium that held a great attraction for Paganini throughout his life.

Cervetto, Niccolò's first genuine violin teacher, relinquished the wonder child to a younger colleague, the opera composer Francesco Gnecco. (Always loath to give credit to his teachers, Paganini later stated that Gnecco had some influence on his musical training.) The busy composer Gnecco passed Niccolò on to Genoa's leading violinist, Giacomo Costa. About this particular event, Paganini later remarked to Schottky, "I think back with pleasure on the painstaking interest of good old Costa, to whom, however, I was no great delight since his principles often seemed unnatural to me, and I showed no inclination to adopt his bowing." Costa taught Niccolò only about thirty lessons, but soon had him playing in the different churches in Genoa, sometimes as often as three times a week, and eventually he prepared him for a performance of a Pleyel concerto at the Church of St. Filippo Neri in 1794.[8]

Whatever Niccolò's early violin teachers—his father, Cervetto, and Costa—had tried to impart was far less significant to the child than the effect of his hearing the violinist Auguste Frédéric Durand in Genoa in 1795. When this Franco-Polish violinist toured Germany and Italy in 1794, his contemporaries tried to analyze and imitate his tour de force, but Durand's violinistic display may have most deeply charged the imagination of the young Niccolò Paganini. Later Paganini allegedly told François-Joseph Fétis, the Belgian music theorist and historian, that many of his most brilliant and popular effects were derived to a considerable extent from having heard this fantastic player.[9]

After hearing Durand's improvisations, Niccolò wanted more than ever to compose his own music. From the age of thirteen he invariably based his concert repertoire on his own violin compositions since these pieces displayed his virtuosity to the best advantage. Although he continued for a time to perform concertos by Pleyel, Rode, or Kreutzer, he added movements to them that he composed himself in order to remold these works to his satisfaction.

In 1830 Paganini told Schottky, "I've often sworn off playing compositions by others and I've already destroyed all such music."

Not that I can't play these works. Everybody knows quite well that I can play the most difficult music at sight, but I want to maintain my own individuality and no one can blame me for this since it seems to satisfy the public.[10]

As the stakes increased during Paganini's youthful career, so did the risks he encountered in his relationship to his father.

I had my violin in my hand from morn till night. It would be hard
to conceive of a stricter father. If he didn't think I was industrious
enough, he compelled me to redouble my efforts by making me go
without food so that I had to endure a great deal physically and my
health began to give way.[11]

These extreme conflicts seem unnatural for most fathers and sons, and
indeed Paganini may have exaggerated: by the time he told Schottky of these
personal antagonisms in 1830, he had learned that Beethoven, his great
musical idol, had suffered from the tyranny of an unfeeling father.

As Niccolò became increasingly alienated from the classical traditions
taught by his Genoese violin teachers, Antonio hit upon the idea of placing
him under the guidance of a celebrated violinist and decided on Alessandro
Rolla, concertmaster of the Royal Orchestra in Parma. Antonio would take
him: to send a thirteen-year-old boy traveling alone to a distant town during
a time of political crisis was out of the question. The venture required money,
both for their pursuits in Parma and for the family left behind in Genoa, so
Antonio arranged for Niccolò to give a gala benefit concert at Genoa's Teatro Sant' Agostino, probably with financial assistance from the generous Marquis Gian Carlo di Negro, an influential patron to whom Gnecco or Costa
had earlier presented the young violinist.

This benefit concert in 1795 and the act of leaving home for Parma
proved important turning points. On 25 July 1795, a notice appeared in
Genoa's newspaper, *Avvisi*:

> There will be a concert in the Teatro di Sant' Agostino next Friday, July
> 31. It will be given by Niccolò Paganini of Genoa, a boy already known
> in his *paese* [native city] for his skill as a violinist. Having decided to
> go to Parma to perfect himself in his profession under the guidance
> of the renowned Professor Rolla, and not being in a position to defray
> the many necessary expenses, he has conceived this plan to give him
> courage to ask his fellow citizens to contribute toward his project,
> hereby inviting them to be present at this event which he hopes will
> prove enjoyable.

There is no extant information regarding this brave debut other than the
announcement in *Avvisi* and Paganini's own two widely divergent accounts
of it; however, most of his performances in Italy took place between the two

parts of a double bill in the form of an "intermezzo concert." For this benefit concert either the celebrated dramatic singer Teresa Bertinotti or one of the last of the famous castrati, Luigi Marchesi, or perhaps both of these singers were involved. As to Paganini's contribution to the program, his intermezzo concert probably comprised the Pleyel concerto he had learned from Costa and his own "Carmagnole Variations," a composition built on a popular French revolutionary tune.

Following the financial success of the benefit concert, father and son set off for Parma in September. To Schottky, Paganini described his meeting with the violinist Alessandro Rolla:

> Since Rolla was ill in bed, his wife showed us into a vestibule where I found a violin and the Maestro's latest concerto lying on a table. It needed but a sign from my father for me to take up the violin and play the composition off at sight. The ill composer was immediately interested and asked who was playing in this way; he couldn't believe it was only a little boy. However, when he had convinced himself that this was so, he exclaimed: "I also can teach you nothing. For goodness' sake, go to Paër [the composer]! Here you'd only be wasting your time."[12]

Ferdinando Paër, the director of the Parma Conservatory, met with father and son, then referred Niccolò to his own teacher, the Neapolitan conductor Gasparo Ghiretti, who for six months gave the boy three lessons a week in counterpoint. ("Under his direction I composed, as an exercise, twenty-four fugues for four hands, without any instrument, just with ink, pen, and paper.") Soon after, Paër took back the reins and insisted Niccolò come twice each day for composition lessons. While the move to Parma had provided no violin teacher, it had again placed the wonder child under the direct influence of experienced composers. Although only fourteen, far from home, and still oppressed by the "excessive severity" of his father's regime, Niccolò found great pleasure and satisfaction in his work as his talent developed and his knowledge increased.

After an absence of ten months from his family in Genoa, Niccolò fell severely ill with pneumonia and returned with his father to Genoa "where he remained for a long time," probably playing at private affairs through the assistance of the Marquis di Negro. On 27 November 1796, the French violinist Rodolphe Kreutzer appeared in Genoa during a music festival in honor

of Mme Josephine Bonaparte. He was entertained by di Negro, who arranged
for Niccolò to play for him. Kreutzer told Niccolò about young Charles
Philippe Lafont, a violin prodigy among his pupils at the Paris Conservatory.
Still curious about Lafont twenty years later, Paganini rushed to Milan when
word reached him that the French artist was playing there.

In midsummer of 1799 with the threat of Napoleon's army at nearby
Tortona and Novi, Genoa was virtually under siege. A national guard was
organized to maintain order and quell the rioting, drafting all males of seventeen and over. With this edict in effect, the Paganini family lost no time in
leaving Genoa to take up residence in Ramairone in the Polcevera Valley.
Once there, Antonio and his two sons turned to agriculture, not only to supply the family's needs, but as a sure means of livelihood now that war threatened to close the nearby ports.

At Ramairone, Niccolò took up the guitar and soon played it master-
fully. As he had with the violin, he developed a unique technique for the
guitar based on his own fingering system. However, more than thirty years
later when Schottky asked him whether he still played the guitar in public,
Paganini remarked: "No, I don't like it and look upon it merely as a thought
conductor. . . . Otherwise, it has no value in my eyes."[13] In the intervening
years he had occasionally used the guitar to work out some compositional
aspects of the accompaniments of his concertos, particularly chordal pro-
gressions, but with that exception he never used any instrument for composing, preferring either to sing or whistle as he worked.

Still unknown and with no personal influence behind him, in his late
adolescence Niccolò confined his appearances as violinist to the smaller
towns where it was possible to rent a hall and entice an audience on short
notice. By the autumn of 1800, Niccolò's father left Ramairone to seek work
on the docks at nearby Livorno (Leghorn) because the French had closed the
port at Genoa. Soon after Antonio arrived there, Niccolò, himself, reached
Leghorn carrying a letter of introduction to the British consul who had not
yet been forced by the French to leave the city, a man who he hoped would
help him engage a hall suitable for two concert appearances in July and
August. The following December, Paganini appeared twice in Modena at
the Teatro Rangoni, assisted by the singer Andrea Reggiantini. On the second of these concerts, he played two concertos and his new "Fandango Spa-
gnolo," evidently an improvised, unaccompanied work during which he imitated bird song on his violin to please the crowd.

With the success of these appearances in Leghorn and Modena, Paga-

nini decided by the end of 1800 to escape his father's domination permanently. At eighteen, the young violinist struck out for his independence and
began the essential transition from late adolescence to intellectual and artistic maturity. Six months later, in 1801, he successfully competed in Lucca
for a performance at an annual musical festival on 14 September, the Feast
of the Holy Cross. In addition, the young violinist had a hidden agenda: a violin position in the orchestra of Lucca's Teatro Nazionale had been announced and he intended to win this appointment. Having agreed to Niccolò's competing for an appearance in Lucca's festival, Antonio sent his older
son, Carlo, along as the boy's companion, knowing his sons would return in
a few days since Carlo was to marry Anna Bruzzo in Genoa on 26 September.

Nearing his nineteenth birthday, Niccolò won the competition and was
presented at the Festival of the Holy Cross in a solemn pontifical Mass. That
morning of his appearance, Minister of the Interior Adriano Mencarelli
directed the clergy to have Niccolò perform following the Kyrie. And perform
he did, for twenty-eight minutes in an unprecedented display of musical
mimicry, his violin imitating the flute, the trombone, and the horn, and finally
joyous bird song which aroused much laughter and great admiration.
Whether Niccolò lacked good judgment in this youthful caprice—perhaps
he should have reserved the virtuosic show for the theater—these were the
years when he often played to the gallery with his imitative effects. The
Jacobins, a group of extreme political radicals that included the indomitable
Niccolò, were in attendance in large numbers and saved the day as they led
the thunderous ovation.

On the crest of his success at the festival, Niccolò may have learned that
he would receive his appointment as concertmaster of the newly founded
National Orchestra in the city of Lucca, for he sent Carlo home bearing the
news that he would not return to Genoa. The brothers were close, so that
Carlo would gladly have done this task. Indeed, he and his bride soon
returned to Lucca to be near Niccolò, and for the following seven years Carlo
Paganini served as a professional violinist in the theater.

Niccolò took a pleasure trip to Leghorn the following year in April 1802
where a new theater, built by two wealthy French businessmen, Livron and
Hamelin, was nearing completion. To both Lichtenthal and Schottky, Paganini related the story of the acquisition of an important violin during this
excursion. To Lichtenthal he said: "Once finding myself in Leghorn without
a violin, a Monsieur Livron lent me an instrument to play a Viotti concerto
and then made me a present of it." To Schottky he remarked, "The wealthy

business man and music lover, Monsieur Livron, lent me a Guarneri because I had no violin with me. However when I had finished playing he refused to take it back." With Livron's Guarneri violin in his possession, Niccolò returned to his post in Lucca well equipped with a fabulous instrument, the first of many he owned over the course of his career.[14]

In Lucca Niccolò grew close to the Quilici family with whom he resided, a family that remained devoted to the violinist throughout his life. He dedicated his Six Sonatas for Violin and Guitar, Op. 3, to their little daughter, Eleanora Quilici ("Alla ragazza Eleanora"). It was rumored that Eleanora eventually became his first love; she was the only person outside his immediate family who was remembered in his will.

These years brought many engagements for the maturing violinist and eventually an appointment at court when Napoleon raised Lucca to a principality and declared Princess Elise Baciocchi hereditary ruler. At Lucca, Paganini continued to compose works of chamber music, among them many sonatas (including the "Napoleon" Sonata), quartets for strings and guitar, and his "Duetto Amoroso," dedicated to the Princess Elise. He also became a conductor and in 1809 at the Teatro Castiglioncello led a performance of Cimarosa's opera *Il Matrimonio segreto* (The Secret Marriage).

The testimony of Bartolomeo Quilici given at the time of the ecclesiastical trial of 1841 after Paganini's death sheds further light on the violinist's Luccan years. To Lazzaro Rebizzo, Quilici said, "There's no doubt that Paganini aroused universal admiration when, as a young man, he went to Lucca, where he obtained an engagement."

He was charitable toward the wretched and especially toward those of his own profession, as far as his means permitted. He was neither jealous nor envious, and though he himself was teaching, he respected the other professors, albeit they were far inferior to him. Sometimes he urged them very courteously and without any display of superiority, to adopt other methods. Although at that time there were few professors who were skilled musicians, he not only tolerated their ignorance, but he also never reprimanded them. He studied and played other stringed instruments besides the violin. In fact, he gave cello lessons to Signor Angelo Torre, to the latter's great advantage. He also took a friendly interest in Professor Francesco Bandettini (at that time first double bass of the Royal Orchestra) and persuaded him to change his method of playing the double bass, which Bandettini found very excellent.

Professor Dellepiane and Professor Giovannetti were two good violin pupils of his; he wrote some music especially for them, with consummate mastery.[15]

Evidence of Paganini's musical genius and violinistic prowess resides in many of his musical compositions, and outstandingly so in his Twenty-four Caprices for solo violin, probably composed before Niccolò was twenty. This masterpiece is a veritable dictionary of violin playing, a complex work that reveals the fundamental, irreversible transformation in violin technique for which Paganini was responsible. Much more than a compilation of performance difficulties, the work in its original form has made a genuine and lasting impression on musicians and audiences alike. In the nineteenth century, Robert Schumann believed that the theme of the second caprice alone assured its composer undeniable artistic status, "first rank amongst the younger Italian composers," while Johannes Brahms reckoned that the caprices evidenced "as great a gift for composing in general as for the violin in particular." Recast by composers ranging from Franz Liszt to Darius Milhaud and Boris Blacher, Paganini's caprices in their new guises are often arresting and occasionally sublime, as in Sergei Rachmaninov's *Rhapsody on a Theme by Paganini*, composed in 1934.

Paganini remarked to Lichtenthal that upon his return to Genoa (from Parma) in 1796 he "composed difficult music and worked continuously at difficult problems of his own invention." Perhaps it was then, or a little later at Ramairone, that the young Paganini first became enthralled by Pietro Locatelli's *L'arte del violino* (1733) with its twenty-four caprices, a work that to Niccolò "opened up a world of new ideas and devices." No doubt it was in his study of Locatelli's music that Niccolò best understood the legacy that reached back to Locatelli's teacher, Arcangelo Corelli, the ancestor of all great Italian violinists. During his first four years in Lucca, Paganini's own twenty-four caprices must have continued developing in his imagination; they emerged on paper with apparently no preliminary sketches and little revision. Probably prepared for publication in the agreeable atmosphere of Lucca, the autograph manuscript of the finished version is still in the possession of the firm of Giovanni Ricordi, the well-known music publisher in Milan that issued the first edition.

About his role as composer, Paganini once told Schottky, "Composing is not so easy for me as you think. My great rule in art is complete unity within diversity, and that is very hard to achieve. . . . This requires reflection."[16] His only important work to be published in his lifetime, Twenty-four Caprices, Op. 1, may have been intended only for the future—there is no record of Paganini's ever having played the caprices in public.

On 27 April 1837, Niccolò Paganini wrote his last will and testament, bequeathing his violin—an instrument made in 1742 by Joseph Guarneri del Gesù—to the city of Genoa to be preserved there forever. The Cannon, as it is called, remains there still, rarely removed from the town hall.[17]

If the death of the legendary violinist in 1840 left Europe temporarily without a leading exponent of violin playing, other virtuoso violinists soon accepted the almost insurmountable challenge to fill the void left by his disappearance from the concert stage.

CHAPTER THREE

A Girl From Leipzig

Clara Schumann

What a creature Clara is! She certainly talked more cleverly than any of us—whims and fancies, laughter and tears, death and life, mostly in sharp contrasts, change in this girl with the speed of lightning.

From Robert Schumann's diary, 1831,
in Chissell, *Clara Schumann: A Dedicated Spirit*

As she lay dying in Frankfurt, Clara Schumann asked her grandson, Ferdinand, to play the piano for her, but she stopped him after the final chord of her husband's evocative Romance, Op. 28, a piece he had composed when they married more than a half-century earlier. "It is enough," she murmured. This was the last music she heard.

Just after four in the afternoon of 20 May 1896, she died, having lived a life that spanned most of her century, an artistic life intertwined with the fate of the three musicians who most profoundly influenced her: Friedrich Wieck, her father; Robert Schumann, her husband; and Johannes Brahms, her friend. Four days later when Robert Schumann's grave at Bonn was opened, Clara was buried at his side. Amidst bird song and flowers, the bells of Bonn rang out at Whitsun to signal her passing, a romantic close to the life of the nineteenth century's most celebrated woman pianist.

Clara Wieck (pronounced "Veek") was born in 1819; she met Niccolò Paganini on 4 October 1829 when she was ten. He had returned to Leipzig to perform four concerts, and her father, who had previously met the illustrious violinist in Berlin, took her to Paganini's hotel where she was at once invited to play. Clara later noted the important event in her diary: "I played my Polonaise in E-flat, which he liked very much, and he told my father that I had a vocation for art, because I had feeling. He at once gave us permission to attend all his rehearsals—which we did."[1] Paganini offered Clara a seat of honor on the platform at his Leipzig concerts. He introduced her to celebrities and encouraged her to present others to him. She played again for him at his hotel before he departed, and Paganini signed her autograph album with a souvenir in musical notation. To acknowledge her singular worth, he wrote the words *"al merito singolare di Madamigella Clara Wieck."* The great Italian prodigy had recognized one of his own.

Friedrich Wieck was a dominating force in Clara's childhood. At her birth he chose her name (Clara for "light") and fully expected that she would become a great virtuoso pianist, entirely trained by him. Imagine his despair when at four the child could not yet speak and seemed not to hear.

As her alter ego, Wieck began writing his daughter's first diary when she was seven and continued this practice until Clara was eighteen. Using the diaries as a way of communicating with his child, he filled the books with, in the words of her biographer, Nancy B. Reich, "information, praise, reproach, condemnation, exhortation—all clearly seen in his black, bold handwriting—but he persisted in using the first person throughout, as though Clara, herself, were writing."[2] Only when she left home at age twenty-one to marry Robert Schumann did her diaries become an expression of her own thoughts.

Wieck began in 1826 by inscribing a brief biographical statement in the first person:

> I was born at Leipzig, 13 September 1819. . . . My father kept a musical lending-library and carried on a small business in pianofortes. Since both he and my mother were much occupied in teaching, and beside this my mother practiced from one to two hours a day, I was chiefly left to the care of the maid, Johanna Strobel. She was not very fluent of speech, and it may well have been owing to this that I did not begin to pronounce even single words until I was between four and five years old. . . . My inaptitude for speech, and my want of concern in all that was passing round me, often caused my parents to complain that I was dull of hearing. Even up to my eighth year this defect was not entirely cured, although it improved as I came to speak better and to take more notice of what was going on.

Marianne Wieck, Clara's mother, left her abusive husband in the spring of 1824 and returned to her hometown of Plauen to arrange a legal separation. Only the following summer was Clara allowed to be with her mother, then returning to her father's custody with her three younger brothers in a motherless home. Despite Clara's apparent disabilities, Wieck began teaching his child to play the piano when she was five by including her in a piano class with two other young children. Surprisingly, she learned music without difficulty. Clara's newly found mode of expression released her from the bond of silence and she began to speak in full sentences, although her impairment lingered for three more years.

The diary that Wieck kept provides precise details of his highly disciplined teaching methods. During the first year of her instruction, he did not encourage her to learn to read music but rather to play by heart the small pieces he composed expressly for her use, piano music that encouraged the little girl to concentrate on physical position, musical phrasing, tone production, and familiarity with the keyboard, aspects that accounted for the superb facility and ease at the instrument that she demonstrated to the end of her life. Wieck planned Clara's hour-by-hour existence from the outset of her studies. While he insisted she spend some time out of doors each day taking long walks to insure the "joyousness of youth" and her physical well being ("Active exercise, in all weather, makes strong, enduring piano fingers"), he kept seven-year-old Clara at the piano for three hours each day. One was spent in a lesson, two devoted to practice.[3]

Clara's fascination with music and her unbelievably rapid early physical and intellectual development made it possible for her to begin studying a Hummel piano concerto in 1827 after only two years at the keyboard. Diary entries from this period alternately reveal her father's pleasure and displeasure:

My perception of music began to develop more and more quickly.
My playing also improved, my attack was good, firm, and sure, and my fingers strengthened so rapidly that I could now play difficult pieces for two hours on end with fair persistency, and my father often praised my aptitude for natural and good execution, which I always liked.

A short time later another entry reveals: "My father specially blames me now for a certain jealousy of disposition—love of pleasure—childish sensitiveness—and a curious inclination never to enjoy the present time or present possessions. This last troubled my father the most, because it made me appear seldom contented."

Because Wieck believed there could be no satisfaction in mediocrity nor could musical accomplishment be achieved without sustained effort, he limited Clara's school attendance in favor of her musical education, and thereby also limited the usual opportunities for her normal social life with childhood friends. For six months beginning in January 1825, she attended a primary school in her neighborhood, then Leipzig's Noack Institute where she pursued her meager education for another year. Wieck was married again that year, this time to Clementine Fechner, the young daughter of a local pastor, and the household regained a semblance of normalcy. Although Clara never returned to school, when the time approached for her first concert tours, her father provided tutors to teach her what he considered necessary for her professional success: reading, writing, and French and English, the languages besides her native tongue that might be required in her travels.

After Paganini praised Clara's playing of her original compositions, her father decided that she must have expert training in harmony and counterpoint to enhance her musicianship. Christian Weinlig, who had earlier taught Richard Wagner, was given the opportunity to teach the young girl. Under his guidance, she labored assiduously at the task of composing chorales and fugues to demonstrate her theoretical knowledge, while continuing to satisfy her own creative urge by writing piano music for her performances.

The child's first appearances outside Leipzig's familiar chamber music circles began in 1828 when at age nine she performed a piano duet in public with her father's pupil, Emilie Reichold, and continued with several successful performances in Dresden. Clara made her debut at Leipzig's old Gewandhaus on 8 November 1830 (the "Cloth House" had been for forty-nine years the home of the Gewandhaus Orchestra, now the oldest symphony orchestra still in existence). In addition to her own solo compositions, she performed three virtuosic works with the orchestra; *Rondo brillant* by Christian Kalkbrenner, Henri Herz's Variations, and Carl Czerny's Quartet Concertante for four pianos and orchestra, in which she was joined by three other Leipzig pianists, including Heinrich Dorn, the music director of the Leipzig Opera, with whom she would later study composition.

With the success of this debut, Wieck decided that Clara was ready to appear outside Germany and was prepared to leave all his Leipzig commitments in order to devote himself entirely to her new career.

Preparations for Clara's first international concert tour began with the learning of new repertoire that Wieck felt would attract attention in Paris, the final destination of the tour. There Frédéric Chopin and Franz Liszt were the reigning pianists-composers of the day. A diary entry (written by her father) on 8 June 1831 traces Clara's first encounter with Frédéric Chopin's Variations, Op. 2, a new work for piano and orchestra based on "Là ci darem la mano," from Mozart's opera *Don Giovanni*: "Chopin's Variations, Op. 2, which I learned in eight days, is the hardest piece I have seen or played till now. This original and inspired composition is still so little known that almost all pianists and teachers consider it incomprehensible and impossible to play."

On this early tour, which lasted from the end of September 1831 until the following May, Clara lived her usual existence, unperturbed by the enormity of the venture. She practiced, studied her new repertoire (including Chopin's Variations), performed, composed, and took her daily walks; in brief she did as her father demanded. In March they visited Weimar where she performed at court and twice played in private for Goethe, the great poet who had previously encouraged the astounding prodigy Felix Mendelssohn. Having deeply impressed both audience and critics, Clara left Weimar with superb press notices and a personal accolade from Goethe, a medal with his portrait and a note inscribed "For the gifted artist Clara Wieck." Next came success in Kassel, where Ludwig Spohr, the eminent violinist-composer, gave the girl invaluable advice about revising the structure of her original compositions and wrote a glowing testimonial to her piano playing: "Such is her skill that she plays the most difficult works that have been written for the instrument with a combination of certainty and skill which is to be seen only in the greatest living artists."[4]

Once they reached France, the Wiecks stayed two months in Paris, the thirteen-year-old reveling in the newness of her life, the father discomforted by the strangeness of his surroundings, although Eduard Fechner (the brother of Wieck's second wife, Clementine), a gifted Leipzig artist who lived in Paris, looked after them well on their arrival. Fechner drew a charming portrait of Clara that was lithographed during her visit and was able to arrange her brief appearances in the salons of several wealthy music lovers, but her playing at these soirees was severely hampered by the obstinate, heavy-actioned French pianos of the day, instruments quite unlike the Viennese pianos by Andreas Stein to which she was accustomed.

Yet the early tour had other benefits. At the musical evenings in Paris she met and heard perform many important musicians of the day, including

Frédéric Chopin, then twenty-two, who played his Op. 2 Variations in a performance that Wieck found "hardly recognizable on Kalkbrenner's rough and stubborn piano."

Paganini, who was in Paris to play a series of concerts at the Opéra, invited Clara to appear with him as assisting artist, but this concert was canceled when the violinist fell ill. Unfortunately, Clara's major concert arranged at the Hôtel de Ville on 9 April was poorly attended—a cholera epidemic had broken out in Paris. The Wiecks left the French capital and returned immediately to Leipzig.

Robert Schumann, an eighteen-year-old from Zwickau in Saxony, had come to Leipzig to study law in 1828 and had also begun studying the piano with Friedrich Wieck, boarding in the Wieck home. It was in the same year that Clara, at age nine, had her first appearances outside the city. Two years later, completely disillusioned with his law studies, Robert solemnly bound himself to continue working under Wieck, but he was never fully satisfied with his teacher, who was often away on tour with Clara. And he was wary of Wieck as a person after he witnessed him physically abusing his son, Alwin, when the boy played badly while practicing his violin. ("I can barely describe it—and to all this—Clara smiled and calmly sat herself down at the piano. Am I among humans?"[5])

In 1831, Robert suffered a permanent injury to his right hand while using a mechanical device to increase the independence of his fingers. This calamity abruptly ended any aspirations for his career as a pianist, but he continued his relationship with the Wiecks, turning his attention to composing, which certainly was his true vocation.

Despite differences in age and temperament, Robert and Clara admired each other from the beginning. Their youthful friendship developed steadily over the next few years into an enduring relationship. After a year's absence from Leipzig during which time he tirelessly revised his early, unpublished symphony, Robert returned from his hometown of Zwickau. Upon seeing Clara again, he wrote his mother, "Clara is as fond of me as ever, and is just as she used to be of old, wild and enthusiastic, skipping and running about like a child, and saying the most intensely thoughtful things. It is a pleasure to see how her gifts of mind and heart keep developing faster and faster."[6]

The young Felix Mendelssohn was the guest of honor at Clara's sixteenth birthday party on 13 September 1835 and presented her his newly composed Capriccio as a birthday present. At the height of the celebration, Clara performed the scherzo from Robert's new sonata at Mendelssohn's request. A few weeks after the birthday party, Frédéric Chopin, now twenty-five, arrived in Leipzig and spent an evening in the Wieck home. Robert Schumann was ecstatic to be with Chopin, his exact contemporary, a composer whom he had heralded in 1831 in the newspaper *Allgemeine Musikalische Zeitung* with a review that began, "Gentlemen, hats off! A Genius!" After Chopin played his best-known nocturne for the house party, Clara played several of Chopin's etudes and the finale of one of his concertos. The young Polish genius lavishly praised her interpretation of his music.

Two years before this birthday, on 13 January 1833, fourteen-year-old Clara had confided to her diary that she had begun to compose a concerto. Ten months later she noted, "I have finished my concerto and Schumann will orchestrate it now so that I can play it at my concert." The composition to which she refers was a single movement for piano and orchestra that ultimately became the finale of her Concerto in A Minor, Op. 7, a work that she premiered on 9 November 1835 with Mendelssohn conducting the Gewandhaus Orchestra. At the premiere, both Clara and Felix broke with German performance tradition. She played from memory with her profile to the audience; he conducted with a baton facing the orchestra. Before this time, pianists always played from music in deference to the composer's notation and often performed with their backs to the audience, while conductors contrarily faced the audience and beat time noisily with whatever was in hand, objects ranging from a mace to a rolled parchment. Robert wrote anonymously about Clara's new concerto in his important, new music journal (he had become the editor of the *Neue Zeitschrift für Musik*). The article began: "What we first heard took flight before our eyes like a young phoenix soaring up from its own ashes."

Yet Clara would continue to battle for her independence. Her struggles, especially those to break away from her domineering father, reflected the complex relationship established during her prodigy years, but now confrontations with Friedrich Wieck became increasingly embittered as his jealousy mounted with the realization that Clara and Robert Schumann had fallen in love.

When Robert called at the Wieck home in 1835 to say goodbye to sixteen-year-old Clara before she left on her next concert tour, they kissed as she saw him out. Clara later confessed to Robert, "As you gave me the first kiss, I thought I was going to swoon. All went black before my eyes and I could barely hold the light which I was carrying to show you the way."[7]

Robert naively imagined that Friedrich Wieck would eagerly accept him as a son-in-law, but in this he was badly mistaken. Wieck had not the least intention of bestowing his gifted and valuable daughter upon any man, least of all upon Schumann. When at last Wieck realized a romance was developing between them, he forbade Clara to correspond with Robert or receive his letters. On 14 January 1836, he took his seventeen-year-old daughter to Dresden to separate the young lovers. When Robert visited her surreptitiously in Dresden, Wieck heard about it and turned sharply against her. In February 1836, his rage erupted at Clara for the first time. He threatened to shoot Schumann if she should meet him again. He entered his thoughts on their deceitful behavior in her diary. From beloved pupil and protégée, a source of all Wieck's artistic and personal gratification, Clara had suddenly become the enemy.[8]

During these troubled years of late adolescence, Clara began to reject the very music that had assured her early career as a prodigy—the works of Herz, Czerny, Kalkbrenner, Pixis—in favor of the music of her chosen composers, her contemporaries, Chopin, Mendelssohn, and Schumann, and the great master, Beethoven, who had died a decade earlier.

In February 1837, she traveled to Berlin with her father where he intended to present her in a repertoire appropriate to her new artistic status, abandoning the insubstantial, virtuosic music of her prodigy years. In a concert at the Hôtel de Russie on 25 February, Beethoven's "Appassionata" Sonata formed the centerpiece of her program, surrounded by such works as Bach's C-sharp Minor Fugue from *The Well-Tempered Clavier* and recent pieces by Mendelssohn and Chopin. She also played her own compositions, Bolero and Mazurka. In the five concerts that followed, she repeated Beethoven's "Appassionata," as well as his "Kreutzer" Sonata with violinist Hubert Ries, other piano works by Bach, Mendelssohn, and Chopin, and her Bellini Variations. Berlin audiences were astounded that she played everything from memory.

The following September, Robert wrote Wieck to plead that he "bless this union of souls, for nothing but a parent's sanction is wanting to our highest happiness," but Clara's father remained adamantly silent. When the young composer approached him in person, there was a confrontation. Robert wrote frantically to Clara on 18 September: "Coldness, his ill-will, his confusion, his contradictoriness—he has a new method of destruction. . . . You must tell me what to do."

Clara set out again in November on a concert tour. She played Robert's recently published *Carnaval* at a private gathering in Dresden before going on to Prague and Vienna. After the first recital in Prague she was recalled to the stage thirteen times; two further appearances brought still more enthusiastic acclaim. Before leaving for Vienna, she wrote a perplexing letter to Robert in Leipzig, one upon which it appears Wieck had cast the shadow of his unyielding reservations:

> One thing I must say to you; I cannot be yours until circumstances
> have entirely altered. I do not want horses or diamonds, I am happy in
> possessing you, but I wish to lead a life free from care, and I see that
> I shall be unhappy if I cannot always work at my art, and that I cannot
> do if we have to worry about our daily bread. . . . am I to bury my art
> now?[9]

Clara had enormous success in Vienna, where the emperor and empress favored her with Austria's greatest musical honor, naming her Royal and Imperial Chamber Virtuosa, a title of which she was sufficiently proud to print it in her programs for years to come. "She is a great virtuosa," the empress commented, "but I am still more pleased with her personality." Wieck wrote to his wife, Clementine: "Clara is the theme of Vienna. The papers have become enthusiastic and emotional and weave laurel wreaths."

In a retrospective review of her concerts, the critic of the *Allgemeine Musikalische Zeitung* commented:

> Her performances created a sensation on each occasion only to be
> compared with the enthusiasm roused by a Paganini; and which was
> excited, not only by her technical bravura, but in an incomparably
> greater degree, by her invariably individual, sympathetic conception
> and interpretation of the music she played.[10]

Robert was never far from Clara's thoughts during this tour. She told her father that he could say what he liked, but she would never give Robert up. To Robert she wrote that her love knew no bounds—if he wanted her life that day, she would give it for him. After concerts in Pressburg and Graz, she returned to Vienna to meet Franz Liszt and later confessed to Robert: "When I heard Liszt for the first time in Vienna, I hardly knew how to bear it, I sobbed aloud, it overcame me so." But it was Liszt's response to Robert's music that thrilled her most. "I played your 'Carnaval' to him, and he was delighted with it. 'What a mind!' he said, 'that is one of the greatest works I know.' You can imagine my joy."[11]

A bitter struggle almost without parallel in the annals of musical prodigies unfolded over the next two years as Clara fought for her independence. Because the prodigy and her lover remained steadfast in their intention to marry, Friedrich Wieck became more recalcitrant, embittered, and vindictive, his unabated fury tantamount to insanity.

Early in September 1838, Clara returned to the stage of the Gewandhaus for a performance of Chopin's E Minor Concerto and three piano transcriptions of Schubert songs by Franz Liszt, her new-found friend. After the success of the concert, Robert wrote her a veiled argument for change that could not go unnoticed: "You played magnificently . . . [but] you are too dear, too lofty for the kind of life your father holds up as a worthy goal; he thinks it will bring true happiness."[12]

Because Wieck had insisted they could not remain in Leipzig if they married, it occurred to Clara that it might be to their advantage if Robert moved the business operation of his music journal to Vienna. While nothing finally came of this idea, Robert had an exciting experience in Vienna when he met Ferdinand Schubert, the brother of the great composer Franz Schubert who had died there of typhus ten years earlier. Robert learned that Ferdinand was his brother's sole heir and kept the composer's manuscripts in a black polished chest. There he discovered the manuscript of Schubert's last, great orchestral work, the C Major Symphony, where it had been laid away for a decade with other priceless manuscripts. This discovery of a lifetime revealed to Robert a transcendental work that "transports us into a world where I cannot recall ever having been before." The manuscript was sent immediately to the Gewandhaus Orchestra in Leipzig, and soon after its arrival Mendelssohn conducted the world premiere of the great masterpiece.

Anxiety and tension had been engendered by the torrent of love letters Clara and Robert exchanged during their temporary separation. Their dilemma worsened when Wieck made new demands in Leipzig, questioning whether they had sufficient money to survive without his fortune, most of which had resulted from Clara's accumulated earnings. Wieck planned another trip to Paris for Clara; then in a surprisingly vindictive move that made her fearful and undecided, he refused to accompany her, under the pretext of his business obligations. Wieck continued to lash out at both of them in demeaning letters, and finally on 24 October he wrote: "You are, forgive me, like a pair of children. You cry, he scolds, and it is still the same as ever. . . . You can't belong to him and to me at the same time. You will have to leave one, him or me."[13]

The proposed trip to Paris became both a private and a public testing ground for Clara's independence. Once she had experienced her father's fury at her defiance, she began to realize the full extent of his hostility: he would permit her to go, but hoping for the predicted failure, he would count on her return to his domination. On the question of this proposed venture Robert was ambivalent: "About Paris, If I were in your place, I would not act as if it means too much, nor would I talk about it too much either. Your father will certainly not stay home all winter. You cannot travel alone: I won't permit it."[14]

In all this confusion, Clara decided to go. She planned to earn money along the way by giving concerts. After a performance in Stuttgart, she met Henriette Reichmann, a young woman of her own age who was prepared to go to Paris as her traveling companion in exchange for piano lessons, and they set off together for France. Although Clara was troubled by headaches, sleepless nights, and the stressful responsibilities of concert management that were now hers alone, over the next few weeks she began to realize she could successfully carry on her career without her father.

In Paris Clara met Hector Berlioz, a great admirer of Robert's music. The celebrated composer quickly became her ally. She was reunited with her friend, the mezzo-soprano Pauline García, and the singer's brother-in-law, the Belgian violinist Charles de Bériot. These young musicians agreed to join Clara as assisting artists in her forthcoming concerts. When both Erard and Pleyel, the leading piano manufacturers in Paris, placed their best pianos at her disposal, her concert life was again underway.

When Wieck read the favorable reviews of the Paris concerts within a few weeks and realized that Clara was doing well without him, he declared his intention to deprive her of her inheritance, including all the money she herself had earned, unless she abandoned Robert Schumann. In an unbridled rage, he threatened to bring a lawsuit against them both.

Under the stress of such escalating threats, Robert began to exhibit remorseful indecision and the disastrous changes of mood that foreshadowed his impending mental illness. As his ambivalence toward Clara's career increased, he wrote her that "young wives must be able to cook and to keep house if they want satisfied husbands and you can have fun learning that." This he swiftly followed by an injunction: "Use your time to compose, to play. Don't be so retiring, let them know what kind of artist they have in Paris."[15] After this barrage of confusing letters, Clara asked Robert to postpone their marriage. He was angry and responded, "Just promise me not to entertain any more unnecessary fears, trust and obey me; after all, men are above women."[16]

When she received two further letters from Robert, Clara realized that their marriage would not be postponed. The first contained a copy of yet another dignified appeal to Wieck for permission to marry. The second was a joint letter to be signed by both of them if Wieck continued to withhold his consent. Saxon law required the consent of the parents for any marriage, regardless of the age or rank of the children. If such consent could not be obtained, it was customary to appeal to the court: the duly signed joint letter was submitted to Leipzig's Court of Appeals prior to Clara's return to Germany.

While the months in Paris had not greatly increased the young pianist's reputation, Clara, at nineteen, had experienced an enormous change in her personal life. She had lived on her own resources, made new friends, composed music, taught piano lessons, played concerts, and had survived without her father or her lover, despite the toll exacted by the emotional turmoil of this existence. Although her independence was imminent, her perilous journey was not yet at an end. When she returned to Leipzig she found herself homeless. All her possessions—her clothing, music, piano, even her childhood diary—were kept from her under lock and key by her vindictive father. Nor had Robert fared well in her absence. The ongoing, embittered struggle had plunged him into bouts of serious depression and torturous thoughts of death. "I am carrying a great burden of guilt—I separated you from your father—and this often torments me."[17] The year ahead would be yet more difficult for everyone. Indeed, the greatest hurdle loomed ahead, for the court litigation was pending.

On 18 December 1839, Wieck was ordered to appear in court. Clara wrote in her diary: "This day has separated us for ever, or at least it has torn to pieces the tender bond between father and child." Throughout the embattled proceedings that followed, Clara managed to sustain a filial concern for her father despite their conflict: "I regret everything so much, and yet was he not cruel? Was he not terrible? Nonetheless I feel such an inextinguishable love for him—one friendly word from him and I would forget all the pain he caused me. . . . I cannot suppress the childlike love I feel. In losing me, he has lost all his hopes."

During a lull in the protracted events at court, Clara left on tour. Even though plagued by pains in her hands and on the brink of collapse, she showed great fortitude and played well, performing Robert's F-sharp Minor Sonata for the first time in public on 1 February.

The court case dragged on. Although Wieck would not acknowledge defeat, by August the court conferred its consent for the marriage of Clara Wieck and Robert Schumann. They would marry without parental permission. "I cannot grasp this happiness," Clara wrote in her diary. On 5 September 1840 she played a concert in Weimar. Robert was there to take her home after her very last public appearance billed as Clara Wieck.

One day before Clara's twenty-first birthday, the wedding took place in the little village church at Schönefeld, near Leipzig. On the eve of her coming of age, Clara wrote: "My whole self was filled with gratitude to Him who had brought us safely over so many rocks and precipices to meet at last. I prayed fervently that He would preserve my Robert to me for many, many years. Indeed, the thought that I might one day lose him is enough to send me out of my mind. Heaven avert this calamity!"

Despite Clara's youthful supplication on her wedding day, Robert Schumann died on 29 July 1856, sixteen years after their marriage. He was quite alone that day in the asylum at Endenich, near Bonn, where for two years he had suffered acute melancholia, varied by intervals of complete lucidity when he composed as before. He was survived by Clara and seven of their eight children, and many of his best friends, including Johannes Brahms. To posterity he left musical compositions of incalculable worth.

Clara lived on for forty years to become a preeminent concert pianist. While she remained the major exponent of the works of her husband and of Brahms, her friend, it was the performance of Beethoven's music that was the crowning achievement of her mature career.

In later life, Clara Schumann expressed her conviction that only a composer—a creator—could achieve immortality; the interpretive artist would soon be forgotten. Yet she is not forgotten. She is remembered as the little mute child who began playing at five, then surged ahead as an astounding prodigy who survived, despite the unrelenting demands of a domestic life devoted to an ailing husband and eight children, as a major pianist until her final years. Not least of all, she is remembered as the champion of the monumental, romantic piano music composed at the apex of her century.

Pablo Casals at five, 1881. Courtesy Marta Casals Istomin.

CHAPTER FOUR

El Niño del Tost

PABLO CASALS

From infancy I was surrounded by music. You might say music was for me an ocean in which I swam like a little fish. Music was inside me and all about me; it was the air I breathed from the time I could walk.
   Casals, interview by Albert E. Kahn, *Observer Review*, 13 September 1970

AT TWELVE, Pablo Casals found his first full-fledged professional engage-ment—playing cello in a cafe trio seven nights a week from nine until midnight for four pesetas an appearance. In 1888 the trio performed in the main room of Barcelona's Cafe Tost in the suburb of García where every night an audience came to hear the music—marches, waltzes, and well-known operatic airs—as much as to have a cup of excellent coffee or choco-late with friends.

   Pablo liked his new job and tried to improve it. He persuaded Señor Tost, the owner of the cafe, to devote one night each week to classical music. The customers liked what they heard. Pablo's plan was a success and more and more people began to come to hear the young cellist, El Niño del Tost, as they lovingly called the boy.[1]

   He was born on 29 December 1876 at Vendrell, a small, Catalan village in Spain, where narrow, meandering streets lined with humble dwellings and busy shops all led to the Church of Santa Ana. Few of Vendrell's five thousand inhabitants ever went beyond sight of the imposing bell tower, but during Pablo's childhood the Casals family occasionally went a few miles south of the hills that encircled Vendrell to enjoy their one luxury, a small

91

cottage in nearby Playa San Salvador, a small beach on the Mediterranean shore.

Pablo's first memories were of that beach and the Ermita, a small, secularized Romanesque hermitage at San Salvador, where he was attracted to the endlessly moving sea: "I stayed for hours, resting my elbows on the windows watching this spectacle, always changing, yet always the same." For more than sixty years Casals returned there at least once each year and throughout his long life felt the powerful attraction of the hermitage and the shores, as well as the little town of Vendrell, whose spell always evoked the wonder world of his childhood.[2]

Carlos Casals, Pablo's father, was born in Sans, a working-class quarter in nearby Barcelona. There he studied the piano, then mastered the rudimentary technique of the organ. When he was a teenager, he organized a successful choral group in his neighborhood with the help of the barber Peret, his friend who played the guitar. When Peret decided to move to Vendrell he encouraged Carlos to move there also. In Vendrell the two friends formed La Lira, a men's chorus that still exists, and were soon making music in the evenings at a favorite gathering place, the Cafe del Centro.

Carlos discovered that the great baroque organ of the Church of Santa Ana badly needed repairs. He convinced the clergy that he could do the work, then labored without pay to restore the organ. By the time he was twenty, Carlos had become the parish organist and choirmaster of Vendrell, the chief musician of the village.

About the same time that Carlos arrived in Vendrell, a widow named Señora Defilló and her two children arrived in Vendrell from Mayagüez in the faraway colony of Puerto Rico. Pilar Defilló, the widow's young daughter, was eighteen. Beautiful, shy, and talented, Pilar continued the piano lessons begun in Puerto Rico with Carlos Casals as her new teacher. A real affection soon developed between them, and in 1874 they married. They moved into their new home, the upper two floors of a modest house at No. 2, calle Santa Ana, near the church. Carlos set up a music studio on the first floor where he continued teaching private lessons. Their living quarters were two small rooms on the second floor.

During their long marriage, Pilar gave birth to eleven children, but only three survived their infancy. Their second son, Pablo, lived almost a century. From his earliest days, music was his natural element, something as natural to him as breathing. "I certainly sang in tune before I could speak clearly. Thanks to my father, I learned to combine sounds at the same time that I expressed myself in words."[3]

Carlos' parental influence on young Pablo was considerable, maybe decisive. "He was quite a remarkable musician in a quiet way," Casals said. "It was he who awoke in me the love of music through his lessons and his example. It was the example of a man who, without departing for a moment from modesty, was nevertheless a true and pure artist." But it was his mother who best understood Pablo's aspirations in music. "Oh, my mother was an exceptional woman! What I owe to her energy, her genuine understanding and her deep humanity! Right through her life she was my guardian angel."

As his first teacher, Carlos gently guided Pablo through his earliest musical experiences. At the age of two or three, the child sat on the floor resting his head against the upright piano the better to hear his father's improvisations or stood behind the piano naming any notes Carlos played at random. At five Pablo learned to sing plainsong when he was admitted to the church choir. As a second soprano he earned eighty-five centavos (about a dime) a night at choir rehearsals. He sang in his first choir concert during *la misa del gall* (Mass of the cock) on Christmas day in 1861. The Casals family had walked through Vendrell's dark streets before dawn and entered the church ablaze with candlelight for the early morning ritual. "My father played the organ and I sang—I sang with all my heart!"

Little Pablo was curious about any new musical instrument he saw and was irresistibly attracted to all of them. First he learned to play the piano. By the age of six he already played the simpler works of Chopin, Beethoven, and Mendelssohn, and Carlos soon introduced him to Bach's *Well-Tempered Clavier*. (This body of music became a lifelong preoccupation for Casals, who began his work every day at the piano playing one set of the forty-eight paired preludes and fugues.) At seven, Pablo began learning the violin and within a year played in public an air with variations by Charles Dancla. The boy began to compose by writing a little mazurka. He presented his first piece to his grandfather, who rewarded him with dry figs and a ten-sous coin. When he was about seven, he helped his father write music for *The Adoration of the Shepherds*, a play staged at church on Christmas Day in 1883. His father had the text and agreed to set special episodes to music, but he was overworked and asked Pablo to help him. When the boy began to work at the task, Carlos was not at all surprised for he thought it was quite natural for this child of seven to write notes and musical signs diligently on the staff.

Among Pablo's greatest desires from the age of six until nine was to play the organ. He would sit next to Carlos when he was playing in church, and kept asking his father to teach him. Carlos insisted that he could not begin this musical undertaking until his legs were long enough to operate the pedals adequately. When he did begin to play the organ, within a few months he could substitute when his father was ill.

A traveling group of entertainers dressed in clown costumes appeared in the Vendrell plaza in 1885. They called themselves Los Tres Bemoles (The Three Flats). These musicians played on guitars, mandolins, bells, and instruments made from washtubs, cigar boxes, and assorted household utensils. One man who played standing up used a primitive one-stringed instrument made of a bent broomstick. Pablo sat on the cobblestones in the front row of the audience, fascinated by this broomstick instrument. A few days later his father built him a similar instrument, using a dried gourd as a sounding board. This gourd-cello exists to this day.

This was Pablo's first cello. He tried it out by playing a few scales, then the tune of Schubert's Serenade. On this gourd-cello with its one string, he soon learned to play the many songs his father wrote and the popular tunes that he heard on the village streets. While his gourd-cello was still new, he performed on it one night in the ruined monastery of Santas Creus outside Vendrell. When he revisited the site thirty years later, he met an old innkeeper who recalled this childhood performance: "An old innkeeper remembered me as a boy of nine playing my queer instrument in one of the cloisters flooded with moonlight. And I remembered the stillness of that night, and the music which echoed so strangely against the crumbling white walls of the monastery."[4]

Pablo's childhood was not all music and moonlight. As a youngster, he was high spirited and daring, sometimes mischievous, with great strength for his age. At school he fought his share of bullies. The family friend Matines, a wine-cask maker well-known for his inventive exploits (he had thrown himself from the roof of his house, wearing homemade wooden wings), took delight in making seven-year-old Pablo a wooden bicycle with a large front wheel. On his first attempt to ride the new bicycle, Pablo descended a steep hill, hit a stone on the road, and fell so violently that he fractured his skull, but he got up, mounted the bicycle again, and this time he rode it successfully. A few months later while playing a game of hide and seek near the station, he ran through a barrier and got snagged by one big nail which went into his head. He freed himself, then went to the middle of the village plaza to lie on his back so that the sun would dry the blood. His father found him there and thought he was dead.

A more serious incident occurred when a mad dog bit Pablo's leg. His parents thought he had no chance of survival but hastily took him to a hospital in Barcelona to undergo Pasteur's new treatment, sixty-four injections of boiling serum. Pablo stuffed his mouth with a handkerchief before the ordeal began, remembering his father's command "Say to yourself that men don't cry!"

In 1888 a chamber music trio traveled from Barcelona to Vendrell to perform in the Vendrell Catholic Center. At this trio concert, eleven-year-old Pablo saw and heard a real cello for the first time. It was played by Josep García, the accomplished cello professor of the Municipal School of Music in Barcelona, who was later to be Pablo's teacher. The boy was fascinated and that same evening said to his father, "*That* is the instrument I want to play!" His earnestness persisted; he began to play his violin upright between his knees as though it were a cello. Repeatedly Carlos made him put it back on his shoulder, but moments later the boy continued the other way. Carlos soon found a small cello and gave his son his first cello lessons.[5]

Carlos had a strong conviction that a life in music would not earn the boy a living. He asked the village carpenter who lived across the street to take him as an apprentice when he reached the age of twelve. Pilar had a different point of view. She opposed her husband in this matter, and the violent rift between them greatly upset Pablo: "They argued with such bitterness that it pained me terribly and I felt very guilty." Since he had first heard the cello and shown such enthusiasm for it, Pilar insisted Pablo have lessons from a real teacher. Because there was no cello teacher in Vendrell, she knew her son would lose time by remaining in the village. Pilar decided that Pablo must go to Barcelona to study, and that she would take him there.

Carlos knew that Pablo's compositions showed promise, that he had become an excellent pianist and a good organist, and that he had been wildly excited about the cello for months. Acquiescing to his wife's decision, he wrote to the Municipal Music School in Barcelona inquiring about the possibility of his son's enrollment. The response was positive, but an audition was required for admission. In the late summer of 1888, Pilar and Pablo boarded a third-class railway carriage bound for Barcelona. Carlos remained behind in Vendrell. Casals never forgot his departure from Vendrell when he was eleven-and-a-half years old. "I was very sad at leaving the countryside where I had been brought up, the background of my happy, carefree childhood."

When Pilar's distant relatives in Barcelona, Benet Boixadoes and his wife, agreed to keep Pablo, his mother accepted their invitation but remained there with him for his first few days of school before returning to Vendrell to give birth to her ninth child. After his audition for the director, Maestro Rodoreda, Pablo was accepted as one of the youngest of the four hundred students at Barcelona's Municipal School of Music where he would attend both the cello and composition classes. On the first day he was so terribly frightened that he just did not understand a thing his teacher explained to him, much less the task that was set for the next day. He got home in a very nervous state and in tears, and told his mother all about it. He was feeling desperate and thought the best thing to do was to write something of his own on the figured bass the teacher had assigned as a harmony exercise. When he produced it the next day in class, the teacher looked at it, seemed to laugh and cry at the same time, and ended by embracing the little Catalan.

Pablo was soon too busy to be homesick, and one parent or the other visited often. In addition to his counterpoint studies with Maestro Rodoreda, he continued to study the piano with the famous Spanish pianist Joaquin Malats. His cello teacher was Josep García, the cellist he had heard in the trio performance in Vendrell. He studied with him for the next five years. García was to be Pablo's only formal cello teacher.

Josep García was descended from a family of musicians, many of them famous singers. Manuel García, for whom Rossini composed the role of Count Almaviva in *The Barber of Seville,* was the patriarch. His daughters, Maria Malibran and Pauline Viardot-García (Clara Schumann's friend) were celebrated sopranos. His son, also named Manuel, became an esteemed vocal teacher in Paris and London and codified his father's teaching system into "the García method." The teacher of Jenny Lind and Mathilde Marchesis, he continued to teach singing until the age of 101.

Josep García was in a sense an ideal teacher for Pablo, a musician whose cello playing eventually epitomized the instrumental singing style. Pablo thought his teacher was an excellent cellist, but even at the first lesson he felt disturbed by the conventional things that seemed absurd to him. He began revising García's instructions and was soon creating a new technique of his own. When the other cello students noticed his way of playing they would say, "What are you doing? You will catch it for this," but by twelve Pablo was already revolutionizing cello playing. As he said later, "Cannot even a child observe and think what he likes of his teacher and notice what may be wrong in his teaching?"

Toward the end of his first year of study, he began his first professional engagement as cellist of the trio at Cafe Tost but soon rejoined his family in Vendrell for the summer. Pilar took him for a vacation at San Salvador. In the late summer he appeared in a concert in Tarragona, and for the first time Pilar was able to paste a press clipping into a clothbound book in which she kept his reviews until his twenty-first birthday. In September, Pilar returned with Pablo to Barcelona and found new living quarters a few blocks from the Cafe Tost, where every evening she sat at her regular table with a cup of coffee and listened to the trio.

Early in 1890, Señor Tost, the proprietor of the cafe, began to take Pablo to concerts. They heard Richard Strauss conduct *Don Juan,* and a recital by the Spanish violinist Pablo de Sarasate. A choral society, which later became the Orfeo Gracieno, used to meet above the Cafe Tost. They made Pablo an honorary member and presented him a diploma, his first childhood distinction. A great Wagner enthusiast called Fluvia, who came regularly to the Orfeo, was the first to introduce Pablo to Wagner's *Der Ring des Nibelungen.* He also gave him the scores of *Lohengrin, Parsifal,* and *Tristan und Isolde,* which they read together with great excitement. Richard Strauss became for Casals "another source of exaltation—a youthful emotion that has never left me."

Sometime in 1890, Carlos visited Barcelona and brought Pablo his first full-sized cello. They set out together in search of more scores for the Tost evenings. They went into a secondhand music store, and as they browsed Pablo found the great discovery of his life, a dusty Grützmacher edition of the Bach cello suites.

> I forgot entirely the real reason of our visit to the shop, and could only stare at this music which nobody had told me about. Sometimes when I look at the covers of that old music, I see again the interior of that old and musty shop with its faint smell of the sea. I took the suites home and read them and reread them. They were to become my favorite music. For twelve years I studied and worked every day at them, and I was nearly twenty-five before I had the courage to play one of them in public.

Throughout his career, Casals was plagued by stage fright. It struck first less than two months after his fourteenth birthday when he made his first real Barcelona concert appearance on 23 February 1891 at the Teatro de Novedades as part of a benefit for the elderly comic actress, Concepción Palá. "My head was going round, fear gripped me fast, and I said, as I got up: What am I going to do? I cannot remember the beginning of the composition I am going to play!" Stage fright before playing never left him throughout his long career. At each of thousands of concerts, the terror gripped him as it did on that first occasion. In his old age, stage fright often brought on angina attacks, but he was never defeated. He rose from his deathbed at ninety-six to play the cello one last time for himself and those who kept vigil.

Once when the composer Isaac Albéniz was in Barcelona with his two friends, violinist Enrique Arbós and cellist Augustín Rubio, with whom he had formed a well-known trio, he heard about the playing of El Niño and came to Cafe Tost to hear Pablo play. Albéniz was so pleased with Pablo's playing that he wanted to take the boy to London with him. But Pilar Casals would not hear of it and told Albéniz that her son had to work and get much better before thinking of this. But the great composer gave Pablo a letter of introduction to the Count de Morphy, an illustrious patron of music, who had been tutor and private secretary to King Alphonso XII. He was at that time private adviser to Doña Maria Cristina, the Queen Regent. Pablo's mother kept this letter carefully for three years, just waiting for the opportune moment to use it.

In adolescence Pablo suffered from excessive emotionality and over-flowing sensitivity. He was still greatly disturbed by his parents' conflicting ideas about his future; when his emotional turmoil was at its height, his mother backed him up with incredible tact and understanding, but his father could not understand him and did not realize how near he was to a fatal crisis. His emotional difficulties were much more serious than those of an ordinary phase of adolescence. At this time he concluded that suicide was the only way out, an idea that pursued him for months on end.

Pablo sought refuge in religion and went through a period of religious mysticism. Each day after leaving the Municipal School of Music, he would walk a few blocks to the church of Santo Jaime, go inside, and look for a dark corner where he could pray and meditate in peace. Yet often, as soon as he left the church, he would hurry back again more anguished than ever. He felt that there in the sanctuary was his only hope of salvation. When he returned home his face showed his mother all his painful anxiety. "What is the matter?" she would say, and he would answer, "Oh, it is nothing." Pablo was too fond of her to tell her of his obsession with suicide, his mental revulsion in the face of the horrible world that he imagined. His religious fervor did him no good. He was not long deceived when he read the socialist doctrines of Marx and Engels, something his critical mind could not accept. "I had only to look about me to see what men were like, and I sadly realized that nothing would change them—that they would never become *brothers*."

When Pablo finished his studies in Barcelona at seventeen, his mother thought he could not learn much more there and that it was time she used Albeniz's letter of recommendation to the Count de Morphy. With his two younger brothers, Pablo and his mother set off for Madrid.

When Pilar gave Albeniz's letter to the count, Pablo also handed him his portfolio of compositions. Wanting to hear these pieces, the count arranged for Pablo to play for the Infanta Isabel, who was a music lover. Soon after, he introduced Pablo to the Queen Regent, Doña Maria Cristina, and arranged a concert at the palace where the boy appeared both as cellist and composer. The queen so admired the performance that she granted Pablo a scholarship that made it possible for the family to remain in Madrid. Tomas Breton became Pablo's composition teacher at the Madrid Conservatory and Jesus de Monasterio his teacher in chamber music. Casals held the highest admiration for Monasterio and later often said that he was the greatest teacher one could have had. "He was the kind who evoked devotion because his art and teaching were guided by a sense of greatness and nobility."

The Count de Morphy made himself personally responsible for Pablo's general education just as he had been the preceptor of King Alfonso. Every morning at his home he gave him lessons on general culture, using the same annotated textbooks he had for the king. In order to make Pablo express his impressions clearly and concisely, he sent him to visit the Prado Museum once each week to study its art works, to the chamber of deputies to hear all the famous speakers, and to the classical theater. Every day Pablo had lunch with the count and after the meal improvised for him at the piano in the drawing room. Pablo was received by the queen without ceremony each week when he went to the palace to play his compositions and the cello.

The count's views on music and musicians seemed important at court where he was known as a musician, having been a pupil of both François-Joseph Fétis and François Gevaert in Belgium. When Pablo had been in Madrid for more than two years, the count began to envision him at nineteen as a future composer of Spanish operas. He wanted him to become a composer. Pablo's mother thought differently: "If he is really gifted as a composer, the cello will not stand in his way, but if he neglects or abandons this instrument, it will be very difficult for him to make up for lost time."[6] As a result of their disagreement, Pilar decided the family should return to Barcelona. The count finally accepted their departure when Pablo promised to go to Belgium to study composition with his former teacher, François Gevaert, then the director of the conservatory in Brussels. The count, ever hopeful, arranged for a small allowance to be renewed by the queen.

Casals recalled his journey to Brussels:

> For the first time I crossed the frontier, in the company of my mother and my two younger brothers. My father could not understand and felt desperate and would say, "What is this woman thinking about?" Neither my mother nor I could guess what adventures awaited us when we left Spain.

At their first meeting, Gevaert told Pablo that he no longer gave compositions lessons because of his advancing age and advised him to go to a big city like Paris where one could hear good music. Just as Pablo was taking his leave, Gevaert invited him to play the next day for the cello professor, Eduard Jacob.

The next morning Pablo went for his interview with Jacob but did not bring his cello. He sat on a bench at the back of the room and listened to Jacob's pupils and thought their playing not exceptionally good. At the end of the class, Jacob called him forward and, naming a great many works, asked him to play. Responding to Jacob's demands, Pablo said, "Anything you like." This so exasperated Jacob, that he snarled, "Well, this boy knows everything, he must be extraordinary," a remark that brought gales of laughter from his pupils. Red-faced with indignation, Pablo seized a cello and performed François Servais' *Souvenir de Spa*, a virtuosic piece then thought to be transcendentally difficult. When he had finished, Jacob quickly took him into the privacy of his office and guaranteed the first prize of the conservatory if only he would consent to be in the class. "No, you have made fun of me in front of all your pupils, and I don't want to stay here another minute!"

The next day with his mother and brothers, Pablo left Brussels bound for Paris. When Count Morphy was informed that the young Spaniard had abandoned the plan for Brussels, he was angry and felt certain things had gone wrong because of Pilar's influence. Since the family had no means without

Count Morphy's financial support, life in Paris was hard. Pablo competed for a job at a music hall and won a place in the orchestra of the Folies-Marigny. From the hovel where they lived near the Porte St. Denis, he walked to the theater twice each day, carrying his cello, to save the fare of fifteen centimes. Pilar stayed at home with the other children and took sewing jobs in order to earn enough to help feed four and buy medicines. Pablo's father, Carlos, sent what he could from Spain, but it was very little.

Defeated by such adverse conditions, they returned to Madrid. It seemed the best thing to do. Once more in Spain, Pablo went on with his studies, strengthened by his growing conviction that musical performance at its best should not be an explosion of feeling only, no matter how sincere, but it should be held together by severe and tenacious discipline. This concept would guide his work in later years: "Performance must rely as much on constant simplicity of expression as on the rich variety of forms to be found in nature." Pablo was soon reconciled with Count Morphy and the court. With her usual kindness, Queen Maria Cristina asked him to give a concert at the palace, after which she presented him with a fine Gagliano cello and decorated him Chevalier de l'Ordre de Carlos III.

Within weeks he made his first appearance as soloist with orchestra, performing Edouard Lalo's cello concerto in Madrid. Tomas Breton conducted. After this initial success and with Count Morphy's letter of recommendation to the great French conductor Charles Lamoureux, Pablo set out again for Paris. He was now twenty-two and Pilar rightly thought he should travel by himself, her company no longer as necessary as it had been before. This marked the end of his perilous voyage and began a timely separation from those who had protected him throughout his youth.

At his Paris audition, he played the Lalo concerto through, then was embraced by Charles Lamoureux who proclaimed, "My dear child, you are one of the elect." Lamoureux asked him to play the first movement of the Lalo concerto at his first concert of the new season on 12 November 1899.

Casals' debut in Paris as a soloist at the Concerts Lamoureux was an even greater success than he had hoped for. A large audience filled the Théâtre de la République and, as Alfred Bruneau recorded in *Le Figaro*, did not stint its bravos for the cellist. His interpretation was praised in *Le Ménestrel*. Pierre Lalo, son of the composer and critic for *Le Temps*, wrote of Casals' "enchanting sound" and "beautiful virtuosity." When he appeared again with Lamoureux on 17 December, the conductor proclaimed him

"Knight of the Order of the Violoncello—now and forever." The boy who had been El Niño del Tost was the most promising European cellist of the turn of the twentieth century. He launched an incomparable international career that in seventy years never lost momentum. When he died in Puerto Rico on 22 October 1973, Pablo Casals was ninety-six and had been considered for almost three quarters of a century the greatest cellist who ever lived.

CHAPTER FIVE

A Family Portrait

The Britts and the Koutzens

O N AN OLD mural map that ornaments the foyer of the Glarnerhof Hotel in Glarus, Switzerland, visitors can still see a small forest called Brittenwald that once lay outside the township. As early as 1350 this wooded tract of land on the Kerenzer mountain belonged to an ancient Glaronnais family named Britt. By the turn of the nineteenth century, those Britts who still lived in the Canton of Glarus were ensnared in a vast economic struggle for survival, but despite this hardship, Jakob and Elsabeth Britt stubbornly remained at Obstalden hoping for a change of fortune. It came in 1815.

Having set sail from Elba with one thousand men, Napoleon returned to France like a thunderbolt. When the deposed emperor came ashore at Cannes to reclaim his empire on 1 March 1815, republican peasants rallied around him swelling the ranks. Soldiers dispatched from Paris to arrest the renegade before he could cross the Alps near Grenoble joined him instead. As he passed near Geneva, rumors of revolution swept across Switzerland and Jakob Britt mounted his horse and rode toward Paris to join Napoleon's army.

As a soldier in the Armée du Nord, Jakob Britt crossed the frontier into Belgium on 15 June. Two days later, Bonaparte lost twenty-five thousand men and suffered his final, catastrophic defeat on Belgian soil, but Britt had survived the fierce fighting at Waterloo. In the confusion that followed the battle he slipped away into the night and began the long journey home to Obstalden. Within the year, he returned to Belgium with his wife Elsabeth to establish a new home in Antwerp. Swiss for almost half a millennium, the Britts would now be Belgians.

The first notable musician in the family was Ernest Britt, Jakob's grandson. Born in Antwerp on 17 July 1860, Ernest Britt was already recognized as an outstanding pianist and promising composer while still a student at the École de Musique d'Anvers. Before he was twenty, he met and married the young soprano Maria Deshayes, the daughter of a retired seagoing man who had commanded the *Vasco da Gama*, a three-masted sailing ship. They moved into an apartment on the rue des Images in Antwerp, where their first child was born on 18 June 1881. His birthday fell on the celebration of the Battle of Waterloo. He was christened with five given names to honor both his parents and his grandparents—Horace Ernest Clément Jacques Maria Britt. He was always called Horace.

HORACE

Horace Britt is what is commonly known as a child prodigy. I have a prejudice against these children especially in matters of musical virtuosity. Generally, one must distinguish their mechanical ability from the feeling of what they play. I hasten to say, Horace Britt in these respects was agreeably surprising. In him musical understanding and technical ability are equal.

La Métropole, Antwerp, 20 May 1896

With the help of his friend and patron, Count Roger de Grimberghe, Ernest Britt established himself in Paris as a musician in the fall of 1887. With their three children, Horace, Roger, and Gaëtane, the Britts made their new home at 82, boulevard des Batignolles, a broad boulevard no more than a dozen blocks long, situated in the northwest of the city. "When we arrived in Paris I already had the idea of learning the cello, but my parents had very definite plans for my musical training," Horace Britt recalled.

> When I turned six, my mother began teaching me solfège. I remember standing on a small podium beside her, a baton in my hand, as she systematically taught me to sing in all six clefs. When I had accomplished a certain difficult sightsinging task my father would join us to hear the happy results. It was made clear to me that I would not touch any instrument until I was expert at sightsinging.[1]

For this early training Britt was later grateful. It prepared his musical intellect for what lay ahead.

In the summer of 1890, the family returned to Antwerp from Paris for a

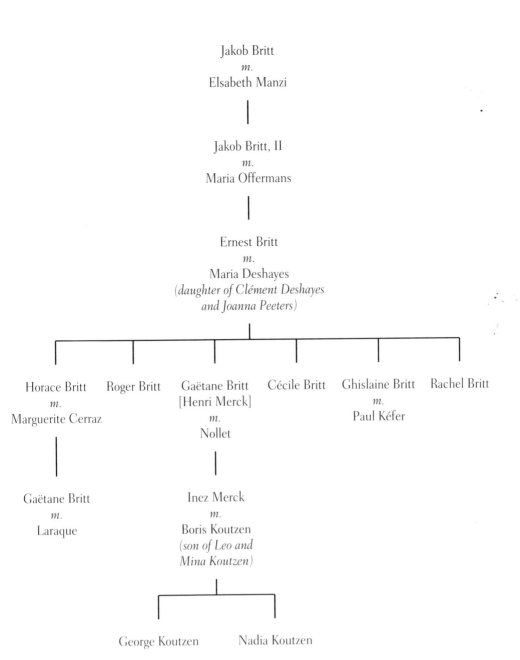

Jakob Britt
m.
Elsabeth Manzi

Jakob Britt, II
m.
Maria Offermans

Ernest Britt
m.
Maria Deshayes
*(daughter of Clément Deshayes
and Joanna Peeters)*

Horace Britt   Roger Britt   Gaëtane Britt   Cécile Britt   Ghislaine Britt   Rachel Britt
m.   [Henri Merck]   *m.*
Marguerite Cerraz   *m.*   Paul Kéfer
                           Nollet

Gaëtane Britt   Inez Merck
m.   *m.*
Laraque   Boris Koutzen
                 *(son of Leo and
Mina Koutzen)*

George Koutzen   Nadia Koutzen

The Britt Family Tree

visit with Horace's maternal grandparents, Clément and Joanna Deshayes. Ernest played his new compositions for them; Horace and his mother sang; Roger, later a fine violinist, proudly showed his early attempts at watercolor using pear stems as brushes. The three girls—Gaëtane and her two sisters born in Paris, Ghislaine and Cécile—were much admired. During this visit the grandparents agreed that Horace could live with them while he began to study the cello with the outstanding Belgian teacher, Gustav Faes. How long would he stay in Antwerp? Until he was ready for the auditions at the Paris Conservatory.

> My father explained that entering the conservatory would be difficult. The Conservatoire National de Musique et de Déclamation is a truly national institution. At that time, only two places for foreign pupils were available in the cello class. The competition was fierce. He felt it would be best for me to begin my study in Belgium, which had a high reputation for cello playing, and promised I could return home to Paris, but only when I was ready to succeed at the auditions. Although I very much liked living with my grandparents, I did yearn to return to my family in Paris, and because of my father's promise, I felt an urgency about my early lessons.
>
> My first teacher, Gustav Faes, who had been a pupil of Joseph Bessems, gave me frequent lessons. He was a fine cellist and for decades had been the solo cellist of the orchestra of the Théâtre Royal. (He had once played the cello solo in the slow movement of Schumann's piano concerto when Clara Schumann was the soloist and Franz Liszt conducted.)
>
> My progress exceeded his expectations. By the end of the year he presented me in public playing the "Gypsy Rondo" trio by Haydn.

Because his grandfather did not want him to be burdened carrying his cello on the streets of Antwerp, he arranged for Horace to leave his own instrument at home and play on another at Faes' studio, thereby only carrying his cello bow from place to place. This soon created a problem when some ruffians along the way saw the boy with his strange stick in his hand and began to harass him. "Some bullies threatened me one day as I walked to my lesson," Britt recalled.

> When I told my grandfather about this unfortunate thing, he had an immediate solution. The next day he bought me a second cello

bow, this one made of metal. "When they approach you, attack!" he commanded, then added, "They are probably only jealous because you play the cello." It was good advice. Later when I learned fencing, I often remembered my childhood experience with the metal bow.

Horace returned to Paris when he was eleven. After only two years' study with Gustav Faes, the amazing child had conquered the demands of Georg Goltermann's third concerto and was ready for the competitive auditions at the conservatory. The jury for this Concours d'Admission comprised members of the teaching staff with Ambroise Thomas, the director of the conservatory, as chairman. The four violin teachers, Garcin, Marsick, Maurin, and Lafort, along with the cellists Rabaud and Delsart, and their colleague, the bassist Verrinust, took such auditions seriously: those few selected would perpetuate not only the quality of the conservatory's performance classes (and the reputations of their teachers), but ultimately the musical life of France.

On 5 November 1892 seventeen hopeful cellists auditioned, and the jury withdrew to a private room to cast their ballots. Horace was accepted into the class of Jules Delsart as the youngest student. Among his older classmates were Louis Feuillard from Dijon, Fernand Pollain from Reims, and the Parisian boy Louis Hasselmanns, son of Alphonse Hasselmanns, the harp professor at the conservatory. Paul Bazelaire was yet to come.

Some jury members at my audition strongly objected to the fact that my little cello had been fitted with an endpin, that device introduced by the Belgian cellist François Servais. Delsart had learned cello playing without an endpin and as an accomplished viola da gambist he was accustomed to holding either instrument between the knees. But Delsart was a champion of new ideas. He used an endpin in his studio, although when he posed for a portrait to be hung at the conservatory,[2] he removed it from his cello for the sake of tradition. Of course, it was Delsart who eventually brought about the final adoption of the endpin for all the cello students at the conservatory.

For the five brief years of Horace's early learning, he had only two teachers: in Antwerp Gustave Faes, and now Jules Delsart.

In the 1860s, Delsart had distinguished himself at the conservatory as a pupil of Auguste Franchomme, Chopin's close friend and recital partner. When Franchomme died in 1884, Delsart succeeded his teacher as professor at the conservatory, having already concertized as a cellist in Holland, Austria, and England, and as viola da gambist of the Parisian Société des Instruments Anciens. As the leading cello teacher in France, Delsart was much in demand. Not the least reason was that during his long tenure as professor at the conservatory, from 1884 to 1900, some thirty-six of his pupils became laureates, having won the coveted premier prix—the first prize— awarded at the conservatory's annual summer competition.

For Horace and his mother, the daily trip from their home on boulevard des Batignolles to the conservatory was a time-consuming but adventurous journey in their horse-drawn fiacre. In 1892, while the automobile had not yet appeared in France, the main thoroughfares of Paris were congested with slow-moving omnibuses each drawn by three gigantic horses. Horace's favorite route took them by the Church of the Trinité, then along boulevard Haussmann, past the stage doors of the imposing Opéra, then only thirty years old and at that time the largest theater in the world. Nearby on the corner of rue Bergère, the Paris Conservatory still stood at its original site, complete with its architectural maze of library, museum, and concert hall.

Each morning the young boys who studied at the conservatory gathered outside the peristyle under which carriages might approach the main doors or across the street at the popular cafe—Crémerie du Conservatoire—not to greet the wonder child with the cello, but to gaze on the fabled beauty of his mother, Maria Britt.[3]

At home, the Britt children, now six in number (Rachel had been born in 1891), were pranksters. Roger Britt recalled their playfulness:

> When Mama entertained her friends on Thursday afternoons, the elegant ladies left their fancy, plumed hats upstairs on a bed while they visited downstairs. Once we removed all the decorations, ostrich feathers and all, from their hats and switched them around, sewing them onto different hats. You can imagine the scene when the ladies tried to claim their hats.
>
> Our best prank was frightening Rose, our country maid. While the very superstitious girl was at the market, with an almost invisible thread we tied together all the pots and pans that hung on the kitchen wall. Hiding behind closed doors when she returned to the kitchen, we gently pulled the threads and rustled the pots, set them to shivering and jingling. Convinced the kitchen was haunted, she fled shrieking and refused ever to go into the kitchen again.[4]

Foreign pupils had the right to take part in the Concours, the prize competition at year's end, only after two years of study at the conservatory. Delsart presented his youngest pupil at the annual event in 1894. With his performance of Bernard Romberg's fifth concerto, Horace won a premier
accessit, a first honorable mention. The next day Arthur Pougin wrote in *Le
Ménestrel*: "This child is charming. He plays very accurately, with perfect
taste and superb self-assurance, but sometimes gets carried away, which
reveals his temperament, his boldness and fearlessness."[5]

Youngsters learning the cello at the conservatory at the turn of the nineteenth century had no private lessons. Everyone was obliged to be present
each time the master taught. Constant exposure to Delsart's pronounce-
ments and familiarity with the common repertoire played ceaselessly by
everyone in the class strengthened Horace's resolve. He learned from the
outset that he must constantly produce evidence of his accomplishment.

In June 1895 when the conservatory announced the set works for the
annual summer Concours, Delsart knew that Horace, then thirteen, was
ready for the challenge and set his pupil's task: to learn, on his own, Karl
Davidov's Concerto in B Minor. There would also be the obligatory sight-
reading.

For three years, Horace had observed his two older friends, Louis Feuillard and Louis Hasselmanns, prepare themselves for the competition and
win the premier prix. With only a month or so to prepare and with no further
guidance from the master, it seemed to the young cellists that there was
never enough time or direction. The sight-reading test piece would not be
seen by anyone but its composer until the manuscript was handed to the
jury an hour before the tests began.

Few musical events in Paris aroused more interest and curiosity on the
part of the general public than the summer Concours. They arrived at the
conservatory by the hundreds, streamed up the fine staircase past the bas-
relief of Minerva and into the Grand Salon. The spectacular concert hall
was subjected to a frenzied mob of spectators (and music critics) suffering
from the high temperatures of mid-July and generating an indescribable
undercurrent of anticipation.

The distinguished jury was assembled well in advance. Of its members,
three were cellists—Charles Lenepveu, Cesare Casella, and Cros Saint-
Ange; the rest were violinists, conductors, or composers. In 1895, Charles
Lefebvre composed the test piece for the sight-reading ordeal. The players
were held virtual prisoners in a large anteroom in order to prevent any dis-

closure of Lefebvre's new work. The competitors drew numbers. Some would wait for hours for their turn to play.

Horace, who had turned fourteen the previous month, drew the number ten. He went to a quiet corner, perhaps to think of his anxious family somewhere beyond the huge stage curtain with its imperial coat of arms, or of Jules Delsart waiting impatiently in his box seat.

After the ninth cellist performed, Ambroise Thomas called for a recess of ten minutes. When the jury had reassembled, Horace Britt was summoned to the stage. His performance was extraordinary for one so young. At the conclusion of the competition, the jury moved out of the concert hall into the foyer where Ambroise Thomas posed the question, "Shall we award the premier prix?" The answer was unanimous. Horace Britt had won the coveted premier prix.

The next day the press was ecstatic: "Monsieur Britt seems already an accomplished artist: it is, of course, he who best deserved his prize, and whose name we must remember," wrote the critic of *XIXe Siècle*.[6] In *Le Ménestrel* Arthur Pougin wrote, "The young Britt, fourteen years old and playing on a three-quarter cello, has the true temperament of an artist."[7]

The wonder child from Antwerp had made history at the Paris Conservatory as the youngest cellist to be awarded the premier prix since its inception. (In 1803 Charles-Nicolas Baudiot's pupil, Louis Pierre Norblin, was the first to win it.) On 23 July 1895, Monsieur Sauni, the Minister of Fine Arts and Culture, wrote to Horace, "Would you please accept one of the medals we had struck for this occasion? I send my felicitations for your beautiful success and I applaud you."[8]

There was a new cello as well. A tradition of patronage had long been established between Parisian luthiers and the conservatory. For years the firm of Gand (later Gand and Bernadel) had honored the winner of the premier prix with one of their finest new instruments, but in 1895 it was Adolphe Maucotel who presented a magnificent new cello to Horace, an instrument on which he performed until 1927.

Ernest Britt was adamant that Horace not be exploited as a prodigy and had devised an exacting plan to insure that his gifted son would suffer no lack of continuity in his growth as a musician. The young cellist returned to the conservatory as a music scholar to study harmony and counterpoint with Albert Lavignac. Horace had consultations with Jules Delsart during the year regarding new repertoire, but his father decided that there would be no performance in Paris until after his son's debut recital in Belgium.

Premier prix. Horace Britt at fourteen, 1895.

On 25 October 1895, the Paris newspaper *Le Figaro* gave a musical soiree in honor of the king of Portugal. The evening began with Jules Delsart and an ensemble of his cello pupils playing a Bach aria and *Valse* by Charles Widor, the famous organist of Saint Sulpice in Paris, who accompanied them. At the end of the evening when the Britts were leaving the concert hall, Delsart introduced them to his newest pupil. Britt recalled:

> This little boy, who held Delsart's hand, was a nine-year-old from Sedan in the Ardennes who had just entered the cello class. My own unusual record was shattered when, ten months later, he won the premier prix at the unprecedented age of ten—an unheard of, a spectacular accomplishment. His name was Paul Bazelaire. He became my friend for life.

During the winter of 1896, Horace progressed rapidly in Albert Lavignac's morning class and met new friends who were studying composition at the conservatory: the Romanian Georges Enesco and Florent Schmitt, pupils of Jules Massenet, and Maurice Ravel, who studied with Gabriel Fauré. He spent his afternoons either at the fencing academy or studying English at home with his tutor, and he diligently practiced his cello in preparation for his debut recital in Belgium.

On 19 May 1896, he appeared in Antwerp with his father as pianist in a program of works by Servais, Popper, and Saint-Saëns. The concert took place at Maison Anthonis before the Cercle Artistique d'Anvers. Gustav Faes, always devoted to Horace, was in the audience to hear his former pupil. The critic of *Le Matin* noted:

> To be technically perfect, to have conquered all difficulties, these skills are acquired through study and will power, but musical feeling, expression—in a word, the soul of music, comes from temperament. And we find these qualities which are the mark of the true artist united in Horace Britt who positively amazed his large audience by his prodigious virtuosity, the absolute perfection of his execution, and above all, by the beauty of his tone, the energy and the expression that he gave to the various works he interpreted.[9]

At Ostende on the Belgian coast, the centerpiece of the magnificent promenade was the huge Casino-Kursaal; its concert hall had been the home of a summer festival for nearly a century when Horace first appeared there in the summer of 1896. He and his father repeated the successful Antwerp program to exuberant press notices. A writer for the new English journal, *The Strad*, remarked the following month that the audience at Ostende found Horace "a consummate artist." He was not yet fifteen.

Horace's success prompted more concerts in Belgium. Ernest Britt's friend, Constant Lenaerts, the founder of Antwerp's Société Royale d'Harmonie and the conductor of its numerous orchestra concerts, agreed to present the gifted boy in an evening of works for cello and orchestra. From the night of 25 September 1896, Saint-Saëns' Concerto in A Minor became Horace's ideal vehicle. Its every page struck some artistic response in the boy, and he was to play its passages over and over again throughout his long, worldwide career. The enthusiasm of the audience knew no bounds. The critics responded extravagantly, and the review from *Le Méphisto* traveled back to Paris to the attention of both Delsart and Saint-Saëns. "His playing defies all criticism. To say that the artist played the work of Saint-Saëns to perfection is to repeat that he is master of his instrument."[10] In December, the Britts again appeared in an Antwerp recital, and the Belgian cellists, both professors and pupils, turned out en masse to take notice of the Britt phenomenon. On hearing sonatas by Locatelli and Beethoven, the critics found new superlatives: "What can be said of the cellist Horace Britt? He is certainly the most captivating virtuoso that we know. What beautiful sound, what clearness, what accuracy, and how poetical his interpretations!"[11]

In an early press notice Ernest Britt wrote, "The young artist has had his talent consecrated in Belgium, and must move to new triumphs." In Paris Charles Lamoureux agreed to present Horace as soloist with his celebrated orchestra of the Association des Concerts Lamoureux. As the concert drew near, Parisians anticipated a springtime debut of one of their favorites. A performance by Horace Britt with Lamoureux's orchestra would be the manifestation of that oldest and most enchanting artistic miracle: yesterday's child of Concours fame transformed into a young artist. Ernest Britt realized that his young son, for all his transcendental qualities, lacked experience performing works with orchestra; however, the decision was made to play the Saint-Saëns concerto, a new concert piece by the Belgian composer Joseph Callaerts, Max Bruch's master stroke *Kol Nidrei*, and David Popper's *Polonaise de concert*.

Delsart dispatched a letter to Budapest asking Popper for his orchestration of the piece, but Popper replied to Horace that he deferred to Ernest

Britt's musicianship: "With great regret I must tell you that I have never thought of making an orchestration of the Polonaise. You should use your father's orchestration. Mrs. Popper and I send our best wishes to my dear Delsart."[12]

The newspaper *La France* championed Horace's Paris debut:

> One would have to look back to the youth of the greatest masters to hear again a performance as artistically moving as the one of 19 March at the Salle Pleyel. There for a duration of a whole evening, a young man of fifteen, Horace Britt, who for two years now is the premier prix winner of the Conservatoire, charmed an enthusiastic audience. . . . One feels that under his large brow, haloed by blond hair, reigns a single inspiration, that of genius. Let the years pass and the future will prove this point.[13]

Understandably, parental attention focused on the amazing Horace, but in March 1897 Ernest Britt presented not one but four prodigies to the public at the Salle Pleyel. Both Roger and Gaëtane had been pursuing studies at the conservatory, Cécile had seriously taken up the violin, and Rachel sang. (Only Ghislaine did not study music.) Cécile was eight, Gaëtane twelve, Roger thirteen, and Horace fifteen when they appeared together in recital for the first time. The young violinist Cécile Britt impressed the critics, but she did not pursue a career beyond childhood. Horace would continue to take the lead.

Jules Delsart decided it was time for him to appear in London, where Delsart had presented many successful concerts and where his friend, the great Spanish violinist Pablo de Sarasate, was a favorite of the English public. At a quartet evening at Delsart's home, Horace was introduced to Sarasate. He later recalled that the Spaniard, so well known for his performances of Romantic music and especially of his own violin compositions, was "a surprisingly magnificent interpreter of the quartets of Mozart."

Taking it upon himself to arrange concert management that would allow the young cellist to appear in London, Sarasate sent this note dated 1 July 1897 to Delsart: "I have heard your young pupil Horace Britt play with the greatest satisfaction. The first rate qualities which he possesses will be the best guarantee for his success in England. My best wishes are with your young laureate."[14]

On 27 June 1897 Horace heard from Delsart:

After the brilliant first prize which you have obtained in my class at the Conservatoire and the great success which has followed your debuts in the domain of art, you can do no better than present yourself before the great English public, which will confirm, I am certain, the reputation of renowned violoncellist which you have gained with us. Best wishes for your success from your professor and friend.[15]

When Horace appeared in London at the English Salle Pleyel on Baker Street, the critic of the *Musical Standard* declared him "a violoncellist of genius!"[16]

The Britts returned to Paris to learn that Édouard Colonne wished to present the young cellist with his famous orchestra. As a prelude to this Paris engagement, Horace played his new repertoire in Antwerp, including the first performance in Belgium of Robert Schumann's great masterpiece of 1850, the Cello Concerto, Op. 129. The Paris concert was scheduled for 9 March at the Salle Pleyel. It was Horace's daring idea to perform Bach's G Major Suite for solo cello between the concertos of Schumann and Saint-Saëns. The suites were seldom played in Paris at this time; only later would Pablo Casals play these works to the consistent approval of French music lovers. "Very well played were Bach's old dances for violoncello alone," wrote the critic of *Le Nord*, "and we are grateful to this young and intrepid virtuoso for having made us understand Schumann's concerto which is complex and difficult."[17]

Three weeks later Ernest Britt staged a major chamber music recital for Horace at the Salle Pleyel. With three young musicians from Colonne's orchestra, the violinists Martinet and Pichon and the violist Chazeau, Horace played Charles Lefebvre's String Quartet in G Minor. Pianist Frans Lenaerts joined him for Saint-Saëns' Sonata, Op. 32. To conclude the recital, all the musicians joined forces for a performance of the new Quintet for Piano and Strings composed in 1886, just over a decade earlier, by Horace's Romanian friend, Georges Enesco.

In his dual role as composer and violinist, the young Enesco enjoyed the patronage of both Queen Isabel of Romania, a picturesque and romantic monarch who wrote poetry under the pen name of Carmen Sylva, and the princess Elena Bibesco who lived in Paris. Elena Bibesco and her sister Alexandra, Princesse de Brancovan, were excellent pianists. Their musical evenings had the reputation of being the most exclusive in Paris—they had presented the Polish pianist Ignace Paderewski to their circle—and a friendly rivalry existed between them on this account as they continued to discover new painters and musicians and to vie for the favor of such literary person- alities as Proust and Colette. In the fall of 1898, Horace became the young cello teacher of the two sons of the Princesse de Brancovan, whose musical soirees were also frequented by her close friend, Camille Saint-Saëns.

On 21 November 1898, Princesse de Brancovan wrote to Ernest Britt (referring to her niece, the Comtesse de Noailles): "Saint-Saëns will be at Madame la comtesse's place Friday at 4:30."

> I have asked that Horace be permitted to be there so he can play
> his concerto for the master. She was kind enough to consent to this.
> You are therefore invited, both of you, Friday at precisely 4:30 at 7,
> boulevard de Boulogne in Boulogne-sur-Seine. I hope I will be there
> too. I will be delighted to have succeeded in bringing about this long
> hoped-for meeting.[18]

What a fortuitous meeting it was between the young cellist and the sixty- three-year old Camille Saint-Saëns! Well-known throughout his life as a bril- liant pianist (he had been a famous prodigy), the master went directly to the piano and the concerto playing began. "Saint-Saëns improvised a marvelous accompaniment as we played," Britt remembered.

> I was to learn later that he was strongly opposed to any transcription
> of his original works to another medium and had a particular dislike for
> creating practical piano reductions of his orchestral scores (Durand,
> his publisher, left that task to the young Georges Bizet). But his
> improvisation that afternoon was entirely convincing and I took the
> bull by the horns and played straight through to the final chords.
> Saint-Saëns seemed delighted with my conception of his concerto, an
> extremely difficult work and a challenge to the cellist, although its
> subtleties are hard to express in words.
>
> After our first meeting, Saint-Saëns invited me to play his early
> Piano Trio, Op. 18, with him and the violinist Joseph White, who was
> having a superlative career in Paris. I was excited by his invitation and
> agreed immediately.

They must have made a spectacular trio—the elegant black Cuban vio- linist, the rotund, bewhiskered French pianist, and the dashing young Belgian, who was but seventeen at the time. It was no surprise then their chamber music playing became a very special offering of the Bibesco salon.

During the summer that followed, the Britts and Édouard Colonne agreed that Horace periodically would join the cello section of Colonne's orchestra but would be allowed to pursue other important concert engagements as well, including a performance at London's Crystal Palace under the direction of August Manns. Roger Britt joined the orchestra as violist and became assistant to Pierre Monteux, the newly appointed principal violist.

GAËTANE

Her tone is pure and powerful, her playing flexible, and her style perfect. . . .
We do not know of any harpist who possesses to the same degree the power of
fascinating. One could listen to her indefinitely.

La Gazette de Liège, Belgium

On the second day of November in 1896, four years after Horace had first auditioned for the conservatory, the secretary of the yearly Concours d'Admission read from the official list of aspiring harpists, "Mlle Gaëtane Britt, Belgian, age eleven, 82, boulevard des Batignolles." A pupil of Mme Tasser-Spencer, the little girl was seeking admission to the class of Alphonse Hasselmanns, the Belgian-born harp professor at the Paris Conservatory who was acknowledged by the time of his death in 1912 as the founder of the modern French school of harp playing.

The friendship of Horace and Louis Hasselmanns, the harp professor's young son, first brought the two families together, but Alphonse Hasselmanns' esteem for Gaëtane's gifts as a child harpist ultimately forged the relationship between the Hasselmanns and the Britts.

Gaëtane was happy at the conservatory where she became friends with the other harpists, including the boy from Bordeaux, Carlos Salzedo, who had recently arrived in Paris. On 21 January 1897, she was successful in her harp examination and won the approbation of the jury headed by Hasselmanns and including Albert Lavignac and the pianists Nollet and the brothers Marmontal.

At home, Gaëtane and Horace now shared the musical attention of their father. Ernest Britt turned from the composition of large-scale works to write chamber music pieces for harp, yielding new works for Gaëtane's forthcoming recitals, including *Bardengesang* and *Trilby*, both published in Paris by Leduc. As he had done for Horace, Ernest Britt was preparing the way for

Gaëtane's career in Belgium where Queen Marie-Henriette, who played the harp well, revered the instrument and its great exponents.

Gaëtane's Belgian debut before the Société Royale d'Harmonie in Antwerp was arranged for 23 September 1899. Although she was only thirteen, Gaëtane, joined by Matthieu Quitlin, the solo flutist of the Théâtre Royal orchestra, performed Mozart's Concerto for Flute and Harp, K. 299. She played a Lyon harp, a chromatic instrument with pedals, constructed in Paris by its inventor, Gustave Lyon. There was great enthusiasm for Lyon's new harp. The conservatories in Paris and Brussels had organized special classes for its instruction and composers André Caplet (Horace's orchestration teacher in Paris) and Florent Schmitt were already composing for it, although not until a few years later in 1904 would Claude Debussy's great masterpiece emerge—*Deux danses* for chromatic harp and string orchestra.

The two Britt prodigies, with their father and flutist Matthieu Quitlin, were off to tour Holland when Gaëtane turned fourteen in 1899. As exciting as it was to perform abroad, after their final concert in Rotterdam the teenagers were eager to return home to enjoy the newest rage, the Paris Métro. With the new century approaching, all Paris was enthralled by the opening of their subway which traversed the Right Bank from the Porte de Vincennes to the Porte Maillot.

Within a year of her tour in Holland, Gaëtane was introduced at court in Brussels, where she became the absolute favorite of Queen Marie-Henriette. Horace later remarked that on that occasion, "the Queen approached Gaëtane before she began to play, and arranged the hem of my sister's gown to create the perfect tableau." Queen Marie-Henriette later gave Gaëtane Britt her own superb Erard harp—and her favorite fan made of mother of pearl and lace.[19]

In Brussels on 21 January 1901, Gaëtane and Horace appeared in a joint recital at Salle Ravenstein performing music by Thomé, Bruch, Zabel, and Saint-Saëns, ending their program with Ernest Britt's *Trilby* and Saint-Saëns' *Le Cygne* (the Swan). In April Gaëtane appeared again at Salle Ravenstein, this time in a major solo recital entitled "La Harpe à travers les ages," playing music for the complete range of historical instruments: the Irish harp, the pedal harp (both single and double action), and the new chromatic harp. She was fifteen.

The following September, Gaëtane and Horace appeared with the American violinist Maude Powell in Belgium at the Casino in Spa before Horace went to live in London and Gaëtane withdrew from public performance to

Gaëtane Britt with the Erard harp given to her by Queen Marie-Henriette of Belgium. Courtesy Nadia Koutzen.

build her repertoire. In England Horace performed Saint-Saëns' *The Swan* on the London stage with Sarah Bernhardt. But the pinnacle of his youthful career came in August 1904 when he gave the first cello recitals in China, Japan, and French Indo-China (Vietnam).

In 1905 Horace was bound for North America and a new life with Marguerite Cerraz, the young Parisian girl with whom he had fallen in love. Through Enrico Tramonti, the European harpist of the Chicago Symphony, a position had been found in the orchestra for the young cellist. In his absence Ernest Britt began searching in Belgium for another cellist to take part in Gaëtane's recitals. In Brussels he met the extraordinary musicians of the Merck family. The father was Belgium's premier French hornist, knighted by King Leopold in 1890 for his distinguished service to the musical world and to the Brussels conservatory where he taught for thirty-five years. All his six children were musicians, four of them laureates of the Brussels conservatory. Henri Merck, the cellist, was outstanding among them. He agreed to appear on Gaëtane's forthcoming recitals in place of Horace. Merck was then thirty-six, sixteen years her senior.

Gaëtane and Henri performed together for two years, first throughout Belgium and France, then in England where their harp and cello recitals at London's Steinway Hall and the Portman Rooms on Baker Street created a furor. Always present in the audience was someone dear to the young harpist. In London, Gaëtane was reunited with her brother Roger, then a violinist in the orchestra of London's Carl Rosa Opera Company.

On 21 February 1907 a daughter was born to Gaëtane and Henri in London, and they called her Inez, the evocative name of the heroine of Ernest Britt's opera, *Inès de la Sierra*. Unfortunately, the couple soon parted. Henri moved to America where he became principal cellist of the Pittsburgh Symphony, then conducted by Victor Herbert. Gaëtane returned to Paris with Inez. There at her parents' home she found Horace and Marguerite, who were vacationing in Paris before returning to America where Horace had become principal cellist of the Philadelphia Orchestra. With them was their baby daughter Gaëtane, named in honor of her now-famous aunt, who was fast becoming the leading harpist in France.

For that brief week in September 1907, Ernest and Maria Britt lavished affection on their new granddaughters, who would both later be outstanding Britt family musicians. Horace's daughter, always called Tatane, became an exceptional child violinist in New York and San Francisco before returning to Paris to study with Jacques Thibaud at the École Normale de Musique.

Gaëtane's daughter, Inez, grew up in the home of her grandparents, which was near the Eiffel Tower on rue de la Motte Piquet near the École Militaire. Her loving grandfather ("Bon Papa") supervised her education, teaching her the piano throughout her childhood in Paris.

Together Bon Papa and Inez often played on the novel rosewood piano commissioned from the Paris firm of Pleyel by Count Roger de Grimberghe, an instrument that Maurice Ravel had greatly admired. For years Grimberghe and Britt had played ensemble music for two pianos on this marvelous instrument with its two keyboards, one going in the opposite direction of the other, until eventually Grimberghe gave the instrument to the museum of the École Normale de Musique in Paris, where it remains today. In 1975, Inez Merck Koutzen recalled: "The double piano I feel is very much part of me. I could not have been more than ten years old when I first played on it. After that, Bon Papa and I went regularly to play on it at the École Normale."[20]

In December 1908 Gaëtane and her sister Ghislaine arrived in New York on the SS *Vaderman* with her Erard harp, the gift of Queen Marie-Henriette, to begin Gaëtane's first tour of America in Pittsburgh.

By the next fall, both Horace and Gaëtane had career triumphs. Arturo Toscanini brought Horace, now twenty-seven, from Philadelphia to the Metropolitan Opera House in New York to be his principal cellist; Gaëtane made her startling debut in Paris at twenty-three. A few months later the critic of *Le Soleil* declared: "Gaëtane Britt, although very young, is a most remarkable virtuoso. She is one of the best harpists of our time."[21]

During the decade that followed Gaëtane's Paris debut, the Britt family survived a world war and experienced changes of fortune just as dramatic as Jakob and Elsabeth Britt's exodus from Switzerland in 1815.

When Roger Britt returned to the United States in 1922, where he had earlier lived for six years as a violinist in the Philadelphia Symphony Orchestra, he was not alone. Gaëtane's daughter, Inez, was with him. She had crossed the Atlantic to seek a new life in America, leaving her Bon Papa alone in their home near the Eiffel Tower, grieving for his wife Maria who had died that autumn. By November when she had turned fifteen, Inez and her Uncle Roger were well-established in Atlantic City. The two resourceful musicians had found engagements playing in the evenings at the resort hotels.

Roger and Inez were surrounded by relatives. Horace and Marguerite, with Tatane, lived nearby in New York City at Hotel Harding on West 54th

Street. Horace had returned to the East Coast in 1921 to join the Hans Letz Quartet after seven years playing quartets, the music he loved best, with Louis Persinger in San Francisco. In New York Horace shared music and friendship with Pablo Casals and his wife Susan Metcalfe, Georgette Leblanc (Mme Maurice Maeterlinck), Harold Bauer, Victor Herbert, and Mischa Elman. Here Horace could also enjoy the companionship of his sister, Ghislaine, and her husband, cellist Paul Kéfer. As Jules Delsart's last pupil, Kéfer had won the premier prix at the Concours in 1901, then went on to establish himself in America as principal cellist of the New York Symphony and, somewhat later, to form a superb chamber ensemble, the Trio de Lutèce, with flutist Georges Barrère and harpist Carlos Salzedo. For young Inez and her cousin Tatane, an evening of chamber music at New York's Aeolian Hall must have seemed a welcome family reunion with illustrious relatives both on stage and in the audience.

Inez met Boris Koutzen in the fall of 1923 in Atlantic City during a playing engagement at the Marlboro-Blenheim Hotel. The splendid young Russian violinist had recently arrived in the United States from Berlin, where he had given successful recitals, made some recordings, and played regularly at the Cafe Ruscho with his Russian colleagues, cellist Gregor Piatigorsky and pianist Leopold Mittman. Nadia Koutzen recounts that, "in the midst of playing a Grieg sonata, they fell in love. . . . Pappa proposed simply by crossing out my mother's name in one of her books, and wrote his."[22] They were married on 3 June 1924 after Boris joined the Philadelphia Symphony Orchestra.

The Curtis Institute of Music was founded in Philadelphia the following September, and Mary Curtis Bok (the wife of violinist Efrem Zimbalist after 1943) engaged Horace as the institution's first teacher of cello and chamber music. Although he continued to live in New York City where he played with the Letz Quartet, then formed a new quartet with Mischa Elman, Horace was in Philadelphia each week to teach and to visit Inez and Boris, whose career as a composer he championed over the decade that followed.

In June 1926 when Inez was just nineteen, the Koutzens had their first child. They named their son George. Four years later on 6 October 1930, a daughter was born. Little Nadia Koutzen would be the ultimate manifestation of the musical prodigy in four generations of gifted children born to the Britts, Mercks, and Koutzens.

NADIA

*There is a widely held notion that all prodigies are merely rubber stamps of
their teachers, obeying mindlessly, just doing what they are told, as if
independence of thought is just not possible. Quite the opposite was the daily
reality for me.*

Nadia Koutzen, "Reflections of a Child Prodigy"

In her journal, Nadia Koutzen's mother described an incident that took place
when Nadia was just three:

> Papa Heifetz (Jascha's father) was teaching a grand niece of his and
> felt she was talented. He asked Boris if he could bring her to our house
> to play for him and give his opinion. This was in October of 1933. They
> came and as long as I live I will see our tiny Nadia sitting in her little
> chair completely absorbed in the playing and tears streaming down
> her face. After they were gone she resolutely stated that she wanted a
> violin for Christmas. Her poor father had an awful time finding one
> small enough, but finally just in time, he found a 32d size in Phila-
> delphia at William Moennig's. . . . Having studied violin myself in
> Paris, Boris felt I knew enough to work with her between lessons,
> though in the beginning he gave her a short lesson each day.[23]

Thus Nadia became the third generation of violinists in the Koutzen
family. Her Russian grandfather, Leo Koutzen, who was born in Kiev,
Ukraine, studied the violin in Odessa, Warsaw, and St. Petersburg, where he
received a diploma of distinction from the conservatory. In Uman, near Kiev,
he established a music school and a decade later was appointed head of the
violin department in nearby Kherson. Born in Uman in 1901, Boris followed
quickly in his father's musical footsteps. He was a composer by six. He displayed great promise as a child violinist and when only eleven performed the
Mendelssohn concerto in Kherson.

In 1918 when the Koutzen family moved to Moscow, Boris entered the
Moscow Conservatory, studying composition with Reinhold Glière. Leo
Koutzen held a position in the orchestra of the Imperial Opera at the Bolshoi
Theater, where seventeen-year-old Boris joined him in the violin section and
soon became friends with fifteen-year-old Gregor Piatigorsky, the youngster
who led the cellos. During the difficult time following the Bolshevik revolution, Mikhail Ippolitov-Ivanov urged the young violinist-composer to go to

western Europe; in 1922, Boris Koutzen left Moscow for Berlin. He was nineteen.

Among the distinctions of Boris Koutzen's outstanding career in the United States—he taught, conducted, concertized, and composed—was his great accomplishment as Nadia's only formal violin teacher. Through him she would share in the legacy of the Russian school of violin playing, which he and his father represented, and he also formulated his own innovative teaching method for beginners which he published in 1951 as *Foundations of Vio-*

Vermont, 1935. Nadia Koutzen, age five, with her father, Boris Koutzen. Photograph by Inez Koutzen. Courtesy Nadia Koutzen.

lin Playing. Nadia described the freedom he gave her to develop her own musical ideas:

> Pappa often expressed unbridled pleasure in his experience with me even as a tiny child, so that many of the musical things I did naturally were left untouched by him. I felt then and I know now that he wanted it just that way. There was never any doubt in my mind about certain musical (and technical) parameters as he knew and felt and understood them and about which he was consistent. Beyond those, whatever I did—until he died—the only prerequisite was that it be convincing. There came many occasions in his last years when my father disagreed, but was convinced. That certainly didn't surprise me, but I was always touched.

When Nadia learned Mozart's Concerto in G Major (K. 216), plans were made for her debut with orchestra. The fearless little violinist would play the work at a matinee concert in December 1938 with the Montreal Symphony Orchestra, conducted by her illustrious great uncle, Horace Britt. Leon Barzin offered an opportunity for her first rehearsal on the stage of Carnegie Hall where the National Orchestral Association played and rehearsed.

> The first time I played the Mozart with orchestra was at one of those rehearsals before I turned eight years old. . . . The hall was empty but for a few invited guests. I felt a glow to be standing on that stage—to say nothing of the excitement of hearing the sounds of an orchestra surrounding me for the very first time.

On 6 October Nadia turned eight, with only two months left before her debut. Her father faithfully continued to coach the Mozart concerto, even though these were demanding times for him. At NBC a new era began in November when Pierre Monteux conducted the first broadcast of the new NBC Symphony Orchestra, in which both Boris and Horace—and later Nadia's brother George Koutzen—would play under Toscanini.

When mid-December arrived, it was time for the trip to Montreal:

> I recall so clearly the extreme excitement to be in the upper bunk of a Pullman car and the brand new flannel pajamas for my first overnight trip. In my heart then, and retrospectively, these things were just as important as the event itself.

I remember the rehearsal more clearly than I do the concert. Uncle Horace began the opening tutti at one brisk clip. I made my entrance and continued playing. I knew that it was faster than I'd ever played it, but would certainly not have known to speak up. I can still see my mother standing at the edge of the stage, her arms outstretched trying to get her uncle's attention. He looked around. "*C'est beaucoup trop vite pour elle*," and he slowed it down. Whew!!

A big audience for the concert was not intimidating, but the crowd backstage was. People came in a rush to see this tiny curiosity. I can still feel the pleasure of sitting atop the manager's shoulders as he told them all that if they didn't give me some room he'd take me away altogether.

Paul and Ghislaine Kéfer lived in Rochester in 1939, where he was teaching at the Eastman School of Music. In an interview with reporters while little Nadia sat on Uncle Paul's lap, he gently made fun of her because she insisted on tuning her violin before a picture was taken. She was in Rochester to make her next concerto appearance, this time with the Rochester Philharmonic, Guy Fraser Harrison conducting.

Conductor Guy Fraser Harrison was patient and kind. What was supposed to be a performance of only the first movement quite spontaneously changed to my playing the whole concerto. A piano was rolled out at the end when I played a couple of short pieces with Mama at the piano. The big treat for this concert was that it was in the evening—way past my bedtime!

"Some child geniuses are stiff, or forward, or a bit taken up with their own importance. Not so Miss K. She is that rare combination of ability, charm, and complete absence of affectation," reported the *Rochester Democrat and Chronicle*.[24]

From the beginning, Nadia's parents protected her from exploitation. The offer of a movie contract for the child was dismissed. The word *prodigy* was never used in her presence. Another took its place: *privilege*.

The word itself was not drummed into me, nor was I constantly reminded of how fortunate I was. It was simply what I felt around me. That explains the keeping of the word "prodigy" from my eyes: the implicit emphasis was not on how special I was, but rather on how special it was to be endowed with the gift of music.

In such a family, the process of music-making never stops. In 1939 Boris was composing several of his largest works. His opera *The Fatal Oath* was progressing and the Symphony in C was near completion. For two seasons he had been a violinist in the new NBC Symphony under Toscanini and would continue for another seven years until his retirement, at which time George joined the orchestra where he remained a member of the cello section for nine seasons. (At his first rehearsal in the orchestra, George sat at the stand with his great uncle, Horace Britt, who had been one of his first cello teachers.) A pupil of János Scholz at thirteen, George launched his career at age seventeen as principal cellist of the Kansas City Philharmonic. From the start, Boris was insistent upon playing chamber music, and time was always found for Inez and the children to play Haydn trios, chamber music ventures that Boris coached.

Nadia's school, P.S. 69, was across the street from the apartment house on 54th Street in New York City where the Koutzens lived. "I remember a sense of order about everything, lining up 'single file' and according to size," the violinist recalled. "I was always first—very small for my age and weighing less that thirty-five pounds."

After school, Nadia and George often went to Central Park:

The carousel, the zoo, the pony rides, roller skating, the playgrounds— all of it was joyful for me. I always stopped to admire horses. One day there was a mounted policeman at our street corner. My mother didn't want me to go too close, but the policeman was very reassuring. He asked me if I would like to touch the softest thing in the whole world, meaning the end of the horse's nose. The sweet pleasure of that tactile joy is with me still.

What I loved most of all was to stop at Emil Herrmann's studio on the way home from Central Park. There was a very big green sign on the repair shop door: No Admittance. I was in there all the time, loving the smells of the varnish and cleaners, fascinated most of all by the charming Mr. Sacconi, who had a warm, broad smile and a strong Italian accent which sounded like music to me. He was one of the finest and most beloved violin experts.

Emil Herrmann, the violin dealer and our very dear friend, wanted to see his generously loaned little treasures once in a while to make sure they were in good condition. At one such visit to his studio, Emil, placing his very thick glasses on top of his head, peering closely at the violin, said to my father in a very firm tone of voice, "Boris, stop making her cry."

Nadia's tears didn't stop, of course (the little girl cried easily), even though on the spot her naive mind thought they might, but the scene in the violin shop paid off. Because the acid in her tears was staining the varnish, from then on when tears were imminent, Nadia protected herself and her violin. "Instinctively and without hesitation, I held Emil's violin in front of my face."

All winter the Koutzen family looked forward to the summer at Woodstock where the entire Britt clan gathered at an annual artists' retreat in the Catskills. To escape the heat of New York City, Horace had taken Marguerite and Tatane up the Hudson to Woodstock for the first time in June 1910. In that rustic paradise, where they lived in Hervey White's Dutch farmhouse, they found complete happiness and joined colleagues and friends to create the Maverick Theater, the colony's summer performance venue.

When Nadia was eight, a special event occurred at Woodstock that would greatly influence her future:

> At the end of a regular Sunday afternoon chamber music concert at the Maverick Theater, Hervey White, who was the impresario of the series at the time, requested that the audience keep their seats—he had a surprise. My mother, my brother, and I performed a G Major Haydn trio, both George and I playing from memory.

Adrian Siegel, whose candid photographs tell the history of the Philadelphia Orchestra, was in the audience that afternoon. When he returned to Philadelphia, he told his friend Eugene Ormandy about the precocious violinist, Nadia Koutzen, then informed her father that in a forthcoming competition Ormandy would choose a young soloist for the Philadelphia Symphony.

> My father's reply was that under no circumstances would he have me compete. Each side was insistent until Adrian finally convinced Ormandy to hear me. Several months later, we went to the Academy of Music in Philadelphia where I played the Mozart concerto for

Ormandy, my father at the piano. I will always remember that when I was finished playing, Ormandy came to the edge of the stage and asked softly, "would you like to play with this orchestra?"

The concert took place on 4 November 1940. "For so small a child," wrote critic Samuel Laciar, "her tone was astounding in its power and brilliance, and she showed a remarkable technical equipment in the solo cadenza. . . . At the close of the movement she was greeted with a storm of applause."[25]

I recall the moment after my entrance onto the stage that Ormandy took my violin to tune it for me. The other very clear recollection at both rehearsal and concert is his urging me to stay close to the front of the stage saying, "the audience won't hear you." As I played I kept easing my way backwards closer to the musicians. During an orchestral interlude at the concert, I felt a gentle hand on my back urging me forward.

This collaboration with Eugene Ormandy was the beginning of a long-lasting musical alliance during which the great conductor continued to urge Nadia Koutzen forward. He reengaged her over the years as violin soloist with the Philadelphia Symphony Orchestra, including the 1952 premiere performance of her father's Concerto for Violin and Orchestra. Along with Fritz Kroll, William Primrose, and Nathan Milstein, Ormandy formed the keystones of support outside her family circle that bolstered her career; as a mature artist she would take her rightful place for a time in the international concert world.

Like Yehudi Menuhin, Nadia Koutzen is still on an unfinished journey as she looks over her shoulder at three generations of ancestors who were musicians before her. Like many of them, she was a prodigy of untold promise. Throughout her career she has remained determined to fulfill her life as a violinist in an unrelenting pursuit of artistic ideals.

During the 1960s she turned away from the negative aspects of concertizing that have so little to do with music-making, instead building a new career as a concertmaster, mostly of touring ballet companies, including the Pennsylvania Ballet, the Stuttgart Ballet, and the Bolshoi. When Henri Elkan invited her to become concertmaster of the Garden State Philharmonic in New Jersey, she accepted and remained in the position for twenty-one years.

"I have been a firm believer in the cause of community orchestras since the days when I performed as soloist with many of them," Nadia Koutzen has said. "People getting together to make music for the love of it is a major contribution to musical life everywhere."

> When it's all said and done, music, for me, is for sharing what the violin and I can do to bring warmth and pleasure, perhaps take people out of themselves. . . . I have considerable conviction about what I am capable of musically, and about what is in me to give to listeners. There are those times when I feel self-reproach for not fulfilling a potential I know was there—for not wholly redeeming God's gift. . . . but I would not have exchanged the other important elements of my day-to-day life.
>
> I couldn't have it both ways—now could I?

Nadia Koutzen at ten, as soloist with the Philadelphia Symphony Orchestra in 1940, Eugene Ormandy conducting. Photograph by Adrian Seigel. Courtesy Nadia Koutzen.

CHAPTER SIX

California Crossroads

JASCHA HEIFETZ,
EMANUEL FEUERMANN,
GREGOR PIATIGORSKY,
AND ARTUR RUBINSTEIN

J ASCHA Heifetz, the twentieth century's most celebrated violinist, played in
two trios that brought together four former prodigies, first with Emanuel
Feuermann and Artur Rubinstein, then with Gregor Piatigorsky and Rubinstein. Both collaborations took place in the artists' home town of Beverly
Hills; RCA Victor was the motivator and benefactor.

All four were born in Poland or Russia and established childhood careers
that led to international fame before World War Two. They immigrated to
the United States and quickly rose to the top echelon of concertizing violinists, cellists, and pianists.

Feuermann's untimely death in 1942 left Heifetz and Rubinstein without a cellist for their trio that had begun recording for RCA Victor the previous year. By 1950 Heifetz again joined Rubinstein, this time with cellist Gregor Piatigorsky. The three musicians gave four concerts of trios and sonatas
in one week at the Ravinia Park festival near Chicago, creating a sensation
that drew the largest audiences of the summer. After the concerts, as Piatigorsky recalled, *Life* magazine bestowed on them "the dubious title 'The Million Dollar Trio,'"[1] and the media promoted the moniker nationwide. Rubinstein found it in bad taste and discontinued appearances of this kind,
bringing the Million Dollar Trio to an end. The two string players soon
formed Heifetz-Piatigorsky Concerts in California where they both lived. By
1960, with several other colleagues they began recording a wide range of
works, including several piano trios with Jacob Lateiner and Leonard Pen-

nario. Ultimately Victor generated individual recording careers for these musical giants that assured success during their lifetimes and beyond.

JASCHA

One of Fra Angelico's seraphs seemed to have stepped from his background of goldleaf, disguised himself in modern dress, and exchanged a trumpet for a fiddle. While the boy was playing, Auer strode nervously about the room with a helpless shrug of the shoulders, as if to say, "Was there ever anything like it?"

Violinist Albert Spalding's first impression of Heifetz, in Weschler-Vered, *Jascha Heifetz*

Joseph Heifetz was born in Vilna, Lithuania (then part of Russian Poland), on 2 February 1901. Later at the St. Petersburg Conservatory his teacher, Leopold Auer, dubbed him Jascha because there were other Josephs in the violin class.

When Jascha was eight months old, his face beamed with joy when his father played a beautiful tune on his violin. His mother, Annie, remembered that later her son's reactions to hearing the violin became so distinct that his father indulged him with a miniature quarter-size violin for his third birthday.[2] Soon Jascha could imitate his father's playing, and Reuven Heifetz began teaching him. "When I played some notes on my violin, Jascha managed to reproduce them accurately on his tiny one. I played some more—and again he was able to repeat the notes. Moreover, if I played a false note, the boy would immediately start to scream. I was astonished."[3]

Although later Heifetz didn't remember being made to practice as a small child, he concluded that his father had persuaded him to undertake the task, and he was glad that he did. Reuven Heifetz had considerable ability as a violin teacher and devoted every ounce of energy to his son, in whose talent he believed implicitly. "There will be a plaque on the house where Jascha lived," he once remarked quite seriously. During Jascha's early career in New York, his father could be seen on the back row at Town Hall at every Heifetz recital, scrutinizing the stellar performer through opera glasses. Not only had he given his son his first lessons, but throughout his life he remained his severest critic. Often at gatherings after a brilliant performance with the New York Philharmonic, the violinist could be seen replying apologetically to his father's merciless account of the evening's flaws.[4]

At the time of Jascha's early childhood, Vilna had two important violin-

Jascha Heifetz at six, 1909. Courtesy Avigdor Zamir (Haifa).

ists: his father, then the concertmaster of the Vilna Symphony Orchestra, and his father's friend and colleague, Ilya Davidovitch Malkin, a former student of Professor Leopold Auer in St. Petersburg who taught at the Royal School of Music. Jascha began studying with Malkin when he was not quite five and made his first public appearance in the overcrowded auditorium of the music school performing Jean-Baptiste Singelée's *Fantaisie pastorale*, Op. 56, with piano accompaniment. By the time he was six, Jascha had mastered the Mendelssohn concerto under Malkin's guidance and performed it for the first time at nearby Kovno, also to a full house. The six-year-old continued to add new works to his repertoire; after only two years of study at the music school in Vilna, the astounding prodigy violinist graduated at age seven.

When Leopold Auer visited Vilna in 1907 during a concert tour, Malkin convinced him to listen to Jascha, although the professor insisted that he had had enough of these little geniuses and wished to be spared hearing yet another. However, an interview was finally arranged, and in the company of his father and Malkin, Jascha went to Auer's hotel room to play for him. The master was impatient with such a troublesome interview, but the seven-year-old was undaunted. He launched into a performance of the Mendelssohn concerto, then played Paganini's twenty-fourth caprice. Auer enthusiastically invited the boy to study at the conservatory in St. Petersburg, then went on his way the following day.

To raise sufficient money to make a new start in St. Petersburg, Reuven Heifetz was forced to sell his entire property in Vilna. When father and son finally stood before the master teacher at the conservatory six months after he had first heard Jascha in Vilna, Leopold Auer did not remember the child, but when Jascha had played a few measures, Auer's memory returned. He hugged the boy and demanded that Reuven enroll him at once.

Now an obstacle arose that had earlier presented a great difficulty for the families of Efrem Zimbalist and Mischa Elman. By czarist law St. Petersburg was a city closed to Jews. For Reuven Heifetz to reside in St. Petersburg and take care of his young child, Leopold Auer and Alexander Glazunov, then director of the conservatory, devised an acceptable plan—*both* father and son were enrolled, a formality that assured the family a residence permit in old Petrograd.

When the wonder child was admitted to the St. Petersburg Conservatory as its youngest pupil, he was not immediately accepted into Auer's class, but instead assigned to his assistant, Professor Ioannes Nalbandian, where he remained in the secondary violin class for a while, but this did not deter his musical activities. Immediately after his arrival in the city and although barely settled in the conservatory, Jascha played a concert in St. Petersburg on 30 April 1911. Before the year was finished, he had appeared in three more concerts in Odessa.

When Jascha was nine Auer finally accepted him as his personal student, which certainly was the turning point in his childhood. Leopold Auer, great master teacher of the violin at the beginning of the twentieth century, built his success on in his ability to develop each student's individuality. The first two important prodigies to come to Auer's class were the Jewish boys Efrem Zimbalist in 1901 and Mischa Elman in 1903. These two astounding child violinists were followed by others of equally stupendous gifts: the Canadian from Calgary, Kathleen Parlow; Cecile Hansen, the daughter of a Dane, born in the Cossack village of Stamiza Kamenska; Toscha Seidel, a prodigy from Odessa; Michel Piastro, born in Kerch in the Crimea; Eddy Brown, the Chicago boy who arrived in Russia from his studies with Jenő Hubay in Budapest; and finally, Jascha Heifetz, who later said of his teacher: "The Professor was a stern, strict, and very exacting teacher, but at the same time, he was very sympathetic . . . a wonderful and incomparable teacher."[5]

Auer's master class in St. Petersburg at that time usually included twenty-five to thirty students. While each gained individually from Auer's personal attention, from his criticisms, corrections, and all kinds of hints about violin playing, Auer was never satisfied with a mere explanation to any one of them unless certain it was understood, and he could always demonstrate his point by picking up his own violin and bow and playing. While all this transpired, young Jascha enjoyed listening to others as he waited his turn to play, especially Miron Poliakin, a talented violinist, and Cecile Hansen.

In 1904 Auer arranged for the Berlin debut of his young pupil Mischa Elman. This appearance threw Mischa into direct competition with the Hungarian wonder child Franz von Vecsey, a pupil of the great violinist Joseph Joachim, and sparked a rivalry between the young musicians that lasted for decades. However, Mischa's teenage career focused world attention on Auer and his pupils, so that by 1912, five years after Joachim's death, Auer's reputation made his pupils welcome in the German capital and paved the way for the Berlin debut of young Jascha Heifetz.

On 24 May 1912, eleven-year-old Jascha played a recital program at the Hochschule in Berlin. The program included the Mendelssohn concerto (with piano accompaniment), *Souvenir de Moscou* by Wieniawski, and a few shorter pieces. Impressed by the boy's playing, a critic pushed Jascha into the competitive fray when he ranked his playing somewhere "behind Mischa Elman and in front of Franz von Vecsey."[6]

Later that year, the Berlin critics were not so kind when Jascha appeared in a concerto performance conducted by Artur Nikisch in the large Philharmonic Hall, replacing the indisposed Pablo Casals. The critics found that Jascha's tone, so expressive in smaller halls, became lost in the Philharmonic Hall, and although he played the Tchaikovsky concerto in a virtuoso manner, the painful questions remained: "Does a mere child belong in the framework of such a concert? Here at least is one not entitled to expect a personality as soloist?"[7]

During Jascha's stay in Berlin, he met the world's reigning concert violinist, Fritz Kreisler, himself a former prodigy. Heifetz recalled meeting his idol in 1912 at a gathering of critics and musicians at the home of Arthur Abell: "Someone suggested that 'the young man from Russia play a number or two' and I was willing enough. What about the piano score? Fritz Kreisler kindly jumped into the breach and played my accompaniments from memory."

The final chords were greeted by a stunned silence. Kreisler rose from the piano, looked at the honorable guests, who included no less than Bronislaw Huberman, Carl Flesch, Joan Manén, Willy Hess, and Jan Kubelik, and said, "Well gentlemen, now we can all break our violins."[8]

After his success in Berlin, Jascha resumed his studies with Leopold Auer at the master's summer studio in Loschwitz near Dresden where musicians as well as impresarios gathered to hear the latest prodigy. At a musical matinee, Auer presented two of his favorite pupils in Bach's Double Concerto—Jascha Heifetz and Toscha Seidel, age eleven and thirteen. Auer later reminisced, "Not only I but all the guests were deeply moved by the purity and unity of style, and the profound sincerity, to say nothing of the technical perfection, with which the two children in blue sailor suits played that master work."[9]

Auer and his students were spending the summer in Dresden in 1914 when World War One broke out. The Heifetz family was permitted to return to Berlin, but as enemy aliens, and finally in December 1914 they were allowed to return home to St. Petersburg. Two years later in the summer of 1916 with the war still raging, Jascha, then fifteen, joined Auer in Norway where a small group of his students continued to study. Jascha and Toscha

Seidel repeated their performance of Bach's Double Concerto for the king and queen of Norway at the royal villa, somewhere outside Christiania (now Oslo). During the intermission of the soiree, Jascha challenged the royal prince to a race in the gardens, then later thoroughly enjoyed himself taking photographs of the landscape with his newly acquired box camera, a proud possession.

By the end of 1916, Jascha played a series of concerts in Moscow where he was becoming not only the focus of Russia's musical society, but also of foreign music agencies. Jascha's best opportunity—a promised debut performance in New York's Carnegie Hall—presented itself in 1917. Fortunately Leopold Auer had good connections with the music world abroad and this offer came to Reuven Heifetz from the Wolfssohn Music Bureau, a New York firm of impresarios. The concert management agreed to bring the entire Heifetz family to the United States and promised Jascha a full year of engagements, some fifty concerts. Twenty-five thousand dollars, an unusually large fee in 1917, was promised to the young, unheard violinist.

While world travel is a relatively simple matter for today's jet-age prodigies, Jascha's first journey to America was extremely difficult. It also was one-way. In 1917 Russia was invaded by the Germans. Vilna, Kiev, and Kharkov fell, and the front advanced quickly toward St. Petersburg. Under these circumstances, any itinerary through war-torn Europe was impossibly dangerous. The entire Heifetz family fled St. Petersburg, a city by then threatened by the German invasion and by the Russian revolution as well. They struggled across Russia to Siberia and on to Yokohama. From Japan they crossed the Pacific to San Francisco, where part of the family remained, while Reuven and Jascha traversed the continent by train, arriving finally in New York City: Jascha's presence was reported in the newspapers on 8 October 1917. The family would be reunited two months later, after Jascha had established a career for himself.

On 27 October 1917, Jascha Heifetz, the sixteen-year-old violinist from Vilna, changed the history of violin playing forever when he appeared for the first time in New York's Carnegie Hall. André Benoist, the pianist recommended by violinist Albert Spalding, accompanied the debut recital. On that autumn afternoon, Jascha galvanized the attention of the audience and paralyzed the aspirations of many other concert violinists. Jascha's violin playing seemed invincible.

The repertoire of the debut recital was not extraordinary; rather it was a typical presentation of *tour de force* violin pieces, beginning with Giovanni

Vitali's Chaconne, accompanied by Frank Sealy on the Carnegie Hall organ. Accompanist Benoist performed the balance of the program, which included Henryk Wieniawski's Second Concerto, then a half-dozen short works ending with Niccolò Paganini's twenty-fourth caprice in an arrangement with piano accompaniment by Jascha's teacher, Leopold Auer. At the end of the recital, the audience rushed the stage waving hats and handkerchiefs, and Jascha returned for encore after encore until the house lights were turned off.

Overnight Jascha became the musical idol of America; he made thirty appearances that season in New York alone. The critic of *Musical America* wrote that the greatest violinists may not be quite serious in their rumored decision "to shut up shop, burn their fiddles, and withdraw to distant wastes to invite oblivion because Jascha Heifetz has come upon us. Nevertheless, this Russian boy is beyond all possibility of cavil a divinely inspired marvel—the supremest genius of the violin."[10]

While the sound of Paganini's legendary violin playing at sixteen is left to our imagination, not so with Heifetz. Two weeks after his debut recital in Carnegie Hall, Jascha was standing before the acoustical horn in the Camden studios of the Victor Talking Machine Company in Camden, New Jersey. On that day, 9 November 1917, he recorded Riccardo Drigo's *Valse bluette*, Edward Elgar's *La Capricieuse*, Henryk Wieniawski's *Scherzo-tarantelle*, and Franz Schubert's *Ave Maria* in the famous transcription by August Wilhelmj. About five weeks later on 19 December, he returned to the recording studio to capture on disk five more flawless performances, including Antonio Bazzini's *La Ronde des lutins* (Dance of the Goblins), a recording that virtually preempted all further performances of that work by other concert violinists. These two sessions in Camden were the beginning of an unparalleled recording career.

Not until 1939 were Heifetz (by then securely established as the world's leading violinist) and his management willing to consider public concerts with another string player. Heifetz began to share chamber music evenings at home in New York City and on his Connecticut farm with the cellist Emanuel Feuermann. In December 1939 RCA Victor presented them to the public as musical colleagues in a recording of Brahms' Concerto for Violin and Cello, Op. 102, with the Philadelphia Orchestra and its then-new music director, Eugene Ormandy.

The success of this Brahms recording prompted RCA Victor in 1941 to ask Heifetz to form a series of chamber music combinations with Feuermann and others. While the choice of a pianist gave the new collaborators some concern, the recording company argued for Artur Rubinstein, who was under contract to them.[11]

They began to rehearse for their chamber music recordings in mid-August of 1941 in Beverly Hills. The first recording project, Beethoven's Trio, Op. 97 ("Archduke"), Brahms' Trio, Op. 8, and Schubert's Trio, Op. 99, took place in Hollywood during a five-day session, 9 to 13 September 1941. By mid-December the recordings were edited and with RCA Victor the trio was planning their public concert debut to introduce the new recordings to the market. This plan was never realized. On 25 May 1942, Emanuel Feuermann, known as Munio to his family and friends, died unexpectedly after minor surgery. He was thirty-nine.

MUNIO

Of all those who have ever been entrusted to my guardianship, there has never been such a talent as this gifted one, Munio. Well, good luck for our divinely favored artist and lovable young man.

Julius Klengel to Wilhelm Fux, 1918,

in Itzkoff, *Emanuel Feuermann, Virtuoso*

Emanuel Feuermann was born one year after Jascha Heifetz on 22 November 1902 in Kolomea, a small town on the eastern plain of Polish Galicia (now Ukraine). Munio was the third of five children in a musical family. His older brother, Sigmund, was an amazing violin prodigy. In her maturity, his younger sister, Sophie, was a pianist of great attainments. Their father, Maier Feuermann, was an accomplished violinist who turned to cello playing to meet the demands of Kolomea's provincial musical life while still devoting himself to his gifted children as teacher and impresario. Their mother, Rachel, was a faithful homemaker and protector of the family's domestic life.

Sigmund developed slowly as an infant and suffered convulsions before he was one year old, but by three he was playing the violin. Despite this unusual beginning to his life, no one in the family imagined that in later life the gifted Sigmund would suffer from mental illness. Like his younger compatriot, the Polish violinist Josef Hassid, Sigmund descended pitifully into musical oblivion, eventually dying of a brain tumor. ("My children all become famous and die young. I wish they had become shoemakers," said Rachel Feuermann after his death.[12])

During childhood Sigmund and Munio were treated very differently by

Emanuel Feuermann, eight years old in 1910, playing his father's cello. Courtesy Seymour W. Itzkoff.

their parents. Sigmund was awakened early each morning for an intensive violin lesson with his father, then left under his mother's supervision to practice throughout the rest of the day. While Sigmund labored under the severe scrutiny of one parent, Munio had no such strict parental guidance. He was left on his own to play his violin as he wished, under his chin or between his knees as Casals had done in faraway Spain a quarter-century earlier. One day when a neighborhood boy was brought to the Feuermann home with his small cello to have a lesson with Maier, Munio grabbed the little cello and demanded to be taught to play it. For Munio this day was the end of violin playing.

In January 1908, the Feuermanns decided to move to Vienna for Sigmund's sake. Maier left Kolomea to search the Austrian capital for a master violin teacher who would accept Sigmund. Otakar Ševčik arrived in Vienna the same year as professor of violin at the Vienna Academy, and he enthusiastically accepted Sigmund as a pupil. Both Feuermann boys were taken often to the academy, Sigmund to be taught in Ševčik's master class, Munio to observe his brother's lessons. At home after these forays, seven-year-old Munio would take time off from his assigned cello etudes to fiddle on the cello as though he were playing the violin for Ševčik. Munio's disarming playfulness seemed to content Maier, and he allowed the young cellist to continue to set his own pace.

Wilhelm Kux, a man outside the family circle, brought a new influence to bear on the lives of the Feuermanns. A wealthy Jewish banker from Czechoslovakia, Kux was a powerful patron of the arts in Vienna and was particularly devoted to the city's most promising string players. Observing the imbalance of attention the father granted his sons, Kux suggested that a teacher other than Maier be found for Munio. He turned the family's attention to Friedrich Buxbaum, and Munio soon began lessons with his first master teacher, the cellist of the celebrated Rosé String Quartet. It was a time of great change for Munio. As a pupil of Buxbaum, he found himself absorbed into a group of privileged children who thrived under Kux's patronage, including young Rudolf Kolisch, who would later lead one of Europe's most distinguished quartets, and little Erica Morini, perhaps Vienna's most spectacular violin prodigies of the time.

Within a year Munio's progress under Buxbaum's guidance came to the attention of other Viennese cello teachers. Eager to claim the boy as his own pupil, Anton Walter, the young cellist of the Fitzner String Quartet, convinced Maier in 1910 to make a change. When Maier was frequently away from home supervising Sigmund's concert tours, Munio progressed rapidly as a student of Anton Walter.

By 1912, Walter had made the boy aware of the great cellists of the age—David Popper, Karl Davidov, and Julius Klengel—and now the young cellist eagerly awaited his first opportunity to hear the sensational Pablo Casals. The Spanish cellist had appeared in Vienna for the first time in November 1910, playing Emanuel Moór's unfamiliar concerto, then a few days later the Brahms Double Concerto with violinist Arnold Rosé. At the end of 1912, Casals returned to play the concertos of Boccherini and Haydn with the Vienna Philharmonic. Munio was in the audience, and the experience changed the course of his musical life, not only because of the incomparable Casals, but also because of the music itself, Haydn's Concerto in D Major.

Munio did not ask Anton Walter to teach him Haydn's concerto but rather demanded that his mother buy him a copy of the music, then set out to learn it on his own. When he finally played the concerto through for his teacher, Walter was stunned by the child's ingenious musical accomplishment.

As Munio's prowess became increasingly well-known in the musical circles of Vienna, other cello teachers found the prospect of claiming the boy as their student something worth bargaining for. Paul Grümmer, a former pupil of Julius Klengel In Leipzig (and later the cellist of the Busch Quartet), visited Rachel Feuermann at her home and proposed that in return for her granting his wish to teach Munio, he would favor the family with scholarships and financial stipends. Although the unsought financial boon was tempting, Rachel realized that Munio was perfectly satisfied to remain with Anton Walter, and Grümmer's aggressive offer was rejected.

Under Wilhelm Kux's influence, Sigmund and Munio began to appear regularly in chamber music evenings in the homes of Vienna's wealthy music lovers. Sensing the disparity in the career development of the Feuermann brothers, both Kux and Walter pressed Maier to present Munio in a debut recital. When it finally took place, the recital was a modest affair in a small hall in the Leopoldstadt during which Munio had a complete memory lapse and sat silent on stage, apparently puzzled as to what to do next.

Soon after this fledgling recital, Munio, not quite eleven, played his favorite solo work with Vienna's Tonkünstler Orchestra, the orchestra in which his father was a cellist. Oskar Nedbal conducted. In February 1914, he performed the Haydn concerto again, this time in an important, official debut with the Vienna Philharmonic conducted by Felix Weingartner. Music critics Julius Korngold and Max Kalbeck pronounced Munio an unusual cello talent and a worthy addition to the family's musical reputation,[13] which in 1914 was based entirely on Sigmund's success. This may explain the critics' faint praise for the younger, less accomplished sibling.

During the hazardous early years of World War One, Sigmund and Munio undertook several modest joint concert tours, appearing in Poland, Bohemia, and Romania. They often performed, with piano accompaniment, one movement or another from the Brahms Double Concerto, the masterpiece that would eventually serve as their most perfect concert vehicle.

When Munio turned fourteen, Maier knew it was time for the teenager to leave Vienna to study elsewhere. Although the idea of studying with Hugo Becker at Berlin's Hochschule was appealing, Munio went instead to Julius Klengel in Leipzig in July 1916. With his borrowed Amati cello in hand and burdened with overstuffed suitcases, Munio said farewell to his family at the train station in Vienna. For the young cellist this emotional moment was the beginning of a timely separation. "Munio, come back a second Casals," someone shouted. "No, I'll come back a first Feuermann," he replied.[14]

Julius Klengel had been a precocious cellist himself, serving as principal cellist of the Leipzig Gewandhaus Orchestra by fifteen. As professor at the Leipzig Conservatory from 1881 to 1933, he taught a legion of gifted cellists, including Auber, Grümmer, Hoelscher, Pleeth, Schneider, Stutschewsky, Suggia, Wallenstein, even Piatigorsky. Now fired by adolescent enthusiasm, Munio at last began to labor seriously at his cello playing in this new artistic environment. When Klengel assigned him a difficult Bach suite at a Monday lesson, he practiced with unimaginable ardor, then brought it back memorized on the following Thursday. Talent was no stranger to Klengel's studio, and both master and pupils quickly recognized Munio's gifts. About his study in Leipzig, Feuermann said, "When I took lessons from Julius Klengel, he thought I was using strange and unusual fingerings only on account of my long fingers."

> It did not occur to the dear old man that I had purely musical reasons in mind. Twenty years ago when I started concertizing, the public and even critics often disliked my way of playing. . . . They frequently criticized me for "playing violin on the cello." The tradition among even music-minded people was to pity the cellists for trying to compete with the violinists; a cello recital was expected to be a boring affair.[15]

Franz Liszt once remarked that Friedrich Grützmacher, II, would assure that the cello dynasty of the Grützmachers would not die out, but the dynasty ended in 1918 when Grützmacher, then professor of the Cologne Conservatory, died at fifty-two. Julius Klengel made an unusual recommendation that sixteen-year-old Munio succeed Grützmacher. After Munio's audition in Cologne, Professor Adendroth announced: "The faculty has had a unique experience. It has witnessed in the playing of the young cellist Emanuel Feuermann abilities of unimaginable scope. His is truly a talent of the utmost rarity. In spite of his age we have agreed to appoint him to the faculty. Feuermann will be a brilliant jewel in our crown."[16] This appointment in Cologne launched Munio's distinguished teaching career and marked the end of his brief childhood. Even though the professorial title was withheld because of his youth, Emanuel Feuermann now set out to accomplish a man's job. In this role he was enormously successful, so much so that in 1929 he was appointed the successor to Hugo Becker at the Berlin Hochschule where he remained until 1933 when the political climate in Germany led the Hochschule to terminate his contract.

During the 1920s Munio performed in more than one thousand concerts in Europe. When he appeared as soloist in Vienna with the Berlin Philharmonic in 1925, he encountered the Russian cellist Gregor Piatigorsky, a virtually unknown young artist whom the orchestra's celebrated conductor Wilhelm Furtwängler had engaged one year earlier as the principal cellist. The orchestra was standing when Munio reached his place on stage near Piatigorsky. Feuermann and Piatigorsky standing side-by-side must have presented a sharp and somewhat amusing contrast. Munio stood only five foot seven inches. Piatigorsky towered over him at six feet four. From that time onward, the ascending careers of these two unique cellists were intertwined.

As a supreme instrumentalist displaced by the Nazi regime, Munio was bound for the United States after 1935 following two world tours. There he began establishing a new career, and in 1939 his pivotal encounter with Jascha Heifetz resulted in their landmark performance of the Brahms Double Concerto for RCA Victor.

On 25 May 1942, Emanuel Feuermann died unexpectedly after minor surgery. He was only thirty-nine and still struggling to claim his place in an international arena in which both the older Casals and Gregor Piatigorsky were aggressively pursuing their careers.

In July 1942, three months after Feuermann's death, Piatigorsky replaced him at the Ravinia Festival and thoughtfully dedicated a performance of a Boccherini adagio to his departed rival. The following November, the National Orchestral Association, with whom Feuermann had repeatedly appeared as soloist in New York, also dedicated a program to his memory.

In his few brief years teaching at the Curtis Institute in Philadelphia, Feuermann had established himself as a teacher of international reputation. Although by 1942 many of Feuermann's pupils had dispersed, some to continue their studies in New York with Dr. Demetrius Dounis, it was no surprise when Piatigorsky accepted the invitation to become the chairman of the cello department at the Curtis Institute. Grisha (as Gregor Piatigorsky was known to family and friends) would build a superlative new cello class in Philadelphia and later at the University of Southern California in Los Angeles.

GRISHA

As a little boy in Russia, I heard music at home all the time. My parents didn't especially encourage or discourage me to become a musician—I was absolutely determined about that myself at an early age. I started to earn money for the family before I was eight years old. As a youngster I had all kinds of jobs. I even wrote music for the silent movies, in Russia, when I was nine or ten years old.

> Piatigorsky, in Bernard Rosenberg and Deena Rosenberg,
> "A Last Talk With Piatigorsky"

Gregor Piatigorsky was born in Russia at Ekaterinoslav (now Dnepropetrovsk in Ukraine) on 17 April 1903, the year after Emanuel Feuermann was born in Poland. A superb raconteur, Piatigorsky wrote the story of his life a decade before his death (he died in California in 1976). In this work he describes, with unexpected candor, his childhood and the eventual flight from revolutionary Russia. As a small child he was spared nothing. He recalls huddling in a dark cellar, terrified by the sounds of a savage pogrom taking place above. Grisha's childhood was in every way a rough and ready existence.

Piatigorsky recalled the night he saw and heard a cello for the first time when his father, Paul, took him to a symphony concert: "I had never heard or seen anything nearly so beautiful before." At home the next day, Grisha armed himself with two sticks, a long one for the cello and a short one for the bow, and pretended to play the cello, those magic sticks lifting him into an imagined world of sound where he could summon every mood at will.

On the morning of his seventh birthday, his father woke him early, and a few minutes later when the sleepy boy stumbled into the living room he found his entire family waiting. There he was given his first cello, the most perfect birthday present of his young life. From that morning onward, the instrument was next to him at all meals and by his bedside at night.

Like Munio's father, Maier Feuermann, Grisha's father was a violinist and gave his son his first lessons, but soon the boy's cello study was entrusted to Mr. Yampolsky, a local cellist. When Yampolsky left Ekaterinoslav, Grisha became a student of Mr. Gubariov, then director of the conservatory. Grisha

Gregor Piatigorsky at ten, 1913. From Cellist *by Gregor Piatigorsky. Copyright © 1965 by Gregor Piatigorsky. Used by permission of Doubleday, a division of Bantam Doubleday Dell Publishing Group, Inc.*

was impressed by two things about his new teacher: Gubariov's cello seemed to stand alone, separated from him by his enormous stomach, and as he played and taught he habitually sucked on mint drops. As small boys will do, Grisha imitated his teacher in every detail. When his father found him practicing at home with a large pillow held against his cello, his mouth stuffed with mint drops, he decided that the emulation had gone far enough and the lessons with Gubariov were terminated.

Another false start occurred when a reputable cellist visiting Ekaterinoslav agreed to listen to the child play. Mr. Kinkulkin, a former pupil of Professor Klengel in Leipzig, listened halfheartedly, then delivered a quick verdict—Grisha should keep away from the cello because he had no talent whatsoever. Fortunately, when it came to cello-playing the boy lived in a magical world of his own invention and was not troubled by any of this. He simply continued to play in whatever way his imagination led him.

Paul Piatigorsky wanted to be a concert violinist. When he left home to study with Leopold Auer in St. Petersburg, Grisha's grandfather, who had vigorously opposed the plan, withdrew his much-needed financial support from the family left behind in Ekaterinoslav. With this harsh turn of events, Grisha took his cello and went looking for work. Following some musicians into a hiring hall, the child was asked: Do you want a job? ("Yes"); Have you played anywhere? ("At home—quartets with my father and brother. I usually sing the part of the viola"); Do you know any gypsy music? The boy played "Marussja Poisoned Herself" and his own variations on "Dark Eyes." As a result of his colorful renditions, Grisha was instantly hired for a job in a nightclub. He was only eight.

Unprotected by privilege, fine education, or musical training, the boy cellist of Ekaterinoslav continued his incredible, early development amidst oppressive musical engagements that brought him into contact with the most suspect characters in town. In the end he was usually fired from these jobs, not because his playing warranted dismissal but because his extreme youth was bad for business. When the only available cellist in town, who was afraid of the dark when sober, turned down a position in the local movie house, Grisha had his chance in the orchestra pit of Ekaterinoslav's Coliseum Theater. After a few weeks of this arduous new venture, during which he played from three in the afternoon until midnight, the boy nearly collapsed while playing the cello solo in Rossini's "William Tell" Overture. When he could no longer continue, the conductor struck him with his violin bow. Rallied by this unexpected attack, Grisha avenged himself by breaking a chair on the leader's head. Tempers flared. Several instruments were smashed in the melee. The job was lost.

With no possible retreat from such a harsh existence, the jobless boy was back on the streets the next morning looking for work. His lonely struggle continued until the death of his grandfather brought his father home from St. Petersburg, where his plans to become a concert violinist had not gone well. In an unexpected turn of events, Paul Piatigorsky moved his family to Moscow where he applied for Grisha's entrance to the Moscow Conservatory. The boy was interviewed by Mikhail Ippolitov-Ivanov, the director of the conservatory, and was admitted as a scholarship pupil, but before a term was over Paul Piatigorsky had yet another plan. He decided that he and his two sons, Grisha and Leonid, would hire on with the Zimin Grand Opera, a traveling company about to tour the small towns on the Volga River.

With the entire company, the Piatigorskys boarded a third-class railroad car and traveled to Samara for a performance of Tchaikovsky's *Eugen Onegin* in which they would join the rag-tag pit orchestra; Leonid as concertmaster, Paul as first violist, and Grisha leading the cellos. On the opening night in Samara, nothing went well. The conductor, who played the French horn from the podium, only occasionally directed the music. The unexpected climax of the performance came when the tenor fell into the pit in a drunken stupor. As the curtain fell, the musicians fled the theater. The next morning they were on their way to Saratov, then to Astrakhan where the ill-fated tour ended abruptly in total chaos.

Since his father had only enough money for two tickets home, Grisha was left behind to play in an amusement park orchestra in Astrakhan. The orchestra's manager loaned the boy a violin and relegated him to the second violin section, where he sat playing the fiddle between his knees. When this failed, he was hired at the Cafe Chantant and placed facing the wall in the orchestra pit to protect him from the obscene sights on stage.

Within weeks Grisha was making his way home to Moscow, stealing rides on freight trains, sleeping in haystacks, selling his belongings as he went. Twelve days later he arrived home in tatters, just in time to celebrate the end of summer and his return to the conservatory where he would continue his study with Professor Alfred von Glehn, a disciple of the famous Karl Davidov.

A not-very-demanding conservatory teacher, von Glehn was content to hear the same cello etude repeated at every lesson, quite unable to catalyze Grisha's enormous potential into any substantial artistic achievement. When the boy requested and was granted an appearance on a student recital, he played a brilliant, if self-taught, performance of Servais' *Souvenir de Spa*, only to return the next day to playing his Duport etude in von Glehn's studio. The misguided teacher dismissed him with the remark, "Please go home. I can't understand you."[17]

After yet another bizarre cafe engagement, Grisha lost his job, his cello, and his rented room. Thanks to the kindness of a janitor, he found refuge at the conservatory where he slept each night in an empty classroom. Because the janitor was acquainted with Feodor Chaliapin's manager, an opportunity arose for Grisha to assist the great Russian basso in three forthcoming Moscow recitals. Assisting musicians who carried out such tasks on Chaliapin recitals were expected to do no more than present a momentary respite for the singer, leaving the audience to chat and amuse themselves until the basso returned to the stage. Unsettled by this servile role, at the second recital Grisha delivered a commanding performance of Popper's Polonaise, forcing the noisy audience to pay attention. After a rousing ovation, Grisha saw the upstaged singer standing enraged in the wings. After the recital, Chaliapin dismissed him, and the beleaguered young cellist was again cast adrift on his perilous journey to maturity.

Gregor Piatigorsky was only fourteen when the Russian revolution began. Unlike Jascha Heifetz, who was safely on his way to his New York debut, Grisha was trapped in the terrifying uprising. His only solace in those bewildering times was music. He regularly played string quartets with some older colleagues, including the violinist Professor Lev Zeitlin, who told him of a competition for the finest cello position in Russia, principal cellist of the orchestra of the Imperial Opera at the Bolshoi Theater.

Job seeking was nothing new to the fourteen-year-old who appeared at the audition with his cello but no music. When the pianist produced a copy of Dvořák's concerto, the intrepid cellist played the first movement for the jury and won the coveted position. The new communist government was established by then, but the aftereffects of the great revolutionary struggle remained. People were weary and hungry, even the artists of the Bolshoi. "I was the only member of the orchestra to receive a child's ration card, and was called a 'chocolate baby.' For some it was funny, but I would rather have had raw fish and potato peels than my endless diet of sweets."

Bolstered politically by his important position at the Bolshoi, Grisha began to flourish before the adoring Moscow audiences. (Jascha Bernstein, a fellow student from von Glehn's class, recalls that by then Grisha was proudly nicknamed the Child of Moscow.[18]) There were recitals with many outstanding pianists and the formation of a new trio. Grisha's string quartet led by Lev Zeitlin was renamed the Lenin Quartet and allowed to play privately for Vladimir Ulyanov, who under the famous pseudonym Nikolai Lenin was the driving force of the Bolshevik revolution.

After the quartet performance, Grisha was detained for a conversation with Lenin, who acknowledged the phenomenon of Piatigorsky's attainments while still so young. "It is strange that only in music and in mathematics can the very young reach prominence. Did you ever hear of a child architect or surgeon?" he asked. "No, but I have heard of child chess players," Grisha replied. "Quite right. Chess has been good for the Russians. It gives them occasion in this country to fight—to win or lose or come out even, on equal terms and merits."[19] Encouraged by Lenin's reception, Grisha asked permission of Mr. Lunocharsky, the Minister of Art, to leave the country to pursue his study abroad in France or Germany. It was refused. He was needed at the Bolshoi. Grisha threatened to run away. Lunocharsky did not believe him.

In the summer of 1921, the nineteen-year-old cellist joined two singers from the Bolshoi and the violinist Mischa Mischakov in a concert tour. When they reached the village of Volochisk on the Polish border, they joined forces with another small group of touring musicians. The morning after their concert, they arranged to be smuggled across the border. On the next dark night, they were led to a low bridge over the Sbruch River. When they reached it, they were commanded to run.

Piatigorsky later told London's *Daily Telegraph*: "I carry cello over shoulder. Suddenly bing–bang–bang! Two soldiers shoot at us. My health remains goods. Shots not hit. There is with us lady opera singer. She is awfully fat. As she hears bangs, she jumps on shoulders. Puts big arms round neck. . . . Cello is no more!"[20]

Grisha did more than cross over; he burned a bridge behind him forever. On the far bank, border guards arrested him and put him in jail. This was the beginning of his new life in Poland.

When he was released from jail, Grisha made his way through Poland, first to Lemberg, then to Warsaw where he found work in the orchestra of the Warsaw Opera. After almost two years in Poland, he went to Germany. In Berlin he had a few disappointing lessons with Hugo Becker. In Leipzig he studied briefly with Julius Klengel before returning to Berlin where he was reunited with his Russian colleagues, violinist Boris Koutzen and pianist Leopold Mittman. Together they found work at the Cafe Ruscho. This Russian cafe was patronized by many well-known musicians and there Grisha soon made new friends, including pianist Artur Schnabel, who in turn brought him to the attention of Wilhelm Furtwängler at the Berlin Philharmonic.

In November 1923, Furtwängler decided to hear Grisha. Their meeting changed Piatigorsky's artistic life. After the audition, Furtwängler invited him to become the first cellist of the Berlin Philharmonic and from that 1923–24 season in Berlin, Piatigorsky's international career was in the ascendancy. By 1928 he was convinced that he must resign his position with the Berlin Philharmonic in order to tour internationally in Europe, Asia, and North America. His first appearance in the United States was in Oberlin, Ohio, on 5 November 1929. On a brief American tour he appeared with the Philadelphia Symphony Orchestra, Leopold Stokowsky conducting. The tour concluded with his first New York performance on 29 December when he played the Dvořák concerto with the New York Philharmonic, conducted by Willem Mengelberg.

In 1931 he met the pianist Artur Rubinstein when they both happened to be performing in Poland. Upon learning that Piatigorsky was appearing at the Filharmonja Hall in Warsaw, Rubinstein and his future wife, Nela, were eager to greet him after the concert, having heard that the great cellist had escaped from Russia at the same time as their friends Vladimir Horowitz and Nathan Milstein.

That evening Piatigorsky performed a work he came to dislike and never recorded, Friedrich Grützmacher's clever arrangement of concerto movements by Luigi Boccherini, once the most recorded, although spurious, Boccherini concerto. "Piatigorsky played very beautifully; he was certainly the best cellist I had heard since Casals," Rubinstein later recalled. "This very good-looking artist turned out to be a charming man. Right then, our close friendship began."[21] Over the years they would come together to perform, in public and in the recording studio, and their friendship continued until the end.

ARTUR

I remember vividly the mornings when my brothers and sisters had to dash to school, invariably late. . . . They would always be shouting and running, quarreling and forgetting things—it was like an army going to war—and then: complete silence; I was left alone with my piano.

Rubinstein, *My Young Years*

Artur Rubinstein was born in Lodz, Poland, on 28 January 1887. He could sing before he could speak. When his two older sisters began piano lessons

Artur Rubinstein at four, with his cousin Fanny Meyer in Berlin, 1891.

at home, he was happiest nestled by their feet beneath the keyboard. Only three years old, Artur was amazingly responsive to all that transpired above him between his sisters and Madame Kijanska, their piano teacher. The little boy was delighted when Madame Kijanska slapped his sister's hands for playing a wrong note: "Sometimes when my sisters were practicing and made a mistake, I was the one who did the slapping."

Like many keyboard prodigies before him, Artur quickly learned to recognize pitches by name and with his back to the piano could identify the notes of any chords played by Madame Kijanska, even the most dissonant ones. First with one hand, later with both, he was able to play any tune that caught his ear. He claimed his place at the keyboard, playing duets with Madame Kijanska. A cheerful, extroverted little boy, Artur would solemnly stop at the right moment to turn the page, pretending that he was reading the music. To his parents he must have seemed a baby Mozart incarnate. By the time he was three-and-a-half years old his fixation was so obvious that his family decided to do something about his talent.

A detailed letter asking advice was sent to the great violinist Joseph Joachim in Berlin. Joachim replied that nothing should be done until the boy turned six, at which time he should be taught by a good teacher. Joachim added that if they could manage to bring the child to Berlin, he would be pleased to see him. Joachim's apparent interest provoked great excitement in the Rubinstein family and there was a decision to go to Berlin for an interview with this distinguished violinist, the friend of Brahms.

In Berlin, Joachim improvised a musical aptitude test in which the child identified random notes and chords played at the piano, hummed in imitation a Schubert theme, then transposed it into another tonality. Joachim was pleased and said to Artur's mother, Felicia Rubinstein, "This boy may become a very great musician. When the time comes for serious study, bring him to me, and I shall be glad to supervise his artistic education."[22]

When they returned home after this successful interview, the newspaper in Lodz published enthusiastic accounts of their visit to Berlin. Artur's piano lessons began at once with Mrs. Pawlawska, a typical exponent of the old school whose chief effort was to make the boy keep his elbows close to his body and to play scales without dropping the coin she placed on his hand. After three months she had to admit her defeat, and his lessons were entrusted to Mr. Adolf Prechner, a strange, slightly demonic person who would always either speak too softly or shout at the top of his voice. Artur made quick progress with Mr. Prechner and was soon able to play pieces of Mozart, Mendelssohn, and Bach.

Artur's father Itzhak had a secret aspiration to send his son to study with Anton Rubinstein, the great Russian pianist who had been the director of the Imperial Conservatory in St. Petersburg and was generally considered the greatest keyboard player after Franz Liszt. Itzhak asked Artur one morning if he knew who had died, causing the innocent child to burst into tears. "Anton Rubinstein," the father revealed. "Now your future is ruined!" Itzhak Rubinstein's dream was shattered, but not Artur's future.

On 14 December 1894, Artur, then seven, joined a violinist and a singer in presenting a charity concert in Lodz. It was his first important public performance. Excited at having seen a large box of chocolates waiting backstage, Artur enthusiastically played his Mozart sonata and two pieces by Schubert and Mendelssohn. With a quick bow, he accepted the warm ovation from the audience that consisted mainly of his family, their friends, and a small group of Lodz's music lovers, then left the stage to claim his sweet reward.

Because Lodz was becoming unsafe for Jews, Artur's parents took him to Warsaw. After hearing the boy play, Alexander Michalowski, the leading piano professor of the Warsaw Conservatory, spoke encouragingly to Artur's mother but was unwilling to accept so young a pupil. He recommended Professor Rószychi, who accepted Artur without even troubling himself to hear him play. In Artur's first lesson, the weary Rószychi fell soundly asleep, but roused by the final chord, mumbled vague instructions about what should be prepared for the next lesson, telling Artur to buy a copy of his published exercises and practice these three hours each day. The lessons that followed produced little results, because Rószychi continued to doze the hours away. After receiving a letter from her young son describing his teacher's "sleeping sickness," Artur's mother arrived promptly to take Artur home to Lodz.

An economic crisis in Lodz soon affected everyone who lived there. Trapped in a financial catastrophe, the Rubinstein family broke up, sending Artur to sleep at the neighbor's house where for the imaginative ten-year-old there was no piano, no lessons, and nothing to do. In these circumstances, the idea of sending him again to Berlin gained new significance.

When Artur and his mother arrived in the German capital, they went from one piano teacher to another. He played for Ernst Jedliczka and Xaver Scharwenka, but not for Ferrucio Busoni who was away on a concert tour. Finally they visited the young Joseph Hofmann, then twenty-two, and his father, himself a piano teacher, before again turning to the violinist Joseph Joachim for further advice.

Having heard Artur play Mozart, Joachim left the room and returned with a bar of Lindt's bitter chocolate for the child, who was then left alone with his treat while Joachim took his mother aside to discuss a plan of action. That hour, the great man took it upon himself to direct the boy's cultural and musical education. The only stipulation that Joachim made was that Artur not be exploited as a child prodigy, insisting that he get a full education until he was artistically mature. Overwhelmed at their good fortune, Artur's parents kept this promise in full while Artur grew up in Berlin.

Joachim decided that Dr. Theodor Altmann would assume the great responsibility for the boy's general education as his private tutor, teaching him German history, Latin, geography, and mathematics for two hours every day. Joachim's choice for Artur's piano teacher was Heinrich Barth. "My new life started right away. Heinrich Barth, the senior piano professor of the Imperial and Royal Academy of Music, accepted me, on Joachim's recommendation," Rubinstein recalled. Barth agreed to teach the boy without pay and to take charge of all money matters on his behalf, paying for all his living expenses and other lessons from a fund created by four generous patrons. Unfortunately, Heinrich Barth was a formidable personality and terrified young Artur. Nobody before had inspired so much fear in him, but when he saw many of Barth's pupils in tears after their lessons, he realized that he was not the only one to suffer.

Barth had his assistant teacher, elderly Clara Hempel, prepare Artur for his lessons. With her zeal for scale practice, she quickly restrained the spirited child with her method. The boy saw nothing but drudgery in the tasks she set and found no incentive to carry them out. "I would easily get discouraged as I watched my fingers run up and down the keyboard, as though they were cleaning some huge teeth." Despite the harsh regime of his piano teachers, Artur relished Berlin's musical life. At ten, he heard Artur Nikisch conduct all the symphonies of Beethoven and Mozart, heard the great pianists Eugen d'Albert and Ferrucio Busoni, the violinist Fritz Kreisler, and his contemporary Eugène Ysaÿe, the Belgian violinist who became Artur's musical idol.

Joachim had concert plans for Artur. With considerable trepidation, Artur played a Mozart concerto in Potsdam. After a great ovation, the audience demanded an encore. Barth sent him back on stage to play one of Mendelssohn's *Songs Without Words*. He began with great assurance, but suddenly his mind went blank, so he improvised his own themes that had nothing to do with the piece. He hardly dared to take a bow, and was shaking with fear when he returned backstage, certain he had incurred Barth's wrath. Much to Artur's surprise, Barth came happily toward him, shook his hands, and exclaimed "You are a rascal—but a genius! I couldn't have pulled that trick in a thousand years."[23]

In December 1900 Artur played an important concert with orchestra at the Beethovensaal in Berlin that included concertos by Mozart and Saint-Saëns. In the large audience was not only Joseph Joachim, but Max Bruch and the pianist Leopold Godowsky, all of whom shared in the joy of the evening. The press was generous in its praise, and engagements for the fourteen-year-old pianist followed in Dresden and Hamburg.

Unfortunately Artur's relationship with Heinrich Barth became clouded when Barth's stringent choice of repertoire no longer suited Artur's musical temperament, his growing pianistic prowess, nor his practical needs. A few months after the gala opening of the new Filharmonja Hall in Warsaw, Artur was invited to appear there. Barth gave his permission, insisting only that, according to their original agreement that he manage the young pianist's money, the earnings would be brought back to Berlin. A crisis occurred when Artur's father did not send the money as swiftly as Barth had anticipated. In a tempestuous exchange in the studio, the anxious Barth insulted Artur and his father in regard to this financial entanglement. Although the matter was settled within the week, the damage had been done.

In the months that followed, the adolescent Artur began to despair over all the details of his stressful life. When his mother declared that she intended to come to Berlin to live with him, he imagined that all promise of independence was lost. He turned to Joachim for emotional support during this trauma, and the noble old violinist promised to try to dissuade her from coming to Berlin, but in this he failed. The domestic situation became intolerable for the distraught teenager, but Joachim hit on another plan and this one worked. He managed to elicit an invitation for Artur to visit Ignace Paderewski, the great Polish pianist, at his villa in Switzerland. There Paderewski would hear the boy play and give Joachim his opinion about Artur's future career.

When the two Polish pianists met and Artur sat down to play, he made an error in judgment, attempting to impress the older man by performing a difficult Brahms work that he had not fully prepared. When this failed, he bowed his head in shame. But Paderewski understood very well ("Don't be disheartened by a few wrong notes") and after confirming his talent invited him to stay on for several days. When Artur played for him the second time, he performed works that genuinely conveyed his ability as a young artist. After Paderewski jumped to his feet and embraced him, he said: "Artists have a hard road ahead of them before they find themselves. . . . Don't take your young worries too much to heart—you will see there are harder things in an artist's life."

In Berlin, Joachim received a letter from Paderewski. He was pleased at the turn of events when he read, "The boy has an authentic talent, without any doubt. I predict a brilliant future for him."[24] Paderewski invited Artur to spend the summer in Switzerland. When Barth learned of this invitation, he was incensed, particularly enraged that the entire episode had transpired between Joachim and Paderewski, leaving him no say in the decision. Within a few months after this, the relationship between Artur and Barth came to an impasse. When Artur informed Barth that he intended to leave Berlin, they parted badly. Artur would remain ashamed of that day.

The final days in Berlin were gloomy, but Artur was intent on gaining his independence. The young pianist returned to Poland. He was seventeen. "That was enough of Berlin for me. In 1903 an important page of my life had turned!"

Artur lived the musician's life in Poland, France, and England during the next few years, but clearly his artistic metamorphosis was not over. On his first important journey to Paris from Warsaw, he suffered a difficult emotional upheaval. The minute the train moved, he burst into tears. An uncontrollable crying spell took hold of him, and he did not stop for hours." It was a release of all the worries I had stored up: the break with Barth, which affected me deeply, the anxiety about my unfinished studies."

In Paris he met Gabriel Astruc, the impresario, whose first directive was for Artur to come the next day to the Pleyel piano house. There he was shown to the hall where Chopin once gave concerts, and there he played the master's piano for composer Paul Dukas, violinist Jacques Thibaud, and Maurice Ravel. His first concert in Paris was set for December: Camille Chevillard would conduct the Lamoureux Orchestra and the young Scottish soprano Mary Garden, who had recently created her famous role in Debussy's opera *Pelléas et Mélisande*, would be assisting artist. On the day of the concert, Artur's anxiety was heightened by the presence of the venerable Camille Saint-Saëns who unexpectedly appeared at the dress rehearsal to hear his concerto. Artur, who felt unprepared and inexperienced, having played so little in public, was overwhelmed by the events of that afternoon, and the critics were sharply divided in their opinions. Yet overall Artur's auspicious introduction to Parisian music life was successful, and more recitals and further meetings with such musicians as Chaliapin and Casals set him well on his way.

In 1906 when he was not yet twenty, Artur signed his first contract for a concert tour of America. What lay ahead was an amazing career that would span almost seven decades. During World War One he played recitals in England with violinist Eugène Ysaÿe, then in 1916 toured Spain and later South America, becoming an ardent exponent of Spanish music as he entered the critical years of his career. At his debut in Madrid, he gave the successful world premier of Albéniz's *Iberia* and played more than a hundred concerts that season in Spain alone.

After a long absence from North America, Artur Rubinstein returned to play in Carnegie Hall in 1936. After his marriage to Aniela Mlynarska, Rubinstein had resolved to mend his free-spirited ways. During the 1930s, his playing transformed by life's experiences and years of sustained, sheer hard work, he took his place among the pianistic legends.

John Rubinstein spoke of his father on the one hundredth anniversary of the pianist's birth:

> My father died quietly in his sleep in Geneva on 20 December 1982 at
> the age of ninety-five. For about eighty-five of those years he had been
> playing the piano in public. He was buried in a forest that had been
> named after him in the hills overlooking Jerusalem. When you've been
> playing in public and are that successful for so long, you do get this
> large sense of yourself. And no matter what effect that had on him
> personally (and it had a lot), that would completely disappear when
> he was involved with music. Whether he was playing, talking about it,
> listening, he had a direct relationship to the music that was completely
> pure. It was devoid of self. And if you put that all together with his
> real, genuine humility that wasn't studied, wasn't even chosen, that
> made him really rare and special.[25]

CHAPTER SEVEN

Midcentury Keyboard Masters

GLENN GOULD,
MARTHA ARGERICH,
DANIEL BARENBOIM,
AND VAN CLIBURN

Le concert, c'est moi.
Franz Liszt, 1839

FRANZ Liszt declared his credo, "I am the concert," to a Roman audience in 1839. By giving a series of concerts (*soliloques* he called them), not with assisting artists as was done at the time but by himself, he created a new tradition. On 1 May 1840 in England, Liszt's solo performances at London's Hanover Square were advertised as "Liszt's Pianoforte Recitals." Ever the dramatic superstar, the supremely egocentric Liszt would frequently leave the concert platform during the London recitals and move among the audience "with the gracious condescension of a prince, conversing with his friends until he felt disposed to return to the piano."[1]

Fifteen years earlier Danneley's *Dictionary of Music* had defined *recital* as "whatever is sung by a single voice or performed by a single instrument," but in 1840 English critics who saw the advertisements still wondered how anyone could recite upon a piano. That would change as solo recitals became an important part of concert life, engaging soloists, audiences, and critics in a curious love-hate relationship. Nonetheless, legions of pianists continue to perform recitals, and the venue has become a critical hurdle in the early careers of prodigies.

By the mid-twentieth century, such prodigy pianists as Leon Fleisher, Malcolm Frager, Emil Gilels, Gary Graffman, Lorin Hollander, Eugene Istomin, Byron Janis, William Kapell, Alicia de Larrocha, Eugene List, Leonard

Pennario, and Ruth Slenczynska represented a new generation of young artists casting their lot before an enthusiastic public. Their stories would fascinate and delight, but four other midcentury masters of the keyboard—Glenn Gould, Martha Argerich, Daniel Barenboim, and Van Cliburn—present especially striking contrasts.

The four were born within a decade of each other. A cultural icon in his native Canada, Glenn Gould abandoned worldwide fame in the concert hall at the peak of his youthful career in favor of the solitude of the recording studio. The Argentinian artist Martha Argerich always loved to play the piano but came to dislike being a professional pianist. Perhaps the endless travel and professional demands that have troubled many artists seemed to her to have nothing to do with her playing or her music-making. Daniel Barenboim, another prodigy born in Argentina, sustained a repertoire of more than three hundred works, spoke five languages, studied the Talmud, and found time to box and to play soccer. Trained as an orchestral conductor from the age of eleven, he had established a dual career as pianist and conductor by age twenty-four. Finally, in this chapter we begin the story of Van Cliburn's journey from a small-town childhood in Texas to quite sudden international celebrity, a hero's tale that continues in chapter 8.

GLENN

As soon as Glenn was old enough to be held on his grandmother's knee at the piano, he would never pound the keyboard as most children will with the whole hand, striking a number of keys at a time; instead he would always insist on pressing down a single key and holding it down until the resulting sound had completely died away. The fading vibration entirely fascinated him.

Herbert Gould, remembering his son's infancy,
in Friedrich, *Glenn Gould: A Life and Variations*

Glenn Gould was born in Toronto, Canada, on 25 September 1932. There was ample evidence of his precocious musical talent by age three—absolute memory of pitch and a nascent ability to read musical notation. His mother began to help him at the piano and remained his only teacher until he was ten.

Florence Gould was a determined woman. Having aspired to a career in music as a pianist, she had become a vocal coach. At forty-one, she tried to prepare the way for her unborn child with daily, persistent prenatal exposure to classical music, hoping that he would be a pianist. In her role as Glenn's childhood teacher, she seems to have been preoccupied with developing his ability to internalize musical concepts through singing. She tenaciously monitored his music-making, correcting all his musical mistakes each time he played the piano. When Glenn began composing at five, she promptly took him to a meeting at a nearby church where he charmed his listeners by playing his little pieces. As Florence Gould catalyzed her son's potential into durable achievement, young Glenn, like Paganini before him, quickly became self-directed and later perceived himself as self-taught.

The Goulds took Glenn to his first concert given by a celebrity performer when he was six. The final performance in Toronto of pianist Joseph Hofmann made a staggering impression on the child, so much so that when his family drove him home half-awake, he experienced a fantasy, the very simplicity of which probably accounted for its intensity and consequent longevity. Hearing the incredible sounds that surged through his mind and no longer aware he was a limited novice, the entranced child felt magically transformed into Hofmann. The sensations of the fantasy lingered in Gould's memory until the end of his life.[2]

When Glenn was ten, his parents decided it was time for a master teacher and entrusted their son to the guidance of Alberto Guerrero, the Chilean pianist who, at fifty-six, had taught for twenty years at the Toronto Conservatory of Music (later renamed the Royal Conservatory of Music of Toronto). Guerrero, who belonged to a generation of Chilean artists of international renown, was known for sharing his profoundly eclectic knowledge with his pupils, "bringing a strong influence to bear on them, one that went well beyond the purely musical."[3]

While it cannot have been Guerrero's easiest pedagogical task to teach this unusual child who was endowed with such mysterious gifts, the great teacher upheld his commitment for nine years, until an inevitable and timely separation took place when the differences in outlook between them became too great. In 1960, after Guerrero's death, Glenn Gould remarked on those differences, commenting that "He was a heart man and I wanted to be a head kid."[4] Gould, whose intellect was extraordinary, evidently felt this dichotomy strongly despite the view of others who admired the humanity of Guerrero's teaching and the superbly poised equilibrium of his performances. Robert Finch described Guerrero as a pianist "who left no musical detail, however minute, no musical structure, however extensive, a victim to whimsical or inspirational treatment."[5]

John Beckwith, the Canadian composer who had been a fellow Guerrero pupil, commented in 1990 on Gould's having discounted his comprehensive studies with Guerrero, which extended from his eleventh to his twentieth year:

> Their disagreement is sad, but I think Guerrero's proper place in Gould's formation does deserve recognition. . . . He [Gould] may later

Alberto Guerrero and Glenn, his prize pupil, enjoying a game of croquet at Lake Simcoe, Ontario. By permission of the Estate of Glenn Gould.

have disagreed with the aesthetic basis, but there is ample evidence that his technical formation and habits as well as much of his musical knowledge came from those sessions and stayed with him.[6]

From the beginning, Glenn had a predilection for polyphonic music, particularly the many-voiced keyboard works of Johann Sebastian Bach that he performed and recorded with unsurpassed mastery over the course of his mature career. By age ten, he played the complete first book of *The Well-Tempered Clavier* and within a few years was learning the partitas.

When the annual Kiwanis Music Festival was established in Toronto in February 1944, Glenn competed. As contestant No. 7 (of twenty-five) in a class devoted to playing piano solos, he performed Bach's Prelude and Fugue in E Major for the adjudicator Max Pirani, an Australian-born pianist then living in Canada. The eleven-year-old won the class and was awarded the Lady Kemp Scholarship.

The following year, Glenn passed his conservatory examination as a solo performer in piano, and on 28 October 1946, one month past his fourteenth birthday, he was awarded the associate's diploma with highest honors, making him the youngest graduate in the conservatory's history.

The eccentricities that characterized his adult life began manifesting themselves in Glenn's early childhood. As an infant he felt his hands so physically sensitive that he refused contact with a rolling rubber ball. Later he could not bring himself to touch the cold ground during a game of marbles, and abandoned the game. After an accidental fall at age ten, he suffered unaccountable back pain for several years, marking the beginning of a lifetime of uncertain health. He later admitted to hypochondria and lived in virtual monastic seclusion, terrified of any exposure to germs. Despite such personal torment, he never abandoned his idealistic search for the perfect musical life.

Also by the age of ten Glenn was already determined upon a career in music. As he later told Bernard Asbell in 1962, he saw himself as a kind of Renaissance man capable of fulfilling many roles, but had no attraction to performing in public. There were fledgling events in Toronto to mark the passing of his early adolescence: a debut at twelve as organist before the Casavant Society ("His playing had the fearless authority and finesse of a master"); five months later, a performance of the opening movement of Beethoven's fourth concerto in Massey Hall with the conservatory orchestra conducted by Ettore Mazzoleni ("The boy's playing showed how beautiful piano music can be . . . and how awesome are the ways of genius in a child"); then, within a year, an appearance with the Toronto Symphony Orchestra playing that entire Beethoven work with Australian Bernard Heinz as guest conductor. Two solo recitals came in quick succession in 1947, one at the conservatory, the other in Eaton Auditorium, the first professional engagement promoted by Walter Homburger, who was to be Glenn's manager for the ensuing twenty years.[7]

Glenn had no difficulty directing his mind. He played multiple chess games blindfolded, memorized complex scores while talking on the telephone, and listened to two radios simultaneously while studying Schoenberg's difficult Opus 23. He aroused attention, however, when he appeared to fidget on stage during the orchestral tuttis of the Beethoven concerto in his first performance with the Toronto Symphony Orchestra. The critic had no idea that before leaving home for the concert Glenn had bid a loving farewell to Nicky, his shedding dog. By the time of the concerto's rondo movement, he realized his black trousers were covered in dog hair and was busying himself picking them off. All went well until he lost track of which tutti was in progress, but he quickly composed his thoughts and played well to the end: "I had learned the first valuable lesson of my association with the T.S.O.— either pay attention or keep short-haired dogs."[8]

As a teenager Glenn idolized an unusual array of musicians and musical works: the piano playing of Artur Schnabel, then Rosalyn Tureck, Leopold Stokowski's conducting the music of Wagner's *Tristan und Isolde*, and, at fifteen when he "came alive to contemporary music," Hindemith's *Mathis der Maler* (Matthias the Painter), the first twentieth-century work to arouse his passion. He was soon preoccupied with the music of Schoenberg, Webern, Prokofiev, Krenek, Casella—and of the Canadian composers Oscar Morawetz, István Anhalt, and Jacques Hétu.

Glenn's fascination with the technology of communications probably began when he and his childhood friend Bob Fulford strung together two tin cans with silk string, attempting a communication between their two homes, an experiment they abandoned in favor of a microphone link that provided a boyhood exchange of news and music. Throughout his adolescence his fascination continued. The early recording technology of the 1950s seemed to Glenn to hold a revolutionary promise for the future; certainly it would change the course of his life as a musician.

In an essay entitled "Music and Technology" he later wrote, "One Sunday morning in December 1950, I wandered into a living-room-sized radio station, placed my services at the disposal of a single microphone belonging to the Canadian Broadcasting Corporation, and proceeded to broadcast 'live' two sonatas: one by Mozart, one by Hindemith."[9] That day his fascination was transformed into a love affair with the microphone. He was eighteen.

By 1955, Glenn had left his tumultuous adolescence behind him, withdrawing to the solitude of the Gould cabin on Lake Simcoe to play his old Chickering piano and contemplate his future plans. Maturity had brought a new simplicity to his life. At twenty-three, he had a clear vision of the music he would play, and in this he would never again be influenced by anyone else's opinion. In the choice of repertoire, his passions dictated his plans, helping him to avoid the pitfalls of tradition that might have incapacitated his free spirit.

As for his so-called eccentricities, on stage and off, he would continue to say exactly what he thought, to play as he intended, and to do with his life what he liked, however inconvenient. Clearly unthreatened by the prospect of leaving music critics discomforted, he refused to play a traditional debut repertoire in his forthcoming American debut recitals in Washington, DC, and New York City.

"Glenn Gould is a pianist with rare gifts for the world," wrote Paul Hume, critic of the *Washington Post*, following Gould's afternoon recital at the Phillips Gallery on 2 January 1955. "We know of no pianist anything like him of any age."[10] Ten days later he repeated the performance in New York's Town Hall. In the *New York Times*, critic John Briggs extolled the performance: "The impression which is uppermost is not one of virtuosity but of expressiveness. One is able to hear the music."[11] Two weeks later in the *Musical Courier* Briggs wrote, "Gould's complete enthrallment with the abstract, abstruse beauties of these contrasting works seems to result in a sense of almost other-worldly dedication. . . . I can only call him great, and warn those who have not heard him that he will plunge them into new and unfamiliar depths of feeling and perception."[12]

Glenn had played what he wished to play—an unusual array of works drawn from three centuries of keyboard music by Gibbons, Sweelinck, Bach, Beethoven, Anton Webern, and Alban Berg. The critical success of these recitals launched a further decade of public appearances, during which he was both adulated for his musicianship and reviled for his eccentricities. He remained determined to create the environment on stage that gave him comfort: the gloved hands, the bottles of spring water, the now-famous extremely low and mobile chair home-built by his loving father, Bert. If onlookers chose to quibble with such a frank expression of what seemed an eccentric stage persona, they had best close their eyes and simply listen, not be concerned with such mannerisms as his singing audibly, endlessly, hovering low over the keyboard, conducting one hand with the other. Glenn himself found it all quite natural and was untroubled by public opinion. For him there was something far more significant at stake. Was recital giving the best way for him to communicate his artistry, or was there a better avenue?

The answer began to reveal itself the day following his Town Hall debut when he received from Columbia Records (after only one New York appearance) an unprecedented invitation. Without hesitation he signed a contract with the company who would unflinchingly sustain his vast contribution of recorded music for almost three decades, until the day of his death in the autumn of 1982. He launched his work for Columbia as no other pianist would. He recorded Johann Sebastian Bach's *Goldberg Variations*.

In the Columbia recording studio in the basement of an abandoned church on East 30th Street in New York, the young virtuoso made himself at home: he had his special chair, his sweaters and scarves, his pills, his bottles of spring water—and his exquisitely musical mind. In this technological environment, he was surrounded by an eager nurturing team that included producer, recording director, engineers, and publicists, each person poised to play a special role in the new life drama that propelled him headlong into his ultimate creative act.

In these intensive work sessions, something distinctly different was happening. The pianist had no intention of simply recreating the conditions of the concert hall, nor of capturing a "live" performance. Instead he would learn to electronically construct his recordings. With the cooperation of a team of experts from Columbia Records, he amassed sufficient recorded materials within one week for his first recording, all the while refining the principles of his new philosophy of music and technology about which he eventually wrote in great detail.

The last working session was devoted to the first thing heard on the record, the Aria da capo that announces the theme on which the variations are built. With the twenty-first take he was at last satisfied. This remarkable first recording for Columbia stayed in print for the following quarter of a century.

A decade after his New York debut and this first recording for Columbia—after hundreds of recitals and concerto performances for which he could never overcome his distaste—Glenn Gould came into his own. He permanently abandoned the stage for the recording studio.

In a backstage conversation in 1971, Glenn Gould and Artur Rubinstein delineated their opposing attitudes toward the public. Rubinstein asked Gould, frankly, whether there never was a moment when he felt that very special emanation from an audience? ("There really wasn't.") Had he never felt that he had the soul of these people? ("I didn't really want their souls. I didn't want any power over them, and I certainly wasn't stimulated by their presence as such.") The conversation ended when Rubinstein pronounced them absolute opposites: "If you would have followed the pianistic career for many years as I have—over sixty-five years, you know—you would have experienced this constant, constant, constant contact with the crowd that you have to, in a way, persuade or dominate, or get hold of."[13] Gould wanted none of this. He wanted the hard-won solitude in which his artistic personality best functioned. He wanted the ecstasy of the recording studio where he tirelessly constructed the recordings that would be his legacy.

During his extensive career as a recording artist, he continued to pursue other roles—author and producer of groundbreaking original radio and television documentaries, essayist, commentator, composer, conductor—driven relentlessly by his need for physical privacy on the one hand and for electronic communication on the other. His efforts resulted in a discography of 248 recorded works and an enormous output of radio and television broadcasts for the Canadian Broadcasting Corporation.

One month before his death at fifty, Gould returned to Columbia's New York studio, a site now enhanced by new digital recording equipment, to re-record the *Goldberg Variations*. This final project was filmed for Bruno Monsaingeon's television series. When the great pianist died on 4 October 1982 following a severe stroke, most of the obituaries noted the irony that the *Goldberg Variations* were his first and last recordings. "On the back of the album," noted Eric McLean in the *Montreal Gazette*, "there is a picture of Gould's piano, and what is obviously Gould's chair . . . but no Gould."[14]

In 1987 two Voyager spacecrafts were launched, each carrying a twelve-inch copper recording, a record player, and pictorial instructions on how the machine could be made to play. The record ended with "sounds from earth," a segment culminating in Gould's recorded performance of the Prelude and Fugue in C Major from the first book of Bach's *Well-Tempered Clavier*. When the spacecrafts, designed to last a billion years, passed Pluto and plummeted toward distant stars, Glenn Gould's vision of music and technology had already traversed an unimaginable distance from one man's past to an unfathomable, universal future.

MARTHA

After hearing eight-year-old Martha perform Beethoven's Sonata, Op. 31,
No. 3, Walter Gieseking told her parents to leave the little girl in peace,
having seen that she was not enjoying the situation, but the work imposed
by her parents continued. "I was glad he told them, because that was what
I wanted."

Dean Elder, quoting Martha Argerich, in Pianists at Play

Martha Argerich (pronounced "Ahr-ge-reech") was born in Buenos Aires, Argentina, on 5 June 1941, a year-and-a-half before her countryman, Daniel Barenboim. A kindergarten pupil when she was two years and eight months old, Martha was taunted by an older friend (he was five) who proclaimed that she couldn't play the piano. She went immediately to the piano and played a tune that the teacher had often played for the class. She played it by ear and played it perfectly. The teacher immediately called Martha's mother to report the incident: according to Argerich, she began her first piano lessons at five all because of this little boy who challenged her.

A fragile-looking woman, barely five foot four, Martha Argerich at fifty-six is considered by many to be in the front rank of her generation of pianists. Few receive such frenzied ovations or are viewed with such awed admiration by their colleagues. Her performances of the solo piano repertoire and her recordings for Deutsche Grammophon have securely established her international reputation. She has recorded concertos by Tchaikovsky, Prokofiev, and Ravel, solo piano works by Bach, Schumann, Liszt, and Chopin, and Bartók's Sonata for Two Pianos and Percussion with pianist Stephen Bishop-Kovacevich. On stage she has collaborated successfully in chamber music performances with violinist Gidon Kremer and cellist Mstislav Rostropovich.

Few prodigies have suffered such difficult rites of passage from their first encounter with the piano to finally reaching absolute mastery. Unexpected, early success exacted a toll from Argerich, who found it so very difficult to deal with the realities of a lifestyle known to almost no other children and few adults. The unpredictability of her early professional life added an extra dimension to the demands on her often-turbulent emotional state. Despite her difficulties, however, she was determined to do one thing at all costs—perform music as a pianist of significant achievement—and her determination has endured because she perceived meeting that challenge as something absolutely essential for her satisfaction, self-expression, and well-being.

As Maria Montessori phrased it, children live in an environment created by adults. Prodigious children may live in a world particularly ill-adapted to their own needs, repressed by their more powerful elders who undercut their will and constrain them. Some musical prodigies survive such dire circumstances and aggressively emerge from their perilous journeys as they approach maturity. Argerich was able to attain such equilibrium only gradually. Until she was approaching twenty-five she lived an unstable existence as a pianist, rebounding from depression to exaltation in an emotional state bordering on dysfunctional. Perhaps at the root of this anguish was the paradox that despite her love of playing the piano, she already disliked being a pianist.[15]

When she was five years old, Martha joined a group of twenty piano students whose teacher taught playing by ear without music, but soon thereafter she began her formal studies with the Italian pianist Vicente Scaramuzza, the former teacher of Daniel Barenboim's father, Enrique Barenboim. Martha remained with Scaramuzza for five years.

When she was eight, Scaramuzza presented Martha in her first concerto performance. She played Mozart's Concerto in D Minor, K. 466, and Beethoven's First Concerto, separating the two with Bach's French Suite in G Major. When she was nine, she again played the Mozart concerto, and at eleven she performed Schumann's concerto.

As a child in Buenos Aires, Martha was heard not only by the famous German pianist Walter Gieseking, but by many other celebrated musicians, including Claudio Arrau, Solomon (Cutner), Zino Francescatti, and Eduard van Beinem. She played for the Hungarian violinist Joseph Szigeti when she was twelve. So impressed was Szigeti by Martha's playing that he wrote her an encouraging letter during his flight back to Europe from Argentina.

Martha and Daniel Barenboim met as young children at a weekly chamber music soiree in the home of the Austrian-Jewish family of Ernesto Rosenthal. Unlike Daniel, rebellious Martha who didn't want to be forced to practice—indeed, didn't want to be a pianist—often hid from the crowd. ("I was told if you soaked blotter paper in water and put it in your shoes, you would get fever, so I would hide in the bathroom and put water in my shoes.") She met Daniel one evening beneath a large table where they were hiding from the Rosenthals' guests. "You never know when you are very young, when you are studying, what this profession is about," Argerich has said. "No one tells you, and the people outside the profession don't have a clue. They think it is marvelous."

Her negative feelings about being a pianist remained essentially unchanged for her early teenage years, but in 1957 when she was sixteen she entered the Ferrucio Busoni International Competition in Bolzano, Italy. Because she had won no international competitions, she had to undertake a private, preliminary round before only a few judges. She didn't expect to get beyond this stage. After she played, the jury rather ambiguously told her, "That's enough. You can leave." Not understanding whether they meant for her to leave temporarily or permanently was almost more than she could bear, but within minutes she learned that she would go forward to the first round.

Throughout the Busoni competition, Martha never worked at the piano between rounds. She didn't want to practice if she wasn't going to get through. She merely waited to see if her name was announced, and when it was, she would go to work for the next round. "I was always thinking *No*," she recalled. "I think the 1957 Busoni Competition was the highest level that I have ever been in a competition. There was Ivan Davis, Jerome Lowenthal, and Ludwig Hoffman. And they could play very well, you know, really!"

Martha won the Busoni competition and immediately prepared to enter the Geneva competition. The pressure was exacerbated when Cesare Inordio, president of the Bolzano jury, responded angrily to her decision to do so because should she not win the first prize in Geneva, it would reflect badly on the judgment made at Bolzano. Yet she went ahead.

The repertoire for Geneva was minimal. Martha had to play Beethoven's Sonata, Op. 10, No. 3, a prelude and fugue by Bach, two Chopin etudes, the Schumann concerto, a work she had performed since she was eleven, and Liszt's Sixth Hungarian Rhapsody which she had never played in public. Suspicious of the nature of competitions and so unsure of her own role in them, she gave way to her eccentricities, refusing to play the Liszt rhapsody all the way through in the practice studio, not even for her own security. It hardly mattered. Martha won the competition as she had in Bolzano, garnering lavish press reviews as the victor in two renowned international music competitions, the Busoni and the Geneva, that had taken place just three weeks apart.

After winning these competitions when she was seventeen, Martha met Szigeti again in Geneva and played sonatas with him. It was her first chamber music experience. She was terrified because she didn't know the music and had to sight-read. Szigeti withdrew to another room to warm up for a half-hour, so that Martha could compose herself. The young girl was deeply touched by this gesture ("I was a seventeen-year-old with no experience. I was just nothing, you know. He was incredible!").

During her early years in Europe, she studied in quick succession with the Austrian pianist Friedrich Gulda (her first teacher outside Argentina), Nikita Magaloff, Arturo Benedetti-Michelangeli, and Stefan Askenase. Martha's study with Gulda was exceptional. Although she felt he was among the most talented people she had met and playing for him was a fantastic experience, she continued to resist the work his teaching demanded. Gulda challenged her when he thought she had become lazy about her preparation, undistracted by the mystical questions with which she often began her lessons. She truly wondered about God and the immortal soul, but she admitted, "I was so worried and he had to answer, but at the same time he knew I was doing this because I hadn't prepared."

After she had been stalled for a month while learning a Schubert sonata, the crisis could no longer be averted. Gulda complained, saying that he had considered her so talented, but now didn't understand what was holding her back. Perhaps no one could have understood, including Martha herself. However, Gulda took a bold approach and demanded that for her next lesson, five days away, she prepare Ravel's *Gaspard de la nuit* and Schumann's *Abegg* Variations. She returned for her next lesson with both works expertly learned, for when such a prodigy doesn't sense that a work is very difficult, it is often easily learned.

Martha was studying with Gulda in Vienna when she met her South American compatriot, Nelson Freire (pronounced "Frayruh"), a famous prodigy pianist from Ipanema near Rio de Janeiro. They became best friends and have remained so ever since. In her opinion Nelson Freire has the greatest keyboard facility she has ever seen and, excepting Friedrich Gulda, is the best of sight-readers, constantly looking for new things to play or read. Freire has called Argerich unconditionally the greatest pianist of her generation.

When Martha was twenty, she and Nelson Freire went by train to Germany so that she could make her first professional recording for Deutsche Grammophon at the Beethovensaal in Hannover. In her inexperience, she had no idea how to proceed in the recording studio and simply decided that she wanted to play everything three times, would never listen to a play-back, and if they wanted something that she could not play, Nelson must play in her stead, a spontaneously conceived subterfuge based on her immature notion that "no one would see." The recording engineer, who was an expert and understood very much about piano playing, was flabbergasted when he found the two young pianists in adjoining rooms, both diligently practicing the same pieces, Nelson constantly advising and teaching Martha because she didn't really play the Rhapsodies, Op. 79, by Brahms scheduled for that day's recording session. Despite all this, the recording was a success.

After studying with Friedrich Gulda in Vienna, Martha went to Italy to study with Arturo Benedetti-Michelangeli, then returned to New York where she endured a devastating emotional crisis. For one year Martha completely withdrew from playing the piano and simply spent her days watching television. Some friends, among them Fou Ts'ong, the Chinese-born pianist and husband of Zamira Menuhin, tried to help twenty-one-year-old Martha recover her identity as a pianist, but without success. In 1963, her mother encouraged her to enter the Queen Elisabeth competition in Brussels, but of course this was an impossibility since Martha was no longer prepared, by this time having been away from the piano for almost three years.

She did go to Belgium and the night before the competition said to herself, "Well, now Martha, it is over for you. You have been a pianist, but now you are not." The next morning she went to seek help from a musician she had known since childhood, the Polish-born pianist Stefan Askenase, then sixty-eight, who was teaching at the conservatory in Brussels. She went with the firm conviction that somehow she would tell him that since she knew languages, she would become a secretary. Once she had arrived at the Askenase home, instead of meeting the famous Chopin-player, she was greeted by his wife, a woman of great strength and fortitude who ultimately would help Martha change the course of her unpredictable professional life.

She went everyday to talk with Mrs. Askenase and soon started to believe that she could, little by little, begin to play again, all the while questioning what was wrong that held her in check. When finally she had broken through her bond of insecurity, she went to Warsaw to compete in the Frédéric Chopin International Competition.

Eight difficult years had elapsed since Martha's success in the 1957 competitions at Bolzano and Geneva, years in which one personal conflict followed another, but in Warsaw in 1965, Martha reigned supreme over eighty-five young pianists from all over the world. One would never have known that the young woman from Buenos Aires had recently been idle for three years watching television in New York, constantly considering whether to withdraw permanently from the piano.

As David Feldman has said, "In the lives of musical prodigies, the importance of balance—of the coordination of a totally appropriate set of conditions necessary for development—cannot be overemphasized. When the motivational force comes from within the precocious child and is on the mark, it is a force to reckon with; when that force goes awry, it can be baffling and destructive."[16]

DANIEL

I grew up in the belief that everybody played the piano and it took me a long time to realize that some people did not!

Barenboim, A *Life in Music*

At the beginning of the twentieth century, Daniel Barenboim's four Jewish grandparents had immigrated to Argentina from Russia to escape persecution. Daniel was born on 15 November 1942 in Buenos Aires where his parents, Enrique and Aida, taught the piano. When Daniel was a child, every time the doorbell rang it seemed to be somebody coming for a piano lesson, and so he believed that everyone played the instrument.[17] His father, Enrique Barenboim, had studied with Vicente Scaramuzza and often gave concerts with other instrumentalists, but teaching was his passion. He taught advanced students; Daniel's mother taught children and beginners.

At four, Daniel became fascinated with the idea of making music with his father after hearing him rehearse with a violinist. When no little violin was forthcoming, the child decided to take his own place at the keyboard, having by then heard his father playing piano duets with his pupils. His mother taught him to read music and gave him his first lessons when he was five. Soon he began studying with his father and continued as his pupil until he was seventeen.

Enrique Barenboim had strong convictions about his teaching method. It was based on natural movement, and its fundamental principle was that there was no division between musical and technical problems. Under his father's guidance, Daniel found learning to play the piano as natural as learning to walk. "After playing the piano for over forty years," Barenboim has said, "I have neither forgotten nor altered what he taught me."

The home of Ernesto Rosenthal was a haven for chamber music in Buenos Aires. The Barenboims went there on Friday evenings to play and to enjoy the company of other musicians. Little Daniel met many touring artists and often performed for them at the Rosenthal home, and two encounters with celebrated conductors greatly influenced his life as a prodigy. One was with Sergiu Celibidache, the Romanian conductor of the Berlin Philhar-

Daniel Barenboim at ten, playing Mozart's spinet in Salzburg, 1952. Courtesy Daniel Barenboim.

monic; the other was with Igor Markevich, the Russian conductor and composer (and son-in-law of Vaslav Nijinsky). Markevich told Daniel's father, "Your son plays the piano wonderfully, but I can tell from the way he plays that he is really a conductor."[18] Barenboim later commented upon this insightful, perhaps prophetic remark: "The neutral piano became an illusory orchestra to me, and perhaps that was why Markevich thought that I was a born conductor."

In 1949, the violinist Adolf Busch performed the Beethoven concerto and conducted Handel's Concerti Grossi during the German season at the Teatro Colón. Daniel went to many of his rehearsals and also played for him. Although Busch had earlier advised Yehudi Menuhin not to play in public but to concentrate on studying first, he encouraged the Barenboims to the contrary. In August of 1950 when Daniel was still just seven years old, he gave his first official concert in Buenos Aires, playing a broad repertoire of pieces, including a work by Prokofiev. When he was eight, he appeared as soloist with Argentina's Radio Orchestra, Bruno Bandini conducting, in a performance of Mozart's Concerto in A Major, K. 488.

On 14 May 1948 the establishment of the new State of Israel was proclaimed. From that time, the Barenboim family, like many other Jewish families dispersed around the world, began to make plans to immigrate there, their main desire being that their son grow up as a member of a majority Jewish population. They left Buenos Aires for Europe in July of 1952. Their final destination was Tel Aviv.

After an exhausting fifty-two-hour trip to Rome, they took a train to Salzburg where Daniel had been invited by Igor Markevich to observe his summer conducting class at the Mozarteum and take part as soloist in Bach's Concerto in D Minor at the final class concert. This was an exciting prospect for the prodigy who was only ten years old.

Upon arriving in Salzburg, the family left their luggage in a rented room and went for a late afternoon stroll to No. 9, Getreidegasse, the house of Mozart's birth in 1756. In that shrine Daniel played Wolfgang's spinet before they continued their excursion to the Festspielhaus, where they learned that Karl Böhm would conduct Mozart's *The Magic Flute* that evening. There were no tickets, but Daniel convinced his parents that he could sneak into the public gallery for his first operatic experience, promising to meet them later at a nearby café.

He succeeded in hiding himself in the crowd, then opened a door to an empty box where he seated himself and waited expectantly for the overture to begin, but exhaustion soon overwhelmed him and he fell asleep, hearing nothing beyond the first few measures of the overture. Much later he woke up terribly frightened, with no idea where he was. "I started crying very loudly, whereupon the usher came and very firmly, if not brutally, took me out of the box where I was disturbing the public and threw me out of the Festspielhaus," Barenboim recalled.

The Barenboims stayed in Salzburg until the end of August 1952, then went on to Vienna before returning to Italy. In Vienna, Enrique gave a lecture at the Vienna Academy and Daniel played a succession of concerts, including one at the American Institute. In Rome, the young prodigy gave a chance recital for the Società Filarmonica Romana, then a few days later departed Europe for Tel Aviv. When Daniel landed on Israeli soil, he was already a seasoned performer at age ten, a wonder child for whom mounting a concert platform and playing the piano had already seemed perfectly normal for half a lifetime.

Life in Tel Aviv was a culture shock for the Spanish-speaking South American boy, even though three generations of his family lived happily together, enjoying a secure family life. Daniel was neither inhibited nor shy and made friends easily, but "to start school in Israel immediately, in the middle of the school year, with a language of which I did not understand a word, not to mention a different alphabet, was not all that easy to say the least!" In 1952, Tel Aviv was just a small town where the young pianist could safely play soccer in the streets when he was not at school or practicing. For the next two years Daniel did not leave Israel. He began composition lessons with the Israeli composer Paul Ben-Haim and continued to study the piano with his father. He was no longer homesick for Argentina, had no wish to speak Spanish, and, because he learned Hebrew quickly, began to excel at school.

In the summer of 1953, Daniel appeared for the first time as soloist with the Israel Philharmonic, conducted by Milton Katims. After he had completed another successful school year in Tel Aviv, his parents decided that the family should revisit Austria where their eleven-year-old son could study conducting at the Mozarteum in Salzburg with Igor Markevich.

Daniel was the youngest student in Markevich's conducting master class in the summer of 1954. All the others were well over twenty. When Markevich told Enrique Barenboim that his son should stop playing the piano and continue his musical career as a conductor, serious arguments began between them. Daniel's father disagreed with the plan, seeing no need to make such a drastic decision when the boy was still so young.

Later that summer Daniel met the renowned German conductor Wilhelm Furtwängler and played for him. Furtwängler's testimonial—"The eleven-year-old Barenboim is a phenomenon"—prompted further appearances. Daniel traveled abroad with his father several times over the next year to play in Zurich and Amsterdam and to give his first concert in England at Bournemouth, where he played a concertino by the American composer Walter Piston. From the America-Israel Cultural Foundation in Tel Aviv, Daniel won a scholarship to study abroad, an award that made it possible for the entire family to move to Paris for the winter of 1955.

Igor Markevich had studied composition with Nadia Boulanger as a young student in Paris in 1926. They remained close friends, so that he could arrange for Daniel to study with her in France. Daniel had private lessons once or twice each week from Mme Boulanger and attended her composition class. From this master teacher he received an ascetic, strict musical education for a year-and-a-half.

In the summer of 1955, Daniel traveled to Switzerland to meet and play for conductor Joseph Krips in St. Moritz. An invitation followed for an appearance as soloist with the London Philharmonic with Krips conducting. The next January, the chubby thirteen-year-old dressed in short trousers made his London debut at the Royal Festival Hall in a performance of Mozart's Concerto in A Major, K. 488. When Daniel "skipped on to the stage with all the assurance of a young Beethoven,"[19] the press took note of the vitality singing out from everything he did and the magnetism of his personal presence. Soon after his London debut, Daniel made his first recording for Philips.

A month before his London debut, Daniel had met the Polish composer Alexandre Tansman in Paris. Tansman soon arranged for the boy to play for Artur Rubinstein, whom the Barenboim family had admired ever since they had met him in Buenos Aires. At his first meeting with Rubinstein, Daniel played for an hour or so, concluding with Prokofiev's Second Sonata. Rubinstein suggested that he should play in America and said he would introduce him to his manager, Sol Hurok. When a second meeting was arranged, the boy went again to Rubinstein's home in the square at l'avenue Foch and played for Hurok.

The famous impresario was impressed. Rubinstein hastened to agree with him that Daniel should play in the United States, but cautioned that Hurok should have the boy's parents accompany him since he was so young and, as Joseph Joachim had insisted to Rubinstein's own parents at the turn of the century, that there must be no exploitation. Although the famous pianist believed that for a number of years Hurok would not make any money from such a venture, he was certain that Daniel was headed for a great career. "Rubinstein practically negotiated my first contract for me! . . . In December of 1956 I went on my first trip to North America."

At Rubinstein's urging, Daniel was later introduced to Leopold Stokowski at Tansman's home in Paris. After hearing Daniel play various pieces in different styles, Stokowski asked if he would like to play in New York. Hearing Daniel's excited response, he then asked what he would like to play. Without hesitation the boy said that he would play Beethoven's Third Piano Concerto. "Very good," Stokowski said—then, in a surprising move, "You shall play Prokofiev's Concerto No. 1."[20] Because he had an enormous repertoire, Daniel agreed to this without further discussion.

"My first concert in New York in January 1957 was what might be described as a fair success: it was not a failure, but no sensation either," Barenboim has said. His agent, Sol Hurok, had to work hard to secure him further engagements. Daniel was at a difficult age for public acceptance. He was no longer a child, and yet not grown-up. However, Rubinstein constantly encouraged Hurok not to lose faith in him, and he never did.

Success came only gradually after 1958 despite appearances in London's Wigmore Hall, five or six concerts each year in the United States, and a first tour to Australia. There seemed no further interest in Daniel as a child prodigy—he literally had lost his identity. Understandably this most traumatic of adolescent crises made the bewildered teenager despair over his future.

His father still guided his piano study, urging him to learn an even broader spectrum of the repertoire. Because he never allowed Daniel to play the same piece in public more than twice, the teenager commanded a vast repertoire of more than three hundred solo piano pieces, including fourteen piano concertos and many of the thirty-two piano sonatas of Beethoven. He could perform everything imaginable except Schoenberg and Alban Berg, music that came later mostly through his contact with Pierre Boulez.

In the spring of 1960 when Daniel was seventeen and completing his last year at school, he met the man who organized concerts in the small auditorium of Tel Aviv's Beit Sokolow (Journalists' House). When asked if he would like to give a few recitals there, the young pianist's response was immediate. "With the recklessness of adolescence I said *Yes*," Barenboim recalled. "I would like to play all the Beethoven sonatas." He learned the whole cycle and played it in eight consecutive concerts.

In London after Daniel's next performance of the Beethoven cycle, Edward Greenfield, music critic of the *Guardian*, admitted that in the beginning he was "dead set against him," imagining ambition at the expense of humility, seeing him as yet another one of the "get-along-quick young men." However, Greenfield wrote that in the end he "was kneeling at his feet."[21] With this performance, Daniel Barenboim had established himself in London—at eighteen—as one of the world's leading pianists. He repeated the artistic tour de force with great success in Buenos Aires, Vienna, New York, and ultimately on phonograph recordings.

Because he had been persuaded from the age of nine to become a conductor, had been superbly taught by such conductors as Igor Markevich and Carlo Zecchi, and had gained the confidence of many leading conductors, it was only a matter of time until he would be able to put this aspect of his career into action. On a concert tour in the Soviet Union in 1965, Barenboim received a telegram inviting him to conduct two performances of the English Chamber Orchestra, one in Reading, the other in Cambridge. With the success of this venture, recordings followed and tours to festivals in Prague and Lucerne. Soon Barenboim was sharing the conductorial responsibilities of the English Chamber Orchestra with Raymond Leppard, who specialized in early music, and Benjamin Britten, who composed for the ensemble.

In December of 1966, Barenboim met the spectacular young English cellist Jacqueline du Pré, whom he married in Israel one year later, three days after the end of the Six-Day War, when Israel's victory came with stunning swiftness.

For a decade, Barenboim continued his collaboration with the English Chamber Orchestra until in 1975 he was nominated music director of the Orchestre de Paris, where he succeeded Georg Solti. In 1980 Wolfgang Wagner attended a concert performance in Paris of the second act of *Tristan und Isolde* conducted by Barenboim and concluded that Barenboim should conduct the work at Bayreuth. This he did with great success in 1981, returning in 1988 to conduct Harry Kupfer's new production of *Der Ring des Nibelungen*.[22] The experience served as a model for the new Bastille Opéra, an institution for which he became responsible in July 1987. Unfortunately, after the 1988 presidential election in France, a Parisian businessman, Pierre Bergé, was put in charge of the opera houses and, following a lengthy political intrigue, Barenboim was relieved of his duties.

Perhaps this was a blessing in disguise: it left Barenboim free to accept the position of music director of the Chicago Symphony Orchestra, where he again succeeded the retired Sir Georg Solti, keeping his personal commitment to continue performing as a concert pianist as well.

VAN

On Saturday afternoon the radio was turned to the Metropolitan Opera broadcasts. On Sunday it was the New York Philharmonic. No one told me to like it. It was just taken for granted as a part of life. As I grew older and wanted live music, my family kept the highways busy between Shreveport, Kilgore, and Dallas. Someone once asked me where I lived, and I told them, "On Highway 80."

Cliburn, in Reich, Van Cliburn

In 1941, Kilgore, Texas, was not the most likely place to find a resident pianist of the stature of Rildia Bee O'Bryan Cliburn. It was a small East Texas oil boom town, population around ten thousand, with a thousand oil derricks lining the main streets. The Cliburn home was a tiny, one-story, white-frame house at 808 South Martin Street, with a back garden through which Rildia Bee's young pupils came for their piano lessons from the nearby elementary school.

Van entered the school's first grade class in January 1941 after his family had returned to Texas from nearby Shreveport, Louisiana, where he was born on 12 July 1934. His father, Harvey Lavan Cliburn, had worked in Shreveport as a sales representative for the Magnolia Oil Company for more than a decade, and there the gifted Rildia Bee had become a respected piano teacher.

As a young girl, Rildia Bee O'Bryan had wanted a career in music. Her parents, who were prominent, well-educated Texans, encouraged her to study music but did not approve of her career plan. While studying piano at the Cincinnati Conservatory, she heard Arthur Friedheim, the great Russian pianist, in recital. A pupil of Franz Liszt in Weimar in the 1860s, Friedheim became "the pianist of her dreams," and by 1917 she was on her way to becoming his favorite pupil at New York's Institute of Musical Art (the forerunner of the Juilliard School). During three years as his pupil, Rildia Bee developed into a virtuoso pianist, learning all the works of Liszt, but in 1921 her family persuaded her to return home to Texas to teach, get married, and raise a family. "A concert career just wasn't considered proper for a young lady in those days," Van Cliburn has remarked, "but she certainly had the ability and could have had a big career. My mother wasn't just a good pianist, she was a great pianist and one of the most talented of all Friedheim's pupils."[23] Fortunately for the world of music Rildia Bee did not pursue the career of a concert pianist but instead devoted her life to teaching her child. Until Van entered the Juilliard School at seventeen, she was the only teacher of her supremely gifted child prodigy.

When he was three, Van spontaneously went to the piano and played by ear Ruth Crawford's "Arpeggio Waltz," a little teaching piece that he had just heard in young Sammy Talbot's piano lesson. The technical difficulties of "Arpeggio Waltz" far exceeded "See the Kite up in the Air" that Van had

Van Cliburn at nine, 1943. Courtesy Van Cliburn.

learned by rote and played in public that year. Rildia Bee understood these exceptional moments in her son's childhood and began giving him his first formal piano lessons when he was four.

In Shreveport that year, Van had heard a radio recital given by Sergei Rachmaninov, and as he listened an important idea came to him: "I just felt I'm going to be a pianist, and I told my parents about it. My father said, 'Well, son, we'll see about that.' He wasn't too happy."[24] His mother's response was more positive. She immediately set to work teaching Van to read music as she taught all her pupils from the beginning of their training. "I remember that we didn't play games, and we were never silly. My mother always treated me like an adult," Cliburn recalled. "She was a serious person and this was serious business."[25] From the beginning, Rildia Bee was wary of any exploitation of her child and tried to teach him humility, reminding him that his ability was a divine gift for which he should be deeply grateful, without taking undue credit for himself.

In families of musicians, parents frequently teach their precocious children over an extended period of time: Bach taught his children, Leopold Mozart taught his, Friedrich Wieck taught Clara, Boris Koutzen taught Nadia, Enrique Barenboim taught Daniel, and Rildia Bee taught Van. Having his mother as his very serious, often stern piano teacher was challenging, but the boy was reminded of her dual role at every lesson: "You know, I'm not your mother now."

Soon Van had no trouble making that distinction when Rildia Bee gave him each daily lesson, supervised his practice time, and, as Florence Gould had done for Glenn, taught him to sing. "My mother made me sing everything first before I played it on the piano, a method we applied even to Bach's Two-Part Inventions."[26]

A profound bond existed between them, and both mother and son kept account of the substance of Van's lessons during his childhood. Rildia Bee never asked her son to do anything she couldn't do. She greatly believed in scale playing, not only to enhance keyboard facility, but to develop a beautiful legato style. She also knew from experience that at those times when one wasn't motivated to practice, scale playing could still arouse a student's fascination with sonority, instrumental timbre, and musical line. Rildia Bee was astute in her understanding of pedaling and its coordination with the fingers on the keyboard. Arthur Friedheim had explained to her Franz Liszt's subtle use of the pedals, and his approach to score marking, phrasing, and analysis of musical architecture. This legacy from the golden age of pianists Rildia Bee passed on to her child.

When he began school in Kilgore at midterm, his musical gifts were already apparent. Oleta Gray, his first grade teacher, invited him to join the class rehearsing "Tom Thumb's Wedding." When Van heard the wedding music from Wagner's *Lohengrin*, he tugged at her skirt and said, "I can play that," then went to the piano and played it to perfection. Eloise Bean, who heard the little boy play, recalled: "He was a showman from the beginning. He just looked like he was destined for the stage."[27]

Joyce Stanley, a fellow classmate, recalled: "He had a marvelous sense of humor, he was fun loving, rarely moody—serious though. He loved people, and he never seemed to get his feelings hurt or get mad. He was usually laughing, having fun."[28]

Van has said of his childhood: "There were others things I would like to have done besides practicing the piano, but I knew my mother was right about what I *should* do."

I was not the kind of child who followed blindly. I questioned things. My parents didn't treat me as a child. They would never answer a question of mine by saying "just because."

There was nothing I ever wanted for, nothing that I ever needed, nothing I ever wished for that I didn't have. Neither of my parents forced music on me. It was just there, always part of the atmosphere.[29]

Rildia Bee encouraged Van's curiosity about the vast piano repertoire, but she carefully selected the basic works for his early instruction. When he was seven, they had great discussions about the first movement of Beethoven's "Pathétique" Sonata; when Van was studying polyphonic works she would explain how each voice must stand alone, and how to accomplish that at the piano.

José Iturbi, the great Spanish pianist, came to Dallas to play a recital when the boy was eleven. Under the thrall of Hollywood's "A Song to Remember," Van was eager to play for Iturbi, who had recorded the soundtrack for the cinematic portrayal of Chopin. "One of the first big-selling classical artists, [Iturbi] got a lot of people, a lot of children, excited about classical music," Cliburn recalled. "They saw those movies and they wanted to play the piano." Soon after playing for Iturbi, Van met Artur Rubinstein backstage after a Dallas recital. This great artist, like Iturbi, was enthusiastic about the boy. These two concert pianists became sources of inspiration for Van, who would not remain a novice pianist for long.

For all Rildia Bee's efforts as his teacher, she remained selfless and anticipated eventual change. "I always was waiting for the time to come when Van would want to go to another teacher, and sometimes I would suggest the possibility. 'I'll quit if you won't teach me,' he'd say. Then we would go on with the practicing."[30] When Van was twelve, he auditioned for and was accepted by the American pianist Olga Samaroff, then head of the piano division at the Curtis Institute of Music in Philadelphia, but before the boy could begin his lessons with the celebrated pedagogue, she died.

When Van won a competition at twelve, he was given a short radio broadcast on 12 April 1947 as soloist in a performance of the first movement of Tchaikovsky's Piano Concerto in B-flat Minor with the Houston Symphony Orchestra, conducted by Ernest Hoffman. Both the date—12 April—and the work—Tchaikovsky's piano concerto—now seem prophetic. A decade later on 12 April 1958, Van Cliburn would shock the international music world into jubilant celebration when he performed the Tchaikovsky concerto in Moscow during the final round of the first international Tchaikovsky Competition and won the gold medal.

Although Lavan Cliburn had aspirations for his son to become a doctor, a pursuit that had once been his own ambition, he said after the radio broadcast in Houston, "Well, sonny boy, if that's what you want, believe me, I'll help you."[31] And in his quiet way, he always did.

"Former Local Boy to Play at Carnegie" ran the headline of the *Shreveport Times* on 18 January 1948. Van had again competed, this time in Dallas with sixteen pianists of all ages, including college graduates, and won his first date in Carnegie Hall. At his first New York performance (on a program with several other youngsters), he impressed a concert manager who approached Rildia Bee with the promise of concerts and travel. She thanked him profusely but explained that she did not want to subject Van to that—she didn't want him to fade away, but to progress. "Life in general has many terribly rough roads," Cliburn has said, "but you can transcend those inevitable difficulties by where you set your ideals. There are so many people who say, 'Oh, I missed my childhood.' Well, I had an absolutely fabulous childhood."

Despite the relative isolation of his life in Kilgore, Van's youthful career gained momentum during his early adolescence. When Rildia Bee returned to New York in the summers of 1947 and 1948 for master classes given by

Ernest Hutcheson and Carl Friedberg at Juilliard, Van went with her to see the school for the first time. He attended music theory classes in harmony, dictation, and sight reading, and he played for the first time in the concert hall of the old Juilliard School on Claremont Avenue. The occasion was a Wednesday noon student recital, the piece was Franz Liszt's third *Liebestraum*.

When Juilliard beckoned, the Cliburn family responded, determined to accelerate Van's progress toward his high school graduation. In New York, Juilliard's dean attended Van's entrance examinations, found him an extraordinary talent, and had no doubt that he was unusual and would be admitted. It had long been Rildia Bee's hope and plan for Van to study at Juilliard with Rosina Lhévinne, continuing in the Russian tradition of piano playing that she had introduced to him. But now the question was whether Lhévinne, who was perennially overburdened with students, would accept the teenage Texan as her pupil. When she interviewed the seventeen-year-old, Lhévinne was doubtful. She proposed that Van study with someone else and play for her every two or three weeks, but this was not a plan he could accept. He wanted stability, not instability. After hearing his entrance audition, Lhévinne found room for Van Cliburn in her crowded class. During Van's student years at Juilliard (1951–54), his mother and Lhévinne became the best of friends and admired each other enormously. About Lhévinne's teaching Cliburn has said, "She corrected only what was wrong, so that her students were not damaged psychologically. She built you up so that you played your best and you were stable as a performer."

For the Juilliard School and Rosina Lhévinne's piano class in particular, the Cliburn years were a time of abundant and extraordinary talent: John Browning, Daniel Pollack, Jerome Lowenthal, and Jeaneane Dowis were all outstanding pianists; the singer Leontyne Price and the violinist Michael Rabin were there. In fact, a whole new generation of American artists on the verge of making national and international names for themselves was taking shape in a single institution.[32]

From the age of twelve, Van was a successful competition pianist. In that rather perverse arena, he was not only a warrior, but a victor. There was no self doubt. As he matured, he continued to take competition in stride, rising above those who were endowed with stage nerves of steel and who played to technical perfection but no further. His performances of certain works in his repertoire—Franz Liszt's "Paysage" and "Mazeppa" (the third and fourth of the *Transcendental Etudes*) and the Twelfth Hungarian Rhapsody, for instance—were incomparable artistic achievements. After entering Juilliard, Van launched a winning streak that was phenomenal in the history of American musical competitions. From April 1952 to April 1958, he won every piano competition he entered. There were five before Moscow: the Dealey Memorial Award in Dallas, the Kosciuszko Foundation's Chopin Scholarship Award in New York, the Michaels Memorial Music Award in Chicago (a competition for various instruments in which he won the second prize), and the Leventritt Award.

Van graduated from Juilliard in May 1954. In June he signed a contract with Columbia Artists Management. Winning the coveted Leventritt Award had assured his New York debut and on 14 November he performed the Tchaikovsky concerto at Carnegie Hall with Dimitri Mitropoulos conducting the New York Philharmonic. He mesmerized both the audience and the critics. More than three hundred crowded the backstage area after the concert to attend Mrs. Leventritt's reception for the young artist.

Many concert engagements followed in the next two seasons, and an appearance on the *Tonight Show* brought the pianist to the attention of millions of television viewers. For two seasons, Van's success had exceeded all expectations.

Then the prospects for the 1957 season came to a halt. Van was called up for induction into the army, and he told Columbia Artists Management to book no further engagements. But when he was standing with hand raised taking the oath at the induction center in Dallas, there was a last-minute reprieve. Military doctors had discovered medical records showing he had been subject to chronic nasal hemorrhages since his youth, and he was rejected from military service.

In July when he performed in Cleveland, his parents drove there to hear the concert. In their hotel room Rildia Bee slipped and broke a vertebra in her back. Van and Rildia Bee returned to New York where she was admitted to the hospital before returning to Texas to convalesce. When his father was injured in an automobile collision seven weeks later, Van returned to Kilgore to look after them both and to take over his mother's large class of piano students.

In New York, extraordinary plans were in the making. The First Tchaikovsky International Competition in Moscow had been announced for qualifying pianists and violinists. Rosina Lhévinne wrote Van a letter begging him to consider the possibility. Eugene Istomin encouraged him. Dimitri Mitropoulos eagerly agreed to help Van plan his repertoire for the competition, knowing that because the requirements were vast, the choices would be difficult.

At this time the Cold War was escalating, and US and Soviet political concerns could have put the trip to a halt, but on 23 March Van flew to Moscow. When he arrived—the trip took forty hours via Paris and Prague—he was momentarily bewildered, then instantly knew what he would do first. He went to Red Square and gazed on the onion-shaped cupolas of the Church of St. Basil. The architectural masterpiece completed in 1560 had fascinated Van since childhood when he first saw it in a child's picture history book of the world, a Christmas present given to him by his parents in 1939. Satisfied to have seen St. Basil's at last, he left Red Square, found his hotel, and the next day set to work.

CHAPTER EIGHT

Discovery

COMPETITIONS AND MANAGEMENT

Contests are as unpredictable as roulette. They are all right for those who have nothing to lose.

Henry Temianka, in *Facing the Music*

WHEN competitions permit the very young to participate, family and teachers on the child's nurturing team might well consider the psychological impact of winning as much as that of losing. They may wisely resist the temptation to allow their children to take part in such risky behavior.

But is either winning or losing a competition too much to bear even for the maturing musical prodigy? Doesn't adolescence have sufficient confusion, loss of esteem, and manic, grandiose, despairing energy of its own without this added burden? Since one cannot light a candle in a high wind, "Competitor beware!" is a worthy injunction, regardless of the urgency of the adolescent's temptation to compete.

During the rough passage from puberty to maturity, the prodigy, if tough and lucky, evolves into a creditable, responsible artist. Despite the promise of success, fame, and financial gain, in many cases what the young musician needs is shelter and safety. To abstain from aggressive competition in this period may be critical for the sensitive and aspiring, but immature, child prodigy.

For every supremely gifted prodigy there may come a unique moment for discovery, but not every competition or professionally managed recital tour will yield such an opportunity. If a young performer of exceptional ability is to compete, competitions must be chosen wisely. Younger artists should avoid too many participations in too brief a period of time and should balance the demands of specific competition repertoire. Even winning a grand tour of sixty concerts for an ensuing season when the prodigy has little experience in touring may not be entirely beneficial in the long run. Because nurturing a prodigy remains a team effort, every step taken by the protagonists—family and friends, teachers of all sorts, and patrons and concert managers in various guises—is crucial to the career development of the prodigy.

Today the drama of competition may be a coming-of-age ritual, but recall that Cliburn was already twenty-four when he triumphed in Moscow in 1958. Glancing back further, the most memorable of modern violin competitions was the first International Henryk Wieniawski Violin Competition in Warsaw in 1935, where blazing paths crossed as never before, as we shall see in the next chapter. By way of introduction, we can consider a curious precursor to the modern competition which occurred several centuries ago.

On Christmas Eve 1781, Wolfgang Mozart and Muzio Clementi engaged in a friendly rivalry at the court of Emperor Joseph II in Vienna. Royalty had instigated a musical performance competition at the Hofburg, the imperial palace. Although both musicians had been prodigies, their wonder years were behind them (Mozart was twenty-five, Clementi was twenty-nine); nevertheless, the contest had many elements of the modern musical performance competition.

Mozart described the formal event in a letter to his father.[1] It had a sponsor, a scheduled time and place, and a reasonably objective format. The competitors, who were of similar ages, each had achieved mastery, and in the various events of the competition performed works of equal difficulty. There was the imposition of new music unknown to the players and a demand for improvisation, an eighteenth-century musical skill expected of mature pianists. The jury, in this case Emperor Joseph II, made the final judgment. No winner was proclaimed and no prize awarded, which sometimes occurs in modern competitions.

Although both Mozart and Clementi had attained unassailable reputations as pianists, their playing differed greatly, as does that of great pianists today. Clementi was primarily a brilliant keyboard technician. Mozart, the foremost pianist in Vienna, was an artist whose consummate musicianship ruled over his virtuosity.

Born in Rome on 24 January 1752, Clementi, like Mozart, was both a performer and a composer. The Englishman Peter Beckford had induced Clementi's father to allow the Italian wonder child to move to Dorset, England, when he was barely fourteen. During his first four years there, Clementi continued to cultivate both his piano playing and his skill as a composer. In 1770, at the age of eighteen, Clementi gave his debut recital in London, then remained there conducting opera from the keyboard in the tradition of the period. In 1781 he set off on a concert tour, playing first in Paris, then in Strasbourg and Munich before arriving in Vienna.

"After we had stood on ceremony long enough," Mozart wrote his father, "the Emperor declared that Clementi ought to begin. 'La Santa Chiesa Cattolica (the Holy Catholic Church),' he said, Clementi being a Roman."[2] After the emperor's deference to the church, the Italian played a short, improvised prelude, followed by a composition of his own, the Sonata in B-flat Major. (Later Mozart borrowed the theme of the first movement of Clementi's sonata for his overture to *The Magic Flute*.) The Italian followed this with a toccata featuring the rapid execution of difficult double-note passages in the right hand, demonstrating an instrumental virtuosity for which he was widely acclaimed.

When Clementi had finished playing, the emperor turned to Mozart and said, "*Allons*, fire away." Mozart performed improvised variations on an original theme; then the Russian Grand Duchess Maria Feodorovna produced some sonatas by Giovanni Paisiello. Both pianists alternately read at sight from Paisiello's manuscript "wretchedly written out in his own hand." Mozart played the allegros and Clementi the andantes and rondos. Finally the emperor asked the musicians to take a theme from Paisiello's sonata and accompany one another on two pianos as they improvised upon it. Unfortunately, Mozart was relegated to a poorly maintained instrument.

The funny thing was that although I had borrowed Countess Thun's pianoforte, I only played on it when I played alone; such was the Emperor's desire—and, by the way, the other instrument was out of tune and three of the keys were stuck. "That doesn't matter," said the Emperor. I put the best construction on it I could, that is, that the Emperor, already knowing my skill and my knowledge of music, was only desirous of showing especial courtesy to a foreigner.

The emperor did not declare a victor, but Clementi later spoke of Mozart's singing touch and exquisite taste with considerable admiration and admitted that he strived to put more music and less technical show into his performances from that point on. In contrast, Mozart's verdict was harsh. He wrote to his father:

> He is an excellent player, but that is all. He has great facility with his right hand. His greatest strength lies in his passages in thirds. Apart from this, he has not a farthing's worth of taste or feeling, in short he is simply a *mechanicus*.

Although each pianist may have had a secret agenda, both musicians took a certain risk by competing since there was nothing to gain and a great deal to lose for the player judged inferior. Yet at the summons of an emperor, even such musical titans as Mozart and Clementi had to think seriously about taking part. It mattered little that in those days no concert manager was poised to forward the competitors' careers: by 1781 both men managed their own affairs independently. Evidently, the emperor considered Mozart an apparent winner (the court sent him fifty ducats for his appearance), but his personal quest for a court appointment was no nearer to fulfillment after the competition than before.

The proliferation of international competitions has been astounding in the twentieth century. The World Federation of International Music Competitions was created in Geneva in 1957 to help regulate what was generally considered a valuable and necessary stage in the career development of young performers. The fourteen founding members of the federation were well-established competitions. Some were patriotically named after important music centers: Budapest, Geneva, Munich, Prague, and Toulouse. Others were named after famous musicians: the Ferrucio Busoni (at Bolzano), Niccolò Paganini (Genoa), Pyotr Tchaikovsky (Moscow), Henryk Wieniawski (Poznan in Poland), Frédéric Chopin (Warsaw), Ludwig van Beethoven (Vienna), Giovanni Battista Viotti (Vercelli in Italy), Marguerite Long-Jacques Thibaud (Paris), and Eugène Ysäye (Brussels), the latter renamed the Queen Elisabeth of Belgium International Competition.

In 1996, the federation announced that 101 musical competitions would be held throughout Europe, North and South America, the Middle and Far East, Australia, and South Africa, in which talented young artists could win the opportunity to perform in concerts, recitals, and recording studios, and on radio and television, in addition to winning millions of dollars in prize monies. The federation heartily encouraged young musicians everywhere to seek these outstanding career opportunities and their sponsors, whether individuals, organizations, foundations, or the media, to continue their generous support of these deserving young artists.

Within North America numerous music festivals, subscription concerts, and summer-season programs enlist the winners of international music competitions and thus create contact between outstanding young performers and the public. In addition to the major New York–based competitions sponsored by the Walter Naumburg Foundation and the Young Concert Artists International Auditions, contests that offer cyclical participation for various categories of instrumentalists and singers, more than forty others from coast to coast range from the student competitions sponsored by the Philadelphia Orchestra to the Los Angeles Philharmonic's awards, Fellowships for Excellence in Diversity, which are granted in competition to Californians from ethnic groups underrepresented in major orchestras.

Contests offer opportunities for woodwind, brass, and stringed instrument players, chamber ensembles, guitarists, harpists, percussionists, singers, and conductors. Piano competitions remain the most prominent with more than sixty annually scheduled events. Perhaps this is to be expected since by midcentury there were more than twelve million piano students in the United States, many of them enchanted by the myth of an imagined, ultimate accomplishment—playing a recital in Carnegie Hall—never realizing that this could be only one step in a major career.

The phenomenon of the mechanicus, a term that Mozart applied to Clementi, is everywhere evident in modern competitions. It is a negative by-product of the exceedingly stressful demand to play the instrument perfectly, to be judged the flawless executant rather than the consummate musician. This regrettable denigration of artistic values in favor of technical prowess is one of the most alarming results of competition fever and seems to afflict many prodigies, no matter what instrument they play. As violinist Ruggiero Ricci recently said, "I want to hear something that is special; not just another 'contest fiddle player' who is good, but has nothing to say that is memorable."[3]

Despite continued controversy, competitions now play a crucial role in the developing careers of emerging young artists, especially as it becomes increasingly difficult to attract and hold the attention of the public in general and of influential groups of supporters and concert management in particular.

Yet Richard Corrado, vice-president in charge of management of artists and conductors for ICM Artists in New York, along with other managers, has made it clear that major concert management does not present unknown artists at a financial risk, which years ago the legendary New York impresarios Sol Hurok and Arthur Judson occasionally did. Usually there is a sponsor, either a corporation or a private individual, who is willing to accept this financial obligation. In unusual circumstances, the directors of high-budget concert series at concert venues such as Alice Tully Hall at New York's Lincoln Center decide whether a young artist is important enough to be presented on a subscription basis. If presented, the artist is paid a fee and, according to Corrado, "is sold to the public in that way . . . but usually it is an artist that does have some New York panache, some New York exposure, and some recognition throughout the world."

Pianist James Kamura Parker, a Canadian prodigy from Vancouver, made his first public appearance at five, began winning important competitions in 1978 when he was nineteen, and came to international attention when he won the International Piano Competition in Viña del Mar, Chile. Commenting on Parker's winning the Leeds International Pianoforte Competition in England in 1984, Corrado said in 1995:

> The Leeds Competition was a very prestigious competition to win at the time Parker won it. . . . He had the advantage that there were certain officers of this corporation that were present there, indeed, wanted him whether he won the prize or not. For that alone, he had the luxury of major management from the time the competition took place until the present.[4]

Young careers may teeter in a delicate balance between competitions, concert opportunities, management, and personal needs. With European tours and several new recordings, Helen Huang's world recognition increased dramatically, building upon her New York panache and exposure as soloist with the New York Philharmonic. With many elements in her life as a pianist already consolidated, she has major concert management to direct the professional aspects of her burgeoning career and may not ever be heard again in a major competition. Further competition could prove psychologically disturbing to her, and should she not be judged a winner, the continuity of the career that has been established for her would be endangered. In the modern era, winning can be no more for the prodigy than a stepping stone to a career, while losing in a major competition, particularly after having previously won a significant prize, can be disastrous.

HELEN

Born in Japan in 1982, Helen Huang moved to the United States with her Taiwanese family at the age of three. Her parents, who are not musicians, encouraged their three children to study musical instruments. Regarding her early encounters with music, Helen has said:

> When I was about three, whenever I came back from church I would play the pieces I had heard on the piano. Whenever my brother and sister would play at their lessons, I would sit next to them and tell them "you had this wrong note or you had that wrong."[5]

Helen began seriously studying the piano at five. Within a year she had won her first competition and performed in public. By the age of six, she was not yet tall enough to climb easily onto the piano bench and once seated she needed a special device to reach the pedals. She soon graduated from giving recitals at her local school auditorium and astounded audiences when she won competitions such as the New York Philharmonic's Young Performer Auditions. At twelve, Helen was invited to perform with great orchestras around the world.

A highly disciplined young teenager, Helen attended public school at Cherry Hill, New Jersey, and when not on concert tours she devoted herself to her piano studies, having weekly Saturday lessons in New York City with her teacher, Yoheved Kaplinsky. She has described the rigors of her self-directed practicing: "I play around thirty minutes in the morning before school and practice three hours at night. Also, if I have time in the afternoon I'll play, but that depends on homework." Helen insists confidently that "It is something I want to do. I want to become a pianist!" When asked why, she responded, "Maybe because you can show people how you feel by the way you play."[6]

While still a young teenager, Helen traveled everywhere with her mother. Invitations took them to Paris, Japan, Israel, and even to Puerto Rico for an appearance at the thirty-ninth annual Pablo Casals Festival. In February 1995, she made her New York debut playing Beethoven's Concerto in C Major, Op. 15, with the New York Philharmonic, conducted by Kurt Masur, who had previously presented the prodigy as soloist in Leipzig with the Gewandhaus Orchestra. Helen made her first major recording with Masur, a Teldec compact disc of Beethoven's first piano concerto and Mozart's Concerto in A Major, K. 488. "As we started to work together, I didn't take her anymore as a child. She was a partner," Masur, music director of the New York Philharmonic, has said. "There is a natural connection to the music and to the instrument when she plays. And therefore she doesn't play as a child, and she never tries to ask somebody if she was good. She knows."[7]

Huang had twelve scheduled performances in 1995. The violinist Hilary Hahn had seventeen, and violinists Sarah Chang and Leila Josefowicz each had thirty-one bookings. Having followed in the professional footsteps of the violinist Midori (Goto), twenty-three at the time, the young girls are all currently at the top of the prodigy chain. Lee Lamont, chairwoman of ICM Artists in New York, has expressed concerns about the professionally managed careers of such young artists, questioning such things as the number of engagements in new places with new conductors and the separation of recitals from concerto dates to assure adequate time to prepare: "If an artist is performing sixty concerts, and is playing twelve different concertos instead of five different concertos, that makes a big difference. . . . Don't make success the prime mover."[8]

Helen Huang has no apparent stage fright and in her performances seems entranced by an unforced intuition of the highest order. "My teacher told me that I should just think that I'm playing in my living room. That's what I do," Helen has said. "It's much easier to play than to talk in front of people. She freely expresses her innocent view of the imaginative artistic processes at work that give order and control to the works that she plays: "Every single note is like a different color and the whole thing is sort of like a rainbow."

THE FIRST TCHAIKOVSKY INTERNATIONAL COMPETITION

Winning a major international competition certainly can bestow worldwide recognition and may help the young performer gain the assurance of major concert management. While such an accomplishment does not guarantee the longevity of a career, it can be the impetus for beginning one. Concert management firms can initially use such coveted credentials to their business advantage, issuing a short-term contract with the understanding that the competition winner must advance further to warrant an extended contract. From the management point of view, public interest in a young violinist, for instance, who can be publicized as having just won the Paganini or the Queen Elisabeth competition, soon dwindles with the certainty of that performer's being superseded by a new winner at the next competition a few years hence.

To look back on the First Tchaikovsky International Competition in 1958 is to be reminded of a remarkable moment in the life of pianist Van Cliburn. At twenty-three he was already a seasoned competitor. He had won every piano competition he had entered over a six-year period, a winning streak that was phenomenal in the history of American musical competitions. There were five before Moscow.

Although the Tchaikovsky Competition sets the age limit for competitors between seventeen and thirty-two, it has always been an event essentially for mature players, one that presents to each competitor the daunting challenge of selecting works from an enormously difficult, prescribed repertoire (one heavily laden with Russian music). For his competition repertoire in 1958, Van Cliburn was advised by his mentor, conductor Dimitri Mitropoulos.

Having drawn lots for the order of their appearances, the fifty competitors awaited their turns. Cliburn's came on 2 April at 9:30 in the morning, an unlikely hour for most performers. He began with Bach's Prelude and Fugue in B-flat Minor from Book I of *The Well-Tempered Clavier*. Next came Mozart's Sonata in C Major, K. 330, and four etudes: Chopin's "Winter Wind," Op. 25, No. 11; Scriabin's Etude in D-sharp Minor; Rachmaninov's Etude Tableau in E-flat Minor, Op. 39; and Liszt's "Mazeppa." As did the other contestants, he ended his program with Tchaikovsky's seldom-played Theme and Variations, Op. 19.

Although the jury was divided in its appraisal of Cliburn's playing of Mozart, they concluded that his performance was expressive in every detail. Judging fifty intermittent performances of the Tchaikovsky variations was a grueling ordeal—the long hours of intense concentration were unsettling for some jurors. Arguments ensued. The voting, based on a scale from zero to twenty-five, was manipulated in various ways, some giving extra points to insure the progress of the favored Russian pianist, Lev Vlasenko, while others, including Sviatoslav Richter and Heinrich Neuhaus, veered in another direction. When pianist Andrei Gavrilov asked Richter why he never attended a jury after the 1958 competition, he is said to have answered, "It was absolutely disgusting because they were trying to boycott Van Cliburn."[9]

Having met the stringent demands of the first round, nineteen competitors went forward to the semifinals, including Van Cliburn, who now shielded his emotions from the rumored intrigue and political maneuvering of an anxious jury. The second round with its intimidating repertoire proved a difficult ascent to the finals, eliminating five semifinalists. In this round, Cliburn played Taneyev's Prelude and Fugue in G-sharp Minor (a choice suggested earlier by Mitropoulos), the first movement of Tchaikovsky's Sonata in G Major, Chopin's Fantaisie in F Minor, and Liszt's Twelfth Hungarian Rhapsody. In the spirit of internationalism, the contest included an innovative requirement: all had to perform a new composition by a contemporary composer of the country they represented. Cliburn ended his program with the finale of Samuel Barber's Piano Sonata (1949), a work over which the intrepid Texan held sovereign mastery.

Some thirty years later his old adversary Lev Vlasenko recalled Cliburn's performance in the semifinal round: "You cannot imagine how well Van played. I can only say that his playing sounded the most Russian of everyone. I mean, he was more Russian that we were. And after all these dismal years [in postwar Stalinist Russia], Van was like a ray of sun penetrating the clouds."[10]

From the more than fifty pianists who had begun the competition, only nine remained. Van Cliburn and Daniel Pollack, the Los Angeles pianist, were the only American finalists. The Soviet contingent included Lev Vlasenko, Naum Shtarkman, and Eduard Miansarov. Milena Mollova from Bulgaria, Nadia Gedda-Nova from France, Liu Shih Kun from China, and Toyoaki Matsuura from Japan completed the roster of finalists.

On stage Cliburn was endowed with supreme charisma. "For many Russians, he was the first live American that they could really touch and feel and see," remarked Vladimir Feltsman, the Soviet emigré pianist. The musical event was among the first in the history of Russia to be telecast live. The pianist Alexander Toradze, who watched the broadcast, recalled that "the people in the hall threw to him on stage their most dear pieces of memorabilia, the dearest mementos of their lives. . . . Unknown people gave him all these things."[11]

On 12 April the hall's overflow crowd was nearly hysterical by the time Van Cliburn walked onto the stage of the Great Hall of the Moscow Conservatory to play the Tchaikovsky concerto; Dmitri Kabalevsky's Rondo, the imposed solo work written especially for this occasion; and Rachmaninov's Third Piano Concerto. Outside thousands more waited to hear the jury's verdict. When Van rose from the piano after the Rachmaninov, a thundering ovation that lasted nearly nine minutes brought even the jury to their feet. But there was still another night of competition and other finalists to be considered.

Van Cliburn had repeatedly played the Tchaikovsky concerto with or-

chestra since the age of twelve when he won the Texas Federation of Music
Clubs contest and performed it with the Houston Symphony Orchestra. In
1954, he had given an acclaimed performance of the great masterpiece at
Carnegie Hall with Dimitri Mitropoulos conducting the New York Philharmonic, and his stylistic and technical command of Rachmaninov's Third
Concerto, an extremely difficult and musically elusive piece, was a certainty.
His performances of it had won him the accolade "one musician whose
prodigious talent marks him as the most important young pianist of his generation."[12] Cliburn's previous performances of these two works gave him
invaluable stage experience, a practical advantage in Moscow.

At the end of the final round the jury reached an impasse, and the minister of culture was dispatched to consult Nikita Khruschev. Since national
pride was involved, he had to solve the dilemma. Realizing that the international community expected equity, the often unpredictable Khruschev simply asked the minister of culture, "Is he the best?" The minister's answer was
unequivocal. "In this case, give him the first prize."[13]

Emil Gilels made the official announcement to the Moscow audience on
14 April 1958. Van Cliburn, "the most deserved of the deserving," had won
the gold medal. A friend in Shreveport conveyed the good news to Kilgore,
and the Columbia Broadcasting System soon arranged a telephone call to
Moscow. "It's official!" Van told his parents. Within hours Van was recording
the Tchaikovsky concerto with Kiril Kondrashin conducting the Moscow
State Symphony. He was feted by Queen Elisabeth of Belgium at a Kremlin
reception and photographed with Khruschev. The startling photograph made
its way around the globe. When the *New York Times* ran a front-page story
that stretched across four columns, the domino effect began. He would go to
New York, then to Washington, DC, to meet President Eisenhower.

Cliburn performed at Carnegie Hall, this time with Kiril Kondrashin
conducting the Symphony of the Air. The next afternoon a ticker tape parade
swept him down Fifth Avenue, a hero's welcome. Outside City Hall after
the parade, Mayor Robert Wagner presented the city's scroll and medal to
the lanky Texan, who said what he felt at that moment: "I shall always
remember this day, and know that it wasn't to me that this happened, but to
the fact that music is a language and a message that we can all enjoy."[14]

Back in his home state seed money was offered for a competition to be
named after him, and in 1962 the Van Cliburn International Quadrennial
Piano Competition was launched, continuing to this day to nurture the
careers of promising young performers.

CHAPTER NINE

Warsaw, 1935

The First International Henryk Wieniawski
Violin Competition

During the competition at Warsaw's Filharmonja Hall, each contestant in turn stood inside a small chalk circle at center stage to play. To step outside of it meant instant disqualification, something to be remembered for a lifetime.

Henry Temianka, in *Facing the Music*

Violinists came from east and west, converging on Warsaw in March 1935 to take part in the first International Henryk Wieniawski Violin Competition. The Polish government took great pride in Wieniawski, who was born in Lublin, Poland, in 1835, and helped launch his worldwide career after he completed his studies abroad with Lambert Massart at the Paris Conservatory. Wieniawski died in 1880, and in 1935, the centenary of his birth, Poland honored his memory by instituting an international competition in his name. The first Wieniawski competition, for many the most memorable of modern violin competitions, was a golden moment for the outstanding pupils of Carl Flesch and Pyotr Stolyarski.

Adam Wieniawski, nephew of the celebrated violinist, and Paul Kochanski, who had been concertmaster of the Warsaw Philharmonic and later a professor at the Warsaw Conservatory, served as vice-chairmen of the jury of twenty-one distinguished musicians from Poland, Yugoslavia, Latvia, Estonia, the USSR, Denmark, Sweden, France, Switzerland, and Germany. Among the prominent jury members were Gregor Fitelberg, the conductor of the Warsaw Philharmonic; Georg Kulenkampff, the leading German violin-

Warsaw, 1935. The first International Henryk Wieniawski Violin Competition. Identified
Henri Temianka, Boris Goldstein, Ginette Neveu, Ida Haendel, Josef Hassid; (back row)
Ljerko Spiller.

...to right by Lorand Fenyves as: (front row) David Oistrakh, Mary Louisa Sardo,
...Neuhaus, Adam Wieniawski, an unidentified man, Gregor Fitelberg, Jose Figuera, and

ist and professor at Berlin's Hochschule; Oszkár Studer, an important violin teacher at the Franz Liszt Academy in Budapest, then living in Switzerland; the Hungarian composer Ernst von Dohnányi; and Poland's esteemed violin pedagogue, Mieczyslaw Michalowicz, the teacher of Bronislaw Huberman, Szymon Goldberg, and Roman Totenberg. The three prodigies Ida Haendel, Boris Goldstein, and Josef Hassid were among the contestants.

As competitors from sixteen countries arrived in Warsaw, they were greeted at the railroad terminal by Adam Wieniawski and a representative of the Polish government, then later interviewed by a government official, who discreetly inquired into their racial and religious background. "Granting the first prize to a Jew would have been intolerable to the virulently antisemitic Polish government," recalled Henri Temianka, one of the competition's winners. Indeed, in those troubled times in a Poland suffering from unbearable political oppression, the Polish press overtly conveyed the prejudiced ideology of the time. In the decade preceding the rise of fascism, violin prodigies from around the world had gone to study and perform in Berlin, and, according to Temianka, "The majority had one thing in common: they were East European Jews or their descendants. An unbroken tradition of great violin playing had emerged from the ghettos."[1]

The repertoire requirement for the first Wieniawski competition was simpler in scope than in more recent Polish competitions but no less demanding, considering Wieniawski's singularly virtuosic compositions. The preliminary round was eliminatory. The fifty-five competing violinists each began by performing several movements from an unaccompanied sonata by Bach, continued by playing three pieces by Wieniawski, then finished with one romantic or contemporary work of their own choice. With this choice, the violinists had their best opportunity to set themselves apart and to go forward to the final round, performing the required two movements from either the first or second violin concerto by Wieniawski.

The favored competitors' age span was startling. At seven, Ida Haendel was the youngest. Two other genuine prodigies were Boris ("Bussia") Goldstein from Odessa, a pupil of Pyotr Stolyarski, and Mieczyslaw Michalowicz's Polish pupil, Josef Hassid. Both gifted boys were twelve. Ginette Neveu from France was sixteen. The Hungarian Lorand Fenyves was seventeen. The older competitors who were ultimately successful were in their twenties and had already established their careers by 1935: Tomás Magyar (the brother of cellist Gabriel Magyar of the Hungarian String Quartet) was twenty-three, Bronislaw Gimpel was twenty-four, and Henri Temianka was twenty-five.

David Oistrakh, the twenty-seven-year-old Russian violinist from Odessa, was the oldest.

GINETTE

Born in Paris on 11 August 1919, Ginette Neveu won the first prize in Warsaw in 1935 at the first Henryk Wieniawski International Competition.

Ginette's father was an amateur string player, her mother was a violin teacher, and her brother, Jean, was a gifted pianist who later joined Ginette on the concert stage as her accompanist. While still an infant, Ginette could sing tunes after hearing them only once and was moved to tears when she first heard Chopin's music played at a concert. Her mother, Mme Ronze-Neveu, gave her a quarter-sized violin when she was five and began teaching her; then Mme Talluel, a prominent violin teacher at the École Supérieure de Musique in Paris, recognized Ginette's vocation and accepted the child as her pupil. Ginette's mother later recalled that her young daughter felt driven to perfect her violin playing and often had to be stopped from practicing while she continued to argue, "But it has got to be beautiful."[2]

Under Talluel's guidance, Ginette made her debut in Paris at seven playing Bruch's Concerto in G Minor with the Colonne Orchestra at the Salle Gaveau. Two years later she won the first prize at the École Supérieure de Musique and the Prix d'Honneur awarded by the city of Paris for her performance of the Mendelssohn concerto. When the concerto performance was repeated in Winterthur, Switzerland, a critic described the little violinist as "Mozart in petticoats."

After studying with Madame Talluel, Ginette was accepted as a pupil of Georges Enesco. When she began studying with him in Paris in 1928, Enesco was among the world's most revered violin teachers. A musician of unimaginable intuitive gifts, little Ginette defended her interpretations of Bach's music when they were at odds with those of Enesco, but the master teacher, in his uncanny wisdom, recognized their understandable differences in perception and acknowledged her rare intuition.

Enesco prepared the child for the entrance examinations at the Paris Conservatory, and at the annual Concours d'Admission in November 1930, she was accepted into both the violin class of Professor Jules and the composition class of Nadia Boulanger. In only one academic season she was ready for the conservatory's summer prize competitions, and in July 1931 Ginette Neveu won the premier prix. Her mastery by age twelve rivaled that of Henryk Wieniawski eighty years earlier. The Polish prodigy had won the conservatory's coveted first prize in 1846 when he was eleven, in competition with fourteen older students.

Having finished her studies at the conservatory, Ginette traveled to Austria in 1932 to compete in an international competition in Vienna. She won the fourth prize. When the competition was over, Carl Flesch, who had been on the jury, sent this message to Ginette's mother at their hotel: "If you can come to Berlin, I undertake, without any thought of personal gain, to make myself responsible for the young violinist's musical education."

The plan was realized two years later and proved to be an important turning point. When Ginette went to Berlin in 1934, Flesch heard the fifteen-year-old violinist for the second time. He was deeply impressed: "My child, you have received a gift from heaven, and I have no wish to touch it. All I can do for you is to give you some purely technical advice."[3]

He did much more. Carl Flesch personally financed Ginette's entire venture in the forthcoming Henryk Wieniawski competition in Warsaw. Though a late entrant, she was accepted from among the 180 applicants, and in early April 1935 Flesch worked intensively with her to prepare, quickly but thoroughly, the required Wieniawski repertoire, including the Concerto in F-sharp Minor, composed before Wieniawski was eighteen. Ginette's choice for ending her program was Maurice Ravel's *Tzigane*. This masterpiece, a virtuosic gypsy piece in the form of a fantasia, would remain an outstanding component of her concert repertoire throughout her career.

The competition in Warsaw aroused great passion in 1935. The international jury and even the population of Warsaw were split into warring factions by nationalistic, chauvinistic, and personal rivalries. Henri Temianka recalled that certain teachers who were members of the jury were grimly determined to prevent the pupils of rival teachers from winning the contest regardless of merit, while outside Warsaw's Filharmonja Hall, "the man in the street bet on the contestants as if we were horses."[4]

When the first prize went to the teenager from Paris, many in the audience were stunned in disbelief. David Oistrakh, a mature concert violinist at twenty-seven, had become a favorite competitor. The official judgment was that Ginette Neveu had placed first by attaining twenty-six jury points more than David Oistrakh, the nearest competitor, but this rationale didn't satisfy everyone. One member of the jury, Gabriel Bouillon of France, later recalled, "Oistrakh had to be satisfied with second prize, perhaps because the sympathy of the Polish members of the jury was with a French woman rather than with a Russian."[5] Debate over the jury's landmark decision continues among violinists to this day, even though the two supreme artists, Neveu and Oistrakh, have long been absent from the world's concert halls.

Fourteen years after she won the first prize in Warsaw, on 28 October 1949, Ginette Neveu and her brother, Jean, perished in an airplane crash over the Azores. She was thirty-one. "Her voice has been silenced for ever," her mother lamented in her 1957 biography of the great violinist, but Neveu had already lived her artistic credo—"Aim high, aim at beauty"—and for those who recall her playing, the memory is indelible.

DODI

David Fedorovich ("Dodi") Oistrakh was born on 30 September 1908 in Odessa, in the USSR. In later life, he spoke of his early childhood encounter with music: "As far as I reach back, I cannot remember myself without a violin."

> I was three-and-a-half when my father brought home a toy violin. I enthusiastically imagined myself a street player, a sad profession quite common at that time in Odessa. It seemed to me the greatest happiness in the world to be able to go from courtyard to courtyard with a violin in my hands.[6]

At last at the age of five, he was given a real violin—one-eighth size—and his absorption was total. Dodi's mother, who sang in the opera house chorus, invited the violinist Pyotr Stolyarski to their home to meet her son. When Stolyarski heard Dodi play, he recognized the child's musical talent and accepted him as his pupil. Stolyarski's pedagogical methods worked well with Dodi over the next fourteen years. He was never to have another teacher.

Dodi gave his first public performance in 1914 when he was only six, opening a school matinee that ended with the graduation recital of violinist Nathan Milstein. The prodigy's greatest satisfaction was that he could easily do things that required considerable effort from others; he later recalled that "It gave me almost physical pleasure." Oistrakh remembered that when he was six, the progress of his musicianship was not remarkable despite his unusual prowess as a prodigy violinist. In his own words, he played "neatly, correctly, but it was boring and without a spark." Stolyarski would tease him with the nickname Old Granny.[7]

In 1923 when he was fifteen, Dodi began his conservatory studies at Odessa's Muzdramin, the music institute. In his first year in Stolyarski's violin class, Dodi appeared with the student orchestra, conducted by Grigori Stolarov, in a performance of Bach's Violin Concerto in A Minor. A year later, he gave his first solo concert, repeating the Bach concerto and including Tartini's sonata, "Devil's Trill," Sarasate's *Gypsy Airs*, and some shorter genre pieces. While still a member of the violin section of the conservatory orchestra, he went on his first tour outside Odessa as the orchestra's soloist, performing the Tchaikovsky concerto in three Ukrainian towns: Korovograd, Nikolaiev, and Kherson, the place where Leo Koutzen had been head of the local conservatory's violin department and his son, Boris Koutzen, had made his prodigy debut in 1912.

Dodi finished his studies with Stolyarski at the conservatory in Odessa in 1927. His graduation recital included Prokofiev's First Violin Concerto, the scherzo of which he would play the following year for the composer, and ended with his accomplished presentation of Anton Rubinstein's Sonata for Viola and Piano, Op. 49.

In the autumn of 1927 in Kiev he performed Alexander Glazunov's violin concerto with the composer conducting. After that engagement's success, an invitation came from the conductor Nikolai Malko for Dodi to perform Tchaikovsky's violin concerto as soloist with the Leningrad Philharmonic in 1928. He made his successful Leningrad debut when he was nineteen and appeared as a soloist in Moscow for the first time the following year.

In 1930, Oistrakh celebrated his first victory at a national music contest when he won first place at the all-Ukrainian violin competition in Kharkov. Later that year, he married Tamara Rotareva, an Odessa girl of Bulgarian descent who had graduated from the conservatory as a pianist. Their only child was born the next year on 27 April 1931. They named him Igor. Like his father, he too would be a concert violinist.

Dodi continued to fulfill the promise of his prodigy years. He competed again in 1935 at the second National Competition of Instrumentalists in Leningrad and won first prize. "Oistrakh's performance at the contest showed him as a violinist of a world class," wrote pianist Yakov Flier. "He stood out like a beacon, towering above all the other participants. His victory was unconditional."[8] Within weeks, he received an instruction from his government to take part in the First International Wieniawski Competition in Poland, where his experience in Russia's competitive arena would serve him well.

When his Warsaw adventure began, Oistrakh was mature enough to anticipate the competition with eager pleasure, yet he was indeed traveling outside Russia for the first time. Aboard a westbound train he began writing a series of letters to his wife, Tamara.[9] Nearing the Polish border on 2 March 1935, he wrote that he felt well and that day had practiced on the train. Two days later he wrote again: "Here I am in Warsaw, now I believe it." At the terminal the Russian contingent was met by the competition's organizer, Adam Wieniawski (the nephew of the composer), representatives of the Polish violinists, and the Russian consul, who brought the five Russian violinists to the embassy and made them comfortable.

On 4 March Dodi wrote about the gala opening of the competition, discussing the merits of the competitors he had heard thus far—a Pole who lived in Paris, the Hungarian Biro, the Dane Christiansen, the Polish woman, Grazyna Bacewicz, whose playing he compared to that of Ruth Posselt, and finally Bronislaw Gimpel, "a wonderful violinist with wide international experience." He mentioned rumors of a very strong Englishman in the competition, meaning Henri Temianka, the Polish violinist then living in England.

When he won the Leningrad prize in 1930, Oistrakh's perilous voyage to maturity had ended. Now, five years later, with his prodigy years behind him and his concert career well established in Russia, he sought international recognition at the Warsaw competition. His letters reveal the emergence of a confident artist, positive in his self image, tremendously focused, yet also generous in his appreciation of his fellow competitors. As the day of his own performance approached, he wrote Tamara that he felt very well, quite healthy, fairly calm, and that his hands were in good condition.

After he had played the program, he wrote her about his great moment saying, "I must tell you that I am terribly happy with my performance at the competition. I think it was the most successful performance of my whole life. Tomorrow I am starting to work on the concerto." In the nine days remaining, Oistrakh must have practiced both Wieniawski concertos because when asked on the day of his final performance which concerto he would play, he said that he had not yet made up his mind. Like Ginette Neveu, he finally chose the First Concerto in F-sharp Minor.

On 17 March, he wrote: "I cannot believe that it all ended so brilliantly: this is how I see the results of the competition. I am happy." He continued by speaking of Ginette Neveu who had won the first prize:

I must admit, Neveu is devilishly talented, I found it out for myself yesterday when she played the F-sharp Minor Concerto by Wieniawski with great force and conviction. Besides, she is no more than fifteen or seventeen [Neveu was sixteen], therefore one cannot say that her winning the first prize is grossly unfair.

HENRI

While David Oistrakh was speeding toward Warsaw on 2 March 1935, Henri Temianka was on an eastbound train from London. Temianka had been a child prodigy like Oistrakh and now was a mature concert violinist. Unlike Oistrakh, he was also an experienced world traveler who already knew, at age twenty-five, the machinations of the music business in Rotterdam, Berlin, Paris, London, Philadelphia, and New York—cities where he had lived, studied, and performed—yet he too had high hopes for what lay ahead at the competition in Warsaw.

On 19 November 1906, Henri Temianka was born in Greenock, Scotland, of Polish parents who were visiting Scotland from Rotterdam, where his father was a reasonably prosperous diamond merchant. When Henri was four, he had his first violin lessons from his father. To celebrate his seventh birthday, he was given violin lessons with Carel Blitz. The first time Henri went to the new violin teacher's house, he was more than a little frightened. He had no idea what a real violin teacher was like. Mr. Blitz greeted him warmly, took his little violin, and stood it upside down on his forehead, then with both arms spread wide, he did a precarious balancing act while crossing the room. He tuned Henri's little violin, then began to play it. "I, of course, had never heard anyone play so beautifully, and instantly vowed that some day I would play like Mr. Blitz," Temianka recalled. "When he handed the violin back, it felt quite different. It felt warm and comfortable. All of a sudden all the notes turned up in the right places. . . . Soon, Mr. Blitz became the fixed star by which I judged all other values."[10]

When Henri first played for Bronislaw Huberman, the great Polish violinist became interested in the boy's youthful career. The fourteen-year-old accompanied Huberman on concert tours in Holland, carrying his violin case and turning pages for his accompanist. On Huberman's advice, Henri moved to Berlin when he was fifteen to study with Willy Hess, a pupil of Joachim who was then professor at the Hochschule, but he soon went on to France to work with Jules Boucherit at the Paris Conservatory. There he labored during the day to attain the fabulous virtuoso career he hoped would be his; at night he played for a circus in Maestro Farinelli's orchestra where he was the last of the fiddlers.

Henri returned to Holland in the summer of 1924. As he walked past a cafe on the boardwalk in the seaside resort of Scheveningen, he met the conductor Ignaz Neumark, a long-time friend of the Temianka family. "Flesch is in town," the conductor announced.

"Flesch was no more eager to hear me than I was to play for him," Temianka recalled, but Ignaz Neumark arranged an audition before the great teacher left Holland for Philadelphia where he was head of the violin department at the new Curtis Institute. After just one minute, Flesch told the boy to put his violin away. Henri was crushed until he heard, "Can you come to America with me on Saturday?" Two days later they were on an ocean liner bound for the United States.

When Henri graduated from the Curtis Institute four years later, the school sponsored his New York debut in Town Hall. The New York critics were full of praise, but within weeks Henri realized that young virtuoso violinists have no prescribed future until they are better known. Flesch urged him to go to England where he was a citizen by birth. Henri went to London, took a room in a boardinghouse in St. John's Wood, and began to call on all the concert managers in town.

During an evening's work in a London theater orchestra, Henri had an accident with his Gagliano violin. It split from top to bottom, but he had little time to grieve because the next day, Harold Holt, the powerful English impresario who had managed Yehudi Menuhin's youthful career in England since 1932, called to say that Bronislaw Huberman had fallen ill and had to be replaced immediately. Henri borrowed a cheap violin and caught the train to Leicester, where he shared a concert with Luisa Tetrazzini, the famous but aging coloratura soprano. With Ivor Newton at the piano, he played Corelli's "La Folia" variations, then took the night train back to London. Hearing of Henri's success the next day, Harold Holt called again, offering him all the remaining concerts in England for which the ailing Huberman had been engaged. Henri accepted.

In February 1935, the Polish pianist Leopold Muenzer wanted to use the piano in Henri's London apartment to practice. One day as he was complaining about a piano string he had broken, he happened to mention the forthcoming Wieniawski competition in Warsaw. Although the deadline for applicants had passed, Muenzer wired the organizing committee, they waived the rules, and Henri was accepted—with three days remaining before he must take the train to Poland, precious little time to learn the Wieniawski caprices that were required in the first round, works he had not played before.

"Three chance happenings guided my career in ways that I could have neither planned nor foreseen," Temianka has said. Because he left Paris to return to Holland for the summer, he ended up studying with Carl Flesch in Philadelphia. Because he happened to have received an unexpected telephone call from Harold Holt when Huberman took ill, he got his first career break in England. "And because I happened to meet Leopold Muenzer in London, I won a prize in the Wieniawski Contest and started my international career."[11]

Boris Goldstein, Josef Hassid, and Ida Haendel gave dazzling performances in Warsaw in March 1935. Because the three young prodigies played in a way known to almost no other children and few adults, their venture in a competition that set the upper age limit of candidates at thirty exacted an immediate toll: at the conclusion of the contest these children had to face the realities of unexpected, sudden fame or momentary failure. The effect on the remaining years of their childhoods can only be imagined. Boris Goldstein, of whom least is known today, disappeared from the concert stage more than a half-century ago. Josef Hassid was tragically stricken with mental illness and died within a decade following the events in Warsaw. Only Ida Haendel, who is now approaching seventy, survived to become one of the century's supreme violinists.

BUSSIA

Born in 1923, Boris ("Bussia") Goldstein was one of several legendary violinists, including Mischa Elman, Nathan Milstein, and David Oistrakh, who grew up and studied in Odessa, where as a small child he became a violin pupil of Pyotr Stolyarski. In early March 1935, Bussia was sent by his government to compete in Warsaw. A few weeks later, he emerged in fourth place after Neveu, Oistrakh, and Temianka, an amazing accomplishment for a twelve-year-old competing against such formidable violinists.

In 1937, Bussia again joined a contingent of Russian violinists, including Oistrakh, Elizaveta Gilels, Marina Kozolupova, and Mikhail Fichteholz, in Brussels at the great international violin competition in the memory of

Eugène Ysaÿe. As he had done in Warsaw, Bussia placed fourth at the first
Ysaÿe Competition, but this time he reached his triumphant hour having
competed against a group of contenders numbering 125, instead of the
twenty-five to thirty violinists initially expected by the Belgian organizing
committee.

"What ever happened to Bussia Goldstein?" is a question one still hears
occasionally from European violinists who knew him and his playing in the
mid-1930s. After Bussia left the USSR and settled in the West, his amazing
violin playing disappeared from the world stage.

What happened to the Polish boy Josef Hassid is simpler to answer
because his adolescent life in England and his artistic success were well-
documented by his admirers.

JOSEF

Josef Hassid was an amazing child prodigy considered by many, notably his
last teacher, Carl Flesch, and Fritz Kreisler, to be among the most promising
instrumentalists of the twentieth century. Kreisler's often-quoted assess-
ment, heard and later reported by the son of Carl Flesch, grew out of a comparison he made between Hassid and another violinist (ever since unnamed)
during a visit to Flesch's home in London in the 1930s. On that occasion,
Kreisler said, "A fiddler such as X (mentioning a very famous name) is born
every one hundred years—one like Hassid, every two hundred."[12] However,
the practical result of the meeting of Kreisler and Hassid at a tea party in the
Flesch home was that Kreisler later helped Josef acquire a better violin, an
instrument made in Paris by J. B. Vuillaume, which Josef used for the
remainder of his playing life.[13]

Josef Hassid was born in 1923 in the small Polish town of Suwalki on the
Russian border. His mother died when he was an infant. As a small child he
studied with the local violin teacher in Suwalki before being taken by his
father to play for Bronislaw Huberman in Warsaw, where he remained to
study first with a violinist named Krystal, then from the age of ten with
Mieczyslaw Mihalowicz at the Chopin School of Music. After studying for
two years with Mihalowicz, Josef represented Poland in the 1935 Wieniawski Competition.

During his final performance at the Warsaw competition, Josef's memory betrayed him, but despite this most-dreaded catastrophe, the boy
received an honor diploma, coming second after the Hungarian Tomás Mag-

yar in the group of fifteen competitors so honored. "After his great disappointment when his memory failed," Lorand Fenyves recalled, "I took the
distraught twelve-year-old to a nearby cafe where for an hour he stuffed himself with sweets, crying all the while with frustration."[14]

At the wise suggestion made two years after the Warsaw competition by
Bronislaw Huberman, Josef was taken by his faithful and adoring father in
1937 to study with Carl Flesch in Spa, Belgium. The following year, the Hassids moved to London so that the boy could continue his work with Flesch,
and Josef gave a memorable performance in a private recital at the house of
Sir Philip Sassoon in Park Lane.

The last day of August 1939 was the last day of peace in Europe. With
the invasion of Poland on 1 September, Germany's ruthless international
tyranny launched a world war. Because no Jewish musician living in Poland
was exempt from the terror that followed, the Hassids decided to stay in
London.

Impresario Harold Holt took up Josef's cause and on 4 April 1940 presented him at the Wigmore Hall in his first formal recital in London. Billed
as "The Polish Boy Violinist" and accompanied by pianist Gerald Moore,
seventeen-year-old Josef performed works by Bach, Corelli, Debussy, Schubert, and Paganini. Three weeks later at the Queen's Hall, his superb performance of the Tchaikovsky concerto with the London Philharmonic, guest
conducted by his compatriot Gregor Fitelberg, generated the fervor of a large
audience. Ida Haendel recalled, "When we saw him step on to the stage, a
charming figure with his unruly black hair and modest manner, we knew he
would win all hearts."[15] Josef's London performances captured the attention
of record producer Walter Legge, who arranged for the young violinist's only
recording engagement. Again accompanied by pianist Gerald Moore, in 1940
Josef performed short works by Elgar, Tchaikovsky, Sarasate, Achron,
Dvořák, Kreisler, and Massenet in the HMV studios on Abbey Road, leaving
four 78 rpm records to posterity.

A sense of foreboding soon overwhelmed those who knew Josef well.
Before a performance of the Brahms concerto in London, his anxious father
decided he could not bear to attend the concert because Josef had not
touched his violin for a whole month, yet in the *Daily Telegraph* critic Ferrucio Bonavia wrote that the Brahms was far and away the finest he had ever
heard.[16]

Josef suffered acute depression. His personal life tormented him, and he
decided to give up the violin. Lord Horder, Winston Churchill's physician,

arranged for him to go to his own hospital where he sent the message, "I am sending you a genius." In a tragic turn of events, Josef Hassid had fallen ill with schizophrenia soon after his recording sessions. He never fully recovered.

Carl Flesch wrote his pupil, "I hope you will do everything within your will-power to get well again as soon as possible. A great artist like you owes it to the world to become active again."[17] After a year in the hospital, Josef returned home and attempted to revive his violin playing but instead tortured himself daily by designing ever-increasing technical challenges for his already formidable abilities.

Defeated at twenty-one, he withdrew from the world. A year later in a hospital at Epsom, he underwent a delicate, dangerous, and unsuccessful operation on a brain tumor. There his life ended, leaving only the legacy of his few recordings, eight short encore pieces captured on shellac.

IDA

Ida Haendel, one of the century's greatest violinists, was born on 15 December 1928 in the village of Chelm, Poland, not far from the Russian border. After she surprised her family by playing the violin spontaneously when she was three-and-a-half, her father recognized her gift and sought a master teacher for his child. On the advice of his violin-playing friend, Dobrowski, Nathan Haendel began his quest in Warsaw in the spring of 1932 when he took Ida to play for Mieczyslaw Mihalowicz, who had been a student of Leopold Auer in St. Petersburg. When Mihalowicz, a violin professor at the Chopin School of Music, accepted Ida as his pupil, the Haendel family moved to the capital where for several years they lived in desperate financial circumstances in one room in the Warsaw ghetto so that Ida could pursue her destiny in the city that had honored music for almost a millennium.

By the time she was five, the wonder child had begun playing the concertos of Mendelssohn and Tchaikovsky. When she was seven, her performance of Beethoven's violin concerto won her first prize in the Bronislaw Huberman Competition. "Whenever an important concert violinist visited Warsaw, invariably there was Mr. Haendel with his baby seeking an audition. Sometimes it was rather difficult to approach these people," Ida Haendel has recalled.[18] During that period, both Szymon Goldberg and Joseph Szigeti listened with amazement to the child's playing. When Szigeti, who was living in Paris, encouraged them, Nathan Haendel decided it was essential that

they go to there. He and Ida traveled to France in 1935 only to learn on
Szigeti's doorstep that the Hungarian violinist could not teach Ida because he
was soon to depart for a North American tour.

The first Henryk Wieniawski Violin Competition was to be held in
Poland in early March, and Nathan Haendel was convinced that if Ida won
there, she would be launched on a great career. A chance meeting with
Ignace Rubinstein (the brother of pianist Artur Rubinstein), who was an
acquaintance of Carl Flesch, gave Haendel a way to make contact with the
master teacher, hoping Flesch would prepare Ida for the competition in
Poland. Flesch began at once teaching her Sarasate's *Carmen Fantasy* and
soon presented her in a recital at Salle Gaveau. The preparations for Warsaw
were underway.

In early March, Ida's father took her to Warsaw for the competition. In
the final round the seven-year-old violinist performed Wieniawski's Second
Concerto, placing seventh among the international winners and winning the
special prize for Polish contestants, a high honor for the little girl from
Chelm. When she was invited to the palace of the president of the Polish
Republic and presented to him, the excitement was almost too much to
absorb.

After the competition, Ida's father took her to Germany where she continued her lessons with Carl Flesch at Baden-Baden. When Flesch decided
to take up residence in London, the Haendels followed. Ida was very excited
about studying with Flesch. She remembers him as a rigorous teacher, but
one who was always kind and affectionate to her, inspiring her great respect.

Ida was again taken to Paris when her father became determined that
she study Bach with Georges Enesco, the great Romanian violinist who had
taught Yehudi Menuhin. This course of action caused a serious rift between
Ida's father and Carl Flesch, but when Haendel brought his daughter back to
London, there was a reconciliation and Ida returned to the fold. She would
later feel that all these changes of teachers during her childhood resulted
from both her father's strong will and his genuine concern for her musical
development.

Although later in life she found it difficult to assess the differences that
she experienced as a child between the teaching of Flesch and Enesco, she
summarized her memories in this way: "Flesch knew exactly how to correct
faults, and like a surgeon pin-pointed exactly what needed to be done, and
made sure that the pupil understood. Enesco would not waste time telling
the pupil that something should be done this way or that, but instead would

demonstrate his point trying to convey its purpose, then say 'Go home and get it right.' And somehow you did."[19]

Although the nurturing team that would eventually steer her course was not yet complete in late 1936, once Harold Holt was engaged as her manager, her London career seemed assured. She recalled their first meeting:

> Harold Holt agreed to manage me, but first he wanted to hear me play so an audition was arranged at the Wigmore Hall. I just played a few bars from a concerto and he immediately rose, went to my father and said, "Mr. Haendel, I think we should try to launch Ida on the same type of career as Yehudi Menuhin—on a very big scale!"

Harold Holt arranged Ida's London debut recital at the old Queen's Hall when she was nine. The accomplished pianist Ivor Newton played for her in a program that included Mozart's Concerto in A Major, Bach's Chaconne, and *Poème* by Ernest Chausson, a melancholy work to which the child was passionately drawn. "Never in my then fairly young life," recalled Yfrah Neaman, a former Flesch pupil who heard the recital, "had I heard any artist, let alone anyone that young, who played with such enormous security and assurance and just as if she knew exactly where she was going both on the instrument and emotionally and musically."[20] Ida appeared again at the Queen's Hall in February 1937, this time playing the Brahms concerto at a Promenade Concert conducted by Sir Henry Wood, an event that marked the beginning of a treasured relationship with the conductor and a lifelong series of appearances at the Proms.

The entire Haendel family was joyfully reunited in 1939 after Ida's mother and sister arrived safely at Knokke in Belgium. Had Ida not been a prodigy violinist of such indescribable promise with the stringent early training that took her away from her native land, the family might well have remained in Warsaw and suffered the inevitable fate of Jewish people in wartime Poland. From Belgium, the Haendels returned to London and found a new home in Hampstead, for several years huddling together through endless nights in the Underground station at Belsize Park to avoid the apocalypse above, but ultimately surviving the war.

Ida's New York debut was planned for 1940 after her first recording sessions in London but was delayed six years by the war in Europe, during which time she gave many concerts in England under appalling conditions. With the war over, she set out for New York in 1946. Publicized by impresario Sol

Hurok as "The New Violin Sensation," she was presented in her Carnegie Hall debut in December. A young woman of eighteen, Ida had successfully made the transition from child prodigy to mature artist and would meet all the new challenges that lay ahead.

In her career, Ida Haendel appeared internationally in recitals and as soloist with orchestra, performing not only the time-honored masterpieces, but twentieth-century concertos by Edward Elgar, Benjamin Britten, and Sergei Prokofiev. Her unsurpassed interpretation of Jean Sibelius' violin concerto moved the composer to remark, "Above all, I congratulate myself that my concerto has found an interpreter of your rare standard."[21]

For those artists who are fascinated and beguiled by music's very nature from their first moments of awareness in early childhood, there may be no clear alternative to a lifelong pursuit of it. Reflecting on a career that has spanned more than sixty years, Ida Haendel has said, "Of course I would do it all over again! There is absolutely no doubt, because that is what I was born for. I am sure there was absolutely no other choice for me."

CHAPTER TEN

Virtuosos of the Twenties and Thirties From A to Z

ALDO PARISOT, ISAAC STERN,
JÁNOS STARKER, RUGGIERO RICCI,
MSTISLAV ROSTROPOVICH,
YEHUDI MENUHIN, AND ZARA NELSOVA

NOTHING dominated the postwar era of the mid-1920s in the United States so much as the new urban life with its movie houses and supermarkets and the mass-produced machine that offered previously unimagined mobility—the family automobile (Henry Ford produced his ten millionth car in 1924). While everyone enjoyed listening to the radio at home —there were already thirteen million in use—concertgoers in increasing numbers were more eager than ever to hear and see their favorite artists in live performances in the concert hall.

When Yehudi Menuhin first appeared in public in 1924, he created a sensation as a child prodigy. Accompanied at the piano by his teacher, Louis Persinger, the seven-year-old violinist performed Charles de Bériot's *Scène de ballet* in a San Francisco Symphony Orchestra concert at the Oakland Auditorium. As Ruggiero Ricci has said, "Yehudi got everyone thinking about prodigies."

Following Menuhin's earliest appearances, the prodigies Ruggiero Ricci, Zara Nelsova, Isaac Stern, Aldo Parisot, János Starker, and Mstislav Rostropovich each captured the imagination of twentieth-century music lovers. In San Francisco in 1928, Ruggiero Ricci made his debut at eight playing the Mendelssohn violin concerto. That same year, the ten-year-old Canadian cellist Zara Nelsova gave a masterful performance of Fauré's *Élégie* in Winnipeg. In 1932, twelve-year-old Aldo Parisot began playing cello recitals in Brazil. In 1933 in Hungary, cellist János Starker played in public for the first time when he was nine. He made his professional debut in 1938 at fourteen, performing the Dvořák concerto. The Russian-born violinist Isaac Stern made his debut in 1935 at fifteen with the San Francisco Symphony, playing Bach's Double Concerto with his teacher, Naoum Blinder. Mstislav Rostropovich also launched his career in 1935, in concert with his sister, Veronica, a violinist. In 1940 in Slaviansk, Ukraine, he gave his first performance with orchestra, playing the Saint-Saëns cello concerto. He was thirteen.

These prodigies had remarkable beginnings; some endured considerable struggles. From A to Z, here are reminiscences of the musical childhoods of seven amazing virtuosos.

ALDO

There is one thing you should know about me. Since the age of fifteen, I have had three dreams: I wanted to become a concert artist and tour all over the world; I wanted to own a Stradivarius cello; and I wanted to teach at a famous university. All of my dreams came true.

Parisot, in Wyman, "Life With a Strad"

One morning during a recital tour in the 1950s, Aldo Parisot and his pianist arrived in a small town in the American southwest to find that the portfolio of piano accompaniments had been left behind. Within minutes Parisot was on the telephone inquiring of a violinist who lived nearby, "Could I borrow some music? A stack of violin music will do." That evening he improvised a world-class recital, playing works rarely heard on the cello. Spontaneity and practicality have been defining elements in Parisot's life. An insightful judge of human nature, he has come to see teaching as his greatest contribution to the music world and has guided a new generation of cellists with his credo, "To make a success is easy. To keep a success is hard." Moving effortlessly between his studios at Yale, Juilliard, and The Banff Centre, he inspires disciplined, hard work, teaching with the same fiery passion that characterized his cello playing for half a century. Parisot, who was born on 20 September 1920, tells his own story.

There was an Italian cellist, Thomazzo Babini, who came to my home town of Natal, in northern Brazil, when it had only fifteen thousand people. (Today there are 1.5 million living there.) He had been playing all over Europe in a quite well-known piano trio. When the trio played in Natal, Babini fell in love with the town, and since he was tired of traveling, he decided to stay. He was offered two jobs and was soon

Aldo Parisot at thirteen, 1933. Courtesy Aldo Parisot.

teaching in a school for girls and at the Natal Conservatory. And he played at my mother's wedding!

My mother married an engineer who used to play flute as an amateur for his own pleasure. In 1924 when I was four years old my father died. I look at his picture now and know that this was my father, but I can't remember that face. A year later my mother married the cellist Thomazzo Babini and after their marriage I heard music at home. When I heard the cello, I immediately begged my mother to ask my stepfather if he would teach me, since I was afraid to ask him myself because I really didn't know him that well then. Because I showed a desire to learn the cello, she did ask him. At first he was not sure he would teach me at that age ("Kids of this age are really not very serious," he said), but finally he decided to teach me, so I started the cello when I was five.

My stepfather had been a pupil of Francesco Serato from the Italian cello school of Gilberto Crepax, Arturo Bonucci, and Luigi Silva. He was a tremendous virtuoso—a wonderful, fantastic player— and he had a pedagogical system based on the one in use in Bologna where he came from. The plan covered nine years of study divided into three equal parts, and one had to learn a certain repertoire every three years in order to command the whole system.

In the *first* year when I was five, I did the entire first three years of the program and later completed it all in only three years, instead of nine. I developed an enormous facility. How did he teach me the cello? First of all, he taught me solfège. I learned all the clefs using the books of Valerio Bona, the Italian theorist. In the last book of Bona, every note is in a different clef. Soon I could read music in every clef. In the cello lessons, my stepfather spent six months just with the bow arm, teaching me how to cross the strings. In the beginning he taught me the thumb position [the high registers], not the usual lower positions. He did this so that later I would not compare the lower positions with the thumb position and become afraid of the high registers. He had transcribed traditional etudes for the high positions. I would play these etudes—Friedrich Dotzauer etudes—in the high register and for the next lesson he would assign the same etude to be refingered. Every note! He would do this with every etude, assigning each one three consecutive times. What that did for me was two things: I was not afraid of the thumb position since I became comfortable there and it made me a fantastic sight reader because I knew how to use all kinds of different fingerings in all the positions.

I used to practice in a room next to him and when my intonation was wrong he used to come in and . . . twice he broke a cello bow over my head! At any rate, he was the only teacher I ever had. I went from the very beginning (at five) to eighteen years old under his guidance. Repertoire? I never saw a Bach suite until I was twenty years old. In our house there were no Bach suites, no Beethoven, no Brahms, but all the concertos of Romberg, Goltermann, Davidov, Servais, Popper. At the age of eleven (I wore short pants in those days) I was going all over South America with my stepfather playing all the most difficult concertos, but I had never seen a Bach suite. He worked with me on technique—everything about technique! There were no difficulties for me whatsoever. With my eyes closed, I used to play Paganini's *Moto perpetuo* on every concert because the public liked that kind of music. So this was the kind of training I got from my stepfather and the kind of training I still believe in. It is very important. Absolutely important.

My older brother, who was eight when our father died, played the violin. He became a banker and is still living in Rio. From my step-father's side, my mother had two girls and one boy, Italo Babini, who was also a student of my stepfather. Once when I played in Munich and saw Italo there (he was studying with a German cellist on a scholarship from Brazil), he wanted me to take him to the United States, so I arranged for him to come to Yale and study with me. But there he got impatient and didn't want to stay too long, so he left soon for a job. Italo is the principal cellist of the Detroit Symphony and has been there for many, many years.

When I was eighteen, I left Natal and went to Rio de Janeiro where there was an audition for principal cellist of the Brazilian Symphony. I won that audition, became principal cellist of the orchestra, and the rest is just history. Before I left home, my stepfather told me, "Now you know how to play the instrument, go and play chamber music, especially string quartet." The first quartet I was in was one where friends got together to read music. When the music was Beethoven's Opus 132, I thought, what kind of music is this? For me it was like waking up today and hearing Penderecki. But my stepfather had said, "go play chamber music," and that is what I have done.

In Rio I joined a quartet called the Jacovino Quartet which was

really the best in Brazil at that time. And that is when I met Heitor
Villa-Lobos. He was very close friends with the quartet and he and I
became very close friends also. I remember we once asked him if he
would write a quartet for us. "Yes, I'll write a new quartet for you," he
said, "but with the condition that you play my first quartet, a suite. I
hate it! but I want the public to also hear my *bad* works." He insisted
he wanted these works to be heard. So he wrote the quartet for us and
we played it . . . and the first quartet also.

The first great cellist I heard in my life was my stepfather. Who
was the second one? It was Pablo Casals in Rio in 1938. On that
recital he played the Locatelli sonata. Then I didn't know how to play
staccato (I learned that later in America listening to Piatigorsky). I was
in the front row and so interested in hearing this. Comes Casals and
. . . *no staccato.* I was so disappointed! Everything was so magnificent,
but no staccato.

At fourteen I heard one of Emanuel Feuermann's recordings at a
neighbor's house played on one of those old wind-up machines. That's
the way to play the cello, I thought, and I haven't changed my mind.
Later I had the good fortune to meet Carlton Sprague Smith, an
American diplomat who was the attaché in the American Embassy in
Rio. He arranged for me to go to the Curtis Institute in Philadelphia
where I had a scholarship to study with Feuermann, the one person
with whom I wanted to study. That was three months before Feuermann died on 25 May 1942. I was so discouraged!

When I was principal cellist of the orchestra in Rio, Ricardo
Odnoposoff, the Argentinean violinist, and I played the Brazilian
premiere of the Brahms Double Concerto in 1940. Just imagine! You
can see my country was one hundred years behind the times. Carlton
Sprague Smith said, "You should not stay in Brazil. There is nothing
here for you. I will arrange for you to go to Yale University."

In 1946 I came to Yale University where I was in the class of Paul
Hindemith. It was a way to come to America. When I was first at Yale,
my life was a little bit critical financially since I left Brazil with only
two hundred dollars in my pocket. I made a big tour all over Brazil to
get that money and I thought it would last longer, but it did not. Finally
one week I had no food to eat, but there were two jobs available on
campus, museum guard and latrine cleaner, and I got those jobs. I'm
very proud of doing that.

I won the Koussevitsky Prize in 1947 (they always pick one young instrumentalist) and made my debut with the Boston Symphony Orchestra at Tanglewood with my compatriot Eleazar de Carvalho conducting. The next year when I played in New York at Town Hall and Carnegie Hall, I got wonderful reviews. Later when I appeared as soloist with the New York Philharmonic for the first time, Columbia management suggested why not ask a Brazilian composer to write a work for me, so I wrote to Villa-Lobos, will you write a concerto for me? He said, "You are the cellist so you know it is so difficult to write for the cello, but I'll think about it. I am going to come to New York soon and I'll let you know." He called me when he got to New York and said, "I will write a concerto for you. I know how you play, but could you come to New York? I want you to practice in my hotel room."

I went to New York from New Haven every day for one week and there I practiced in his hotel room—scales, etudes, concertos—while he was writing. On one side he had the cello concerto, on the other side a symphony, and he was jumping from one to the other. And who was there during all those sessions? Andrés Segovia! He was a very close friend of Villa-Lobos and he was there, sitting and waiting for the lunch! Segovia loved Brazilian food, so he was always waiting for his lunch and wouldn't say a word!

When Villa-Lobos had something ready in the concerto, he'd let me try the passage. Then he would say, "No, no, Aldo. Not that way, this way." He loved to hear sliding on the cello, not shifting connections, but real slides. And he would demonstrate. In one week he had the whole thing blocked out. Tailor made. I performed it with the Philharmonic on 5 February 1955, with Walter Hendel conducting. Villa-Lobos was in the audience, and as usual he never stood up to acknowledge the applause. No way! And I was trying to get his attention—I even spoke in Portuguese above the heads of the audience— wanting him to come to the stage, but he would not. He was a wonderful man and very funny, especially telling Brazilian dirty jokes.[1]

ISAAC

I studied with Naoum Blinder until I was seventeen and after that I never studied with anyone. I was responsible for my own mistakes. It is a process of intellectual and personal involvement with music as an idea and a way of life, not as a profession or career, but a rapport with people who think and feel and care about something. You have to find your own way of thinking, feeling, and caring.

Stern, in Collins, "Isaac Stern"

Isaac Stern was the soloist in a performance of the Brahms violin concerto. I remember the exact moment in the finale when he shared such a passionate dialogue with the cellos that I thought to myself, this is the grandest violin playing I have ever heard. Stern was thirty-five. Three years later in 1959, he demonstrated to the world of music that he was more than a great musician. He was an extraordinary leader. In New York, he organized, then spearheaded, the citizens' committee that saved Carnegie Hall from demolition. In recent decades, Stern helped establish the National Endowment for the Arts in the United States and the Jerusalem Music Centre in Israel where he has guided the America-Israel Cultural Foundation, (the Mishkenot is a center for creative artists and scholars). For a life's work devoted to music and to humanity, Isaac Stern received the first Albert Schweitzer Music Award in 1975. The documentary film *From Mao to Mozart*, made during his visit to China in 1981, portrays Isaac Stern in one of his most important roles, that of a teacher nurturing young artists from all over the world.

Isaac was born on 21 July 1920 in Kremenetz, a small town on the Polish-Russian border. His parents were well-educated, middle-class Russians who revered music. His mother had studied singing at the St. Petersburg Conservatory in a city closed to Jews by csarist law and, like Jascha Heifetz and others of the period, was only allowed to do so by special decree. In the spring of 1921 when Isaac was only ten months old, the Stern family escaped the chaos of their village to build a new life in San Francisco.

Isaac's music lessons began at home when he started playing the piano at age six. When he was eight he heard a neighbor practicing the violin and knew instantly that he preferred the violin to the piano. In 1930 when he was ten, he entered the San Francisco Conservatory to study with the Russian violinist Naoum Blinder, who had been a pupil of Adolf Brodsky at the Moscow Conservatory. In 1928 Blinder had succeeded Louis Persinger, who taught both Menuhin and Ricci, as concertmaster of the San Francisco Symphony when Persinger left to teach at the Juilliard School. Isaac's training with Blinder, like that of David Oistrakh with Pyotr Stolyarski, was in the early twentieth-century tradition of the Moscow-Odessa school of violin.

From 1932 to 1937, Isaac worked exclusively with Blinder and after the late 1930s had no further formal training.

Unlike Menuhin and Ricci who were pushed into the prodigy limelight before they were ten, Isaac's childhood was not unduly strained. Naoum Blinder helped create for the young boy a marvelous environment of fraternity with the musicians of the orchestra during his formative years. Isaac frequently played chamber music with these musicians and they treated him as an equal, although he was two generations younger than any of them. He was soon "one of the fellows" and this mattered greatly to the gregarious Isaac. In their company he learned the chamber music repertoire, attended orchestra and opera rehearsals, and heard and met the great soloists of the day.

In 1935 when he was fifteen, Isaac made his debut with the San Francisco Symphony playing Bach's Double Concerto with his teacher. The following year he appeared with the Los Angeles Symphony, conducted by Otto Klemperer, playing the Tchaikovsky concerto.

On 11 October 1937, Isaac made his New York debut at the age of seventeen. He performed a recital at Town Hall, accompanied by Arpád Sándor. His playing was well received by the New York critics, but he was troubled at this crossroads, questioning whether he should continue to pursue a soloist's career or turn aside. The day after his recital he disappeared for a lonely bus ride. During the interminable eight hours of his journey around Manhattan, he made his decision. He would continue.

When he returned to play again at Town Hall on 18 February 1939, his performance was a resounding success, and he took his place among the most significant American concert violinists. "It was an instant love affair to be on stage and to see people," Stern has said. "To this day I enjoy being on stage. It is home for me. I felt at home almost from the beginning."

In 1943 Isaac made a triumphant debut in Carnegie Hall, the great bastion of music that he would help save from demolition in 1959. A few months later he performed with the young and exuberant Leonard Bernstein. When the two came on stage for their curtain calls before an enthusiastic audience, Bernstein whispered to Isaac, "Isn't it marvelous to be young and famous?" The success must have been sweet indeed for Isaac Stern. Although he had been the third great San Francisco violin prodigy, his youthful career had unfolded without the early exposure that this might have brought. He keep faith with those who nurtured him: Naoum Blinder, his sole teacher; Alexander Zakin, his pianist; Sol Hurok, his impresario; and Columbia Masterworks for whom he began recording in 1945.[2]

In 1996, the San Francisco Conservatory of Music established the Isaac Stern Distinguished Chair in Violin to fund a professorship in violin in honor of Stern, who continues to support the institution where his career began.[3]

JÁNOS

When I reached the grand old age of nine, I loudly declared that I was going to play the cello as long as I lived and would try to play it as well as possible. . . . I was a child prodigy, but it was an unexploited passing fad. When I realized that this is not what makes a musician, I began to study seriously.

Starker, in Rooney, "Calm Mastery"

I first heard János Starker playing Kodály's Sonata for Solo Cello on a phonograph recording in 1951. What a revelation! When we became friends and teaching colleagues twenty-five years later, it was my best fortune to be in his musical presence, to hear his inimitable, patrician performances on stage, and to witness his pedagogical mastery in the teaching studio, where he works exclusively from his extraordinary memory. In an interview for the *New York Times* in 1972, Starker remarked, "Sometimes I am inclined to say that temperamentally I am much more of a pedagogue than a concert artist. In my mind, teaching is far more significant than playing concerts because what I do as a teacher affects generations."[4]

Alexander and Margarete Starker and their two older sons were living in Budapest when János was born on 5 July 1924. Because both his brothers were studying the violin, their teacher, Deszö Rados, advised his parents that János learn to play the cello. He was sent to the Franz Liszt Academy when he was seven to study with Adolf Schiffer and there he spent his prodigy years. Adolf Schiffer guided generations of Hungarian cellists, first as David Popper's assistant, then as his teaching successor. Among them were Miklós Zsámboki, Géza Belle, Pál Herman, Vilmos Palotai, and Gabor Rejtő. The amazing Starker child was to be Adolf Schiffer's final pupil before his retirement, but Ernst von Dohnányi, director of the academy at that time, extended Schiffer's tenure at the school so that he could establish a pedagogy class in cello. In this changing intellectual environment, János became a fledgling teacher and by the age of twelve had eight students. "I had to explain *why* this is bad, or *how* to put the thumb here instead of there. For this I am eternally grateful," Starker has said.[5] Articulating musical and technical thoughts so early in his life proved enormously helpful to his growth.

János Starker at twelve, with his teacher Adolf Schiffer at Cortina d'Ampezzo,
Italy, 1936. Courtesy János Starker.

"These circumstances helped to create the climate that made it possible for me to spend a lifetime trying to find all the problems and various answers."[6]

At the academy he came under the influence of the composer Leo Weiner and the avant-garde violin pedagogue Imre Waldbauer ("These two men were the ones who gave me the first tools that enabled me to justify and explain what I was doing"), both of whom taught him chamber music. The boy's cello playing developed exceedingly quickly. By eleven he had played the Bartók string quartets. The following year he was playing professionally and, between the ages of twelve and fifteen, earning a living. When he was fourteen, János made his debut in a performance of the Dvořák concerto, the masterpiece he would perform hundreds of times in the five decades of his mature career.

János' perilous journey to maturity began in the grim realities of World War Two, when like millions of others he suffered personal tragedy—his brothers were killed and his own life frequently endangered. In the war's final year, he stopped playing the cello altogether, but after he returned to it, within a month he was playing recitals in Romania and joined the Budapest Philharmonic and Opera orchestras in 1945. After a debut in Vienna, one critic wrote that he played with "the security of a sleepwalker."

Yet János began to have self doubts. "It was then that I, who played very well and never had any particular problems, began to think: 'What if I started having problems?'" János had witnessed the demise of prodigy careers and felt that the failures came from not understanding the challenges involved. He didn't play in public again for seven months, during which time he lived in Paris and began to formulate what became his now-famous *Organized Method of String Playing*. Speaking of this period of disillusionment, Starker has said, "What happens to the bird who sings and doesn't know how it sings?"

> That's what happens to child prodigies. They wake up and ask themselves dangerous questions about how they do it—and have no answers. I nearly had a nervous breakdown. Consistency is the difference between the professional and the amateur. I was grown up and could no longer depend on instinct.[7]

Starker came to the United States in 1948 when Antal Doráti invited him to become principal cellist of the Dallas Symphony. That year in Paris his first recording of the Kodály solo sonata had won the Grand Prix du

Disque, marking the onset of a career before the microphone that has continued until the present. He soon joined the Metropolitan Opera orchestra, conducted by Fritz Reiner, then in 1953 became principal cellist of the Chicago Symphony. Five years later, he launched a career as soloist and at the same time joined the staff of the School of Music at Indiana University. For the next forty years, János Starker sustained an international career doing the two things he loves best—playing and teaching. "I am deadly serious about what I do in music, but not about myself," Starker has said. "Anyone who has proven that he can do something exceptionally well or better than others, has a right to be proud, but only with regard to that accomplishment. For the rest, I am individually no different to anyone else."[8]

RUGGIERO

The violin is probably the most hellish invention ever conceived by man, a beautiful and treacherous work of art that demands our constant attention but can never be completely dominated.

Ricci, in Campbell, *The Great Violinists*

Even though it was past time to take Ruggiero Ricci to the concert hall, my friend and I still sat drinking coffee with him at his hotel, excited at the prospect of asking one or two more questions about his Paganini recordings. "How did you record the fifth caprice at such a fast tempo with *that* bowing?" brought a quick response from Ricci. "Three things: I put some cotton in my left ear so as not to hear my Guarneri [that job was for the microphone], I had the technician turn off the red light, then I played and didn't let anything or anybody stop me until I was finished!"

Later when we lingered with him before the concert, the stage manager admitted a quiet lady with a battered violin case. "I think it is a Vuillaume," she murmured, handing him the fiddle, "but it hasn't been played in years. Old strings. A few cracks." Imagine our surprise when a little later Ricci walked on stage with that strange fiddle in hand and launched into a superlative performance of Bruch's *Scottish Fantasy*.

Ricci is a daring violinist! On 10 January 1987 in Ann Arbor, Michigan, Ricci (then sixty-seven) filmed Paganini's twenty-four caprices in only one day. This unedited video masterpiece, along with his three sound recordings of the caprices made in 1947, 1960, and 1978, form an unparalleled document of violin virtuosity.

For a time they called him Woodrow Wilson Rich to disguise his Italian background from an anglophile public. The third child of seven in a large Italian family, Ruggiero Ricci was born on 24 July 1920 in San Bruno, California. Four years later Yehudi Menuhin's sensational debut as a child prodigy sparked an obsession in Papa Ricci. The struggling trombonist from Genoa, barely able to support his family, decided to produce a violin prodigy of his own. He began giving the boy lessons at home, certain this child held the promise to the family's future.

"I started before I can remember," said Ricci. "If it weren't for Menuhin, I wouldn't be here."

Elizabeth Lackey, Louis Persinger's assistant, with the Ricci brothers in 1927: Giorgio, at the left, and Ruggiero, then five, at the right. Courtesy Ruggiero Ricci.

Believe me, when you find a prodigy, you find an ambitious parent in the background. My father was some kind of musical maniac. He bribed me with fiddles. I'd wake up in the morning and there would be another one. Once I had five fiddles under my bed.[9]

When he was seven, Ruggiero was auditioned by Louis Persinger, whose fame as a teacher had escalated after Menuhin's debut. After hearing the boy play variations on "The Blue Bells of Scotland," the perceptive Persinger came to his aid. He taught him regularly, but also arranged for the boy to have daily lessons with his assistant, Elizabeth Lackey. It was a winning combination.

On 28 January 1928, Ruggiero took part in a violin playing contest at San Francisco's Emporium Auditorium sponsored by Boys' Achievement Club. He played "with amazing feeling on a quarter-size violin, and got a clear, resonant tone full of sweet charm." It was Sigmund Anker, William Bickett, and John Vogel who judged "Roger Rich," a pupil of Miss Betty Lackey of Berkeley, as the gold medal winner. It was his first prize, but later that year Ruggiero was awarded the Oscar Weil Scholarship, to continue his studies.

On 15 November 1928, Ruggiero gave his first public recital at San Francisco's Scottish Rite Hall. Louis Persinger was at the piano to accompany works by Vieuxtemps, Saint-Saëns, and Wieniawski—and the Mendelssohn concerto in a performance hailed as "nothing short of genius." With the boy's value as a prodigy established, a struggle erupted for control over his childhood. Ruggiero spent more and more time with Lackey. Her home became his, he saw no other children, didn't go to school, visited his family only on Sundays. The adults in his life committed him to playing the violin with no reprieve. He practiced four hours in the morning, studied with a tutor in the afternoon, practiced again, ate his supper, did his homework, then went to bed.

In October 1929, a concert was arranged in New York. Henry Hadley conducted the Manhattan Symphony Orchestra at the Mecca Temple when Ruggiero performed a Mozart concerto, the Mendelssohn concerto, and Vieuxtemps' *Fantasia appassionata*. After hearing Ricci's New York debut at the age of ten, Olin Downes wrote in the *Times*, "It was the playing of one born to play his instrument." The *New York Telegraph* described the boy as "the greatest genius of our time in the world of interpretive music."[10]

By 1930 Elizabeth Lackey was the legal guardian of both Ruggiero and his brother, Giorgio. (George Ricci later became a distinguished cellist.) After a separation of sixteen months from his sons, Ruggiero's father attempted to regain custody. In the opening court proceedings, he alleged that his boys were now "forcibly and wrongfully detained and deprived of their liberty." During the forty-one hearings that took place over seven months, a patron who had subsidized Ruggiero's studies sided with the father in claiming financial and physical exploitation. A neurologist testified that a pending tour would be excessive, but others argued to the contrary. Lackey's attorneys cited the concert activities of other prodigies. A music critic testified that genius needed public appearances. The California court dismissed the parents' appeal for custody, and Ruggiero completed the tour of ten scheduled concerts during which the New York Society for the Prevention of Cruelty to Children observed him. On 30 December 1930, the New York Supreme Court decreed that parental custody be restored.[11]

In 1929 Yehudi Menuhin went to Europe to study with Adolf Busch; after following Persinger to the Juilliard School, Ruggiero was sent to Leopold Auer's pupil, Michel Piastro, concertmaster of the New York Philharmonic. With the departure of Yehudi and Ruggiero from his studio, Louis Persinger lost his two famous prodigy pupils to other teachers.

Ruggiero's study with Piastro was not successful: "When I was nine or ten, it was beautiful fiddle playing. By the time I was twelve it was a fiasco," Ricci has said. "They took me and they changed me."

> Persinger was of the Belgian school, and when I was taken away from him they sent me to Michel Piastro. He was trained in the Russian tradition, and he thought I was a genius or something, so he threw the Brahms concerto at me.[12]

Adverse criticism began. The Stradivarius violin he played was too large for him and he didn't play well. Ruggiero was used to adoration, and now it was withdrawn. His youth had become an embittered struggle. "I wasn't a child anymore and I wasn't grownup. I was fighting my image."

On a successful tour of twenty concerts in Germany in 1932, Ruggiero played in Berlin, where he was received by Gerhart Hauptmann and Chancellor Franz von Papen and met Albert Einstein, for whom he played and who in turn played the violin for him. Ruggiero's further study with the Berlin violinist Georg Kulenkampff brought only confusion and frustration for the young violinist.

He limited his performances and began a period of intensive, self-directed study. He was inducted into the United States Army Air Force in 1944 for three years and at the end of World War Two played extensively for the troops abroad. Ruggiero also studied the music of Paganini, mastering the fingering, shifting, and bowing needed in the twenty-four caprices. Ricci has said, "I learned more about technique from Paganini than I did from any of my teachers."[13]

Although Mischa Elman advised him against excluding the traditional violin repertoire with piano accompaniment, when Ricci returned to the stage of Carnegie Hall in November 1946, he played a successful concert of unaccompanied music by Bach, Ysaÿe, Hindemith, and Paganini. The following year he made his first recording of the complete Paganini caprices. Despite the adversity of his childhood, Ruggiero Ricci, heir to Paganini's legacy, has remained one of the greatest violinists of all time.

SLAVA

According to Tolstoy, music begins where speech ends. The process of musical communication is, indeed, absolutely specific. Music speaks to mankind and addresses the human heart with a particular language much more profound than the spoken word. For me, the spoken word is to music as earthly life is to life in the hereafter.

      Rostropovich, in Samuel, *Mstislav Rostropovich and Galina Vishnevskaya*

"Sputnik!" someone yelled out when Mstislav Rostropovich entered the dining room of the Hotel Meurice in Mexico City. It was 15 January 1959, and we were gathering for a short journey to Jalapa for the second International Pablo Casals Competition. Rostropovich would be on the jury. We were impressed by this young cello professor from the Moscow Conservatory. He was only thirty-two and both Prokofiev and Shostakovich had already composed concertos for him.

In Moscow in 1964, he performed most of the basic concerto repertoire over a nine-month period. He repeated the feat in 1965 in London's Festival Hall. In New York in 1967 he played a cycle of twenty-nine solo works with the London Symphony in Carnegie Hall. In each marathon, Rostropovich's vast repertoire ranged from the music of Vivaldi, Tartini, and Haydn, to new twentieth-century masterpieces composed for him by Dmitri Shostakovich, Sergei Prokofiev, André Jolivet, Walter Piston, and Benjamin Britten (the Cello Symphony, Op. 68), among others.

At all the events of the 1959 competition in Mexico, Rostropovich was surrounded by his countrymen, a vanguard of Cold War bureaucrats, body-guards, and interpreters. Over the next fifteen years as his world fame increased, his strained relations with the Soviet authorities intensified each time he left his country. Sheltering his friend, the dissident writer Alexander Solzhenitzyn, finally led to Rostropovich's exile from Russia. In 1978, he and his wife, soprano Galina Vishnevskaya of the Bolshoi Opera, were stripped of their Soviet citizenship. A Russian patriot to the core, then and now, Ros-tropovich is a citizen of the world. The International League for the Rights of Man in New York has recognized his courageous stand for artistic freedom.

Mstislav Rostropovich at thirteen, performing at Slaviansk, 1940. Courtesy Mstislav Rostropovich.

Rostropovich has said, "Shostakovich once told me, 'Slava, we are all soldiers of music. There are no generals among us. If people throw stones at
you, don't leave the stage. Stand firm. . . . Play to the end.'"[14]

Slava was born into a family of musicians in Baku, Azerbaijan, in the Soviet
Union on 27 March 1927. His grandfather, Vitold Rostropovich, had been a
professional cellist and teacher; his father, Leopold, was also a cellist, a pupil
of Alexander Verzhibilovich and Pablo Casals; his mother, Sofia, was an
excellent pianist; and his sister, Veronica, became a professional violinist in
the Moscow State Philharmonic. When asked who decided he would
become a cellist, Rostropovich remarked, "There was no 'decision;' everything happened naturally."

> My father was an absolutely phenomenal cellist. He was also an
> excellent pianist. He played everything by heart. And he was an
> extraordinary sight-reader; I must say that I never met another
> performer as gifted in the art. He wanted to acquaint me with the
> piano repertoire, and I recall how he sight-read a Rachmaninov
> concerto; it was miraculous! I don't say all the notes were right there,
> but it was on the whole absolutely extraordinary.[15]

When he was four, Slava had piano lessons from his mother and began
to compose. His father decided that he should study with a master teacher
and moved the family to Moscow in 1934. Destitute except for a fake Persian
rug and a Japanese ivory carving, both made in a village outside Moscow, his
father found no work. An angry landlord who had rented them a corner of his
room confiscated the "treasures" and pushed his lodgers into the street. An
Armenian family living in a communal apartment with seven other families
took them in. For two years the boy and his father both practiced the cello in
a corner of that one-room dwelling where there was never any sunshine.
"Evenings we crowded around the piano," Rostropovich has said, "and my
father played a tango called 'Tougher than Death.' I was only six, but I
remember that tango and I often play it for myself."[16]

Slava appeared in public for the first time in 1935 when he played in a
concert with his sister, Veronica. Five years later he gave his first performance with orchestra, playing the Saint-Saëns concerto in Slaviansk, Ukraine,
where his father was a member of the orchestra. "That first concert was
unforgettable. I was thin as a rail then; I barely had any strength, and the first

time I played with an orchestra, I had a lot of trouble making myself heard. I suffered. That was during my adolescence."

In 1942 the family was evacuated to Orenburg in the Ural mountains. During the frigid winter, Leopold's heart failed. The trauma of his death brought on a serious illness for Slava at thirteen, but his godmother, a schoolteacher, took the family in and by gradually emptying her rooms, bartered her possessions for food for them. Villagers brought them a stove: "They dragged it in and left. Total strangers. Can I ever forget such things, or what my obligations are for them?"

At the Second American Cello Congress in Arizona, Mstislav Rostropovich, the distinguished cellist and conductor who commands the absolute attention of the world's musical community, told a story of his childhood, a story of a child who had begun giving cello lessons to earn a little money for his starving family, a boy who joined a small group of traveling musicians, members of an evacuated Leningrad opera company who were giving concerts in nearby towns. The three hundred cellists gathered that June evening in Arizona won't easily forget Rostropovich's emotional tale, which unfolded in a voice trembling with passion.

"During the winter of 1942, six of us were on the train from Orenburg going on to the next place," Rostropovich began:

> Each of us was given one thin blanket, but it was so cold in that unheated train car that my teeth would not stop chattering. So terribly, terribly cold! And my father was gone, my mother suffering. I lay down and thought this would be a good time to die. I fell into deep sleep. And woke up warm! Six blankets—all the blankets we had—were piled on top of me. One by one, the others had covered me with their blankets during the night. . . . This is the debt I must repay. This is why I want to give something back with my music. It is a debt to all people, but most of all to *my* people, who gave me what they did. Who made me a person and a musician.[17]

For Rostropovich, the inner life and imagination are much more important than the material world around him. "I have all of Russia in my mind and never detach myself from it."

YEHUDI

*My parents took me to concerts when I was a small child and intuitively
I reached out for an instrument that I sensed would be able to express my
feelings. So at that stage I sought out the violin not so much for the purpose
of playing to an audience, but simply to fulfill my need to find an outlet for
my emotions.*

Menuhin, in Daniel, Conversations With Menuhin

When my string quartet first visited the Yehudi Menuhin School in England
in 1972 to play a concert, Menuhin was away, but his presence was felt
everywhere in the little Surrey village of Stoke d'Abernon. Because he had
created a well-balanced artistic environment for learning music, it was not
the pony or the swing in the oak tree, nor the treasured music lessons that,
in themselves, seemed to matter most in that idyllic setting; it was their magical synthesis, the way that all the elements worked together in this unusual
boarding school for greatly gifted children.

Ever since Menuhin was a boy, concert audiences have loved not only
his magnificent violin playing, but the strength of his artistic conviction and
his humility. Once during the slow movement of a great violin concerto he
had played for a lifetime, his bow began to tremble on the string. Every one
of several thousand listeners took a deep breath and waited for this unwel-
come moment to pass. It did. Menuhin went on, the music went on, life
went on. Greatness unfolded. More than for the public image projected by
concert managements and governments, Lord Menuhin, at eighty, is loved
for himself, for his seven, valiant decades on the world's stages.

When the final chords of Beethoven's violin concerto sounded, the audience
in Carnegie Hall, overwhelmed with wonder, rose in a sustained, ecstatic
ovation. It was 25 November 1927, and an eleven-year-old violinist in a white
silk blouse and velvet knickers had given a miraculous performance of the
great masterpiece. The next day, Lawrence Gilman, critic of the *Herald Tribune*, commented: "What you hear takes your breath away and leaves you
groping helplessly in the mysteries of the human spirit."[18]

Although the young child had already played many important concerts,
Yehudi achieved international fame as a child prodigy in his celebrated debut
in Carnegie Hall with the New York Symphony, conducted by Fritz Busch.
Critics, audience, and orchestra shouted and cheered. Many cried, profoundly moved. Yehudi brought his teacher, Louis Persinger, on stage to

Yehudi Menuhin at eight, 1925. Courtesy Lord Menuhin.

share the ovation. No one would leave until the little boy put on his hat and coat. Of course, he would be back on that stage, and soon.

Born in New York on 22 April 1916, he grew up in San Francisco where his childhood as a prodigy was both well-protected and orderly. Menuhin has recalled listening to the San Francisco Symphony, his attention focused on concertmaster Louis Persinger.

> I asked my parents if I might have a violin for my fourth birthday and Louis Persinger to teach me to play it. . . . Quite simply I wanted to be Persinger, and with equal straightforwardness proposed the means of bringing this enviable situation about.[19]

After an initial rejection from Persinger, who made no profession of teaching little children, Yehudi was taken to study with Sigmund Anker ("His method was to set up a target—correct intonation, full round tone, or whatever—and whip his pupils toward it by unexplained command"), but Menuhin's mother soon tried again to place her son under Persinger's guidance. This time she was successful. Hearing Persinger play Bach in his studio, Yehudi and his mother were transfixed, and the boy knew that this musical world was what must surely lie ahead for him. "I knew this sublimity was what I must strive for," Menuhin has said, "and that [my mother] expected my striving no less than I did myself."

The season after his San Francisco Symphony Orchestra concert at age seven, he joined the orchestra again for Lalo's *Symphonie espagnole*. Before he was nine he gave his first full recital at San Francisco's Scottish Rite Hall. When Persinger moved to New York to teach at Juilliard, the Menuhins returned to New York as well. Yehudi would play his first New York recital at the Manhattan Opera House on 25 March 1925.

It was off to Europe the following year when the entire family, including Yehudi's gifted sisters Hephzibah and Yaltah, went to Brussels. Yehudi played not very convincingly for Eugène Ysaÿe, then begged to be taken to Georges Enesco on the next train to Paris. This proved the beginning of a fulfilling period.

After his Carnegie Hall performance of the Beethoven concerto in 1927, Yehudi had returned briefly to California to work further with Persinger, who was there for the summer. Victor sent recording engineers to Oakland, and Yehudi, twelve years old, made his first recordings before he and Persinger set out on a transcontinental concert tour. With Persinger at the piano,

Yehudi played a concert for each of fifteen weeks and upon his arrival in New York performed the Tchaikovsky concerto at Carnegie Hall.

In an unexpected turn of events, a patron of the arts, Mr. Henry Goldman, told the boy to choose any violin he wanted. At the shop of Emil Herrman, Yehudi found the "Prince Khevenhüller" Strad, a magnificent violin made in 1733 when Antonio Stradivarius was ninety. A week after the 1929 crash of Wall Street, the violin was paid for and Yehudi had his first Strad.

On Enesco's advice, the boy was taken to Basel, Switzerland, in 1929 to study with the great German violinist Adolf Busch. On 12 April, a few days before his thirteenth birthday, Yehudi appeared in a demanding performance of three great concertos with the Berlin Philharmonic, conducted by Bruno Walter. The concert aroused such passion among the audience that management summoned the police to restore order. Albert Einstein came into the artists' room directly from the stage, hugged Yehudi, and said: "Now I know there is a God in heaven."

Success followed success. In 1932 at the age of sixteen, Yehudi Menuhin and Sir Edward Elgar made musical history in London at the Abbey Road studios of His Master's Voice when they recorded Elgar's violin concerto. They repeated the performance several months later before the English public at the Royal Albert Hall. The early Menuhin performances of Elgar's masterpiece remain the standard of the musical world. And they mark the close of the amazing prodigy's childhood career. In his maturity, Yehudi Menuhin has continued to perform as a concert violinist and conductor for six decades.

The concept of the Yehudi Menuhin School came to the violinist during his visit to the Central School of Music in Moscow at the end of the Second World War. "The school was the happiest place I saw," said Menuhin. "The children were beautifully looked after. The place was a shining example of what a music school should be." It took eighteen years for his dream of such a school in England to become a reality. On 16 September 1963, Menuhin opened its doors to fifteen pupils. Students between the ages of eight and sixteen are admitted by rigorous audition. From the outset, in addition to the highest standard in the study of instruments, there has been a breadth of activity, a far-reaching overall vision of cultivating well-balanced human beings.[20]

"Many children have gifts," Lord Menuhin said of his more recently initiated innovative program to take music, mime, and dance to disadvantaged children. "All children have some gifts. But very few children have the good fortune to have the right background, the parents, the teachers, the opportunity, the encouragement, the love that I had."[21]

ZARA

The power which has sustained me throughout my life—as a young player and throughout my development as an artist—is the love for music and the love for the cello.

Nelsova, 1995

Surely everyone has a prized memory of a great performance that can be savored at will. I recall a warm August evening in London in 1969 when the Royal Albert Hall was filled to capacity for a Proms concert. In the tradition of Victorian England, a large fountain was splashing under the sky-high dome, and the stage area was choked with the audience of young people who promenade before these concerts. The noisy hum of humanity reverberated until a hush fell over the crowd. Carrying the "Marquis de Corberon" Strad, the regal Zara Nelsova came on stage to play the Elgar concerto, followed by Sir Charles Groves, who would conduct the BBC Symphony Orchestra. When Nelsova challenged the orchestra from the highest reaches of her cello during the first movement, a shock overwhelmed the rapt audience. I agreed when pianist Brian Harris sitting beside me whispered, "She's gone to heaven!"

I have known and admired Zara Nelsova most of my life. Our friendship has given me many treasured memories, but the one that time will never extinguish transports me back to the Albert Hall on that warm August evening long ago and directly to the heart of Elgar's cello concerto.

Zara was born on 23 December 1918 in Winnipeg. She shares her story.

My very early studies began in Winnipeg with my father, Gregor Nelsov, in 1922 when I was almost five years old. My father was determined to have a "sisters trio" and since my two sisters, Anna and Ida, were already playing the piano and violin, he was impatient to have me start the cello. He produced a full-sized instrument which, of course, was much too large. I cried with disappointment! Several days later he brought a viola converted into a cello complete with strings and end pin.

Zara Nelsova at ten, 1928. Photograph by Gregor Nelsov. Courtesy Zara Nelsova.

I remember making my early debut in Winnipeg in 1924 when I was about five-and-a-half years old. Soon after I became a student of Deszö Mahalek, a wonderful cellist who had immigrated to Canada from Hungary. (Years later I learned that Deszö had been one of David Popper's favorite students.) I just adored Deszö because he was so interested in me, and very anxious to help. He and my father would work together to figure out the best way to overcome a particular problem. I remember while practicing when I was about seven years old that suddenly the thought came to me that this—playing the cello—would be what I would be doing all my life. It was the promise of my artistic future.

In those days, another one of Deszö's students was Lorne Munroe, the solo cellist of the New York Philharmonic until his retirement in 1996. I remember Lorne bringing me a gift of a beaded necklace which he had strung himself. He would have been about nine.

During the Manitoba Music Competition Festival, my sisters and I were heard by the invited adjudicators.[22] They were Sir Hugh Roberton (not yet knighted at that time), conductor of the Glasgow Orpheus Choir, Edward Bairstow, and Ralph Conn—all noted musicians from England. They advised my father to come to England to continue our musical education. We arrived in London in 1928 with almost no money, excepting what had been raised by the music lovers of Winnipeg.

Life in London at that time was a cruel experience for me and my sisters because we were very poor. It was the Depression and my father was unable to find any work. We had not commenced school, but as children we could not help him in any way. For the first six months we lived in abject poverty in two rooms—my parents and four children, including my brother. Meals had to be taken in relays since our tiny kitchen, which was also our dining room, was much too small. However, my father was determined that our practicing should continue. I remember having to practice in the same room as my violinist sister, she in one corner and I in another. We were forced to work for six hours per day (with a five-minute break after each hour) under my father's constant supervision. In this way I acquired the gift of learning how to concentrate during my work, and this is an experience which has proved to be invaluable during my life.

When I was ten years old, I had a dream. It was that I had gone to a concert, but when I arrived there were no seats available, so I stood at the back. On the stage was a female figure in a flowing white garment, sitting on a podium and playing the cello. The sound of her cello that I heard in my dream is the sound I have tried to recreate all my life.

My father tried to enroll me at the Royal College of Music, but I was much too young to be admitted. It was at that time that I went to play for Herbert Walenn, the great cello teacher. He immediately offered to teach me at his London Violoncello School. I was loaned a Gagliano cello by Lady Parmoos, a great patroness of the arts, and later this instrument became mine as a gift from Margaret Ellis, the niece of Lady Parmoos.

Many of Herbert Walenn's famous students had already left his school, but I do remember Michel Cherniavsky, Laurie Kennedy (later the first cellist of the BBC Symphony), John Barbirolli, Boris Hambourg, Boris Rickelman (a brilliant player), and Colin Hampton, who joined the famous Griller Quartet. At my time there was William Pleeth, Eleanor Warren, who later became Mrs. Walter Susskind, and many other fine players.

Our debut as the Canadian Trio at the Wigmore Hall when I was ten consisted of Beethoven's C Minor Trio and Anton Arensky's trio, plus my solo offering which was the *Kol Nidrei* of Bruch. Two years later at the age of twelve I made my debut in London with the London Symphony Orchestra conducted by Malcolm Sargent. Sargent was wonderfully kind and inspired me with his great confidence. It was my first orchestral experience and the memory is still vivid. I can so easily recall the excitement I felt at hearing the introduction to the Lalo concerto. It was an unforgettable experience.

When I was sixteen, my sisters and I, accompanied by our father, left for a concert tour of Australia and South Africa. This trio tour kept us away from London, my mother, and young brother for almost eighteen months. I was almost eighteen when I arrived back in London at which time my parents decided to leave for South Africa, which they did. The political situation was extremely tense, and shortly afterward war was declared. My pianist sister Anna had already left England for the United States and I was left alone in London with my other sister, Ida. After my recital at the Wigmore Hall, I felt I must return to

Canada. We had only sufficient funds for our steamship tickets with nothing else. After attempting passage on the SS *Athenia* (it was torpedoed and sunk), we left on the next sailing for Canada.

Back in Canada, life was extremely difficult as we had almost no funds. I remember going to Toronto at Christmas in 1939 and staying at the YWCA with my sister. I was not permitted to practice in my room, but was given permission to practice in the boiler room. As an indirect result, this was how I started my "second career." One day I looked up when I was playing to see ten musicians peering at me from the open window. They had been rehearsing for a CBC concert in the church next door and, attracted by the sound of the cello, came to see who was playing.

After this unusual meeting, they arranged to have me play for any important artist who came to Toronto. Arthur Fiedler came and after he heard me play he invited me to play with him in Boston at the "Pops" with the Boston Symphony Orchestra. As a result of this performance, Charles Munch invited me to be guest soloist on the BSO series the following season. When Munch became ill, Ernest Ansermet was invited to conduct instead. When he heard me, he invited me to be his soloist with the Orchestre de la Suisse Romande in Geneva. And so I became known and my career blossomed.

Artists who greatly inspired me were Casals, Piatigorsky, and Feuermann. I studied with all three. When I was ten, John Barbirolli took me to play for Casals, but it was not until I was twenty-five that I had the opportunity to study with him. All three cellists were an important influence in my musical life. I remember hearing a recording of Ernest Bloch's *Schelomo* played by Feuermann and the Philadelphia Orchestra under Stokowski. I was so inspired, not only by the playing but by this magnificent work. All I wanted was to meet Ernest Bloch and work with him on his cello compositions. This was arranged by his friend Colin Hampton and I went to Oregon. As a result of our meeting, Bloch invited me to be his soloist in London at the Bloch Festival in 1949. I played *Schelomo* with him and several days later recorded it with Bloch conducting. With Bloch at the piano, I also recorded his "Prayer," "Supplication," and "Jewish Song," the three pieces from his suite called *Jewish Life*.

The Strad cello that I play belonged to a very great friend in London, Audrey Melville. I was in California in 1961 when I received

a letter from Mrs. Melville telling me she had decided to leave me her
Strad for life. The letter was dated 11 April 1953. I knew she had been
very ill and thought she had mistaken the date. I wrote to her telling
her how important it was for her not to give up playing (she was an
amateur cellist) and how much I looked forward to seeing her again
and to playing some duets. A week later a letter arrived from a mutual
friend telling me that Audrey Melville had died. Her letter to me
had been written in 1953, and although I had visited her frequently,
nothing was ever mentioned about what she intended to do with the
Strad. The decision was almost certainly due to the influence of
Guilhermina Suggia, who was her close friend. I have never played
on another instrument since.[23]

Little Gary Karr with members of his bass-playing family. From left to ri̵

PART TWO

THE INNOVATORS

cle, Bill Nadel; his cousin, Milton Nadel; and his grandfather, Esaak Nadel.

CHAPTER ELEVEN

Against All Odds

ANDRÉS SEGOVIA,
GEORGES BARRÈRE,
WILLIAM PRIMROSE,
AND EVELYN GLENNIE

ANDRÉS Segovia called his quest an obsession. At sixteen, he vowed to bring his ancient folk instrument to the world's concert halls—that he would be the "Apostle of the Guitar." Before he died in 1987 at the age of ninety-four, the supreme guitarist had won millions of devotees, perhaps more than any other classical performer at that time.

Georges Barrère, "the monarch of flute players" as critic Olin Downes once called him, began his musical life in France playing the penny whistle and the fife. When he finally had a flute, his superb career unfolded.

During an evening of quartet playing at Le Zoute in Belgium, Eugène Ysaÿe suggested to his pupil, William Primrose, that he should play the viola instead of the violin. This strengthened the young Scotsman's resolve to follow his own yearnings, and when he abandoned the fiddle for the noble alto, the world of the viola saw a new day.

Evelyn Glennie has become the world's premiere solo percussionist and a great musical innovator despite her profound deafness since childhood. She established herself as a consummate musician in her student years at London's Royal Academy of Music and, at the outset of her youthful career, launched a courageous one-woman crusade that brought the music for percussion instruments to international prominence. She has created a new and viable performance tradition that promises a previously unimagined future for percussion soloists.

A performance career may be notable but may not transform the field. The life's work of Andrés Segovia, Georges Barrère, William Primrose, and

Evelyn Glennie, four performers who began their musical lives as unusual prodigies, proves an exception. Against all odds, they each embarked on a courageous odyssey that no one had dared before them. Even in the astounding world of musical prodigies, their innovations set them apart from all others.

ANDRÉS

My life has been a slowly ascending line. Everything came. But I was not to be distracted, not to answer another call. . . . I am surprised at the miracle of my will that persisted in the road I have taken, but I think that luck has also happened.

Segovia, in *Andrés Segovia: The Song of the Guitar*

The modern guitar, whose precursors can be traced to early Babylonian and Egyptian cultures, appeared in Italy before 1780 and soon spread throughout Europe. It quickly became the most popular folk instrument in Spain. In the hands of the flamenco guitarists, its poetic, melancholy voice echoed along the streets in every village, capturing the imagination of all who heard it, but especially the Andalusian boy, Andrés Segovia. During Segovia's youth at the end of the nineteenth century, the guitar was considered the perfect instrument to accompany songs and dances in the popular amusements, but entirely unsuited for playing classical music. Segovia saw the guitar differently and set out on a most remarkable musical quest.

He was born at Linares in Andalusia on 21 February 1893, but a few weeks later his parents returned to Jaén, their native city where the child spent the first years of his life. Because of their poverty, they left Andrés at the age of four in the care of his childless aunt and uncle who lived in the village of Villacarrillo. Feeling abandoned, the little boy wept bitterly, but his Uncle Eduardo—bearded, completely bald, and without a tooth in his head —sat down in front of him and, hoping to distract him, pretended to strum a guitar held to his chest as he sang:

> *Tocar la guitarra* (strum!)
> *No tiene ciencia* (strum!)
> *Sino fuerza en el brazo* (strum!)
> *Y perseverancia* (strum!)

(To play guitar,
You need no science,
Only a strong arm
And perseverance.)

He repeated the ditty again and again until the boy calmed down and smiled back at him. Then, taking Andrés' small right arm, he made him beat the rhythm of the *strum*, which gave him such intense delight that he remembered it always. Eighty years later, Segovia recalled, "This was the first musical seed to be cast in my soul and it was to develop, as time passed, into the strongest and most rewarding constant in my life."[1]

When he was six his guardians sent him for violin lessons with Francisco Rivera, a bad violinist who lived in their neighborhood. "Neither memory, measure, nor ear," was Rivera's harsh criticism that made the child fearful. Unconvinced by this judgment that his nephew was unmusical, Uncle

Andrés Segovia at seventeen, Córdoba, 1910.

Eduardo brought the lessons to a halt, deciding to wait for more auspicious circumstances and a better teacher before continuing the boy's music lessons. Soon after, a strolling flamenco guitar player found his way to their house, produced his battered guitar, asked for a sip of wine, and began playing. At the first flourish, there was an explosion of sounds when more noise than music burst from the strings, followed by his tapping on the face of the broken-down instrument. Segovia recalled his fright:

> Having sat down very close to him and rearing from the impact, I fell over backward. "Do you want me to teach you," he asked. I nodded several times. In a month-and-a-half I had learned everything the poor man knew—that is to say, very little.

When Andrés was ten he was taken to Granada to be educated formally. From his bedroom window in his grandmother's house he could listen to street musicians playing flamenco and in the distance see the Alhambra, the medieval fortress of the Moors. In the gardens of the Alhambra he spent hours in quiet contemplation, listening in ecstasy to the sounds of nature. When he was eighty-four, Segovia returned to the Alhambra to make a film during which he reminisced:

> I came here for the first time to this place of dreams when I was ten years old. It was here where I opened my eyes to the beauty of nature and art . . . and believe me, to be here is to feel near, very near to Paradise.[2]

Andrés knew as a young child that close to his uncle's house in Villacarrillo there was a guitar shop ("Curiously, the spirit of the instrument came to my cradle. It was the first call of my destiny"). Later in Granada, his instincts told him that to make beautiful sounds, he needed a finely crafted instrument. When his school friend, Miguel Cerón, took him to the guitar workshop of Benito Ferrer, he stood transfixed, looking at the row of new guitars hanging before him. Miguel agreed to buy one of Ferrer's guitars for him if he would repay him little by little with the pocket money his uncle gave him. Miguel also would give him weekly lessons and teach him all he knew about the guitar.

With the acquisition of his new guitar, Andrés became completely distracted, neglecting his studies to practice hours on end. Almost daily he sought permission from his uncle to study his school lessons next door in a neighbor's garden, saying it had nicer trees than their own, for there he secretly kept his guitar and practiced. From then on Andrés was to be both his own teacher and pupil. Explaining the genesis of his life as a self-taught musician, Segovia has said:

> The vocation for music I received from Heaven, but when I held the guitar, unconsciously I fell in love with it. I had been captured for life by the guitar, absolutely the most beautiful instrument that man has created. It was my destiny. With complete dedication, I have been totally faithful to it all my life.

During his lonely struggle to master the guitar, Andrés often heard about Francisco Tárrega, who lived in Barcelona and played classical music on the guitar, but he never met this teacher who might have encouraged him with lessons. Tárrega died in 1909, the year that sixteen-year-old Andrés made his debut in a concert arranged at the Granada Arts Center by his friend Miguel Cerón. The day after the first public performance in his life, a moderately favorable review, written by Alberto Cienfuegos, appeared in *Noticiero Granadino*. Reading Cienfuegos' words, Andrés naively believed he was famous in the world: "Suddenly I decided to be the Apostle of the guitar. I set out with a firm stride."

In 1912, having appeared in recitals in Granada, Cádiz, and Seville, Andrés performed for the first time in Madrid at the Ateneo concert hall, playing on a magnificent new guitar made by Manuel Ramírez, luthier to the Royal Conservatory of Madrid. After his successful recital, it was said that the gods would punish him for bringing the lowly guitar into concert halls, but such foolishness was Andrés' least concern. He knew now that only with the creation of a new repertoire could the classical guitar succeed: "The hardest task that I assigned to myself was to enrich the repertoire of the guitar. I was deeply saddened by the fact that the guitar, an instrument so rich in shading and so suited to the dreams and fantasies of a composer, should be so lacking in beautiful works."

This sentiment was soon shared by composers who heard the young Andalusian play in Madrid. Some realized that if they knew the instrument better and if the guitar were to attract enough virtuosos, the solution would be to create a typical Spanish repertoire for it, one removed from the music played in the cafes. The first to answer the call was the Spanish symphonic composer, Federico Torroba. Over the next fifteen years, Segovia's triumphs encouraged other composers to write for the guitar and for the man who performed with such distinction. After Torroba came Manuel de Falla, Joaquín Turina, Manuel Ponce, Alfredo Casella, Alexandre Tansman, Heitor Villa-Lobos, and Mario Castelnuovo-Tedesco.

Encouraged by Pablo Casals, Segovia made his debut in Paris on 7 April 1924. In the audience at the Paris Conservatory were composers Paul Dukas, Manuel de Falla, and Albert Roussel. Roussel was eager to hear his new composition, simply called *Segovia*. Concerts followed throughout Europe, and after a debut in Berlin, further afield in Scandinavia and Russia, where the young guitarist appeared in Moscow and Leningrad.

Fritz Kreisler encouraged his own concert manager to arrange Segovia's first tour of the United States in 1928. Following a private performance in Proctor, Vermont, a front-page article appeared in the *New York Times* that excited public interest. His debut in New York's Town Hall on 8 January 1928 set the press ablaze with enthusiastic reviews by critics Olin Downes and Lawrence Gilman. Five more sold-out New York recitals followed, then a tour of twenty-three other cities. In 1929, he went to the Far East and made a lasting artistic impression in Manila, Hong Kong, Shanghai, and Tokyo.

The great guitarist was always attracted by the communications media. Between 1927 and 1939, he made twenty-seven records for HMV in London before World War Two cut short his early recording career. Segovia left his home in Madrid to live in Montevideo, Uruguay, when Spain was thrown into the tumult of civil war, then later moved to New York City where Sol Hurok continued to manage his worldwide concert tours as he resumed recording for a small American firm. In the late 1940s, he began working with the Decca producer Israel Horowitz, recording the multimovement sonatas composed for him by Manuel Ponce.

Segovia accepted the advent of television as an important way of reaching as many people as he could. He appeared in such diverse productions as the *Bell Telephone Hour* and the *Ed Sullivan Show* in the United States, the European documentary *Segovia at Los Olivos*, filmed at his home on the Spanish Costa del Sol, and another film made in Madrid at the Prado Museum.

"To teach is to learn twice," this self-taught master often said, encouraging a new generation of classical guitarists that included Alirio Diaz, John Williams, Michael Lorimer, Oscar Ghiglia ("It was my time to learn and his time to teach"), Christopher Parkening ("Segovia is really to the guitar what Paganini was to the violin or Liszt to the piano"), and Eliot Fisk ("I think we could say that all classical guitar playing is a *footnote* to Segovia. He is the person that sketched out the parameters of everything we are still trying to do today").

Prodigiousness in music appears at widely different times within the years normally encompassed by childhood, the timing affected, in part, by the culture's ability to respond to extraordinary talent. Segovia's ascent from early precocity to creative adult achievement was shaped largely by the absence of opportunities to play classical music on the guitar in a concert milieu when he was a child. The public had to wait until he was a mature artist and had created an accepting environment for his performances before they heard the accomplishments of genius.

Andrés Segovia became an international figure on the concert stage, enjoying a tremendous career that continued until his last performance, a recital at the Miami Beach Theater in Florida on 4 April 1987, two months before his death on 3 June 1987 at the age of ninety-four. Queen Sophia of Spain eulogized Andrés Segovia not only as a celebrated guitarist, but as a great artist and a man of genuine intellect devoted to Spain's literature, poetry, and artistry, as well as its music:

> Though Segovia became a citizen of the world honored wherever he played, he continued to feel that his soul belonged to Spain and his beloved Andalusia. His legacy will always remain alive, and thanks to him, the name of Spain will have one more reason to be revered throughout the world of culture.[3]

GEORGES

My older brother seemed to be the musical white hope of the family. He had learned to play the tin whistle only ordinarily, when somebody gave him a cheap violin. I grasped the discarded penny whistle, finding my way to scales and tunes on the six-holed primitive instrument.

Barrère, in *Georges Barrère*

Georges Barrère, the great French flutist, was born in Bordeaux, France, on 31 October 1876. His family moved to the small town of Epernon near Paris when Georges was three. His life as a young musician was carefree. He played the penny whistle, then the fife. In 1889 when the prodigy turned twelve, he got his first flute. After playing the flute for only six years, he won the premier prix at the Paris Conservatory in 1895 and launched a career that would bring him great distinction as an eminent chamber musician and orchestral flutist.

Barrère's moment of opportunity to go abroad came in 1905 when he auditioned for Walter Damrosch, who was visiting Paris. Damrosch invited the young Frenchman to be the first flutist of the New York Symphony Society, and one month later, on the morning of 13 May 1905, Barrère discovered America from the pier at Christopher Street. In New York Georges Barrère was in his artistic element. He would live out his long life there, creating a musical sensation whenever he performed as flutist or conductor.

In his essay of 1928, "When Georges Barrère Played the Flute," Dr. Frank Crane asked the question, "Do you know who Georges Barrère is?" and then answered it, "He is one of those persons who can do something better than anybody else in the world can do it."[4] Eventually Americans who loved the flute and flute playing, chamber music for woodwinds, and the charm of a witty raconteur who could talk about new music agreed that Georges Barrère was a consummate master. Patrick Gallois, the French flute virtuoso, has said, "Georges Barrère created a new way to be a flutist in the twentieth century."

The first prize winners at the 1895 Concours that celebrated the centenary of the Paris Conservatory. Georges Barrère, at nineteen, stands in the back row, fourth from the right.

Unlike the nineteenth-century flutists who composed their own music, much of which has not survived into our century, he did not compose. Instead, he worked with many composers to help create new music and in this way he was the first contemporary musician of our instrument.

You must know who you are to play music! Barrère asked questions first, then found the reason to search for answers. He had the courage to destroy everything he knew each day in order to find new answers. He knew it was important to love music, to understand music, and to urge composers to create.

Perhaps Barrère went to America to escape the restrictions of the Old World, to escape them in order to create something new. To speak with composers. Yes, perhaps he escaped to be able to freely speak his mind—to find a space to be with other artists who understood this pursuit. He was very strong to move in this way![5]

Gabriel Barrère, Georges' father, was a furniture maker. "I sang even when a little tot," Barrère recalled. "Father and Mother couldn't detect imperfections; first, because love is as deaf as it is blind, and again because my dear parents were decidedly not musical."[6]

Georges began school in Epernon. When he would pipe out tunes on his penny whistle at recess, the other school boys left their marbles to gather round him. Soon the toy store in Epernon couldn't supply whistles fast enough to meet the demands of all his friends who wanted to learn to play with him. The director of the school was the municipal bandmaster and when the band marched in Sunday parades, Georges fell in step, playing by ear on his penny whistle to the encouragement of every member of the band.

Like his contemporary, Pablo Casals, who played popular tunes on the streets of Vendrell on his one-stringed gourd-cello, Georges piped on his tin whistle in Epernon, but playing such primitive instruments garnered no critical acclaim for these children. Unlike the instruments favored by most prodigies—the piano, violin, and cello—penny whistles and gourd-cellos have no classical repertoire, claim no place in the concert hall, and even when played amazingly well attract little attention. What then was the influence of such unusual childhood activity on these prodigies? Perhaps the element of play explicit in their early musical expression presaged the later, significant development of both children.

In 1888 when he had turned twelve, Georges left Epernon and went back to Paris. The boy's ability to develop exceedingly quickly, the hallmark of the prodigy, must have been considerable. Joining a military class at the Bataillons Scolaires, he took up the fife, immediately becoming sergeant of the fife and drum corps of the school cadets. On Bastille Day, 14 July 1889, the corps paraded before the grand reviewing stand at Paris City Hall, a great day for Sergeant Barrère, who led the Ninth Battalion.

An even greater day came soon when a teacher who had studied at the Paris Conservatory recognized Georges' remarkable talent for music. Although this perceptive first teacher had no far-reaching reputation, he played an important role in helping the self-taught child gain the confidence to follow a new path. He persuaded him to leave his fife behind and begin a more serious pursuit—to study the flute. After seven years of playing the penny whistle and the fife, Georges took his first flute lesson on 11 April 1889. He was twelve-and-a-half years old.

Georges became an auditor in the flute class of Henri Altès at the Paris Conservatory, and by October 1890 passed the conservatory entrance examination and became a regular member of the class. "At that time I was the chum of many older flute players who were the stars of my limited musical firmament," he recalled. "These boys were in their upper teens and some were as old as twenty-five. They looked upon the small fourteen-year-old lad as little more than a baby in their midst."

When Georges was seventeen, still living at home but already playing at the Folies-Bergère, he bought himself an upright piano for daily practice of scales and exercises. One afternoon his older brother taunted him by playing a "profane tune" on this valued possession. They quarreled, and Georges locked the cover of the keyboard, causing a violent scene. Compelled to obey his parents, he surrendered the key but threatened to leave home. "That evening I left the house to play my engagement at the Folies-Bergère where I was first flute, but I didn't return," Barrère recalled. He rented a room in a dingy hotel, so small that he had to open the window to find elbow room to practice. He was prepared to live this new bohemian existence, even perhaps to negotiate for a place in an act at the Folies-Bergère should he have to leave the conservatory, but a reconciliation with his family brought him back home. He had asserted his independence, and serious work lay ahead.

The elderly Henri Altès retired in the fall of 1893, and Paul Claude Taffanel, the greatest of all French flute players at that time, succeeded him. The following year, while also playing second flute at the Concerts de l'Opéra, Georges intensified his study with Taffanel in preparation for the annual summer Concours. After a remarkable performance, Théodore Dubois, president of the jury, awarded Barrère the premier prix on 29 July 1895. Graduation marked the end of his regular flute studies, as well as the one-hundredth anniversary of the founding of the Paris Conservatory in 1795. With eleven of his fellow laureates, Georges was photographed by the Parisian journal, *Le Monde Musical,* on the great occasion of the conservatory's centenary.

The young flutist returned to the conservatory in the fall, having obtained the privilege of postgraduate attendance in the flute class. Taffanel was pleased with his request to stay with him an extra year and took care to enlarge and refine Barrère's solo and chamber music repertoire. "Taffanel was an inspiration," Barrère has said, "and I doubt if anybody who has approached him wouldn't bear in his heart the loveliest memory of that great master and wouldn't entertain the deepest veneration and respect for the man and the artist."

That same fall, Georges launched his professional chamber music career in Paris. Reviving an idea of Taffanel's, he founded his own woodwind ensemble: the Société Moderne d'Instruments à Vent, the Modern Society for Wind Instruments. The success of the ensemble soon rivaled that of Taffanel's famous chamber music group of two decades earlier, which had consisted of two woodwind quintets.

Georges toured France, Spain, Portugal, Switzerland, and Belgium with his new colleagues. These chamber music artists—Foucault (oboe), Vionne (clarinet), Bulteau (bassoon), Servat (horn), and Aubert (piano)—gained such renown that their ensemble was soon subsidized by the French government. By the end of a decade, the group was responsible for the writing and introduction of eighty-one new compositions by leading composers in France and throughout Europe. "Music was scarce for our combination and with the intrepidity of my twenty years I dangled myself on every composer's doorbell to induce him to write for us," recounted Barrère. In the Modern Society for Wind Instruments, Barrère had created the prototype of the great ensembles he would organize later during his enormously successful career in North America: the Barrère Ensemble of Wind Instruments, the Trio de Lutèce, the Barrère Little Symphony, the Barrère-Britt Concertino, and finally in 1932, the Barrère-Salzedo-Britt Trio, the ultimate trio for flute, harp, and cello.

As Patrick Gallois said, "He knew it was important to love music, to understand music, and to urge composers to create." Barrère began prompting the composition of new music when he was twenty-two: the resulting compositions were in the hundreds and included new music by Robert Russell Bennet, Arthur Bliss, Alfredo Casella, Claude Debussy, Arcady Dubensky, Paul Hindemith, Boris Koutzen, Quinto Maganini, Wallingford Riegger, Bernard Wagenaar, and many others. In 1935 Edgard Varèse celebrated Barrère's new platinum flute by composing *Density 21. 5.* (The curious title refers to the density of platinum, calculated using a chemical formula to divide grams by cubic centimeters at twenty degrees Celsius.) Varèse's new work exemplified the revolutionary music that he sought to create based on a whole new world of unsuspected sounds, rhythms, and structures that he imagined.

Barrère had moved from penny whistle to fife, from the silver flute of his student days to a flute of gold made by William Haynes in 1929, to the platinum dream of his final years. His flute was near him on 14 June 1944 when he suffered a fatal stroke at his home in Kingston, New York. He was buried at Woodstock in the Catskills where he had been part of the artists' colony in annual summer retreats since 1910. Looking like a professor of Greek, as writer Frank Crane once observed, his marble bust stands sentinel over the quiet library of the Chautauqua Institute near Jamestown, New York. This image of Georges Barrère is lifelike, but silent. There is no hint of the penny whistle's little voice, no more ethereal melody or intimate loveliness that once sounded on the platinum flute.

BILL

My father owned a very beautiful viola—a Brothers Amati. As a youngster, when he wasn't around, I found a way to open the latch on the cupboard where the Amati was kept and played it with considerable satisfaction. I preferred its sound to that of the violin. I thought someday a string quartet might ask me to fulfill the role of violist. If so I would be ready.
Primrose, in Walk on the North Side: Memoirs of a Violist

Although the viola may be the most ancient member of the violin family, having come into existence sometime around 1520, by the nineteenth century its players had fallen into ill repute, being for the most part failed violinists. In Germany, for instance, the viola was often referred to as the *Pensioninstrument* because orchestral violinists who had lost their touch were relegated to the viola section. In England and France, where the viola was

William Primrose at twelve, on the occasion of his first concert in St. Andrew's Hall, Glasgow, 1916. Courtesy Primrose International Viola Archive, Brigham Young University.

also looked upon as the pensioners' instrument, real principles of modern viola playing were laid down for the first time by the indomitable Englishman Lionel Tertis and his contemporary, the French violist Maurice Vieux. They thus prepared the way for the viola's long-overdue acceptance as a supreme solo instrument.

William Primrose believed from the outset of his career as a violist that there were significant, basic differences between the playing of the violin and the viola, that the notion held by many violinists that performing on the viola was no more than playing the violin at the interval of a perfect fifth lower was anathema. In Primrose Tertis' dream was fulfilled. The noble instrument would be, as Tertis said, "Cinderella no more."

Bill was born into a privileged life in Glasgow on 23 August 1904. While his early childhood in Scotland represents the more traditional prodigy beginnings—by four he was performing on the violin—his ultimate achievement in music, like Segovia's, came only in his maturity when he moved from the violin to the viola and raised public awareness of that instrument's true potential.

His earliest childhood recollection was of watching his father teaching violin at home in the parlor of the family's exceedingly small apartment at No. 18 Wilton Drive in Glasgow. As an infant, Bill often sat on the floor of the parlor watching his father and imitating his movements as he played the violin: "When he, relishing my apparent enthusiasm, bought and placed a quarter-sized violin in my eager hands in 1908, I began at once really to play."[7]

His father arranged for him to become a pupil of Camillo Ritter, an Austrian national who had studied with Joachim and Ševčik and who was the most prominent teacher of violin in Scotland at the time. Among Ritter's pupils in 1908 was another four-year-old—David McCallum, Bill's rival. Forty-five years later at the height of his international career, Primrose recorded Hector Berlioz's *Harold in Italy* with Sir Thomas Beecham conducting London's Royal Philharmonic and David McCallum as the distinguished concertmaster of that great orchestra.

Bill's training with Ritter was rigorous. The disciplined Ševčik pupil passed along a meticulous pedagogical regime and in 1914 even arranged for the boy to go to Prague to study with Ševčik, a plan that collapsed when an epidemic and a threatening war made it implausible. Both Bill's father and Ritter never acknowledged the boy's talent or precociousness, at least in his presence. He was constantly admonished not to get above himself and to understand that he was not as good as he might believe. This was the way of dour Scotsmen.

Bill had already appeared in recitals at the Congregational church, at local schools, and finally at Glasgow's Palette Club before he came under the influence of Emil Mlynarski and Landon Ronald, conductors of the Scottish Orchestra in which his father was a member of the violin section. The boy took in the concerts of the Orpheus Choir, conducted by Hugh Roberton, and heard great chamber music performances for the first time when the London String Quartet appeared in Glasgow, not guessing that this ensemble held the key to his future. ("I almost went out of my mind as I encountered such sweet joy.")

In the summers, his father took the Primrose family to Blackpool, a coastal resort in Lancashire where Landon Ronald conducted the orchestra season. There Bill heard the singers Enrico Caruso and Emmy Destinn and many great violinists of the day—Joseph Szigeti, Rafael Kubelik, Mischa Elman, Fritz Kreisler, and Eugène Ysaÿe, who was later to become his master teacher.

Bill's school in Glasgow was demanding and the academic discipline it imparted helped hone the boy's considerable intellect. In his youth he read Dickens and Thackeray voraciously, discovered he had an ear for foreign languages, and devoted himself to perfecting his chess game, but for all that, his secret dream was "a perpetual vacation with unceasing soccer," once he had discovered the exhilaration of sports, especially of the soccer field and later the boxing ring.

When he gave his first stunning performance of Mendelssohn's violin concerto at St. Andrew's Hall in Glasgow at the age of twelve, he attracted the attention of his father's friend, R. D. Waddell, a Glasgow businessman who owned a fine collection of string instruments. A few years later, Waddell made a generous gesture to Bill's career. Nan Holmes, who was a secretary at the Glasgow sausage factory owned by R. D. Waddell, later told her daughter, Isobel Moore, about the exciting event at work in 1921 when "every one of the employees lined up to witness Mr. Waddell present seventeen-year-old Bill Primrose with a Strad violin."[8] It was this Stradivarius violin, the famous "Betts" made in 1704, that accompanied him back to London where the family had moved in 1919 so that he could study at the Guildhall School of Music with Max Mossel.

On 12 November 1922, Glasgow's *Sunday Post* devoted its front page to "Glasgow Boy's Rise to Fame—How Willy Primrose has amazed the critics with his fiddle." The nineteen-year-old violinist was making his mark in London's musical circles where his father had broken into the orchestra field.

"My life was rather free and easy at the Guildhall. It was very similar to the life of a young man of wealth and class who went to Oxford or Cambridge, except that I didn't have the wealth, and the 'class' was latent," Primrose recalled. However, he soon made his debut as soloist on the "Max Mossel Concerts" at the Queen's Hall in London in 1923.

Conductor Landon Ronald, who had helped to arrange the debut, presented Bill before an important London guild, the Worshipful Company of Musicians, and as a result the young man was awarded a medal and sufficient funds to enable him to play two important concerts; an appearance with orchestra at the Queen's Hall—he performed both Lalo's *Symphonie espagnole* and Elgar's violin concerto, with Ronald conducting—and one week later a solo recital at the Wigmore Hall that set him on his way.

He graduated with distinction from the Guildhall in 1924 and began extensive concertizing and broadcasting, but this early phase of his career as a violin soloist was badly managed. "There was no plan, no one to guide me along the path that leads to success," Primrose recalled. His first recording for His Master's Voice was Saint-Saëns' *Introduction and Rondo capriccioso* with piano accompaniment. It took place in the days before electrical recording when a huge apparatus that looked like an old-fashioned gramophone horn was sticking out from the wall. "The artist would tilt his instrument toward it and play into it for four-and-a-half minutes, with the hope that when he untilted his instrument he would have recorded some four-and-a-half minutes of passable performance."

When Bill began the third season of his professional career, a good friend, the pianist Ivor Newton, offered him some much-needed advice. Newton suggested his going abroad to study with Eugène Ysaÿe in Belgium. He took the advice and was soon at work with Ysaÿe at La Chanterelle, the Belgian master's villa at Le Zoute. As his tuition with Ysaÿe progressed, so did his yearning to play the viola, and Ysaÿe was responsive. Ysaÿe is said to have commented to a friend that both Paganini and Vieuxtemps played the viola from choice, that Joachim loved the timbre of the bigger instrument, that his friend Lionel Tertis was doing much missionary work for his viola, and that "I have had a young man from Scotland who will blaze new paths in the years to come."[9]

Bill's early concertizing had been limited largely to the United Kingdom except for an exotic but brief concert tour to East Africa with Percy Hemming, a singer from Covent Garden. In 1928 he appeared in Paris for the first time as violin soloist in a performance of Mozart's masterpiece, the Symphonie Concertante, K. 364, for violin, viola, and orchestra. Lionel Tertis was the viola soloist and Sir Thomas Beecham the conductor. "By this time I had definitely made up my mind to switch to viola, but I didn't tell any-one," Primrose later recalled.

> I'm reasonably sure, though, that if I had advised Tertis of my secret ambition he would have welcomed me with open arms, because he was *the* great viola protagonist. As my decision finally became known, some people were aghast and my father deeply despondent. One individual, a very distinguished orchestra player and highly respected, told me, "You're making the biggest mistake of your life. You will regret this as you've regretted no other thing."

In 1927 James Levey had resigned as first violinist of the London String Quartet, and Warwick Evans, who had founded the ensemble in 1908, planned to approach Primrose, but John Pennington presented himself and was immediately invited to lead the group. The London String Quartet had achieved international status (they were the first modern quartet to perform the cycle of Beethoven quartets in public, and their repertoire embraced more than five hundred works, including 150 new compositions, many from contemporary British composers). Yet it was fortunate for the chamber music world that Primrose did not become the first violinist. In fact he had been preparing himself to be a quartet violist ever since sneaking his father's Amati viola from the cupboard when he was a boy in Glasgow.

In 1930 when the London String Quartet's violist Harry Waldo-Warner retired, Primrose, then twenty-six, contacted Warwick Evans and expressed his interest in joining the quartet. Another violist had already been engaged to replace Waldo-Warner, but after three months he collapsed under the strain of travel and Warwick Evans cabled Primrose from New York, asking him to come immediately. He crossed the Atlantic in March 1930 and joined the London String Quartet for the last third of its United States tour, then sailed to South America where the quartet appeared in Chile. Primrose had not yet played the viola parts in much of the quartet repertoire and had exten-sive preparation ahead. He later recalled:

> I was left pretty much to myself to sink or swim when we first ap-peared in Chile. I had become a violist full-fledged. I had burned all my bridges. I had walked the Damascus road, seen the light, repented of past transgressions, and turned to the viola.

Besides providing Primrose with a successful and rewarding beginning to his career as a violist, his membership in the quartet for five years gave him his first exposure to international audiences. After the quartet disbanded in 1935, Primrose joined Arturo Toscanini's new NBC Symphony Orchestra in New York City. In 1938, the NBC music department invited the violist to form the Primrose String Quartet with violinists Oscar Shumsky and Joseph Gingold and cellist Harvey Shapiro. "I am quite convinced," Primrose said, "that no quartet ever played that had the instrumental ability of my quartet."

Richard Crooks, the celebrated American tenor, asked Primrose to join him on a concert tour as his assisting artist in 1941. One tour evolved into five tours in four years and led to the solo career that distinguished the violist worldwide. Primrose was to reach international prominence in his late thirties, against all odds.

Throughout the long career that followed, he continued to define the new age of the viola. Until his death at seventy-seven on 1 May 1982, Primrose remained a vigilant artist, responsive when innovation beckoned. The new music composed for him by William Walton, Benjamin Britten, Arthur Benjamin, Peter Racine Fricker, Edmund Rubbra, and Darius Milhaud— and of course, Béla Bartók, whose last composition was the viola concerto commissioned by the intrepid Scotsman—created a new musical legacy.

EVELYN

When I see something, I hear it. If you dropped your pencil on the floor, I am assuming that is making a noise, therefore I use my imagination and therefore I hear it. And that is basically how my whole sound world is made up. It is entirely through my imagination, entirely through touch, through feel, and what I see.

Glennie, in *Breaking the Silence Barrier*

Arthur Glennie, Evelyn's father, was one of seven children who grew up on a farm in Aberdeenshire in the northeast of Scotland. He met young Isobel Howie at a country church at New Deer where she was the village organist. In 1959 they married. They decided to live in the district of Ardo where they could raise their sons, Roger and Colin, on a farm as they themselves had been brought up. Their third child, Evelyn, was born on 19 July 1965 in Aberdeen. She was christened at the parish church in the village of Methlick, two miles from the Glennie's farm, Hillhead of Ardo.

The mid-nineteenth-century stone farmhouse atop the hill became a comforting sanctuary for Evelyn and her two older brothers; with the exception of one trip to Orkney, the Glennies never took holidays away from Hillhead. Whether the encircling fields were covered with snow or verdant with grain, the family tenaciously nurtured their land and animals in all seasons, surviving each harsh Scottish winter to revel in the spring that followed. "I loved the farm and often think about my days as a farmer's daughter," Glennie has said.

> I have only to close my eyes to see the dear familiar white house amidst those peaceful green fields, and the pressures melt away; I am a child again, idling in the sunshine or hanging off the top of the grain

Evelyn Glennie at eighteen, during the 1984 Shell/London Symphony Orchestra competition with (left to right) John Chimes, Michael Frye, and Kurt-Hans Goedicke. Courtesy Evelyn Glennie.

tower, craning my neck to see further and yet further into the blue distance above my head.[10]

Arthur Glennie's secret dream as a child was to be a musician, but there was no money for instruments or lessons, although he eventually owned an accordion. Once each year, when the rest of the family attended the midnight church service on Christmas Eve in Methlick (Isobel played the organ for hymn singing), Arthur would stay home with Evelyn to play the traditional Scottish songs and reels for her on his accordion, a celebration of folk music that the child remembered all her life.

There was a piano at Hillhead, but it was not often played until little Evelyn first climbed on the bench and discovered how to plonk away with two fingers. One day she gave a perfect rendition of the Youngers' Special Bitter jingle, music from a television commercial that had lodged itself in her memory. Glennie recalled: "Prodigy and genius were, perhaps fortunately, not my family's immediate reactions! Music became increasingly important to me in a quiet and relaxed way, so that I was able to experiment and play without external pressures."

At Cairnorrie Primary, the country school near the Glennie farm, Evelyn was soon entertaining the class with her keyboard jingles: "When I heard 'Play us a tune, Evie,' my fingers would happily oblige." Her teachers began to understand her need—and her ability—to express herself in music. Piano lessons followed, then clarinet playing, in what became a long, rewarding association with Cults, the Aberdeen Music Centre where she went for Saturday classes.

At the local Ellon Academy where examiners from Trinity College of Music periodically adjudicated young musicians, Evelyn took her first piano examination in June 1974. The Glennies waited to hear the results, but not for long. When a week had passed the good news arrived at Hillhead. Evelyn had achieved the highest marks in the United Kingdom. "The immediate and very exciting effect was that I was invited to give a short performance at Aberdeen's Cowdray Hall," Glennie recalled.

This was the first musical milestone in my life, and, to begin with, a rather daunting experience. The performers had to sit among the audience until it was their turn to go up to the stage. When it was time for me to go up, I didn't hear my name being called out and the man behind me had to tap me on the shoulder to take my cue.

As Evelyn bowed and left the stage, she told her teacher, "I want to be a concert pianist." Practical Mrs. Merriless replied, "So do a lot of other people," but argued no further when the child insisted, "But I have decided!" Glennie said, "I liked being on that high stage, looking down on all the faces, and feeling a real sense of authority, and I suppose this was the beginning of it all, my thinking, Golly, I like this!"

By the time Evelyn was eight the first signs of deafness occurred. By eleven when she was due to leave Cairnorrie to attend Ellon Academy, her hearing was so poor that her parents were advised to send her to the Aberdeen School for the Deaf. The little country girl to whom music had become so vital was undeterred and decided that somehow she would cope with her deafness, that it was "just a matter of getting used to it." Evelyn was fitted with the most powerful hearing aids available and went on to Ellon Academy, along with most of the other children from her country school. Later that year, her parents took her to Glasgow for extensive hearing tests. They returned to Hillhead knowing that she had become profoundly deaf.

Having abandoned the clarinet, Evelyn decided that she wanted to play percussion instruments. When she asked permission at school, Hamish Park, head of the music department, was rather surprised because of her poor achievement on all aural examinations. ("He was too tactful to say it—'Percussion! You haven't got a hope!'—but I could see what he was thinking.") Park finally agreed that she could speak with Ron Forbes, the academy's percussion teacher. At their meeting, Forbes asked her to play some scales on the xylophone. Although she had never used sticks before, she picked them up and played with no stiffness or awkwardness—and doing so Evelyn crossed the threshold to her future.

Concealing her hearing aids beneath her curls, Evelyn had told no one at the academy that she could not hear, but now she began losing her balance and coordination because sounds were extremely distorted and it was increasingly difficult for her to identify where they came from. While playing in a percussion group she could only hear noise and began to play louder and louder in order to hear herself, no longer able to relate to what others were doing. She became so frustrated that she abandoned her hearing aids and retreated into total silence. To her delight, she was no longer distracted by unidentifiable noise and began to understand how to compensate for being deaf. "I found I could control my movements so as to make soft or loud sounds. I was beginning to recognize how much pressure I needed to strike a xylophone bar, and how the dynamics of a sound worked," Glennie recalled.

A perfect memory of pitch informed her acute musical sensitivity. Because she could hear inwardly with amazing precision, she could place one note exactly in relation to other notes. This was one of her great advantages. Focusing intently on her inner vision of the music she played, Evelyn searched for all possible ways to hear music in any way she could and never doubted herself as she attempted to achieve what she wanted. The music interested Evelyn most: "To be a good musician, there must first of all be the seed that comes from the heart, something to grow from. . . . I discovered that I had something inside me that had nothing to do with the technical side of music." As her deafness increased, so did her involvement with music and with the audiences who loved her performances but beyond that had little curiosity or concern. "Over the next few years I was to enjoy more and more frequently the curious experience of audience applause and recognition which I could see and feel, but could not hear."

In her adolescence Evelyn became a regular member of the academy's percussion groups and was soon playing solo pieces such as Mozart's *Rondo alla Turca* that Ron Forbes had arranged for the xylophone. Forbes encouraged her to explore the possibilities of a vast array of percussion instruments, including xylophones, marimbas, drums, timpani, vibraphones, tubular bells, glockenspiels, and the sound-effect instruments, tambourine, triangle, and castanets. She made her own transcriptions to be played on the tuned percussion instruments and began to compose, a creative act that she accomplished by simply sitting down and thinking about it as only the most gifted creative musicians have done.

When the percussion ensemble from Cults traveled to Croydon, England, for a three-day summer competition, their prize winning was rewarded with the chance to play in the Schools Prom at London's Albert Hall the following November. "Once I was on stage in front of this great throng I felt huge and powerful, and I remember my sticks flying as I played my heart out to them all." For Evelyn this began an ongoing adventure of travel and discovery, of public appearances with the ensemble, proudly dressed in a distinctive Scottish tartan.

In 1979, the ensemble traveled to France for the first time, crossing by ferry from Hull to Rotterdam on their way to Autun. The following summer they returned to Autun and added a performance at Vaison-la-Romaine. When Evelyn was thirteen, there were concerts in Aberdeen, where she met Roderick Brydon, the artistic director of the Scottish Chamber Orchestra. By sixteen, she was discovered by the media. A feature article in *People's Jour-*

nal set off a publicity siege that unfortunately focused on her deafness, a matter she later never mentioned on her professional concert programs. She intended to make no issue of her deafness, either in her professional or personal life.

In Aberdeen on Guy Fawkes' Day in 1980, Evelyn met James Blades, who at age eighty was one of the world's great percussionists. Together they performed a timpani duet, a piece called *Circles* on the marimba, and a snare drum duet. "We got on like a house on fire," Glennie said. "When we had finished playing, he nudged me in the ribs in his friendly way and said, 'You ought to think about going to London.'"

With her final examinations looming ahead, Evelyn asked the school whether she could have some tutoring from Sandra Buchan, an itinerant teacher for the deaf who regularly visited the Ellon Academy. When Buchan learned of Evelyn's discouraging encounter with a career adviser to whom she had confided her interest in a professional career in music, she took immediate action. Hoping to improve Evelyn's situation, Buchan wrote an impassioned letter to Ann Rachlin, the founder of England's Beethoven Fund for Deaf Children. Her welcome response was kind and positive. She invited Evelyn to visit London to play for Ezra Rachlin, her American husband. Once a celebrated prodigy pianist, Rachlin had been a favorite conducting student of Fritz Reiner at the Curtis Institute in Philadelphia and was by then a distinguished conductor with a worldwide career.

At the Rachlin home in St. John's Wood in North London, Evelyn impressed Ezra Rachlin with her musicianship, but he questioned rightly how she would manage a career. What conductor was prepared to guide a deaf percussionist? That evening when the Rachlins heard Evelyn perform at the Albert Hall as xylophone soloist with the Cults ensemble, they were amazed. Convinced that Evelyn had a future in the music world, they arranged auditions for her with Pamela Dow and Martin Gibson, principal percussionists of the Scottish National Orchestra, and four months later a second meeting with James Blades.

Meanwhile Evelyn pressed ahead to study in London. She was the first deaf student to apply the Royal Academy of Music and perhaps to any other major conservatory, and her application was considered highly controversial. Her deafness was believed so serious a disadvantage that some felt strongly that she shouldn't even be considered. However, she was offered an audition on 29 March 1982. In the end, Evelyn's talent was so undeniable that the Royal Academy admitted her. "But there was an important condition," Glen-

nie recalled, "that I would only go in for music if I could specialize in solo percussion playing."

At times during her childhood, Evelyn's prodigiousness may have been
eclipsed, even doubtful. Her impending deafness, beginning when she was
eight, thrust her into unimaginable musical situations. That the musical culture at first responded slowly to her unique abilities also stemmed from the
dearth of soloists and hitherto only marginal repertoire in her chosen field of
percussion playing, unlike the domain of violinists and pianists that so abun-
dantly reveals child prodigies. These factors may explain the time elapsed
between Evelyn's early achievements as a hearing, fledgling performer and
her final ascendancy to mastery at the age of twenty, an age when other prodigy performers often have already enjoyed an extended career.

Evelyn bid farewell to Scotland in June 1982 and moved to England to
become a student at London's Royal Academy of Music. Immediately upon
her arrival, she performed privately for members of the royal family for the
first time. Following a fundraising concert for the Beethoven Fund for Deaf
Children at the Royal Festival Hall, Evelyn performed at the reception for the
concert's headliner, the jazz singer Nancy Wilson. With the superb pianist
Ezra Rachlin accompanying her, Evelyn played two solo transcriptions by
Ron Forbes, Jenő Hubay's *Hejre Kati* recast for the xylophone, and Vittorio
Monti's *Czárdas* as a marimba solo. The following day Peta Levi's article,
"Never take no for an answer," was published in the *Guardian* and Evelyn
Glennie was on her way to well-deserved recognition as a serious musician.

Living in a modest student dwelling and with no instruments of her own
for practicing, Evelyn quickly established an efficient daily routine at the
academy where she shared a small basement practice room with ten other
percussionists and worked before and after hours in the empty corridors.
Although her private percussion lessons with Nicholas Cole, principal percussionist with the Royal Philharmonic, were encouraging, she struggled to
keep up with the music theory and history classes where she did her best to
lip read. The usual listening facilities frequented by other students were of
no use for her, but the music library became her most nurturing haunt for the
solitary hours when she memorized hundreds of scores.

"Evelyn would be very upset if she thought we had made any allowances,
and we tried not to," said professor David Robinson. "In fact, I think we went
overboard to make quite sure that she had a 'tough ride.' She wanted to be
assessed as a musician, not as a deaf, handicapped musician."[11] During her
academy years, Evelyn was sometimes shunned by her fellow percussion-

ists who resented her singlemindedness. But that very dedication brought her success at the Barbican Centre in the 1984 Shell/London Symphony Orchestra Music Scholarship Competition. As one of forty-four competitors, Evelyn won the competition's gold medal and prize money for her performance of Andrzej Panufnik's Concerto for Timpani, Percussion, and Strings, and received a heartfelt congratulatory telegram from Buckingham Palace, simply signed "Charles."

During her final year at the academy, Evelyn performed Béla Bartók's Sonata for Two Pianos and Percussion for the first time when she appeared with the American duo pianists, Ralph Markham and Kenneth Broadway, and timpanist Chris Thomas in the Great Hall at Farnham Maltings. A month later she gave the premiere of Kenneth Dempster's *Concerto Palindromos* in the Duke's Hall at the Royal Academy. Sensing a major career in the making in the spring of 1984, impresario Nina Kaye invited Evelyn to join the roster of performers represented by the Kaye Artists Management in Chelsea. Evelyn accepted. Strengthened by her artistic success that season, Evelyn surged ahead, attempting to improve her playing. Always the intrepid traveler, she went alone to Berlin to meet with the illustrious Japanese marimba virtuoso, Keiko Abe, who subsequently invited her to study in Tokyo.

Arthur and Isobel Glennie came from Hillhead of Ardo to be with their daughter when she graduated on 10 July 1985. Still only nineteen, Evelyn had the great distinction to be the final student to step onto the platform, at which time she received not only her degree but the Royal Academy's highest honor, the Queen's Commendation Prize for all-round excellence, presented on that occasion by Princess Diana. "So much time, so much effort, so many hopes and dreams—and suddenly I was there, home and dry, a graduate of the Royal Academy of Music," Glennie has said.

In choosing a career as a solo percussionist, Evelyn had created another challenge for herself. Because serious musical compositions for percussion were almost nonexistent, she set out on her one-woman crusade to expand the repertoire by commissioning new works from composers such as Richard Rodney Bennet, Dave Heath, James MacMillan, John McLeod, Dominic Muldowney, Thea Musgrave, Malcolm Singer, and Loris Tjeknavorian. With the advent of this new repertoire, Evelyn was soon on stage performing new music that clearly reflected the age.

Now considered a leading solo percussionist, Evelyn Glennie appears internationally on four continents and has successfully recorded a series of nine compact discs, one of which won her a 1989 Grammy Award in Los Angeles. At her studio and home in the English countryside, she continues her intense exploration in sound surrounded by a collection of more than seven hundred percussion instruments, supported by the technical expertise of her talented husband, Greg Malcangi, a producer and recording engineer who takes time out to fly her by helicopter from their own backyard to her concerts throughout the United Kingdom.

Her many accolades include thirty-one major awards. In 1990, she was voted "Scots Woman of the Decade," and a year later she won the Royal Philharmonic Society's Charles Heidsieck "Soloist of the Year" award. Six universities have conferred honorary degrees upon her: the universities of Aberdeen, Bristol, and Portsmouth, the Honorary Doctorate of Music; the universities of Warwick and Loughborough, the Honorary Doctorate of Letters; and the University of Dundee, the Honorary Doctor of Laws. In London she has been elected a Fellow of both the Royal Academy of Music and the Royal College of Music. In 1993, she was made an Officer of the British Empire (OBE). "My aim is the same as it always has been," Glennie said, "to make music to the best of my ability and to communicate my delight in it to audiences of every kind all over the world."

CHAPTER TWELVE

Pocket Toscaninis

PIERINO GAMBA,
JOSEPH ALFIDI,
AND LORIN MAAZEL

I hated those rehearsals, I hated walking on stage, standing in front of all those people and trying to impose the authority of a ten-year-old mind on all those forty-year-old-plus minds.

Maazel, in Matheopoulos, *Maestro: Encounters With Conductors of Today*

IN THE twentieth century, maestros Artur Nikisch, Felix Weingartner, Thomas Beecham, and Arturo Toscanini reached the pinnacle of their artistry as octogenarians still blessed with physical vigor, penetrating insight, and extraordinary magnetism. One might well ask what role a child can have in such a complex enterprise as conducting. Certainly it is fascinating to see a gifted child conduct an orchestra of adults, and prodigy conductors, even if unnerved at times, have indeed captivated their audiences worldwide. Thus the allure of three little boys—Pierino Gamba, Joey Alfidi, and Lorin Maazel—brought them to international prominence in childhood.

The art of conducting was still primitive when Jean-Baptiste Lully stood before the court of Louis XIV at Versailles. Lully conducted by striking the floor vehemently with a sharp-pointed cane, hoping that the noise would be heard above the spectacles unfolding on stage. On 8 January 1687 while conducting his Te Deum, he accidentally struck his foot with his formidable baton; gangrene set in, and he died of blood poisoning three months later.

As we watch Leonard Bernstein conduct the New York Philharmonic, Zubin Mehta the Israel Philharmonic, Keri-Lynn Wilson the Dallas Symphony, or James Levine conducting for almost eight consecutive hours a gala performance telecast live from the Metropolitan Opera House, Lully's accident is worlds away. Today's conductors practice a highly cultivated but energetic art, controlling their orchestral forces with a small, hand-held wooden baton. In rehearsal and on stage, the musicians' attention is focused on the conductor's facial expression and body language, on every choreographed movement of the hand, the finger, the eye, and of course, the lightly held, flexible stick that subtly conveys the conductor's artistic intentions.

PIERINO

In May 1947 before a critical Paris audience, Pierino Gamba led the symphony orchestra of the Association des Concerts Lamoureux in a program of Beethoven, Rossini, and Schubert. When the last chords sounded, the listeners cheered him for twenty minutes. Critics hailed him as a "pocket Toscanini." Pierino was ten.[1]

Born in Rome on 16 September 1937, Pierino Gamba was the son of a pastry chef. His father, an amateur violinist, began giving the boy piano lessons when he was six in the hope of their later playing music together at home. After only eight lessons, Pierino was able to learn a Mozart minuet in a quarter-hour. Wary of child prodigies and appalled that his son might become a keyboard virtuoso, Pierre Gamba decided to teach him score-reading instead. The boy had a remarkable musical memory and surged ahead in this pursuit so quickly that by the age of eight he had learned the details of Beethoven's First Symphony.

Romeo Arduini, a conductor at the Rome Opera, took an interest in Pierino and began teaching him to conduct. He soon arranged for him to lead a rehearsal of the Beethoven symphony with an orchestra of players from the opera. Pierino's progress was so exceptional that Arduini presented him in public that season and continued to devote his retirement to nurturing the child as a prodigy conductor. The following year, the sensational Pierino again conducted in Rome, then continued on tour to Milan, Zurich, and Paris.

The Parisian audience found him boyish and friendly, yet dignified. However, after seven curtain calls with the Lamoureux orchestra, Pierino forgot his dignity and ran happily up and down the stage, which endeared him all the more to the crowd eager for prodigy entertainment. After a press conference on stage, the wonder child played with spent photographer's flashbulbs, throwing them all over the stage, them stamping on them, much the same as Mozart had immediately turned to a game of marbles after his performance for the historian Charles Burney. After his tour to France, Pierino went on to Switzerland, then returned home to Rome to his sandbox and his electric trains, which he liked almost as much as conducting.

In 1948 Pierino made his English debut conducting a Beethoven symphony at the Harringay Arena in London. The critics found his musical logic ruthless, everything in its place and sharply defined, and that Beethoven's music was not smeared with the prodigy's own personality, "perhaps because he hasn't yet developed a personality that will smear."[2]

In 1952 when he was fifteen, Pierino went to live in Madrid and began extensive tours of Europe and North and South America. Twenty years later he moved to Canada where he became the music director of the Winnipeg Symphony Orchestra. By then he had conducted orchestras in forty countries and in more than three hundred cities.

JOEY

"There are many, many things about Joey Alfidi which are very special. There is no superficiality in Joey's musical gifts. He has a strong personality, an impulsive temperament, and a delightful ability of enjoying almost anything which happens in his young life." Thus wrote Michael Privitello, Joey Alfidi's music tutor, about the triple-threat musician who was pianist, composer, and conductor.[3] Born in Yonkers, New York, on 28 May 1949, Joey was the son of American-born parents of Italian descent. His father, Frank Alfidi, was a trumpet player who ran a music school in Yonkers. Joey was only three when he started to play several instruments which he found in his father's studio. Much to his parents' surprise, by the time he was five, he frequently improvised little compositions at the piano in the middle of the night and soon became fascinated by symphonic music as well. A half-year after his sixth birthday, Joey Alfidi came to public attention when persuasive concert management found him professional engagements to conduct the Miami Symphony Orchestra in Florida and, somewhat later, members of the New York Philharmonic in a concert on Long Island.

On 18 November 1956, seven-year-old Joey Alfidi appeared in Carnegie Hall conducting one of America's greatest orchestras, the Symphony of the Air. The ambitious program included two overtures—those to Mozart's *The Marriage of Figaro* and Rossini's *William Tell*—Haydn's "Surprise" Symphony, and Beethoven's Fifth. Joey's authority on the podium garnered a rave press review. He had held a steady beat, had ideas of his own, and used a set of enviable gestures. However, the critic of the *New York Times* was skeptical: "Adults, it seems, are willing to present boy conductors at progressively younger years." Lorin Maazel was introduced at the New York World's Fair when he was nine. In 1948, the Italian wonder child, Ferrucio Burco, was presented at Carnegie Hall when he was eight. Now Joey made his bid at seven. During his performance, Joey had turned the pages of his Beethoven score erratically and his baton had flown out of his hand. The critic questioned whether the boy really led the orchestra or whether it went its own way while the child made gestures of being a conductor of a most fiery and dramatic type. Of course, he might well have asked that question of any conductor leading the former NBC Symphony, except perhaps Leopold Stokowski, then the orchestra's maestro.

During the intermission, Dr. Dante Catullo, the physician who had brought Joey into the world, addressed the audience on behalf of St. Joseph's Hospital in Yonkers, where the child was born, and the Sisters of Charity of that hospital who were the beneficiaries of the concert's earnings. The screen idol, Buster Crabbe, (known to millions as Flash Gordon) presented Joey with a gleaming red bicycle, then Steve Ridzik of the New York Giants gave him a baseball and bat on behalf of the famous team.[4]

Further appearances in New York with the Symphony of the Air followed in 1957, 1958, and 1960, and Joey conducted in many other American cities and toured Europe. He attended rehearsals and concerts led by Leopold Stokowski, Guido Cantelli, Pierre Monteux, Sir Thomas Beecham, and Leonard Bernstein. He learned about Toscanini's art from his record collection, but never meet the Italian maestro. According to Privitello, Toscanini had expressed a desire to meet the prodigy conductor, but died before such a meeting could be arranged.

Joey continued to perform as a piano virtuoso and to write symphonic compositions, chamber music, and piano works as he mastered conducting. On a European concert tour in late November 1960, the eleven-year-old musician appeared with the Antwerp Philharmonic and was hailed as "the greatest child prodigy since Mozart." A few days later on 1 December 1960, Joey gave a royal command performance at the Palais des Beaux-Arts in Brussels before the Dowager Queen Elisabeth of Belgium and a distinguished audience. At that gala concert, he appeared in his multiple roles as pianist, conductor, and composer.

When he came on stage in Brussels dressed in white tails, his mane of curly black hair tousled, the youngster made his way to the piano with all the physical ungainliness of his youth but with a seriousness of purpose that indicated his preoccupation with the task ahead. With the Belgian Jef Alpaerts conducting, Joey performed Beethoven's Third Piano Concerto, then returned to conduct his Eighth Symphony.

The traditional call to the royal box for an audience with Queen Elisabeth came in the intermission. With the typical boyish excitement of an eleven-year-old, Joey presented her with the manuscript of his new piano concerto he had dedicated to her in recognition of her internationally acclaimed patronage of music, the new work he would play for her for the first time within minutes. Before they parted, Joey remembered to ask a question that had been much on his mind. He asked permission to compete in the annual international piano competition in Brussels. The Queen, whose name is honored by the Belgian competition first established in 1937, responded wisely: "But why? You have enough talent already. You are very famous, greatly admired and loved. You have no need to enter any contest."

Once more on stage, Joey ended his gala appearance triumphantly by performing his new Piano Concerto No. 2 in G Minor, a work written the previous year when he was still only ten, inspired by the recent death of his younger sister.

The next morning, Joey Alfidi's performance was front-page news in Brussels. The critic of *Le Soir* hailed his appearance as pianist, conductor, and composer: "He played Beethoven's Piano Concerto No. 3 with a force and energy not common in a child. One has a strong impression that he is a born musician with a strong personality," and regarding his composition: "The Concerto No. 2 in G Minor . . . reveals intelligence and a high sense of musical expression. It shows the sensitivity of this young composer." The review concluded with an account of his conducting: "For a child of his age, he proves to have authority, will, memory, knowledge of his scores, and undeniable musicality. Very much at ease in front of the public and the orchestra, he gives proof of his understanding and his musical taste which is correct and natural. He has certainly received from nature the gift of the orchestral leader."[5]

Joseph Alfidi later returned to Brussels to continue his studies. In 1972, twelve years after his gala performance for Queen Elisabeth, he did enter the Concours Reine Elisabeth as a pianist and won the third prize. A decade later when he was thirty-two, he recorded George Gershwin's Concerto in F

Major with the Philharmonie van Vlaanderen conducted by Theodore
Bloomfield and made several other recordings of the music of Chopin,
Rachmaninov, and Samuel Barber. Joseph Alfidi continues to live in Bel-
gium where he is active as a conductor for Radio-Télévision Belge.

LORIN

In 1960, Lorin Maazel, the most famous conducting prodigy of the twentieth
century, had already left his wonder years behind when he made his Bayreuth debut with Wagner's *Lohengrin*. Yet at thirty he was the youngest conductor and the first American conductor to establish himself at the famous
Wagnerian festival. In the decades that followed, he distinguished himself as
both opera and symphony conductor. His allure was undiminished when he
appeared in 1990 as violinist and conductor with the Vienna Philharmonic
in a gala holiday performance on New Year's Day and captured the attention
of almost one billion television viewers around the world.

Born at Neuilly-sur-Seine, just outside Paris, on 5 March 1930, Lorin
Maazel moved to the United States in 1932 with his American parents. His
was a family of musicians: Lorin's grandfather was a violinist, his father and
his uncle were both singers, and his mother was a pianist. At home in Los
Angeles, Lorin's father encouraged him when he noticed that his precocious
son had perfect memory of pitch. Karl Moldrem began teaching him violin
when he was five and Fanchon Armitage the piano when he was seven.

When Lorin discovered Haydn's "Surprise" Symphony in a piano reduc-
tion, he became fascinated with the notion of conducting the work. In response to the boy's great interest, his father arranged for him to begin studying conducting with Vladimir Bakaleinikoff, then associate conductor of the
Los Angeles Philharmonic. Bakaleinikoff was an excellent teacher and Lorin
made such rapid progress under his guidance that in 1938 he was allowed to
conduct a rehearsal of the Los Angeles Philharmonic. Later that season,
Bakaleinikoff arranged for his eight-year-old pupil to appear on a concert of
the University of Idaho orchestra when they visited Los Angeles. Lorin made
his debut on 13 July 1938 conducting Schubert's "Unfinished" Symphony,
and his career as a prodigy conductor was launched.

The child spent two summers at the National Music Camp in Inter-
lochen, Michigan. Olin Downes, music critic of the *New York Times*, heard
him conduct an orchestral concert there and was so impressed that he used
his influence to have the boy conduct the National Music Camp Orchestra

at the Court of Peace at the New York World's Fair on 18 August 1939. Lorin was only nine. He conducted Mendelssohn's "Italian" Symphony and Tchaikovsky's *Marche Slave*, and after he had finished, "the maestro toddled down, . . . tugged at his shorts and ran toward the waiting arms of his father and mother," reported Louis Biancolli in the *World-Telegram*. "You had to rub your eyes to believe it—this chubby little figure in a white linen suit pace-making for an orchestra of seventy, and giving every cue on the dot."[6]

Later that summer he appeared again in California, this time leading the Los Angeles Philharmonic at the invitation of Leopold Stokowski who was conducting the orchestra at the Hollywood Bowl. The next season when Vladimir Bakaleinikoff was appointed associate conductor of the Pittsburgh Symphony Orchestra, the Maazel family moved east so that Lorin could continue to study with his devoted teacher.

New York concert manager Arthur Judson signed Lorin to a conducting contract that brought him an appearance in 1940 as guest conductor of the New York Philharmonic in a summer concert at Lewisohn Stadium. In 1941, Arturo Toscanini invited Lorin to conduct the NBC Symphony Orchestra, at which point the boy learned what happens when success, fame, and adulation are conferred upon a child of eleven. Yet he would prove his mettle in a test that would have undone many an adult.

At his first rehearsal with Toscanini's NBC orchestra, the musicians were outraged at the appearance of a mere boy on the podium and glared at him in open defiance while sucking lollipops to show their displeasure. A wrong note was purposefully played. Lorin immediately corrected it. The complete orchestral score was locked in his memory. From that small gesture, Lorin began to create a rapport with the veteran players, and they were soon rehearsing without further incident. A certain respect gradually arose for the child who reacted to their previous taunts with efficiency and courtesy. "So far as I can remember, by the second or third rehearsal things would have fallen into place simply because I was well-prepared," Maazel recalled. "I was really a little professional; I knew the score, had a good ear and a good memory, and musicians always appreciate that."[7]

Although Lorin's professional appearances were limited to about ten a year and confined to the school holidays—he appeared with the great orchestras including the Chicago Symphony, the Pittsburgh Symphony, and the Cleveland Orchestra, of which he would later become music director—his friends at school made him acutely aware of being somehow different. He has said that he would rather have led a normal childhood, but he does not blame his parents for pushing him into an early career, which in any case enabled him to adapt to the professional world of music at a very receptive age. "The Maazels were certainly not motivated by greed," Helena Matheopoulos has said. "Misguided ambition is the term [Lorin Maazel] would use."[8]

When asked in 1985 about his prodigy years, Maazel replied with candor, "I don't remember the period all that clearly. I do know I found the experience utterly normal. I still went to school and played baseball, and actually I gave very few concerts." Between the ages of nine and fifteen, Lorin conducted about sixty programs—and developed a healthy view of what notoriety and fame meant. "This I learned very early on, and it prevented me from becoming conceited and kept me sober with regard to being a public figure."[9]

He has commented that his childhood adventures as a professional conductor did not make him entirely happy. His early fascination with conducting was real, but Lorin's professional career was launched because the music business was searching for phenomenal performing child prodigies in 1940 and concert managers found something alluring in the eight-year-old—an authentic prodigy conductor. Yet orchestral conducting poses special challenges for the prodigy: the child conductor must be unusually verbal for his age to communicate effectively with orchestra members, even though paradoxically this particular realm may be the most solitary since few have access to the complex, living instrument that is the modern orchestra.

Despite accelerated progress from novice to master, the musical prodigy still endures endless hours of thinking and practicing. Lacking accessibility to the instrument upon which he or she will develop the craft of conducting, carry out actions, produce results, and experiment, how can the prodigy conductor fully grasp the practical meaning of the conductor's art? Moreover, while fledgling conducting prodigies may show more promise in this unique field of music than others of the same age, they must be able enough in practical matters to be judged by the most demanding criteria *regardless of age*: from the beginning they must compete with seasoned adults. These daunting circumstances make the childhood accomplishments of Piero Gamba, Joseph Alfidi, and Lorin Maazel seem all the more astounding.

CHAPTER THIRTEEN

The Rose Tree, *An Opera*

SAMUEL BARBER

I have written this to tell you my worrying secret. Now don't cry when you read it because it is neither yours nor my fault. . . . To begin with I was not meant to be an athlete. I was meant to be a composer, and will be I'm sure.

Barber, age nine, in a letter to his mother

WHEN Samuel Barber was barely two, his mother wrote to her family that he was making up tunes on the piano. By the time he was seven, he had begun to sign his pieces: "Sadness," his first composition; "Melody in F"; and "Sometime," a song dedicated to his mother based on a poem by Eugene Field. Of the ten youthful pieces he wrote during the next two years, half were for the piano, which he played intuitively and where he could most easily explore his musical ideas. The others were songs set to poetry he knew well.

Why the boy's inclination to compose vocal music should reveal itself when he was so young is as much a riddle as it was for Mozart, Schubert, or Rossini, but it was a powerful drive that endured throughout his life.

His father, Samuel Le Roy Barber, was a doctor in the village of West Chester, Pennsylvania, where Sam was born on 9 March 1910. His mother, Marguerite (always called Daisy), was a young woman of English and Scottish-Irish descent whose family had lived in New England since the American Revolution. The musician of the family was Daisy's sister, Louise Beatty, a celebrated contralto who would eventually exert a powerful artistic influence on her nephew, Sam.

In 1895, Louise married the composer Sidney Homer in Boston, then went with him to Paris where she studied singing and dramatic acting. She launched her operatic career in Europe and returned to the United States in 1900 to make her debut with the Metropolitan Opera. She triumphed in the role of Orfeo in 1910 when Arturo Toscanini conducted Gluck's opera in New York.

During Sam's childhood, Louise and Sidney Homer became the boy's most ardent musical supporters. When he was six they invited him to attend

Samuel Barber at seven, 1917.

his first opera performance, a production of Verdi's *Aida* at the Metropolitan Opera in which Enrico Caruso sang the role of Radames and Louise Homer sang Amneris. Later he was present at the Victor recording studios in Camden, New Jersey, when his aunt Louise and Caruso recorded "Aida, a me togliesti." Entranced by the music, Sam was particularly eager to observe the musicians playing in the orchestra.

He often spent his summer vacations with his aunt and uncle at Homeland, near Bolton-on-Lake-George in upstate New York. On these visits, Sidney Homer always reviewed Sam's new compositions, they sometimes studied music together, and to Sam's delight he often heard his aunt sing Homer's vocal works. The Homers' abiding confidence in Sam's talent bolstered the boy's aspirations and helped him withstand the provincialism of West Chester, a conservative Quaker town where musicians and theater people were regarded with some suspicion and where his own parents were not very enthusiastic about their son's calling. They hoped he would become an athlete instead.

While he was still very young, Sam sensed his parents' guarded reaction to his vocation; by the time he was nine he confronted their emotional restrictions in a determined letter to his mother. After his manifesto, his parents became more sympathetic to his needs. They engaged William Hatton Green, a former pupil of Theodor Leschetizky in Vienna, to give their son his first formal piano lessons. The town's best piano teacher, Green was an occasional recitalist who accompanied Louise Homer when she performed in West Chester. He taught Sam for the next six years.

On 7 April 1920 at the local First Presbyterian Church, Sam performed his own compositions in a recital of Green's piano pupils. The ten-year-old composer proved himself an accomplished ensemble player after only a year of study by performing with his teacher two of his own piano duets, "At Twilight" and "Lullaby," then accompanying soprano Charlsie Eddins when she sang his new song, "Child and Mother." A few days later, the *West Chester Daily Local News* noted that Sam was at his best in these performances: "The manner in which he executed different selections brought round after round of applause."[1]

Annie Noble, the Barbers' Irish cook, captured Sam's imagination by singing her apparently unlimited repertoire of Irish songs to him while commanding the kitchen of the family's red brick house on 107 South Church Street. When Sam decided to compose an opera, Annie Noble became his librettist. The romantic language of her Irish songs, which always remained in his memory, generated the poetic structure of *The Rose Tree,* the little opera that he wrote when he was still but ten. By seventeen, he began composing songs to Celtic poetry by James Stephens, James Joyce, and William Butler Yeats. His fascination for ancient Celtic texts influenced his great masterpiece of 1953, *Hermit Songs,* Op. 29, a song cycle based on tenth-century Irish poems.

The Rose Tree tells the story of a Metropolitan Opera tenor who comes to a small American town on his vacation and falls in love with a local beauty. In 1960 Barber told John Ardoin wistfully: "Somehow, after the words and music were written for the first act, Annie ran out of ideas and the opera went no further."[2] But it had gone far enough to give life to a cast of characters: Juanita Alvarado, the heroine (a role Sam composed for his little sister, Sarah); the Stranger (Sam, by then a contralto, sang the hero's role); and the supporting characters, the Landlord, an Old Man, and a Band of Gypsies, for which Sam wrote a chorus and dance, a habañera he later arranged for violin and piano in 1922.

Juanita's Serenade provides the climax of the only completed act of *The Rose Tree.* In this duet, the Stranger sings, "And so I come tonight, to sing my love to you," as he unfolds the tale of one who seeks love beneath the rose tree. The sentimental text of the Serenade was probably inspired by Annie Nobel's intimate knowledge of such songs as Robert Burns' "O my luve is like a red, red rose."

Although *The Rose Tree* remained unfinished, the young boy cleverly advertised on its inside back cover, "Other songs by same composer sold at $.60."

In addition to his early opera, by early adolescence Sam had composed a cantata, *Christmas Eve* (a trio with solos) and a dozen of the eventual sixty-eight songs that remained unpublished in his lifetime, including the Nursery Songs ("Mother Goose Rhymes set to music"). His instrumental works included various compositions for solo piano, two pianos, and pipe organ, an instrument he had begun to study. When he was twelve, Sam got a job as organist at the Westminster Presbyterian Church in West Chester, where he earned one hundred dollars a month until he was fired for refusing to follow the lead of the hymn singers when they chose to pause unduly long at cadences.

That winter Sam sought Sidney Homer's advice in a letter dated 19 December 1922: "Do you think from these works of mine that I can become a composer? And if so, what should I do to further my musical career?" Al-

though not wanting to go against the wishes of Sam's parents, Homer gave
the boy wise counsel: he should develop his musical taste for the best music
in all forms, find a good teacher in composition, and master a practical instrument.[3] No doubt it was this advice that eventually led the young composer to
pursue his studies beyond the confines of West Chester. When at fourteen
Sam played for Harold Randolph, director of the Peabody Conservatory of
Music in Baltimore, Randolph recommended that the teenager leave school
and direct himself toward full-time study of composition and music.[4]

In nearby Philadelphia, the Curtis Institute of Music opened its doors on
1 October 1924. The violinist Max Aronoff, who later played in the Curtis
String Quartet, was the first to enter. Samuel Barber was the second.[5] Sam
commuted the thirty miles to Philadelphia every Friday from West Chester,
where he was still a high school student, to study piano with George Boyle,
which he continued to do until 1926, at which time he began working with
Isabelle Vengerova.

In 1925 in his second year at Curtis, Sam began to study composition.
The Italian Natale Rosario Scalero taught him composition and music theory throughout the following decade and the rigorous, traditional education
Scalero dispensed in counterpoint, the experience in writing for all genres,
and training in all musical forms—large and small—left an indelible mark on
his student.[6] Although Scalero no longer played the violin in public after
1919, he brought an instrumentalist's sensibility to his teaching. When a
photograph of Scalero as a twenty-five-year-old violinist was sent to Samuel
Barber in 1970, he responded, "I was delighted to have the picture of my
dear teacher, Scalero, as a young man—for I had never seen a photograph of
him when he was a violinist. Menotti, too, was very interested to see it."[7]

After he began singing lessons in 1926 with Emilio de Gogorza, Sam
was the first at Curtis to achieve triple mastery as pianist, singer, and composer. He was well-read and accomplished in foreign languages and a scholar
of English literature. His affability and wit assured him a close circle of
friends, among them Rose Bampton, Jeanne Behrend, Benjamin de Loache,
and the members of the Curtis String Quartet. Carrying a letter of recommendation from the wife of Arturo Toscanini, a young Italian composer
named Gian-Carlo Menotti arrived at Curtis in 1927 to study with Scalero.
The first person he met was Samuel Barber. "I arrived and spoke very little
English," Menotti recalled. "He was the only pupil there who spoke fluent
French and some Italian. And so of course we became friends immediately
and became friends for life."[8]

Sam went to Europe for the first time in the summer of 1928. With David Freed, a cellist from Curtis who was his traveling companion, Sam frequently performed chamber music on board the SS *de Grasse* during the passage to Le Havre. The young composer's summer itinerary began in Paris ("as far from West Chester as it is in my power to be") where he heard Stravinsky conduct his new ballet, *Apollon musagète*. By the end of June, he was in Brittany, then on to Gressoney where he visited Rosario Scalero and his family daily. After a brief visit to Venice, he heard a real gypsy orchestra for the first time in Budapest, met the American composer George Antheil in Vienna, heard performances of Mozart's *The Magic Flute* and Beethoven's *Fidelio* in Salzburg, and then in Munich attended a performance of Wagner's *Parsifal*, a work he thoroughly disliked.

Realizing that summer was nearly over, Sam began to compose vigorously during his stay in Munich. He returned to Philadelphia in the fall with his Sonata for Violin and Piano completed. In 1929 the new sonata won the Joseph H. Bearns prize awarded by Columbia University.

For the annual concert of Rosario Scalero's composition students at the Curtis Institute on 10 December 1928, Muriel Hodge, David Barnett, Carl Bricken, and Samuel Barber presented their works. The concert opened with Sam's Prelude and Fugue for organ and ended with his new violin sonata in a performance by violinist Gama Gilbert, with the composer at the piano.

Later that month, Sam finished work on his Serenade for String Quartet and wrote to Sidney Homer that his two big compositions were complete, certainly an accomplishment for the eighteen-year-old who had studied less than three years with Scalero. While the violin sonata soon fell into oblivion, the serenade became a useful work for furthering Sam's career and a good vehicle for the young Curtis String Quartet, who later performed it on a national NBC radio broadcast and during a quartet tour of Europe in 1936. The serenade, published as Sam's Opus 1, has not survived in the string quartet repertoire, but it underwent a metamorphosis in 1943 and emerged in Sam's new version for string orchestra, a medium that brought out its true voice and guaranteed many further performances.

By May of 1929, Sam and Gian-Carlo sailed to Italy on the *Conte Grande*. Rosario Scalero and his daughter, Maria Teresa, were on board. They landed in Naples and then visited the ruins of Pompeii. On their return to Naples, the two young composers witnessed an eruption of Mount Vesuvius. They joined Rosario Scalero to visit Rome, then toured to Milan and Florence and finally to the Italian side of Lake Lugano to spend two weeks at the

Menotti villa at the village of Cadegliano. This was an idyllic interlude, their solitude broken only by family dinners and excursions into the countryside.

By the end of June, they were en route to Gressoney for lessons with Rosario Scalero. Sam wrote his parents: "I began to write the Concerto [for piano and orchestra] the other day and one cannot feel happy until it is finished." This work occupied the composer for the rest of his summer abroad (and far beyond that time), but its progress was uneven and sometimes disappointing. By August when he had finished the first movement, he returned to Curtis, where during the winter he began the orchestration of the concerto. The following summer Sam and Gian-Carlo were again in Italy, studying with Scalero who was living in an ancient castle in Montestrutto. With great tenacity, Sam continued to struggle with his piano concerto, often destroying large segments of the score when his compositional plans went awry. In August when Gian-Carlo went to visit his family in Cadegliano, Sam returned home to West Chester.

During the fall when the piano concerto was in its final stages, Scalero seemed genuinely dissatisfied with the work and Sam had some self-doubt as well. He submitted the finished work to Leopold Stokowski, then conductor of the Philadelphia Symphony Orchestra and at that time interested in looking at new scores, but he rejected the piano concerto. When Sam unburdened himself to Sidney Homer, his uncle responded with heartfelt sympathy, understanding that Sam, then only twenty, had simply not yet reached his maturity. He wrote, "Resentment eats the heart, but philosophy is an armor that protects the source of future work which is the one thing that must be kept inviolate."[9]

No one could have foreseen in 1931 that in his early struggle to compose a piano concerto Sam was gaining his mettle to create a masterpiece thirty years later. A sublime work, the Concerto for Piano and Orchestra, Op. 38, of 1962 would have astounded Rosario Scalero, who died in 1954, even though he may have guessed Sam's potential.

Many masterpieces were on the horizon in 1931: the Overture to *The School for Scandal*, *Dover Beach*, the Sonata for Cello and Piano, *Music for a Scene from Shelley*, and finally the String Quartet. These five works, along with numerous songs, mark Sam's ascendancy to mastery.

In the summer of 1931, Sam returned with Menotti to Cadegliano and every two weeks went to Montestrutto for his composition lessons with Scalero. In early July his idea for a new piece for orchestra met with Scalero's approval. The result was his Overture to *The School for Scandal*, a musical reflection of the spirit of Sheridan's eighteenth-century comedy of manners. It was two years before this work was given its first performance, conducted out-of-doors by Alexander Smallens on the last concert at the Robin Hood Dell summer series near Philadelphia. In April 1933, it won a second Joseph H. Bearns Prize that enabled Sam to spend yet another summer abroad studying with Scalero.

With the overture finished, Sam refined his new setting of Matthew Arnold's melancholy poem "Dover Beach" during the winter of 1931 in Philadelphia, dating the completed score 7 May 1931. This chamber work for voice and string quartet, a surprisingly mature creation for a young man of twenty-one, reminds the listener of nothing in everyday life, but rather of dreams and visions. Sam would sing this music many times in public, entrusting only contralto Rose Bampton to perform it on those occasions when he chose not to sing it himself. In May 1935 he recorded *Dover Beach* in Camden, a recording of his singing so admired by the French composer Francis Poulenc that he offered to write some songs for Sam to sing.

The Cello Sonata, which Sam started in the summer of 1932 in Cadegliano, was the last work he composed under Scalero's guidance after six years of study with the master teacher. When Sam returned to Curtis in the fall, he showed the partially completed work to his colleague, cellist Orlando Cole, who was to be the work's earliest champion. Sam dated the completed score 9 December 1932 and less than a month later performed it with Orlando Cole for the first time at the Art Alliance in Philadelphia. An eloquent moment in the sonata resulted from Sam's afterthought—he appended two miraculous adagio passages to embrace the fast sections of the second movement. The genesis of these slow-moving fragments will remain a mystery: they appear to have manifested themselves fully formed, spontaneously brought into existence by Sam's powerful creative urge.

In Italy at Cadegliano in the summer of 1933, Sam began work on his second large-scale orchestral work, *Music for a Scene from Shelley*. After examining more than 150 manuscripts by American composers, the conductor Werner Janssen chose it for a premiere performance at Carnegie Hall on 24 March 1935. No one was allowed at rehearsals, but Sam and Gian-Carlo hid between the rows of empty seats to witness the work's only rehearsal during which only a segment was played through. After the performance, critic Francis Perkins wrote in the *New York Herald Tribune* that "the score deserves to be rated as one of the most appealing new works by a native American that has been heard here during the last five or ten years."[10]

In the spring of 1935, the American Prix de Rome was awarded to Sam as "the most talented and deserving student of music in America," and the young man from West Chester was off to Rome to study at the American Academy for two years. This accolade and the many successful performances of his early works prompted the New York publisher G. Schirmer to publish the Overture to *The School for Scandal*, *Dover Beach*, and the Cello Sonata.

Among the many compositions that came from Sam's pen in the mid-1930s, including his Symphony in One Movement, the String Quartet is of singular significance, not so much for its prominence as an entity (it has not survived in the contemporary quartet repertoire), but for its slow movement, an adagio that ultimately achieved worldwide recognition.

In 1933 Sam paid several visits to Arturo Toscanini at his home on Isola de San Giovanni, one of the four islands in Lago Maggiore. On these visits Toscanini spoke of Louise Homer's performance of *Orfeo* that he had conducted in 1910 and he showed the young man many of his personal treasures, including a rare portrait of the youthful Beethoven and the last fragment of music Wagner wrote. A bond was forged between them, and a few years later Sam sent Toscanini the scores for *Essay for Orchestra No. 1* and a five-part arrangement for string orchestra of the adagio from his string quartet that he now called Adagio for Strings.

Toscanini conducted these works on a broadcasted NBC Symphony concert on 5 November 1938. After the broadcast's success, Toscanini recorded the Adagio for Strings in an empty Carnegie Hall (it was his first recording of an American work), then took it on tour to England and to South America. During the half-century that followed, the Adagio for Strings withstood the test of time. Along with the masterpieces of Barber's maturity, it now holds an undisputed place in the twentieth-century repertoire.

On a 1982 BBC retrospective broadcast about Samuel Barber, a group of musicians was asked why the Adagio for Strings was such a "perfect piece of music." American composer William Schuman remarked, "The emotional climate is never left in doubt . . . when I hear it played I'm always moved by it." Aaron Copland said, "It comes straight from the heart, to use old fashioned terms. . . . it makes you believe in the sincerity which he obviously put into it."[11]

To develop a unique compositional style, a composer must be committed in at least one of three directions: to himself, to his time, or to his tradition. From childhood, Samuel Barber practiced a tonal art, developing a romantic style distinguished by a striking lyricism. Unlike many of his colleagues, he showed little interest in pursuing the avant-garde. Instead, he sustained a personal vision of music and of the tradition that had influenced him most. This conservatism sometimes brought adverse criticism or neglect from those most interested in new trends; however, with the creation of Adagio for Strings in 1936 Samuel Barber fulfilled the promise of his wonder years. He composed music that spoke from the mind and heart of the composer to the minds and hearts of his listeners into posterity.

CHAPTER FOURTEEN

The Spirit of the Gypsy

KATÓ HAVAS

*Emerson was among those who believed that every human being contains
a divine spark. The task for artists, whether writers, sculptors, painters, or
musicians, is to become aware of this spark and develop it into a flaming
torch without allowing it to become an unruly, destructive fire. The very
process of nurturing and tending it is what I think artistic freedom and the
responsibilities that go with it are all about.*

Havas, "What Is Artistic Freedom?"

I MET Kató Havas while doing a backstage chore—unloading folding chairs
from a van for an Oxfam benefit concert in Dorset, England. The first
time I saw her with a violin in her hands was the next morning, a balmy July
day in 1967. A small group of musicians had gathered in the music room of
Kitchie House, Kató's idyllic cottage at the foot of Nine Barrow Down on the
Isle of Purbeck, a few miles from the English Channel. She entered the
music room relaxed and clear-minded, greeted us, then sat quietly on the
stone steps, determined not to intimidate us by her presence as so often happens in the traditional master class. Yet in the engaging and sophisticated violinist I could still sense the once-famous child she had been. The spirit of the
gypsy shone brightly in her eyes, an unexpected, exciting aspect that was a bit
unnerving despite her self-effacing stance.

She was born in the Transylvanian town of Kolozsvár in Hungary on 5
November 1920. Her youthful career unfolded in the 1930s, reaching an
enviable climax in her Carnegie Hall debut at eighteen, after which she

First recital in Transylvania. Kató Havas at seven, 1927. Courtesy Kató Havas.

undertook a demanding concert tour across the United States. In her little book *The Violin and I*, she recalls her feelings at the time:

> I was no longer a child prodigy. Though I remained small, and looked no more than fourteen, I considered myself a fully fledged artist (with all the problems and responsibility that such a position entails) and a grown up girl: and to the amazement of everybody, including myself, by the time the year was out I was married to an American writer.[1]

Kató did not give up playing the violin at once—it was a gradual process—but while bringing up her three daughters in New Hampshire, she withdrew from professional life. It was during this period of withdrawal that she evolved her revolutionary method of teaching that was based on finding logical and simple solutions for release from the tensions and anxieties that beset many violinists during performance. Her book of 1961, *A New Approach to Violin Playing*, had drawn us all to Kitchie House.

When a young man stepped forward to play Vitali's Chaconne that July morning in 1967, our odyssey of discovery had begun. A professional orchestral violinist, he played well and conveyed the meaning of the music as best he could, but he abruptly stopped with a sigh of resignation. It was obvious that he was not pleased with himself or his violin playing. The intimacy of the music room was so charged with unexpected emotion that it seemed incredible that the sheep just beyond the sun-drenched windows could continue to graze untroubled. The young violinist found himself entrapped, his self-esteem suddenly lost. In the brief silence that followed we waited to see what would happen next. Was this simply to be the familiar ritual of the music lesson or would something quite different reveal itself, the new approach we all hoped for?

At that critical moment, Kató Havas did not overwhelm him by playing Vitali's Chaconne herself. Before she uttered a word, she calmly stroked her strings, then coaxed an innocent note from her violin. The sound was incandescent, reverberating endlessly. I realized that she had begun teaching. Kató Havas was already deeply involved in helping the young violinist light his own divine spark and in that moment I knew she was a keeper of the flame.

Once we had heard the free-spirited voice of her violin, we yearned for more, but we were to have no claim on a prolonged hearing of the great violinist. This was her way. With each phrase she played during the weeks that followed, whether from a lilting Hungarian folk tune or the dazzling finale of the Mendelssohn concerto, we learned that her teaching was not based on her ability to melt our hearts with her bittersweet tone or to thrill our senses with the power and clarity of her projection. We were there to work together, to join her in searching, thinking, and discovering—things that she had done since childhood. She was determined that we would each draw something of consequence from within ourselves. She would be our guide.

At the end of the day she returned to her violin, again playing a single note that took on a life of its own. We wondered from what human depths such a tone could emerge, but we understood what she had written in her autobiographical account—that there was no question of a teacher-pupil relationship, that she was only trying to solve some problems that applied in different degrees to all string players, that she did not set out to criticize and destroy, but to build and perhaps to offer some help, and that she was just as ready to learn from her students as they were from her. As I walked away from Kitchie House that day, she said to me, "This is so simple that it may take some time for you to believe in it."

In 1984, nineteen years later, the Kató Havas Association for the New Approach (KHANA) was founded to communicate with the many people throughout the world who had adopted the New Approach ideals. By 1996, this association (of which Havas is president) encompassed twenty-four countries. In 1991, an important teaching video was created,[2] and one year later the American String Teachers Association gave her their international award in recognition of her "unparalleled achievements" as a teacher. In November 1995, her students around the world helped celebrate her seventy-fifth birthday. For seventy of those years she had played the violin, a life pursuit that began in Transylvania when she was five.

Ever since our first meeting, this remarkable woman has shared her reminiscences with me about the ways in which her childhood was infused with music and the spirit of the gypsy:

A first recital is always a big event, especially if one happens to be seven years old. I clearly remember the pink rococo-style taffeta frock with the matching bow in my hair and the two things that were dinned into me. The first was that I should look on the audience as if they were so many cabbages and on no account was I to take any notice of them. The second was that I should go on playing no matter what happened.

The cabbage idea I did not understand at all. Why should I turn the audience into cabbages when I could hardly wait to play for them?

So the moment I stepped on stage and heard the applause I forgot all thoughts of cabbages, and I remember to this day the face of the woman in the front row. But I followed the second idea and when, due to a short circuit, all the lights went out, I dutifully continued with the fast bit of the Brahms "Hungarian Dance," even though the pianist did not.

I clearly remember being taken to Emil Telmányi one day early in the morning, a few months after my first public recital in Kolozsvár. I remember noticing with some pleasure how untidy his hotel room was, with his patent leather shoes peeping out from under his unmade bed, and the end of his tail coat carelessly sweeping the floor from a chair. He had just been giving a concert the evening before, and was in a hurry to catch a train. But however hasty that meeting may have been, the upshot of my playing to him was that he persuaded my parents to move to Budapest with me so that I could study at the Academy of Music under Imre Waldbauer.

Waldbauer had been a pupil of Jenő Hubay, who was the director of the academy and was acclaimed by many violinists in central Europe as one of the gods of the great schools of violin playing. Hubay in his turn had been a pupil of Joseph Joachim and that by itself would have been enough for people to flock to him from all over the world for lessons. Whatever the truth may have been, it was generally accepted that the only pupils of Joachim who flourished were those good at imitating. The rest fell by the wayside. In Hungary, Imre Waldbauer was the first to turn away from this imitative Old School of teaching. To my knowledge, he was the first in the history of violin pedagogy who began to experiment with the *Gestalt* in his teaching.

I was an only child at that time and he and his family practically adopted me after we moved to Budapest. I stayed for days on end in their house in Buda learning to play football from his son, Iván, and learning from Márta, his daughter, what fun it was to be naughty. Waldbauer was the leader of the quartet bearing his name which was known all over Europe, and which was the first to introduce Bartók's first four string quartets to the public—quite a courageous act in those days. Waldbauer and Bartók were close friends and I remember time and time again filtering in from the garden quietly so that they wouldn't notice me, listening to those rehearsals and passionate discussions.

But though there are many pleasant memories of those days, the pressure of work was very great indeed: five hours' practice every day, four lessons a week, two mornings of master classes, two afternoons of chamber music, piano and viola lessons, harmony, lectures on the history of music—all this apart from continuous public appearances. However, it was soon made clear to me that to be a student at the academy was a great privilege for everyone, but to study with Waldbauer was a very special privilege indeed. This was particularly true for me, because as far as I can remember, I was the only child violinist in his class at the academy at that time.

He considered the ordinary educational system a waste of time, but arranged for me to attend an exclusive private school for one or two mornings a week. There I was looked upon as an honored pupil, and my parents were exempt from paying fees. Waldbauer also saw to it that I had private English and German lessons. He was eager for me to equate the history of music with a parallel history in art, so I was exposed to the visual arts as well. He also made me into an avid reader.

He was adamant that I should hear all the great artists who came to play in Budapest and saw to it that I could always get a free standing ticket in the organ gallery of the concert hall at the academy. As I was too small to see over, I have distinct memories of having to stand on a rung so that I could lean over the top. It was often the young violinist Misi (Michael) Kuttner who hung onto my shirt tail as I climbed on the rail during these performances to see the players.

Waldbauer was a great believer in physical exercise (which was not the fashion in those days as it is now), and in the summer I had to swim every day and in winter I had to go ice skating on flooded tennis courts every evening after my day's work. The cold was often severe and I was bundled into a thick, heavily padded coat, fur-lined cap, and mittens on top of my woolen gloves. These were huge, like boxing gloves, to keep my hands warm and safe. No one else looked like me, but I dare say no one else was a child prodigy either.

In Kolozsvár, my teacher, Paula Kuba, had been a woman who had told me endless stories about the magic of the violin being connected with friendly (and not so friendly) devils. As we lived in a flat, she had also provided me with a patch of my own in her garden and with a tiny spade and hoe. In Budapest, I was still homesick for her and her garden. She had made me sing every piece with note names while clapping the rhythmic pulse with my hands before she allowed me to play it on the violin. (It was only later in Budapest that I realized I had been taught by the Kodály system.) Thanks to her, I had learned to count through note values way before I was acquainted with regular numbers, so one way or another, I was able to hold my own in Waldbauer's chamber music classes.

Imre Waldbauer would not make any concessions for me for being a child, and made sure that no one else did either, no matter how small and frail I may have looked. So, thanks to him, I was referred to as "little Havas," rather than by my first name, which made me feel marvelously grown up, as the "little" seemed to refer only to my size, and not to my stature. He believed that the best preparation for a concert career was to play as much as possible in front of people. He also knew that a performance in intimate surroundings was more exacting than on the stage in a concert hall. So, apart from the master classes and numerous recitals at the academy, he also introduced me to the wealthy patrons in the great houses of Budapest. The soirees given for me were lavish affairs, and were sometimes preceded by a dinner party for more than twenty people.

I don't remember having to do much preparation for these soirees. These events were supposed to be taken lightly, though I could not help noticing that Waldbauer's ears always turned purple while I played. The programs were usually light too, to suit the occasion, like Dohnányi's *Ruralia Hungarica*, Wieniawski's *Scherzo-tarantelle*, a Paganini caprice or two, though there were always one or two violin and piano sonatas, mostly Mozart, but sometimes Schubert and Beethoven, and later on, unaccompanied Bach.

When Waldbauer referred to me as "my dear little golden one" with suppressed fury in his voice, I knew I was in trouble. On the other hand, "my Kató," without any diminutive affixed to my name, meant approval. In the beginning, it wasn't always clear what caused the fury or the approval. On the occasions of these soirees, I was definitely addressed as "my Kató" without any diminutive. "Golden one" was reserved for the master classes with an unspoken understanding that the privilege of these soirees was never to be mentioned at the academy.

At my first recital at the academy in Budapest when I was fourteen, I would have given a pretty penny for the audience to turn into cabbages, especially when at the beginning of Tartini's "Devil's

Trill" I saw Hubay, Kodály, Weiner, Dohnányi, and Bartók appear, one by one, in the balcony. They had come to find out what the girl from Transylvania sounded like. Hubay with his long white hair and white beard not only resisted all ideas of turning into a cabbage, but looked like a dignitary from Heaven itself, ready to dole out the most terrifying punishment. So all I could do was lose awareness, and all I remember is coming to only at the sound of applause at the end.

Most performers, regardless of whether they are actors, dancers, or musicians, tend to be different from other people. Their requirements are the same all over the world. They have an overwhelming need to be loved and to be favorably thought of. They all strive to achieve those, alas, only too rare moments of pure communication, when performer and audience alike are suspended in a transcendental moment of truth. For me, it happened many, many years ago, in a railway carriage, when I was about fifteen years old.

For some reason or other, the train was delayed at a small station, somewhere in Hungary. I do not remember where this station was, or where I was going. I only remember that it was early in the morning and that in order to while away the time, I thought I would play some Bach—the Chaconne to be exact. Soon, I noticed that some window cleaners and other workmen were gathering in front of my carriage window, signaling to me to let the window down so that they could hear. It was then I first felt that overwhelming necessity to transmit my deep-seated and profound feeling for the Chaconne, without the burden of having to play for approval. And the miracle began to happen. Their immobile silence and the spell of their rapt attention transferred both them and the Chaconne into a blissful unified entity. To equate the limited, harsh reality around them with the limitless, omniscient world of Bach was a very heady experience indeed. That was when I realized that "giving" the music and not trying to play well was the real secret of performance. But even with that realization, I could never, ever again recapture that first experience. I had many other memorable performances, but they were never quite the same. Also, I never, before or after, had the same marvelous reward as the large hunk of black bread and bacon, sprinkled with paprika, which they produced for me.

I was eighteen when I first became aware of the fluidity of time. It was when I first saw the sea. It was an overwhelming experience and

the effect of it remains with me to this day. In 1938 I was in Cherbourg on my way to New York via the SS *Aquitania* to give my debut
at Carnegie Hall. I was in an emotional state anyhow, as I was leaving
behind everything and everyone I knew, including the familiar land
mass of the European continent. I have always loved the sound of
water, the chatter of brooks, the endless whisper of rivers. Their music
has always given me a sense of space and peace. But the sight and
sound of the sea was a different matter altogether. I felt dissolved in its
vastness, in its sound, and in its seemingly infinite timelessness. It was
a feeling similar to that when, at the age of five, I saw my little violin
lying in its case, with real strings and a real little bow next to it. I
remember even now how strongly I sensed its fluid, transient power,
although I couldn't then have put it into words.

Since that day in Cherbourg I have spent time by many seasides
and have swum in many oceans around the world. And since my first
encounter with my little violin I have had many other violins, which
have grown in size with me until slowly, imperceptibly, one seemed to
have become even bigger than I. By the time I'd played my successful
New York debut and undertaken a hectic tour across America, it had
begun to present an actual threat. I knew it was trying to tell me
something, but I didn't know what.

Three daughters and a world war later it became clear. I realized
that the demands on my playing in that still-alien country, the pres-
surized feeling of constantly running against time, had taken their toll.
I had developed tensions which were blocking my hitherto natural
"inside-outward" energy flow. Playing Paganini was no problem, but
the gypsy-fiddler-like liquid, golden sound of my violin had receded.
It became obvious that this threatening aspect was a signal of its dis-
approval of being deprived of its life-giving nourishment—my energy
drive. Without being aware of it, I had been butting against the flow
of time. So I began to evoke the playing of the almost-forgotten gypsy
fiddlers from my childhood. And I began anew to track down the
causes and to find possible solutions to the problem in an attempt to
regain this natural equilibrium.

The Hungarian gypsies in Transylvania, where I was born, had no
problems with musicology and research. They knew how the violin
came to be. According to their folklore, as I was often told as a child,
the violin was created by the devil himself. The story goes that there

were two lovers who were parted by fate. As they could not endure the pain of separation, the woman took it upon herself to sell their souls to the devil. So, he turned her into a violin and her lover into a bow. At once, their pleasure at being together was immeasurable, and affected all the other bowed instruments as well. They conquered the world with their magic spell.

If we give credit to this gypsy legend that the devil created the violin (and my experience in years of teaching makes this theory only too plausible), we can understand that, besides its magic spell, the violin is also obliged to dispense pain and grief in equal measures on the player. So the devil saw to it that violin playing became systematized with different and sometimes totally opposite methods and he also arranged the appearance of countless tutor books, study books, and scale books.

Luckily, the gypsies in my childhood could read neither words nor music, and had no violin lessons. So their spellbinding affinity with their violins continued to enchant the listeners. Through them, the unique, haunting voices of the lovers were able to cover the whole spectrum of human emotions.

Anybody who has heard a real country gypsy play the violin knows that the quality of his tone with its infinite variety, his incredible rhythmic pulse, his almost devilish technical facility, rank him among the few top violinists in the world; and his ability to become one with his listener is phenomenal. There is a Hungarian proverb that the Magyar peasant becomes intoxicated on a glass of water when a gypsy fiddler plays for him.

One of the most important factors in the gypsy's power of communication is his "rhythmic pulse," an organic pulse which involves his whole body, not only his arms and hands. Even if we do not get anything else from the gypsies, we could derive from them their total interplay of motion and balance, through their rhythmic pulse. This is what differentiated Fritz Kreisler from all other players in his time— what made audiences stand up all over the world when he appeared on the stage—his ability to combine the ease of a gypsy with the music of Bach.

Even as a child I sensed that perhaps the red mark on the neck, the calluses on the fingertips, the effort and fatigue that went with violin playing were unnecessary. After all, didn't the gypsies play with incredible ease? Especially my particular hero, a plump, elderly gypsy with a shiny dark face and large, fiery eyes, whose name was Csicso (pronounced "Chicho"). He lived in a village by the Danube about thirty miles from Budapest where I used to spend my summer holidays. And even now I can count on one hand the people I have heard play who can equal the quality of his tone with its warmth, its flexibility, and its endless subtle variety. It was the nearest thing to the human voice I have ever heard. And the pleasure he took in playing was a feat to watch by itself. I can still see his smile, with his white teeth showing, his eyes lighting up as he acknowledged an order for a favorite song.

There was, and I sincerely hope still is, a custom in Hungary which is called *Mulatni*. This word, so far as I know, is untranslatable but describes a peculiarity unique to the country, practiced mostly in the villages. It is a sort of "letting off steam" process. If a peasant is visited by a great sorrow or a great joy, or sometimes both at once, it becomes necessary for him to express this in music in front of and with the help of as many people as possible. So he goes to the inn which is also a restaurant, or to a restaurant which is also an inn, and spends hours, sometimes days, ordering songs from the gypsies to suit his mood.

As often as not these occasions end in a fight, so I was usually kept away, but the restaurant Csicso played at was by the bank of the Danube very close to our house, and I have seen enough to be amazed at his complete identification with any given song, and his ability to cast a spell of sorrow or joy over us all. In fact, without knowing it then, I witnessed the epitome of perfect artistic communication.

Csicso and I were friends. His letters when I was in America and even after I was married always began "Draga Katoka," the equivalent of "Dear little Kató." Then, after a while, the letters (which he always dictated because he himself could not write) stopped. I heard later that he had died shortly after the war; and that at his funeral his violin, with all the strings cut, was carried on a red velvet cushion behind his coffin, and was lowered into the grave and was buried along with him.[3]

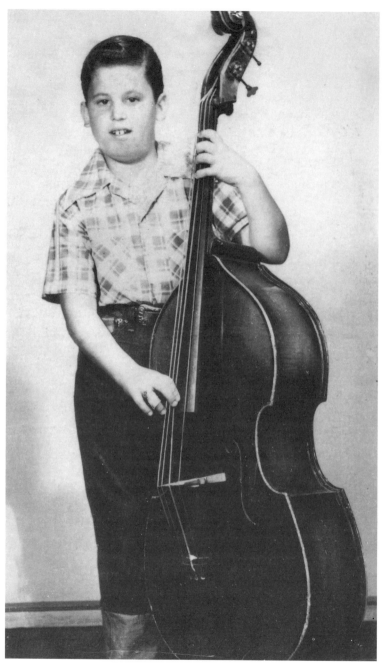

Gary Karr at eight, playing on a family heirloom, a one-eighth size double bass, 1949. Courtesy Gary Karr.

CHAPTER FIFTEEN

Bass Is Beautiful

GARY KARR

There is no question in my mind that starting even the so-called unwieldy double bass at a young age is extremely beneficial and I feel I can do the most for the youngest students, because after the fourth grade they're set in their ways, almost inflexible.

Karr, 1996

THE CAREER of a phenomenal teenage bassist named Gary Karr was in its ascendancy in the late 1950s in Los Angeles. He became the most celebrated solo bassist of our century, perhaps of all time, joining the distinguished company of the legendary bassists of the past: Domenico Dragonetti, Giovanni Bottesini, and Serge Koussevitsky. Karr had already made the musical world aware of the possibilities of the double bass as a concert instrument when *Time* magazine called him "the world's leading solo bassist"[1] After his debut with Leonard Bernstein and the New York Philharmonic in 1962, he performed with major symphony orchestras around the world, often playing the new music he had commissioned from such composers as John Downey, Hans Werner Henze, Wilfred Josephs, Robert Rodriguez, Lalo Schifrin, and Gunther Schuller. Recordings and television appearances followed. Nine recordings taped and released in Japan soon ranked among "top-of-the-charts" favorites in Asia, and twenty million viewers enjoyed his recitals on Italy's most popular classical music program on television. In 1972, he formed the Karr-Lewis Duo with the American keyboard artist Harmon Lewis. For more than two decades their distinguished recitals have taken them around the globe.

Gary Karr was determined to play the bass when he was five, but even when he stood on an orange crate he still wasn't tall enough to manage an eighth-sized instrument. Throughout his life, this lovable, good-humored artist has always remembered how important his early training as a prodigy was to him, and he remains devoted to teaching all children who yearn to play the instrument. Karr seems born for the stage. Hugging his 386-year-old Amati bass made in 1611 (the concert instrument of the late Koussevitsky), he lives his motto, "Bass is Beautiful!" His extraordinary, spontaneous virtuosity and ability to communicate what is in his heart create a heady musical experience for every audience, whether he is improvising an informal recital for elementary school children somewhere in the American heartland or playing a command performance at the palace of the emperor of Japan.

Gary Karr was born in Los Angeles on 20 November 1941, into a family who already had a tradition of bass playing.

I came from a family of seven generations of double bassists. I tried to start the study of the double bass when I was five because there was an instrument in my family that had been passed down through the generations. It was one-eighth size, two inches smaller than a normal cello. It was a nice little instrument, an unusual instrument because until recent years very few such small basses seemed to be in existence. I was pretty lucky to have something like that in the possession of my family.

When I tried to begin, I had to stand on a wooden orange crate. I was quite a short child, and even with the help of an orange crate I still wasn't tall enough to manage an eighth-sized double bass, but I'll never forget the first physical sensation when I drew the bow across the string or plucked the string while standing next to the little instrument that shook and vibrated.

My formal training started at the age of nine, probably at the time of the death of Serge Koussevitsky. Later I learned that Madame Olga Koussevitsky really did believe that her husband's spirit inhabited my body. Not long before she died, she took me to the cemetery where he was buried near Tanglewood and much to my amazement I discovered that when I began my serious study of the double bass in 1951, it was, perhaps to the day, the exact time Koussevitsky died.

I was first taught by Uda Demenstein, who also taught my grandfather, my uncle, and my cousin. Demenstein was a Russian musician who was born in Lithuania at Vilna, the same town as my father. I was lucky enough to have Demenstein living across the street from my family in Los Angeles. Although he suffered terribly from a weak heart, his working with me as a child seemed to be one of the activities in his later years that kept him alive, because he looked forward to our daily contact. What he achieved in my case was teaching me how to practice because I did see him almost daily as we went through the most traditional techniques.

I suppose even in Russia during Demenstein's time, the Franz Simandl Method was the bible of double bass playing.[2] While obviously it did not permanently hamper my development, studying this method was something I have regretted for most of my playing years. It caused a lot of problems that I still have not been able to resolve to this day.

My inspiration for playing the bass came from my teacher, Uda, who like so many of the Russian musicians of the time, was very expressive, poetic, lyrical. He always made me play lyrically on the double bass. I don't know if it was because of his insistence or because of the sound I envisioned (or a combination of both which is the more likely thing), but from the time I began I heard the double bass not so much as an instrument but as a *voice*. Even at a young age I liked to play slow pieces because it would give me a chance to sing through the bass. The great inspiration for my heading in the direction of a solo career came from my grandfather, a wonderfully cultured man who played the bass—and the trumpet. Music was his soul. Music was the best way he could express himself. On the trumpet, he played for me the *Kol Nidrei* of Max Bruch. I thought it was so beautiful! From that moment my main goal was to be able to play the *Kol Nidrei* so beautifully on my bass that I would be asked to perform it in the synagogue, which I did at the age of eleven.

After Uda Demenstein died, I resumed my studies with another man who had also taught two generations of my family. His name was Herman Reinshagen. He had been the first bassist of the New York Philharmonic under Toscanini before retiring in California. By the time I began to study with him, Reinshagen was already ninety years old. He was very much a philosopher. I loved to go to my lessons and hear him talk because he made me realize that music was more than just an academic pursuit. It was a way of life, a philosophical existence that appealed to me.

Reinshagen loved to copy music and worked laboriously at this task using a special manuscript pen on onionskin transparencies. He constantly transcribed pieces for the bass, perhaps nothing of great importance, but transcriptions that were lyrical pieces, idiomatically well-suited to the double bass. I was so excited by the enormous amount of work he had done! I knew that if I played my lessons well I would receive one piece of music each week, which in fact was the case. During that time I played an enormous amount of what today would be considered very "corny" repertoire. But it was playing that repertoire that gave me the insight to appreciate greatness. When you start with "corn" and have to make it seem important, then finally get a fine piece to play, you begin to realize what goes into the making of great music and how best to interpret it.

Los Angeles in the 1940s and 1950s was the mecca in America for great music-making. After the Second World War when most musicians playing in symphony orchestras were having a tough time, many of the finest found that the most lucrative work internationally was in the Hollywood movie studios such as MGM and Twentieth Century–Fox, studios that had their own orchestras. At one time the various studios in Los Angeles had contracts with eleven orchestras, and musicians from all over the United States—indeed from all over the world—were brought to play in them. In one city they comprised a group of musicians the likes of which may not have ever occurred anywhere else. It is for that reason that many of the students who grew up in Los Angeles at the time I did had the enormous benefit of work-ing with some of the great musicians of our time.

Because during the war so many of the great teachers in Europe and Russia were Jewish, or sympathetic to the Jewish situation, they escaped persecution by fleeing their homelands. I learned only last year when I returned to Russia how complete is the circle when I saw where my training had come from. Of course, many of the great teachers in Russia had escaped much earlier in the century and there is a great gap now in Russia in the kind of musical training I received from my Russian teachers in America who were very poetic musicians, very expressive musicians—musicians who taught from the heart.

During that golden age of music in California, Los Angeles was home to many great string players, including Gregor Piatigorsky and Jascha Heifetz, to name only two. I had a firsthand opportunity to observe them in performances and later on in master classes where I got to meet them, which was terribly exciting. I was so particularly impressed by Jascha Heifetz's bowing technique that I adopted many of the things that he did. Although I knew that many violinists regarded him as having a very peculiar bow arm, I thought that it was the perfect bow arm! I incorporated many of his technical ideas on the double bass, and I think it was because of Jascha Heifetz more than anybody else that I learned to play so close to the bridge and learned how to do that without forcing my tone. Because of my early training with Uda Demenstein, I was terribly sensitive to the vocal arts and in Los Angeles I listened not only to many instrumental performances, but to a lot of vocal concerts where I met artists like Igor Gorin, who was a great baritone at the time. I think my genuine interest in both instrumental and vocal performances was responsible for molding my technique.

While I was still in high school, I entered a contest sponsored by the Young Musicians Foundation of Los Angeles. I played Domenico Dragonetti's concerto. The judges were so surprised by my virtuosity on the double bass that they wanted to give me the first prize, but after the board met they decided a double bassist simply could not receive what they felt was such a prestigious award, so I did not win. However, in all their subsequent printed brochures they always called me one of their award winners, when in fact I never did get their award. What I did get from them was an opportunity to play the Dragonetti concerto in public with Henry Lewis conducting the performance. He was one of the inspirations of my youth. At that time he was married to Marilyn Horne and toured around the world with the great soprano as her vocal coach and conductor. Henry Lewis was a great, great double bass player. I heard his college graduate recital, something I shall never forget. He had an incredible flexibility on the double bass—an enormous technique, something to aspire to.

Before Herman Reinshagen died, I had already reached college age and started my studies at the University of Southern California. Because by then I wanted to expand my musical horizons, the administration gave me permission to divide my instrumental studies, continuing my work with Reinshagen, who was on the faculty, and also

studying with the Hungarian cellist Gabor Rejtő. It was Rejtő who first
presented significant cello playing ideas to me. He gave me some wonderful baroque pieces to play, introduced me to Bach, and suggested
that I transcribe Beethoven's cello works.

I never wanted Reinshagen to know I was studying with Rejtő, so
that was always kept a secret, even though studying with both men at
the same time sometimes presented unusual circumstances. Often I
would take a piece of music that was familiar to Reinshagen, like the
Eccles sonata, play it for Rejtő, incorporating various cellistic ideas for
him, then go to Reinshagen's house and play the same work for him
in the old, traditional Simandl way. I think all this helped me gain an
enormous amount of flexibility that served me well throughout my life.

My first important career break came in 1960 when I was nineteen. I was given an award by Local 47 of the American Federation of
Musicians that enabled me to attend the union's Congress of Strings
which that year was based in Puerto Rico. Everyone there thought of
me as a kind of jokester, and I became so popular with the other kids
that they elected me president of the congress. But I was not eager to
perform for anyone and never auditioned for any opportunities to play,
although I practiced diligently.

One day in Puerto Rico when I was practicing, I didn't realize that
outside the door of my room, two teachers—Sidney Harth and Rafael
Druian—had gathered with some students to listen. When I finished
practicing my piece, they broke into applause. This was very exciting
for me, and believe it or not, that event led to an important engagement. Sidney Harth, then concertmaster of the Chicago Symphony
under Fritz Reiner, recommended to conductor Thor Johnson that he
hire me as soloist to tour with the Chicago Little Symphony. Since this
was my first important solo engagement, I've always felt that my career
as soloist began in 1961.

A part of the arrangement was that although I was a student at the
University of Southern California, I would continue my studies for one
semester at Northwestern University in Chicago where Thor Johnson
was on the faculty. I agreed to this and during the months when I was
at Northwestern I entered another contest, this one sponsored by the
Artist Advisory Council of Chicago. Sada Cowan, the wonderful
president of the council with whom I loved to talk almost on a daily
basis, once said to me, "Don't forget, my dear, that the sky is the limit.

The sky is the limit! You should pursue a solo career. You should do all the things that nobody has ever done."

But the same thing that had happened to me in a previous contest in Los Angeles happened again in Chicago! They just felt that their prestigious organization could not give an award to a double bassist and decided not to give any first prize, but instead to give two second prizes. This judgment flattered me no end since I shared the second prize with Toby Saks, who was in my youth one of the great cellists. (She founded and is director of the Seattle Chamber Music Festival.)

The next summer I went to the Aspen Music Festival where I met Stuart Sankey, who was to become my next teacher. He had a very broad academic background, knew a lot about music, and was able to steer me in the direction of great music. Had it not been for Sankey, I would never at that time have played the Schubert "Arpeggione" Sonata, or the Boccherini sonatas, or a lot of other great music that Sankey transcribed for me. He later published these transcriptions that have since become standard in the double bass repertoire. Of course, I am glad that I was the first one to play these transcribed pieces. At the Aspen School of Music I also met Zara Nelsova whose passionate cello playing and intensity of focus was astounding to me and so moving that I played for her whenever I would get the chance. Her wise remarks were so helpful that I am eternally grateful to her for the kind of leadership she gave me.

My love of the voice continued at Aspen and my great god from that time was soprano Jennie Tourel. When I heard her sing Schubert songs, I was so moved by her performance that for the first time in my life I wrote a fan letter. The result was an invitation to dinner at her house and that began a very long friendship. She invited me to bring my instrument, and after dinner we made music together. I'll never forget that as long as I live. As she sang, I wove all kinds of obbligato lines and discovered that I had a hidden talent for this, especially with Russian songs. "You are going to have a solo career on the double bass, and I'm going to help you make it possible," she told me that evening. Later at Alice Tully Hall in New York we gave a recital together that included music of Glinka and Tchaikovsky. It was very exciting!

After my summer at Aspen, I went to New York in the fall and continued studying with Stuart Sankey at the Juilliard School. There I met the cellist Leonard Rose, who became another powerful influence on me. I got wonderful musical instruction from him when I played pieces like Ernest Bloch's *Prayer*, Bruch's *Kol Nidrei*, and the Beethoven cello sonatas. Because he didn't like the fact that I played with the traditional German bow, he persuaded me to learn to play with the French bow [the fingers resting on top of the bow stick] because visually that seemed to him a more comfortable way to play. Then he gave me tremendous insight into how to use the right arm for the most efficient kind of bowing. I still remember his advice to this day. I also studied chamber music with Leonard Shure, who was a great pianist and an enormously gifted coach. Shure was a Schubert expert. My interpretation of the "Arpeggione" Sonata was inspired by the kind of musical advice he gave me.

While living in New York, I also had the opportunity to study with Alfredo Antonini, who was for about thirty years the conductor for CBS and at one time Toscanini's rival. This man was an expert on Italian bel canto, especially the music of Verdi. For him I played all my Giovanni Bottesini repertoire, as well as all the lyrical pieces from the bel canto era that I had learned with Herman Reinshagen. For the insight Antonini gave me into the true bel canto style I am still grateful.

After I had started my studies in New York, Jennie Tourel told Leonard Bernstein about having heard me in Aspen. As a result, he invited me to audition for him. When I played Paganini's "Moses" Fantasy and Bloch's *Prayer* for him, Bernstein was so excited that he decided to present me on one of his televised Young People's Concerts at Carnegie Hall. He asked me if I had orchestrations for the two pieces I had played for him and I told him that Alfredo Antonini had already made an orchestration of Bloch's *Prayer* for me. I also said that I had an orchestration of Paganini's "Moses" Fantasy, which was not quite true, so I went back to my room and wrote one. Although a theory professor at Northwestern had felt I didn't know the academics of orchestration, having been raised in orchestras since my youth, I could hear every single instrument in my mind and didn't need to look up the range of a flute, for instance, since I could hear what it was. When I showed my orchestration for Paganini's "Moses" Fantasy to Leonard Bernstein, he accepted it and we soon performed it on my television appearance for NBC.

I played my New York debut recital in Town Hall in 1962, performing Schubert's "Arpeggione" Sonata, a Boccherini sonata, Giovanni Bottesini's Fantasy on Bellini's *La Sonnambula*, and a new work, *Small Suite* for double bass and piano, written by Alec Wilder. I didn't know this composer and had received his composition out of the blue. I think Wilder had seen my NBC telecast with Bernstein, was excited by it, and just wrote this piece and gave it to me. This was the only time I got music from any composer that I didn't have to commission. He wrote it because he wanted to. It is still one of my favorite pieces. Later I received more music from Alec Wilder—a sonata for double bass and piano and a suite for double bass and guitar—and recorded it all.

Jennie Tourel brought Olga Koussevitsky, the widow of Serge Koussevitsky, to my debut recital at Town Hall. The day after the recital Madame Koussevitsky telephoned me. She had such a thick Russian accent that I thought it was a friend of mine playing a practical joke. When she said, "Zees eez Mrs. Koussevitsky calling," I said jokingly, "Yeh, Baby. I'll bet!" She didn't laugh. She invited me over to her apartment. I thought I'd find out what was really going on and I did show up, not expecting it to be Madame Koussevitsky at all. When the door opened, there she was. Behind her was the great Amati bass made in 1611 that had belonged to Serge Koussevitsky. Later she told me that after hearing my concert, she felt it was an omen that she saw a vision of her husband embracing me on stage and knew, then and there, that I was the one to carry on the legacy of her husband and that the only way I could do it was to have her husband's double bass.

Later, after Madame Koussevitsky had given me the Amati bass, I began to wonder what I would do with this instrument in my later years or upon my death. I consulted with my lawyer who advised me the only way I could guarantee that the instrument would not be sold, but would be given to another person in the same way it was given to me, was to do something that would make it impossible for it to be sold to a collector. I should form a foundation, then leave the Amati to that foundation, which would not dispose of it but make it available to very talented musicians who could not afford to possess an instrument of that quality.

The Karr Doublebass Foundation, Inc., was formed in 1983 to repay in kind the gift of the Amati. Since that time, the foundation has purchased four instruments and these instruments are now being played by talented young bassists. Eventually the Amati will go to the foundation and be a part of a larger collection, since I am planning to leave most of my instruments to the foundation.

I envy string players who can start so young. Recently in Switzerland I heard a bassist who, at the age of seven, is already playing the Eccles sonata, and I think that is an historical "first" on our instrument. In my own case, I am grateful for having had the opportunity to begin at the age that I did, then to be able to continue my pursuit throughout my life. I love performing. I want to reach people's hearts. I don't know anything more wonderful![3]

CHAPTER SIXTEEN

Born for the Cello

JACQUELINE DU PRÉ
AND YO-YO MA

JACQUELINE du Pré and Yo-Yo Ma were born into contrasting cultural backgrounds and grew up in quite different physical environments. Only later were their adult careers as concert cellists linked in the minds of the music lovers they inspired the world over.

JACKIE

I remember being in the kitchen at home, looking up at the old-fashioned wireless. I climbed onto the ironing board, switched it on, and heard an introduction to the instruments of the orchestra. It didn't make much of an impression on me until they got to the cello, and then . . . I fell in love with it straightaway. Something within the instrument spoke to me, and it's been my friend ever since.

du Pré, in Easton, *Jacqueline du Pré*

Since its completion in the summer of 1919, Sir Edward Elgar's cello concerto was a work seeking a champion. Although Felix Salmond, Beatrice Harrison, and Pablo Casals, among others, had left their mark, Jacqueline du Pré's performances in 1965 caused a revival of interest in the work outside Great Britain.

The BBC Symphony Orchestra visited the United States for the first time in the spring of 1965, playing fifteen concerts in a three-week tour with both Pierre Boulez and Antal Doráti conducting. Three young English musicians were the soloists: pianist John Ogdon, soprano Heather Harper, and cellist Jacqueline Du Pré, who was appearing for the first time in North America. The American press lauded the concerts, especially drawn to Jacqueline du Pré's performances of Elgar's cello concerto. About her appearance at Carnegie Hall on 14 May 1965, Raymond Ericson, critic of the *New York Times*, wrote, "Miss du Pré and the concerto seemed made for each other."[1]

A new supernova was on the horizon. As du Pré's fame swept the world of music in the 1960s, she and her colleagues made London's Royal Festival

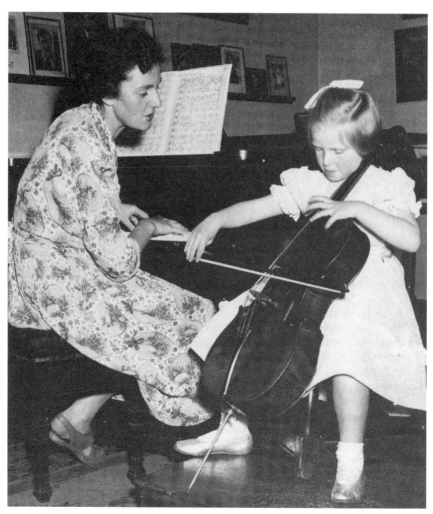

Jacqueline du Pré at six, rehearsing with her mother for a concert at the London Cello School, 1951. Courtesy Harper Collins.

Hall their summer retreat during the annual South Bank Summer Music Festival. Her husband, Daniel Barenboim, presided over the first festival in 1968, an eleven-day chamber music event that featured the artistic collaboration of du Pré, Barenboim, and their friends, pianist Vladimir Ashkenazy, violinist Itzhak Perlman, soprano Janet Baker, guitarist John Williams, and clarinetist Gervase de Peyer. At a subsequent festival, a singular appearance took place that united du Pré and her eminent teacher, William Pleeth, in a performance for two cellos and orchestra of Federico Ronchini's transcription of a Handel work. How touching to see them enter the stage together, master and pupil, two artists bound in friendship and respect, two cellists of vastly different temperaments and accomplishments, yet two musicians who spoke to each other—and to the audience—directly from the heart.

The passing of time had proved the truth of critic Colin Mason's prediction on 2 March 1961, after du Pré's debut recital at London's Wigmore Hall: "She is that rarity, an infant prodigy of the cello, and rarer still in that at the age of sixteen she is already well on the way to a place in the top flight of cellists."[2] In retrospect, almost every concert that followed her debut (and there were hundreds of every kind) revealed a remarkable continuity of development, an unfolding of her greatness. On stage with her Stradivarius cello, the "Davidov" from 1672, she played a vast repertoire; from 1961 to 1979 du Pré made two dozen recordings. Her technical mastery of the cello was absolute, her musicianship unquestionable, and in the end she had become a supreme artist.

On 19 October 1987, fourteen years after multiple sclerosis forced her to abandon her successful international concert career, the world of music mourned the passing of Jacqueline du Pré. She had died at age forty-two at her London home. Over the course of her long illness, her mother wrote an essay about her for the tribute, *Jacqueline du Pré: Impressions*. "Born for the Cello" is Iris du Pré's loving reflection on the musical childhood of a gifted daughter.[3]

> Jackie could sing in tune before she could talk. One day after her bath I was drying her on my lap and I started to sing "Baa, Baa, Black Sheep"; she began to sing with me—just the tune. After a short while I stopped singing but she continued right through to the end.
>
> Jackie, our younger daughter, was born at Oxford on 26 January 1945. As her father was a member of the Senior Common Room of Worcester College, the Provost gave permission for the christening to

be held in the college chapel. Her godparents included Mrs. Theodore Holland, wife of the composer—then professor of composition at the Royal Academy of Music—and Lord Lascelles (now Lord Harewood), who was a fellow cadet at Purbright with Jackie's father.

My other recollection from those early years of her musical abilities was when she was about three or four. It was at Christmas time and quite unexpectedly she said she would like to sing "Away in a Manger." So she duly stood up and sang it quite perfectly. I was very conscious that there was a great deal more to it than just a little girl singing. There was a special quality about it, quite devoid of the slightest precociousness. It was a perfectly rounded little "performance."

The whole of our family have their musical interests. Our eldest daughter, Hilary, is a professional flautist and teaches. Piers, our son, is an airline pilot and a keen singer although, admittedly, only as a hobby.

Jackie's choice of the cello as an instrument was firmly established one afternoon when we were listening to various instruments being demonstrated in a *Children's Hour* programme. As soon as she heard the cello, she said: "Mummy, that's the sound I want to make."

The first time she actually grasped a cello to play was when she was four. Mrs. Garfield Howe, who was the pianist Denis Matthews' mother-in-law, came down to our home when we were living in Purley, Surrey, to instruct a small class of local children and brought with her a cello for Jackie to play. When I said to her afterwards: "Jackie, good, that was very nice," she was absolutely enraptured.

"Oh, mummy," she replied, "I do so love my cello." She said this with such a wealth of feeling, or so it seemed to me at the time, that I remember I started seriously speculating to myself about the future. For the following three months Mrs. Garfield Howe continued coming each Saturday and it soon became obvious that Jackie was improving rapidly, far more quickly than any of the other children; her progress was quite phenomenal.

It was about that time that I began to write little pieces of music for her, pieces suitable for someone of her age and ability. I illustrated them with small sketches around the sides and slipped them under her pillow while she slept. In the morning she would waken early, leap out of bed to get her cello and play the latest composition, before even bothering to get dressed.

Her father and I were a little concerned about what next was best to do with her, as it was clearly apparent that she not only wanted but needed individual tuition. The dilemma was eventually solved by her godmother, Mrs. Theodore Holland, who knew Mr. Walenn, then running the London Cello School. He was extremely impressed and at once suggested she have lessons with Alison Dalrymple, who taught at the school and had a great reputation for being good with children. On our way to her lessons, we would call in at a nearby cafe for an ice cream or a cold drink. That was really the big moment of the day, because at the cafe there was a chef with a tall hat, and tall hats of every type had always held a great fascination for Jackie.

After her lessons she would usually go to see Mr. Walenn and sit on his knee for a short chat. On one such occasion she interrupted the conversation by putting her head on one side and listening intently to the chimes of the grandfather clock in his office. After a moment or two she said: "Do you know that that clock is out of tune?" She has always had the most amazingly good ear. After Jackie had been having lessons for about three years at the London Cello School, sadly, Mr. Walenn died. It was anyway time for her to move on to another teacher and it was agreed that she should go to William Pleeth. She was supremely happy with him both as a teacher and a friend. He has a rare gift as a teacher; he is not merely a good instructor, he has the outstanding ability to coax from his pupils their latent potentialities. Under his gentle guidance Jackie developed apace.

When, aged ten, she competed for the Suggia Gift she was by far the youngest of the competitors and was in fact the first ever to receive this award. Her winning it meant that her lessons were paid for and all manner of wonderful things were done for us; Jackie and I—she was too young to go alone—were sent one summer to Zermatt, Switzerland, where she had lessons with Casals. He, of course, had not heard of her. It was a summer school and each pupil played for him in turn.

After Jackie had played, he said to her: "Are you English? No, of course, you are not." And she replied: "Yes, I am." Then he asked her: "What is your name?" When she told him he roared with laughter, being fully convinced that she could not possibly be English if she had such a name (her father's family is from the Channel Islands) and played with such uninhibited feeling and intensity. It was, I recall, a memorable moment, for the great cellist was clearly very deeply impressed with her vital performance. She admitted to being rather "bolshie" [rebellious] with Casals because she was so proud of her own teacher, William Pleeth, and was rather unreasonably reluctant to accept things Casals was trying to convey to her.

We always kept a firm restraint on our younger daughter as far as public performance was concerned. We were absolutely determined that in no way would her talent be forced or prematurely exploited. However, she did make what was her first real public appearance when she played the first movement of the Lalo concerto on television at the age of twelve. Not long after that she returned to the television studio to play the Haydn D Major.

When, after a competitive festival in London, a concert was given by the prizewinner, at which Princess Marie Louise presented the prizes, I recollect very clearly that we had a disappointed and rather dejected daughter to cope with because the Princess was not wearing a crown.

Her first real concert-hall appearance was a recital at the Wigmore Hall in 1961 when she was sixteen, although she had previously played at the Sir Robert Mayer children's concerts.

There was, I believe, at one time, some talk of Jackie giving cello lessons to the Prince of Wales, who has shown a keen interest in the instrument. I can remember the Prince sitting in front of us at the Royal Festival Hall, during a performance of the Haydn C Major Cello Concerto. I was told at the time that he was too shy to go round to see Jackie afterwards but, of course, I have no idea if that was true. They had met, though, some years before, after a children's television concert in which Jackie played. Prince Charles would have been about ten. He was most interested and afterwards asked if he might examine the cello. Jackie happily agreed. But when the Prince got astride the instrument and started to ride it like a hobbyhorse she became absolutely furious, saying very angrily: "Please don't treat my cello like that." Another encounter with the Prince was at St. George's Chapel, Windsor, when Jackie and her husband Danny gave a recital which he attended. That meeting was enthusiastic if a little less exuberant. They all three talked happily together afterwards.

Between the ages of sixteen and eighteen Jackie won most of the available musical prizes and awards. But after her first batch of concert appearances and the excitement of them she became greatly

depressed, mainly because she would then accept only a few engagements and she seemed to be developing doubts about her ability. It
became imperative for her to find something else to do. As if to create
some yardstick, she took up all sorts of activities. She painted, she
fenced, she did yoga; all manner of things were embraced in her efforts
to overcome her frustration. It was not until a long time later that one
felt she had finally come to terms with herself and made the decision
to become a really good cellist. All this was possibly the metamorphosis
of teenager to adult and one must accept that she doubtless felt a little
bit lost, particularly after so much early success. Everything seemed to
be resolved for her when she went to Dartington for master classes
with Paul Tortelier, and afterwards to Paris for private tuition with
him. Later she went to Moscow for lessons with Rostropovich. She
told us that her studies with her three brilliant masters of the cello
were, as one would expect, not only exciting but completely fascinating, although she has always considered Pleeth her real mentor and
what she liked to call her "cello daddy."

She first became really busy when she returned from the Tortelier
master classes. This was her first taste of traveling abroad alone and
she thoroughly enjoyed the experience. In 1965 she toured America
with the BBC Symphony Orchestra which was also there for the first
time, winning a new and enthusiastic audience for the Elgar concerto.
She had a ten-minute standing ovation in New York. She recorded the
concerto with Barbirolli and later on, again in America, with her husband, and she took it to Russia.

Winning the Suggia Gift in London set Jackie on a course of private
tuition which was fortunate since school had been a misery for her as a child.
On occasion she had endured the chant "We hate Jackie" from children
dancing in a circle round her. "When I left, at the age of ten, it was a golden
day," she said.[4] In 1978, talking with a *Sunday Telegraph* reporter about her
childhood, she said, "Other children didn't like me. I was very introverted and
desperately shy. Children are so quick to spot this."

They knew of the existence of the cello and taunted me with it. That's
when I went and talked to it, saying, "Never mind; they have no idea
how to play." I loved the fact that one could be very private with the
cello and communicate one's innermost thoughts to it. . . . It was the

saving grace of my childhood, but in a sense it is a pity now, that one had to put all one's eggs in that basket.[5]

Soon after winning, she went to William Pleeth for her first lesson. He had not taught young children, but he was entranced by the "simple little lass with blond hair" and guided her early, prodigious advancement. Pleeth has said, "The speed at which she could progress was so rapid that it was like trying to keep pace with a good thoroughbred horse that must be given its head."[6]

When Jackie was fourteen her mother enrolled her in Queen's College where special arrangements were made for a reduced academic load so that she might carry out her cello studies, but on the condition that her work be on a level with that of her class. As she steadily slipped beneath the expectations of the college, the year eventually proved the most miserable in her young life. Pleeth was aware of Jackie's distress; there were tears during lessons but no explanations.[7] In December her parents decided to withdraw her from the school at the end of term, and her examinations were canceled. After that Jackie turned her attentions exclusively to the cello and when she was sixteen played a brilliant London debut at the Wigmore Hall. Although confident, fulfilled, often ecstatic on stage, when off the platform she was confused, unhappy, and immature, struggling with her perilous journey through adolescence.

Jackie had studied briefly with Paul Tortelier, then Mstislav Rostropovich. One evening after a recital by Tortelier at the Dartington Summer School in England, she asked him to help her with Bloch's *Schelomo*. They began working just after midnight and continued for several hours, playing and discussing the music. "She stands out not only for the radiance of her playing," Tortelier has said, "but for her personal radiance as well. . . . I've never met a more ardent young musician."[8] Encouraged by her mother, Jackie went to Paris to continue working with Tortelier, but after a few months in his master class at the conservatory, she felt restricted and depressed; she even questioned whether she wanted to continue playing the cello. Already a world-class soloist at seventeen, she was emotionally ill prepared to be only one of many in Tortelier's master class. She returned to London in February of 1962.

Jackie first played for Mstislav Rostropovich when she was fourteen, at the home of her godfather, Lord Harewood. In 1966, she played for him again, this time at Jeremy Siepmann's London flat. With her friend, pianist

Richard Goode, she performed Beethoven for the Russian master. An invitation was made. Jackie accepted. She would study again, this time in Moscow.

Once the work began, Rostropovich's conservatory studio was always packed when Jackie played. In addition to his master class, he had promised her two private lessons each week. These working sessions took place at the Rostropovich apartment, began late, and lasted into the early hours of the morning, as he reviewed her concert repertoire and set new goals. While she valued the Moscow experience and greatly admired Rostropovich, by March, as had happened in Paris, she was eager to return home to England.

Her final days at the Moscow Conservatory coincided with the Third International Tchaikovsky Competition. Gregor Piatigorsky and Pierre Fournier were on the jury. Rostropovich encouraged Jackie to enter the arena, but the concept of competition was foreign to her. He later whispered to Pierre Fournier, "Don't you agree that if she would compete, she just would swallow all of them—like that?" On her last day at the conservatory, Jackie played the Haydn C Major Concerto with Rostropovich conducting the student orchestra. After the performance, Rostropovich told her, "Of all the cellists I've met of this generation, you are the most interesting! You can go the farthest—farther than me."[9]

Five years later, after her final appearance in New York in February 1973 when her early symptoms of multiple sclerosis became known, her cello fell silent except for brief, private moments. In 1983, the actor Anthony Hopkins wrote: "The cruel extinction of her meteoric career was something to destroy one's belief in any justice, divine or otherwise. At least, though, she knows what it is to achieve an absolute summit as an artist, and in doing so to inspire not just admiration and wonder but also love."[10]

During the last year of du Pré's illness, her biographer Carol Easton observed that "The essential Jacqueline—generous, bright, gifted, with an inordinate capacity for giving and receiving love—never changed. Taught early on that some of her deepest feelings were unacceptable, she learned to camouflage them with a smiling mask. Behind it lay a complex, private, and paradoxical personality."[11]

At the end, Jacqueline du Pré kept notebooks in which she jotted many random thoughts, among them: "Elgar's photo now hangs on the wall. . . . How his face haunts me, and always will; Never mind about present affliction—any moment may be the next; A genius is one who, with an innate capacity, affects for good or evil, the life of others; Don't let the sound of your own wheels drive you crazy." And best of all, "If the sunshine beckons you, accept its invitation and love the golden quality of it."[12]

YO-YO

As soon as we moved to America I had to deal with two contradictory worlds. At home, I was to submerge my identity. But I was also American, growing up with American values. My conflict was apparent to Pablo Casals, to whom I was presented when I was seven. I don't remember what he said about my cello playing, but he did suggest that I should be given more time to go out and play in the street.

Yo-Yo Ma, in Blum, "A Process Larger Than Oneself"

Yo-Yo Ma's father, Hiao-Tsiun Ma, was born in Ningbo, a town near Shanghai. He played the violin and eventually became a professor of music at Nanjing University where he met his future wife, Marina, a gifted mezzo-soprano from Hong Kong who studied music theory with him. He went to France in 1936 to study musicology at the University of Paris, surviving the tedium of his isolation during the Occupation by tenaciously memorizing movements from the works of Johann Sebastian Bach. When Marina moved to Paris in 1949 to study at the École Normale de Musique, they married.

Yo-Yo was born in Paris on 7 October 1955, four years after the birth of his sister, Yeou-Cheng. Both children studied music from infancy. Yeou-Cheng, who later became a pediatrician in the United States, played the violin, which Yo-Yo also began studying when he was three. But he soon left it when he saw a double bass at the Paris Conservatory: he wanted to play the big instrument.

Yo-Yo was four when he first encountered the cello at the shop of Étienne Vatelot on the rue Portalis. When a small chair couldn't be found, he sat on three telephone books to try his new instrument. From that day, his father was a strong influence in his musical life.

> My father had a true gift for teaching children. He really set high standards and was very strict, but didn't demand long hours of practice. Each session was done with intense concentration, but he also created little steps so that I could learn from one day to the next.[13]

To the amazement of Yo-Yo's first cello teacher, a kind lady named Michelle Lepinte, his father had started him right away at the age of four on a Bach suite. The first day the child learned two measures, the next day two more, and so it continued. Gradually he could combine all these bits of information and by the end of two weeks he had learned the better part of a movement.

Yo-Yo gave his first public performance at age six at the Institute of Art and Archeology at the University of Paris. On the first half he played the piano; on the second half, the cello, in a performance of Bach's first suite. "My parents, being musical, obviously hoped that I would love music," Ma recalled.

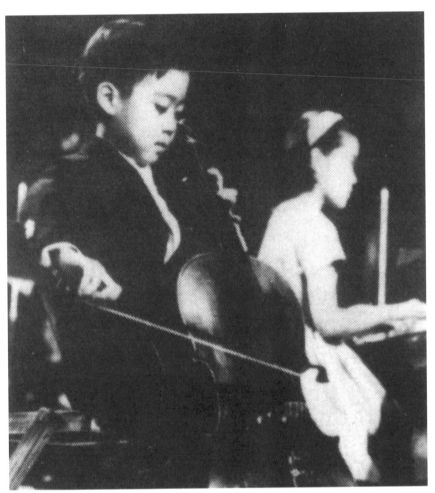

Yo-Yo Ma at nine, performing in New York with his sister, Yeou-Cheng Ma, 1964. Courtesy Yo-Yo Ma.

They were ambitious for me to do my best and set very high standards, and yet they were careful not to exploit me as a child prodigy. I am grateful for this. They seemed to understand that an early physical facility has to be combined with a mature emotional development before a healthy musical voice emerges.[14]

The following year, the family moved to New York where Yo-Yo's father formed the Children's Orchestra of New York. Seven-year-old Yo-Yo attended the Trent School in an innovative program of learning, and later the École Française, a school that specialized in bilingual education. On the recommendation of Arthur Grumiaux, Yeou-Cheng's violin teacher, Yo-Yo began studying in New York with his first master teacher, the Hungarian cellist János Scholz, a long-time member of the Roth String Quartet. "He proved to be the most extraordinary, the most charming and simple little boy imaginable," Scholz recalled. "He was so eager to acquire musical knowledge that he just lapped it up."[15]

During those first crucial years in New York, Yo-Yo progressed so rapidly under the guidance of János Scholz that by age nine he entered the preparatory school at Juilliard. Isaac Stern, who had heard Yo-Yo play his first concert in Paris, introduced the boy to Leonard Rose, with whom Yo-Yo continued working until he was seventeen. "When I first came to Leonard Rose, I could do a lot of things quite naturally, but my tone was small and my playing didn't convey much personality," Ma recalled.[16] Rose guided him through a large repertoire with a wide range of emotions. By twelve he began studying Schubert's "Arpeggione" Sonata and a year later the Dvořák Concerto. In Leonard Rose, Yo-Yo had a teacher with infinite patience and above all one who knew when to teach and when to let go.

At fifteen, Yo-Yo went to study at Meadowmount, a summer school for string players founded by Ivan Galamian in Essex County, New York. "As a kid, I think I was pretty lonely. So when I went to summer camp that was really the first time I was among other kids who did what I did, who loved music and wanted to play."

I had always kept my emotions bottled up, but at Meadowmount I just ran wild. The whole structure of discipline collapsed. I would leave my cello outside, not worrying if it might rain and run off to play ping-pong. I exploded into bad taste at every level. I took some white paint and decorated the stone walls with graffiti. When Galamian found out, he was horrified. I knew I had gone too far, and spent a whole day washing the walls.[17]

Yo-Yo struck out on his perilous journey to maturity, rebelling against the strict decorum of his childhood. He returned to Juilliard in the fall and, clad in a leather jacket for his lesson with Leonard Rose, offered his teacher an outpouring of swear words. "But Mr. Rose took it in his stride and saw me through this phase. All I was trying to do was to be accepted as one of the guys, and not be considered a freak."

At this critical time in his adolescence Yo-Yo began to doubt whether he wanted to become a professional musician. Having played the cello since he was four, he found it difficult to separate his personal identity from his musical one: "It seemed as if the course of my life had been predetermined and I very much wanted to be allowed a choice."

When he was sixteen, Yo-Yo went for the first time to study at Rudolf Serkin's summer music school at Marlboro, Vermont. "I was there four summers, and I think my love for chamber music really developed," he has said.[18] He became engrossed in playing chamber music with his peers and has ever since believed that the basis of all music making is found in a chamber music approach. At Marlboro he found the sense of community that he had felt lacking during his lonely pursuit as a soloist, and this seems to have resolved his conflict. He was inspired by the presence of Pablo Casals: "I thought if he can feel that strongly about music at ninety-five, then I can stick with this for the next fifty years."[19]

At Marlboro, Yo-Yo also met the Polish-born American pianist Emanuel Ax, who had emigrated to New York with his parents in 1961. They formed a duo partnership in 1979 and ever since have toured several times during each season to play sonatas for cello and piano; they have recorded the repertoire for an enthusiastic world audience.

When Yo-Yo graduated from high school at sixteen, he began his college education at Columbia University in New York while continuing to study with Leonard Rose. He desperately wanted to find a piece of life's puzzle that was missing, to go out on his own and pursue something other than music if being a musician was eventually to be his life. He visited his sister at Harvard, liked it, and decided to give it a try, which he reckons is one of the best decisions he ever made.[20] He went in 1972 and soon discovered many teachers who were idealistic about what music should be. They gave him the confidence to look at music and ask questions about himself—and answer them. It was at Harvard, where he distinguished himself studying the humanities, that he realized that music has as much to do with philosophy, history, psychology, and anthropology as it has to do with playing an instrument well.

In the spring of 1977, Yo-Yo made his boldest departure from traditional Chinese culture. He asked Jill Hornor, a young woman he had met at Marlboro, to marry him. She accepted. Their marriage caused a rupture within the Ma family, but in time Yo-Yo's parents accepted Jill. While Yo-Yo established his international career as a cellist, the young couple learned to adapt their lives to the demands of his concertizing career. "You realize that life is finite, and that you absolutely have a limit to your energy. You give, you love, you care, and it's all different. I have yet to find something that beats the power of being in love, or the power of music at its most magical."

At forty-four, Yo-Yo Ma is considered one of the century's supreme instrumentalists. Perhaps what sets him apart is that he doesn't aspire to the accomplishments of other cellists, but concerns himself with his own growth as an artist. His musicianship is unmistakably unique. He has retained his great individuality whether he is playing a Bach sarabande alone, a jazz improvisation with Bobby McFerrin, or a tango, with bandoneón, by Astor Piazzolla.

> I think of myself as me. I am a product of all the influences of my life—born in Paris, Chinese family, educated at Harvard. The pieces are all within me and it is interesting to try to put them together into a workable whole.[21]

EPILOGUE

Bejun Mehta, fifteen years old, after the release of his first recording in 1983. Photograph by Rick Meyer. Courtesy Bejun Mehta.

Prodigies are often more mystified by their gifts than anyone else.

Bejun Mehta

AT FIFTEEN *Bejun Mehta had reached the culmination of his prodigy career as a boy soprano. By his twenties he was finally able to talk about it. Others had long been offering superlatives: on hearing Bejun sing, Leonard Bernstein remarked, "It is hard to believe the richness and maturity of musical understanding in this adolescent boy."[1] Bejun's ethereal recorded performance of music by Handel, Brahms, Britten, and Schubert left listeners aghast, wondering at the mystery of such supreme artistic accomplishment.*

Although his musical precocity found a natural place in the Mehta household, the revelation of extreme vocal talent is always stunning. What coincidence of nature and musical culture allowed this boy such rare expression? He was born on 29 June 1968 in the little North Carolina town of Laurinburg and as a small boy moved with his family to Ann Arbor, Michigan. His Bombay-born father, pianist Dady Mehta (cousin of conductor Zubin Mehta), taught at Eastern Michigan University, having concertized and taught in Europe and the United States after studying in Paris and Vienna. Bejun's mother, Martha Ritchey Mehta, born in Pennsylvania, was his first teacher and a singer and journalist who received her vocal training in Vienna with the celebrated Elisabeth Rado, first as a student and later as a teaching assistant. His older brother, Nuvi, is an accomplished violinist and conductor who studied with Joseph Gingold at Indiana University.

Bejun's first compact disc, recorded by Delos when he was fourteen, won a host of awards, including the coveted "Debut Recording Artist of the Year" from Stereo Review. Yet the perils of Bejun's transition to maturity were unequivocal: shortly after his remarkable boy-soprano voice changed, Bejun embarked on a difficult adolescent odyssey. "Every prodigy has to reinvent himself as he grows up," he has said. This Bejun began doing when he left home to study the cello in New Haven with Aldo Parisot.

He turned to ensemble playing as a member of the Yale Cellos. In May 1986 in Yale's Sprague Hall, the thirty-five cellists, all students of Aldo Parisot, recorded a new compact disc for Delos that included Bejun's arrangement for solo cello and ensemble of Sergei Rachmaninov's Vocalise, Op. 34, No. 14, a work that Parisot encouraged him "to sing on the cello." This persuasive performance placed him among the most outstanding of young cellists.

After traveling throughout Germany and Austria, then writing a thesis on Heinrich Heine, in 1990 the versatile artist graduated from Yale University magna cum laude with Distinction in Germanic Languages and Literatures. By then, his burgeoning musical life in New Haven had brought him to the conductor's podium: he coached with Leonard Bernstein; founded, conducted, and performed with the Yale Symphony Chamber Players; and, at the invitation of conductor Eleazar de Carvalho, conducted a series of concerts in South America.

Bejun also brought his musical knowledge to the recording studio. His production of cellist János Starker's A Tribute to David Popper was nominated for a Grammy Award in 1989, and his later production of the cellist's final recording of Bach's Six Suites was honored with a Grammy in 1998.[2] Bejun's CD reissue productions for Sony Classical, numbering several hundred, have garnered critical acclaim, especially his work on the Masterworks Heritage and Essential Classics series. Bejun Mehta Productions, Inc., his own classical audio production company, has linked him to many outstanding recording artists, including Claudio Abbado and the Berlin Philharmonic, Kathleen Battle, Dietrich Fischer-Dieskau, Wynton Marsalis, and Itzhak Perlman, among others.

In 1991 Bejun returned to singing after a seven-year hiatus and began an uneasy but productive relationship with his baritone adult voice. He appeared again as a recitalist and soloist in liturgical works (a boyhood specialty), and in 1995 he performed the role of Papageno in Mozart's The Magic Flute in a production of New York City Opera Education.

However, the baritone voice never felt natural. In 1997, after a period of considerable struggle, Bejun again stopped singing, his vocal future uncertain. Yet within six months, quite by chance, he came upon an article about the countertenor David Daniels. The story it told paralleled Bejun's own experience so exactly that he decided he had nothing to lose by experimenting with this range in his own voice. The success of these experiments was immediate. Within his first four months as a countertenor, Bejun had signed with Columbia Artists Management, was slated for two recitals and a broadcast with the Marilyn Horne Foundation, and had secured a debut in a new production of Handel's Partenope at the New York City Opera. Most importantly, the joy of music-making had returned. In more ways than one, Bejun had finally found his voice.

During an exciting two-month-long exchange,[3] he talked to me about his life as a celebrated boy soprano and his own experience of the wondrous elements of prodigy. He described his most vivid memories of music during those years, and put into words the feelings of joy and loneliness that he was unable to articulate even to himself until he had gone some distance from the crisis of his adolescence. His gift to posterity includes this glimpse into his "Muse world," the inner world of his musical sensibilities, its loss and hard-won recovery, and his struggle toward understanding.

A Process of Prodigy

BY BEJUN MEHTA

M Y EARLIEST musical memories are from the time when I was a baby and crawled around under my dad's piano. While he played I remember lying there looking up at the struts and sounding board, and the sound would come down and envelop me. I loved being there under the piano while he practiced. Over time, the experience brought many musical things to bear upon me—a first sense of how sounds can come together to make music, a feeling of the physical tension notes make in different combinations, and a nascent understanding that music can be taken apart and put back together.

One day, my father took me on his lap at the piano bench, put his arms around me, and began playing some Bach. (I was small enough for him to play in this way.) My father particularly loves Bach's music and has specialized in playing it his whole life. He played very slowly as he showed me the different voices and how they flowed through the piece. Experiences like this were what taught me voice leading, counterpoint, and a good deal of my music theory—listening to my father emphasizing the soprano line at one point, then bringing out the alto line and merging it with the tenor as the voices switched back and forth. The experience is close to my heart because while my father showed me very specific things about the piece at hand, he also showed me how much he loved music, and by sharing these things, how much he loved me. It took me many years to realize how important this was, and when I did, I also realized that a truly wonderful thing about having grown up in our family, given my particular gifts, was that there was an atmosphere in which you knew that artistic things were noble.

336

For someone who would end up singing and for whom language and self-expression would be major themes, I was ironically nonverbal as a baby. I exhibited little interest in speech for most of my first year-and-a-half, and my taciturnity was a subject of some discussion between my parents. Then one day, I suffered quite a fall from my high chair, smacking my head on the kitchen table on the way down. After the crying had subsided, bones were checked, and I was safely reinstalled in the chair, my mother recalls that I immediately began speaking in complete, correct sentences. The baby-talk stage was essentially skipped. Apparently I had been steeping in language and understanding all along, and had just been waiting and observing until I felt I had learned enough to commit to it myself; the blow loosed the flood-gates. My mother relates that she and my father looked at each other in amazement at this leap—together, my parents and I were beginning to dis-cover evidence of my accelerated faculties.

Language soon gave way to song, and as a small child I was always sing-ing. When there was music in the house, which was all the time, I would imi-tate what I heard. If I heard a record, I would sing that. My brother, Nuvi, who is five years older, recalls many an afternoon trying to do his homework while I was embarked upon what he has since affectionately named "Opera for One." I would go into my room and put on an opera recording, (usually Mozart), and he would count the minutes (usually around seven) until I would start to sing along. And then I would sing every part, every word, every-thing—I would stay in my room and sing the entire opera. Nuvi remembers listening to this, impressed with the freedom with which it occurred.

Even without an external stimulus, I would sing. Our home in Ann Arbor had a big, resonant kitchen, and when I was slightly older and alone in the house, I would walk around the kitchen table and sing whatever came to mind. I would sing for hours upon hours, sing until I was hoarse, just sing on and on. I remember circling that table a thousand times, taking with me the Queen of the Night, complete with high F, or poor Konstanze from Mozart's *Abduction from the Seraglio* with her aria, "Martern aller Arten." Singing was spontaneous with me. On car trips, I'd sit in the back and make up songs about whatever I felt like. My mother particularly remembers one song about the sun, which she encouraged me to write down. Alas, I never did. And I sang at school—not in any sanctioned forum, either. When I was seven, my teacher sent home a report card which commented, in part, "Bejun has very good powers of concentration; however, he frequently sings or hums during inde-pendent work time. This does not hinder his ability to complete his work, but it is disturbing to those who are working near him. Would you kindly talk to him about this?" And my parents, of course, did not talk to me about it at all.

My parents' stewardship in the early years of my life was marked by considerable freedom. When it became apparent that school presented me little challenge, for example, my parents were quite free about letting me find my own way to things that did engage me. My mother, particularly, was just as happy to have me at home with a serious book in hand, or Beethoven on the turntable, than in school every single day. In fact, on numerous occasions the three of us colluded in having me skip school so I could do just those things. This freedom would also mark my mother's early stewardship of my voice. It did not resemble formal teaching, but was more a "gentling" of me along my own path. This free approach both to school and to my voice made me feel good, because I felt trusted in these years to find my own way.

I didn't consider why I sang all the time, why a tune bubbled in my throat twenty-four hours a day. Something just made it so. I was a joyful child, but I also sensed that somehow I was substantially different from everybody else, and that made me quite lonely at times. What I thought made me different was not that I could sing, but that I seemed to feel everything very deeply. My inner world was so active, and the power of my imagination accelerated to such a degree, that I could make emotional connections far beyond the scope of my years. I realize now that my singing stemmed from this combination of joy and gifted loneliness. I had a powerful need to express myself to others in the hope of finding emotional resonance, of being seen and reflected in a way that might help me understand myself and my gifts. Indeed, the combination of joy and loneliness informs all my impressions of childhood and the prodigy time, and, I'm sure, has fueled everything I've done since. At the time, though, I just sang. And sang, and sang, and sang.

When I was five years old, I played a little Siamese child in a local high school production of *The King and I*. It was my first stage experience, and I was one of the kids who got to perambulate around, doing little extra things. When I was six I was in a performance of Puccini's *La Bohème* directed by Josef Blatt at the University of Michigan. I was one of the Parpignol kids in Act II, one of whom sings a little line about wanting a toy horse, all of seven notes. They hadn't yet picked the person to do this. We were all standing there in rehearsal—twelve of us kids—and Blatt, after looking us over for a bit, abruptly pointed to me and said, "You sing this," and I did. It was the first time anyone had ever singled me out for a solo, and it felt good.

Between the ages of five and ten, my singing was very free and easy. I never really thought or worried about anything. But I do remember very clearly a woman who came backstage after a performance of *Amahl and the Night Visitors* when I was ten. She was in tears because she just couldn't get over what she had seen. I didn't think I had done anything special, yet there she was, crying, going on about the beauty of my voice. I had never experienced a reaction quite like that. It was the first time I realized that what I was doing onstage could have a serious effect on people, but I didn't understand what that effect was, nor what I was doing to bring it about—I was just singing. The next night when I had to sing the piece again, just like a snap it was fundamentally a different experience. Waiting for the performance to start, I had a different kind of nervousness than I ever had before. The feeling was not debilitating, and the performance was as much fun for me as ever, but I was now aware that something mysterious, something separate from me, occurred when I sang. It was a feeling that never left me, a feeling that both increased my joy and heightened my sense of isolation. Joy, because I was thrilled to have evidence of my communication; isolation, because the reactions always seemed to have to do with my voice, and not me, particularly.

At twelve, I was reengaged as soloist for a series of *Messiah* concerts. I had sung the same series the year before, and had been nearly overwhelmed by the experience and the majesty of the piece. In fact I got so choked up in the first performance during the great "Hallelujah" chorus, what with two-hundred-voice choir, orchestra, and five thousand audience members all united in the splendor of this incredible music, that I was quite unable to sing myself. I was thrilled to be doing the series again, and couldn't wait to get underway. All the other soloists came from New York, and finally we were all set and ready to go. After the Overture, "Comfort Ye," and "Ev'ry Valley," there was a pause, and the lights were turned up for latecomers. Barely able to contain my excitement, I turned to the alto soloist and asked her how her voice was feeling. I was about to continue, probably something about glorious Handel, when she turned to me and said, "Oh, Honey, my voice feels like shit." Never before had I been ripped quite as unceremoniously from the precious world of my imagination, a world where Handel was miraculous, and where we might all be lifted up with joy and thanksgiving at being part of such an event. For the next half-hour, while the performance swirled on around me, I couldn't find my grounding anymore, wondering with my child's mind how it was that my internal make-up seemed to remove me so from other people. Then the Angel music came, with its "good tidings of great joy," my first entrance. I began to sing, and slowly my grounding returned.

Three years earlier, at age nine, I began casting about for another instrument to play. I knew in an abstract sort of way that my voice was going to leave me someday, and that I would want another musical outlet. After a brief *contretemps* with the French horn, a battle I quite lost, I followed my parents' suggestion and settled on the cello. My teacher was the very accomplished Winifred Mayes, the first woman to be principal cellist with the Philadelphia Orchestra. She introduced me to the wonders of the instrument in a gentle, profoundly nonjudgmental way. It was immediately apparent that I had both talent and facility for the cello, yet I was content to let it remain in the background throughout most of my singing years. I practiced regularly, but not until I stopped singing, at age fifteen, would I devote my full energies and heart to it. Winifred understood this and did a good job of tailoring her teaching style to accommodate my level of interest, never once making me feel like my dedication to our work together should be any other than it was. I have few memories of these early cello years, with the notable exception of something Winifred once said to my parents. We were all walking out to the car after a lesson, when I heard Winifred say, in parting, "Please don't make him hate the cello." I had no idea what she meant, but the phrase struck a painful chord in my heart—a pain that, over time, demanded explication.

As a child, I never thought much about my parents' position vis-à-vis my talents, but it must have been difficult and somewhat frightening for them to have a child prodigious in their own field of expertise. I think the families of children who are gifted in areas other than those of the parents must have a slightly easier time of it. These parents, if they are in-tune and intelligent, soon realize their limitations in dealing with the outward manifestation of the child's genius. Knowing little about the voice, cello, or piano (or figure skating or gymnastics, for that matter), they do their best to get the child to the teacher, coach, or mentor appropriate to his or her particular needs. Unburdened of this teaching responsibility, the parents can then concentrate on providing the child an atmosphere in which he feels seen and supported for who he is, so he can explore the nether-regions of his accelerated imagination and ability with fearless abandon. Prodigies are often more mystified by their gifts than anyone else, and internal exploration is one of the many ways they seek to understand the presence of such gifts in their lives, and themselves as a whole. Support for the prodigy and his inner world, a world the parents themselves may not understand, is vital in this regard.

There is no question that in the early years my parents provided just such an environment. When I was a baby and young child, my imagination

was free to wander, and I exhibited courage, self-reliance, and a natural ebul-
lience of spirit. The story is told of my father finally throwing up his hands in
bafflement because, even as an infant, I seemed undaunted by any challenge, fearless of any danger. Enigmatic though these traits may have been at
the time, that they have all found their corresponding adult form is the
soundest proof of the quality of my parents' early care. Around the age of
ten, however, I began to notice my parents concerning themselves more and
more with the outward manifestations of my talent, including voice, cello,
and scholarship, and less with the simple maintenance of a supportive, reflecting atmosphere. The new atmosphere was marked by criticism: criticisms of phrasing, comparative critiques of performances and work, and
caustic, at times even violent, rejections of my musical and intellectual
expression.

With the passing of the years, as I have encountered the thrills, insecu-
rities, and disappointments of adult life, it has become easier for me to understand and empathize with most of the actions my parents took during this
time. Given their backgrounds, the desire to bring their child the benefit of
their experience must have been great, not to mention the added pressures of
parental responsibility they must have felt because of their knowledge of my
field. Since that time, my parents and I have worked hard at forging a new
understanding, and, in retrospect, much of what happened seems to fall
within the range of a family struggling with extraordinary circumstance.

However, to describe accurately my experience of the prodigy time, it
must be noted that these new critiques were far different in their import
from my father's earlier hug-theory-lessons at the piano. Without the supportive, reflecting atmosphere along with the teaching, the message I now
learned was that believing in me as I was had taken back-burner to "fixing"
me, and I began to feel invisible to my parents. With every new criticism, I
felt increasingly pulled from the world of my imagination, less trusted, and
more and more alone. Being struck occasionally only cemented these feelings
in place. At the time she said it, I hadn't understood Winifred's plea to them,
"Please don't make him hate the cello." It has since become emblematic to
me of the shift in my relationship to my parents, for Winifred was the first
person I noticed articulating concern about my parents' increasingly harsh,
if well-meaning, efforts.

In my child's heart, though, Winifred's painful phrase would soon
become a herald call for change. The experiences of these performing years,
ages nine to thirteen, were setting me off down a new road. The crying

woman backstage at *Amahl*, the alto soloist from *Messiah*, to name just two, and now the new feeling of invisibility to my parents were teaching me that the keys to my self-understanding were not to be found in the external world. In its reactions to me, the world was showing me *itself* and not the reflection of my soul I so desperately needed to see. This knowledge compounded my sense of isolation and made me want to discover and follow my own path. Such self-determination, a process marked by prolonged, intense, and often painful doubts and introspection, is probably the greatest challenge faced in artistic life by prodigies and nonprodigies alike. It is eventually a require-ment of all artists and the adult world in general. However, the process can be particularly difficult for prodigies because they begin confronting its rig-ors so early. For those prodigies like me who take up the task of self-deter-mination with only the tools and references of childhood and adolescence at their disposal, its trials are heightened. There are many examples of prodigies whose deferment of this process resulted in great personal harm. However difficult, the heightened pains and doubts of early self-determination are, I think, the price prodigies must pay to come into easy relationship with their very isolating gifts.

For me, the price would be large. For the moment, though, I was only beginning to heed the path of my innermost convictions. As I became increasingly determined to make my own decisions, the depth of my artistic expression increased as well. Although I was now often locked in battle with my parents, these last two prodigy years contained my greatest successes as a singer and culminated in one final project: the recording of a CD of my favorite music, signature pieces from my career. The CD was a commercial venture, but the recording company placed much emphasis on the autobio-graphical nature of the undertaking, on documenting my achievement. For artists in the middle of continuing careers, such documents are viewed more as snapshots of a particular time, a freeze-frame from an extending arc of artistic effort. For a retiring boy-soprano, however, this CD would be a por-trait. And, after having performed with an instrument as ephemeral as the trumpet of the swan my whole life, it is a portrait that I now feel lucky and grateful to have.

At the time of its making, however, I was not concerned with posterity. I was so unprepared for the eventual loss of the voice that the need for an his-torical document was not much on my mind. My principal memory of the sessions was recording "The Shepherd on the Rock" with David Shifrin and Carol Rosenberger. This work is very likely Schubert's final song, one of the most profound statements in his songwriting oeuvre. Its treatment of the clarinet as a full-fledged second voice, not just an obbligato instrument ornamenting the singer's line, has made it a staple of that instrument's repertoire as well. In their intimate interplay, these two voices pass lines back and forth, completing thoughts, inspiring the next emotion, and requiring the players to be at one with each other. Yet David and I had met for the first time just that day, nor had the three of us ever worked together before. As there was no time to rehearse, we just went into the studio and began to record, trusting in our individual knowledge of the piece to get us through.

And a wondrous thing happened. The moment Carol struck the first notes at the piano, the atmosphere changed. I can't describe it fully, save to say that musical time suddenly felt different, less linear, and more like a great unfolding in all directions. David began to play and I began to sing, and although we both had done the piece many times before and knew perfectly well where we were going, the contribution of our parts felt utterly spontaneous, as though we were making them up on the spot. When music unfolds like this, it feels as though there is all the space in the world between notes, no matter how fast the tempo may be—and in that space, one can feel every emotion, every musical motivation, all at once. In that zone, there is no judgment, and one sings and watches oneself sing at the same time. It is an elevated experience, an experience of the Muse, and I learned that day that it functions only on the most essential level of the human soul. Our first take was one of these rare moments of enlightened music-making: the Muse was present because we as performers were enough out of our own way to be borne up by it for a little while.

When we reached the end of the piece, we three just looked at each other, knowing something amazing had occurred. David broke the silence with a resounding, "Wow!" He then went on to apologize for his bad knee possibly having disturbed such a great take, because it made popping sounds as he moved with the music. Such is the difference between the concerns of the regular and Muse worlds! We went on to record for another five hours, patching up little things, but we never again matched the level of that first take. This take makes up the "Shepherd" on the finished CD, with minor corrections.

I had been lucky enough to experience this type of musical elevation before, albeit not often and never exactly the same. There was a performance of Haydn's "Lord Nelson" Mass, for example, and a small evening singing some songs written by a friend of mine. Later on, as a cellist, I would experience something similar when I was seventeen and recorded my arrangement of Rachmaninov's Vocalise for soloist and cello orchestra, with my teacher, Aldo Parisot, conducting. But the Schubert experience was unique. Looking back now, I believe that it was so satisfying because it provided, at long last, resonance for the world of my imagination: I had communicated with David and Carol from this magic inner world, and they had been able to understand and respond. Furthermore, the inner world itself became less mysterious to me. I now thought of it as a "Muse world," that most essential level of the human soul where all else has been cleared away, the platform from which elevation is possible. Although the language of the Muse world was a rarefied one, I had discovered it could be understood and reflected. I didn't know then if the world in general could recognize and provide these things, or whether I would only feel them in the company of other musicians like David and Carol. Frankly, I didn't care. All I knew at the time was that, finally, I felt deeply seen and wanted the feeling never to go away.

The CD would essentially mark the end of my boy-soprano career. I knew this while we were recording, yet it didn't register much with me on an emotional level. Now having turned fifteen, I was determined never to have a voice-crack disaster onstage, so my performing days were numbered. A final appearance was set for New York, at which I sang favorite songs and Cherubino's arias from Le Nozze di Figaro of Mozart. One of the songs, appropriately, was Britten's setting of "The Last Rose of Summer." Again, the emotional significance of this was lost on me. After the concert, a woman approached me on the receiving line and declared: "On behalf of myself and all the other sopranos in New York, we're glad you're retiring." I laughed at her joke, thanked her, but felt nothing. Shortly thereafter, a plan in the works to sing the soprano solo in Mahler's Fourth Symphony with Leonard Bernstein was scuttled, the first casualty of my changed voice.

It is still uncomfortable for me to recognize the boy I was during this transition. I was struggling for identity from an increasingly difficult position within my family, and was so overwhelmed by the loss of the voice that I couldn't allow any of it to register emotionally. I avoided facing the loss directly for many years. That my life was moving very fast during the transition aided in my denial, however. Almost immediately upon returning from New York, I had a concert performing the Elgar Cello Concerto, the result of having previously won a competition. People commented upon how expressive I was with the cello, and everyone assumed, as did I, that I was already set in my new "voice." This might explain why no one came forward during this period to try and help me understand the loss I was experiencing. I probably would neither have listened nor understood, but the knowledge that someone had tried might later have provided some comfort. With cello suddenly at the forefront, the overall circumstance provided me a neat way of exchanging one mode of expression for another. It also provided a way completely to avoid feeling or understanding what I was going through.

There is a saying in the vocal world that singers, unique among musicians, must die twice: first when their instrument no longer becomes publicly usable, and second when their body actually dies. Violinists and pianists have longer active careers, with conductors traditionally having the longest careers of all. Although other musicians must give up performing long before they actually expire, singers suffer this loss more acutely as a death-experience because of the human nature of the voice as an instrument.

Singers develop an incredibly personal relationship with their voice, which is, after all, not separate from the body, as is a violin. The paradox of the singer's instrument is that, while of the body, it also can feel like a separate entity with its own will. The singer is therefore called upon not only to relate to himself, but also to the instrument, his somehow autonomous flesh and blood. It is an intimate relationship—many singers speak of "partnering" or "parenting" their voice—that requires great emotional integration, the attainment of a certain transparency and free interplay of heart, mind, and soul. We usually experience such intimacy only in relationships with our dearest loved-ones, which can make the loss of a voice feel like a loved-one's death. And, while emotional integration is required of any musician hoping to make a communicative performance, with no other instrument than the voice does emotional integration become a part of the instrument itself. The grounding of the breath, the trust that the air will support the voice, the image of the sound, and the intention of the text all flow from a free, active imagination, the possession of which bespeaks such integration. In many ways, emotional integration is as much a part of the vocal instrument as are the vocal folds, the resonating chamber of the mask, and the breathing apparatus.

My experience of the loss of the voice was no different for my having gone through it at age fifteen, except that I did not have the references of the adult world to help me with the trauma. I had spent my entire life up to that point trying to understand my inner world, trying to find pathways into it and ways that could make it visible to the outside world. Singing had always been my best hope for this. Over ten years of singing, my relationship to my voice had grown into one of deep love and trust, since this voice was my connection to the Muse world and, hence, to myself. As the voice was so identified with the Muse world, its loss induced the nearly incapacitating fear that I would never again be able to make myself understood. The experience of recording the Schubert was still fresh in my heart, and here I was, already losing access to that euphoric feeling of visibility. How could I have known then that I would, indeed, be able to establish such connections with the world again? That these new connections would be visible to people other than specifically inclined musicians? That my boy-soprano voice would not prove to be the only conduit of joy and transparency of soul available to me? How could I have known that the call of self-determination I was heeding was already leading me along a path to self-understanding that would be more grounded, more true, and less dependent upon its outward manifestation?

I couldn't know these things, and so I thrashed about, looking for ways to fill in the space where my voice had been. I use the word *space* advisedly, in both its figurative and literal meanings. I remember feeling an almost palpable hole in my chest during the transition time, as though all the activity in my solar plexus had been frozen. I was driven by an intense need to reestablish a connection to the Muse world; at sixteen, barely a year after the loss of the voice, I left home against the wishes of my parents to pursue cello studies as a private student of Yale professor Aldo Parisot. It is clear to me now that my actions during this period were necessary parts of the self-determining process, actions that both produced the greatest personal benefit and exacted the highest price. Starting over alone in Connecticut, I could explore new aspects to my imagination. The distractions of establishing this new life also allowed me mostly to ignore the hole in my chest, which, while not growing, never went entirely away.

It would be seven years before I could connect with the events of the transition on an emotional level and grieve for the loss of my childhood's voice, seven years of vocal silence, seven years, I realize now, of getting ready. I was in a lesson with Phyllis Curtin, the renowned teacher who would carefully and lovingly steward my first sustained explorations with a changed, baritone instrument. I had been singing well that day, when she asked me a routine question about my earlier voice. Suddenly I was broadsided with such a wave of emotion that I had to leave the studio. We were working in her country house in Great Barrington, and I went out over the back hill into the lower cornfield, where I remained for quite a while, inconsolable. Grief, I learned, is an unmistakable condition, even if one has never experienced it before. It is oddly comforting in that way, and I was secure in the knowledge, even as I wept, that this was what I had been avoiding all these years, that this would start filling up the hole in my chest. In the days and weeks that followed, level upon deeper level of understanding surfaced, and it soon became apparent that my new clarity illuminated not just the experience of vocal loss itself, but the entire prodigy time. At twenty-two, I was finally able to begin facing my own peculiar process of prodigy, the process of coming to terms with my gifts and their presence within the larger context of my life. In so doing, I uncovered new facets to many aspects of my past. In particular, I discovered that my childhood relationship to my voice had been greatly more complicated than I knew at the time.

Looking back from this vantage point, I believe that my process of prodigy had been, from the start, an attempt to be seen as I thought myself to be. Throughout my boyhood, I certainly never thought of myself as a *prodigy*. Frankly, I didn't even know what the word meant. By the time I did (at age twelve), I'd already been singing happily for seven years and couldn't figure out this word's sudden applicability to me, simply for knowing its meaning. *Singing was just something I could do.* It was a source of some mystery to me how this ability of mine, which I considered as natural and as uneventful as my brown hair and blue eyes, could evoke and inspire such deeply held and powerful reactions in people—first in my parents, then in friends and colleagues, and ultimately in audiences at large.

While I certainly loved the attention, this mystery was also a source of considerable loneliness for me, as the distance between the world's reactions to my gifts and my own relationship to them only grew as I grew and became more accomplished. I had the nagging suspicion that I, my true self, somehow wasn't being seen. Years later, with the first experience of grief in Great Barrington, I could finally recognize that I possessed a rare combination of gifts as a child that truly had made me and my musical contributions unique. But that was not how I experienced the events as they occurred. My experience was that the worldview of my prodigiousness mostly centered on my perfect coloratura and the fact that I had absolute dynamic control over any note in any register of my voice—things that, by themselves, didn't matter much to me.

What *I* found special about myself was that I felt emotions acutely and was possessed of an overwhelming capacity and need to express myself to others. I was far from being awed or even concerned with my vocal agility, except that it was great fun. The expressive need, however, was as wondrous to me as a child as it is to me now: it felt like a miraculous stream of sparks and bubbles, flowing from my stomach up and around to behind my eyes, tickling all the way. The medium of expression wasn't very important to me then; such concerns are the province of the prodigy's audience, and the adult performer—not the prodigy himself. All I knew was that I was driven into song by this wonderful inner world, a world that would later, and more consciously, drive me into cello-playing, conducting, and all subsequent endeavor. When I was a young child, my voice was special to me only in providing connection and visibility for this Muse world and thus for myself. My love of the voice was about this access, not about timbre, diminuendos on high notes, and the like. For me, my special qualities all flowed from the Muse world, and I never identified these qualities with the fact of the voice itself—the voice was just the vehicle.

This relationship to the voice changed, however, and in a most subtle way. As I grew more accomplished, the outside world seemed to concern itself ever more exclusively with my vocal prowess, apparently missing the Muse world and my expressive need. These very specific reactions, by dint of their number and sheer intensity, came to challenge sorely my own view of myself and my voice. Although I was discovering that the keys to my self-understanding were not to be found in the outside world, I was also influenced, given my equally profound need to be seen, by the world's uniform reactions to my gifts. And so, somewhere in the middle of my prodigy career, I gradually began taking on the outside world's perceptions as my own, all the while thinking I was maintaining my own view. Ever so slowly, I began to transfer the special qualities I had always identified with the Muse world onto my voice itself. My voice grew and grew in importance to me, until it finally superseded even the magic of my imagination as the repository of all my special qualities. My voice was something that was universally seen, recognized, and reflected in a way that my inner world rarely had been, and soon I couldn't help identifying myself almost entirely by this outward manifestation of talent, by what I could *do*: how high, how soft, how fast. The encroachment of this worldview and its precipitation of such a profound shift in my own view of myself and my voice constitute perhaps the greatest loss in my entire process of prodigy. Although I mourned the loss of the voice itself, the discovery that my childhood relationship to my own voice had been so taken over by the opinions and expectations of the adult world proved to be the major revelation of my grief in Great Barrington.

This is, of course, an expression of loss of innocence, and in many ways the experience of prodigy and the loss of innocence are tantamount to the same thing. For prodigies, however, the onset of loss is as accelerated as are the outward manifestations of talent. This further separates the prodigy from his peers and intensifies the overall experience of loss. Children who lose their innocence early begin traveling in a superficially adult world, but don't yet have language to describe the experience of loss and their corresponding needs in adult terms. Though inarticulate, the underlying sensation of something being taken away is a powerful constant in the prodigy's world. For me, it felt as though I were a balloon that had sprung a slow leak, and I was always mindful of that little hiss of escaping air. This is one area where adults need to work especially hard on the prodigy's behalf, remembering their own childhoods' passage and filling in those needs that the prodigious child can't articulate for himself. Because they have few or no peers with whom they can compare experiences and test reality, prodigies come to rely exclusively on the adult world for example and guidance. For prodigies, then, even more so than for other children, the concerns and views of the adult world carry special weight.

I did not figure out as a prodigy that the weight of adult opinion and expectation had helped me to lose sight of myself. The shift was too gradual, and had taken place too deep within me, to be readily apparent. By the time I even started to sense, in my child's heart, the burden my voice had taken on, the end was already in sight. Intellectually, I kept telling myself that the Muse world would continue on after the voice, soon to be accessed with the cello, and that all I needed to do was to make myself understood in it again. What was really going on, however, was that my voice had quietly *become* my sole sense of identification, so that the nearly incapacitating fear I had felt during the voice-loss stemmed not so much from worries about making myself understood in the Muse world again, but from the subconscious feeling that I was teetering on the edge of an existential abyss. That I had successfully transferred to the cello did nothing to alleviate this fear, because the issue at hand was not one of simply establishing a new musical outlet, but of maintaining basic self-identification. Who would I be when my voice was gone? How could I be special without it? What would be left? What catastrophic change would occur in me once I could sing no more?

In fact, one of the most confusing things about the loss of the voice was that it actually changed nothing inside me at all. Far from suddenly being an empty vessel, I found that all the things I originally thought made me who I was—that gave import to my musical contributions, that enabled the emotional integration which drove my music-making in the first place—all these things resurfaced, shining as brightly as ever. The loss itself was stunningly simple: one day I had a voice, the next day I did not. The fertility of my imagination remained undiminished. It was a cruel joke: the voice-loss helped me rediscover these many special qualities about myself, qualities I didn't even know I'd come to ignore, but now left me no voice with which to access and share them. Little wonder, then, that I was able to deny all these things to myself for seven years, until enough time had passed and a concerned remark from a caring teacher would connect me back to the boy and close the circle.

And so, as I sat in Phyllis' cornfield, I reconnected with the boy I had once been. For the first time, I began to feel his joy and pain and fear and freedom, all commingled with the adult sorrow that I had neglected him for so long. I was amazed to discover how easy it had been to lose track of myself, and what a fragile thing it is, one's sense of self. I had always been told how strong and self-assured I was, but people were mainly responding to the outward, visible manifestation of my talents. In truth, I was a boy with a hole in his chest, listening to the omnipresent, slow hiss of escaping air. In the end, the greatest sorrow that day in Great Barrington was not that I had lost my voice, but that I had stopped being able to recognize the boy I had once been. I was scared as I reached back to him now, wondering who he might be and what he might mean for my adult life. But as I took his hand, I felt a resonance echo deep from the bottom of my soul and was warmed by the possibility of a partnership, of perhaps a turn in the road.

I was filled with an overwhelming gratitude for the special sparks and bubbles, that I had even had them, that they fueled an intoxicating world of imagination and Muse, and had given me the glorious experience of song, whatever the price. My true prodigiousness, it was now clear, had always been the world of my imagination, my special connection to the Muse, and certain emotional gifts that allowed my voice to be what it was and express the things it did. I hadn't done anything to make it this way, or asked to be accelerated. All together, these things simply constituted the immutable "just-is-ness" of me. It was wonderful to be reaffirmed in this conviction, and given that it was a conviction hard won through grief, I was determined never to lose sight of it again. The great discovery that I would always share in the Muse, whatever the "voice," cleared the way for my erstwhile prodigious sparks and bubbles finally to begin taking on their adult form.

I think many grown-up prodigies generally view their prodigious childhoods within the light of loss. They might not have actually lost their instrument, as did I, but they certainly lost their innocent childhoods to travel, hotel rooms, concerts, photo sessions, and to the special loneliness of being seen mainly within the context of the outward manifestation of their talent. If there is any characteristic that all prodigies share, it is a certain free-flowing, heightened, and *trusting* connection between intellect, heart, and soul, and an attendant need for this connection to be recognized. The resulting lack of psychological impediment makes the technical mastery of an instrument easy. Technical mastery is mostly beside the point for prodigious children because it is, in fact, so easy for them to attain. I spent my youth in the magical world of my heightened imagination, a place more real to me than any other, for out of it came music. I was left to wonder why seemingly few people could find me there, and eventually left it myself. The irony for me as a grown-up prodigy is that I now know that the adult world truly experienced all that I had to offer as a child, including my magic inner world, yet was mostly unable to reflect it back to me. Hence my feeling that I was being both seen and overlooked at the same time. I now realize that most adults experience the world of the prodigy, and their own imaginations, like the last echoes of a shouted voice in a canyon: they can still tell that it is a human sound and are drawn to it, but can no longer quite make out what it says.

It is in this way that people tend to assume that prodigy is about the thing in itself—about the violin, about the piano, about magic fingers and lightning octaves and double thirds. In fact, all these things, like my former diminuendos on high notes, are merely byproducts of the true miracle of prodigy. If I impart nothing else, it should be that there is a very "just-is-ness" to the prodigy's life and his relationship to that which makes him prodigious. It is important to remember that prodigies are not prodigious unto themselves: it is the world and its relationship to the gifted individual that turns him into a prodigy. Therefore, it is the prodigy's task, as he grows, to unite and integrate this "just-is-ness" with the world at large, the world which he shares with everybody else but which views him as unique. This struggle for integration, both external and internal, is the fount from which all his or her advantages, disadvantages, trials, doubts, euphorias, and deepest loneliness flow. It is the world's task to listen to the voice evoked by the prodigy echoing in its own soul and, with courage, embrace this aspect of the child.

Notes

Unless otherwise indicated, translations of quoted excerpts are by the author.

Preface

1. Yehudi Menuhin quoted in liner notes for *Vintage Menuhin*, Orion Records, ORS 7271.

Prologue

A Personal View

1. Yehudi Menuhin to the author, London, 12 September 1974.
2. Timothy Gallwey to the author, Los Angeles, 23 February 1975.
3. Quoted in an unsigned review, *Winnipeg Free Press*, 17 April 1964.
4. Eric Wilson, "Waiting for the Unicorn," *Notes* 4 (spring 1980): 29–30.
5. Leonard Rose, testimonial statement, New York, 20 October 1966.
6. Shauna, Thomas, and Isobel Rolston, interview by the author, tape recording, The Banff Centre, July 1995.
7. George Willey, review, *The Strad*, September 1972.
8. Leonard Rose to the author, New York, 12 October 1982.
9. Clayton Lee, review, *Edmonton Journal*, 25 November 1979.
10. Pierre Fournier, interviews by the author, typescript, November 1981, September 1982.
11. Jean Fonda Fournier to the author, Geneva, 18 November 1995.
12. Joanne Talbot, review, *Classic CD*, April 1996, 40.
13. Elizabeth Cowling, *The Cello* (New York: Scribner's Sons, 1975).

Reader's Guide

1. Thomas Gataker, *A Vindication on the Annotations on Jeremiah, Chapter Ten, Verse Two* (London: Calamy, 1653), microfilm, 50.

2. Barbara Jepson, "A Prodigy Still, But Uneasily Older," *The New York Times*, 22 January 1995.

3. Unsigned review, *Leipziger Musikalische Zeitung*, Leipzig, 1829.

4. Francesco Bennati, "Notice psychologique sur Niccolò Paganini," *Revue de Paris*, May 1831.

5. *Sarah Chang: Young Violin Virtuoso*, Altovision Production, 1993, videocassette.

6. Elyse Mach, ed., *Great Contemporary Pianists Speak for Themselves* (New York: Dover, 1991), 54.

7. Hans Gal, ed., *The Musician's World* (London: Thames and Hudson, 1965), 170.

8. Marie Winn, "The Pleasures and Perils of Being a Child Prodigy," *The New York Times Magazine*, 23 December 1979, 39.

9. David Denton, "Reflections of a Suzuki Guinea-Pig," *The Strad*, September 1993, 804–805.

10. Elizabeth Mills, ed., *The Suzuki Concept* (Berkeley and San Francisco: Diablo Press, 1973), 112.

11. Albert Gillis, "An Interview With Erica Morini," *Texas String News*, Summer 1951, 23–24.

12. *Ida Haendel: Voyage of Music*, Program I, Richard C. Bocking Productions, Ltd., 1988, videocassette.

13. Yehudi Menuhin, *Unfinished Journey* (London: MacDonald and Jane's, 1977), 42.

14. David Henry Feldman, *Nature's Gambit* (New York: Basic Books, Inc., 1986), 123.

15. Feldman, *Nature's Gambit*, 10.

16. Ruth Slenczynska, *Forbidden Childhood* (New York: Doubleday and Company, 1957).

17. Renee B. Fisher, *Musical Prodigies: Masters at an Early Age* (New York: Association Press, 1973), 52–53.

18. Quaintance Eaton, "Hofmann's Golden Jubilee," *Musical America*, 25 November 1937, 7.

19. Menuhin, *Unfinished Journey*, 89.

20. Norbert Wiener, *Ex-Prodigy: My Childhood and Youth* (Cambridge, Massachusetts: MIT Press, 1953), 161–162.

21. Suzanne Langer, *Philosophy in a New Key* (Cambridge, Massachusetts: Harvard University Press, 1951), 188.

22. Charles Rosen, "Should Music Be Played 'Wrong'?" *High Fidelity*, May 1971, 58.

Part One: The Grand Tradition

Chapter One: The Miracle From Salzburg

1. "Memoirs of Mozart's Sister, Published in the *Allgemeine Musikalische Zeitung*," in Otto Erich Deutsch, *Mozart: A Documentary Biography*, trans. Eric Blom, Peter Branscombe, and Jeremy Noble, 2d ed., rev. (Stanford: Stanford University Press, 1965), 493–494.
2. Johann Schachtner to Marianne von Berchtold, in Deutsch, *Mozart*, 452.
3. Marianne von Berchtold, "Data for a Biography of the Late Composer Wolfgang Mozart," in Deutsch, *Mozart*, 462.
4. Schachtner to Berchtold, in Deutsch, *Mozart*, 454.
5. Letters 27 and 28 in Emily Anderson, trans. and ed., *The Letters of Mozart and His Family*, 2d ed., vol. 1 (New York: The Macmillan Co., 1938), 47–48.
6. Berchtold, "Data for a Biography," in Deutsch, *Mozart*, 456.
7. Daines Barrington, "Report to the Royal Society in London," 15 February 1770, in Deutsch, *Mozart*, 98.
8. Slava Klima, ed., *Memoirs of Charles Burney 1726–1769* (Lincoln, Nebraska: University of Nebraska Press, 1987), 164.
9. Berchtold, "Anecdotes About Mozart Published in Leipzig," 22 January 1800, in Deutsch, *Mozart*, 493.
10. Letter 31 in Anderson, *Letters*, 52.
11. "Series of Notices in *The Public Advertiser*," in Deutsch, *Mozart*, 33–45.
12. "Second Advertisement for Frankfurt Concert," 30 August 1763, in Deutsch, *Mozart*, 24.
13. Friedrich Schlichtegroll, "Johannes Chrysostomus Wolfgang Gottlieb Mozart," 5 December 1791, in *Nekrolog auf das Jahr 1791* (Gotha: Perthes, 1792), 91.
14. Harrison James Wignall, *In Mozart's Footsteps* (New York: Paragon House, 1991), 33.
15. Letter 55 in Anderson, *Letters*, 82.
16. Letter 88a in Anderson, *Letters*, 130.
17. "Papal Patent, Rome, 4 July 1770," in Deutsch, *Mozart*, 124.
18. Letter 127 in Anderson, *Letters*, 76.
19. Letter 130a in Anderson, *Letters*, 180.
20. Letter 143 in Anderson, *Letters*, 196.
21. Letter 64a in Anderson, *Letters*, 219.
22. Letter 87 in Anderson, *Letters*, 127.

Chapter Two: High Venture

1. The inscription signed Anton Giulio Barrili (1836–1908) is quoted in G. I. C. de Courcy, *Paganini: The Genoese*, vol. 1 (New York: Da Capo Press, 1977), 7.
2. Peter Lichtenthal, untitled biographical sketch, *Allgemeine Musikalische Zeitung* (Leipzig), April 1830.
3. Lichtenthal, untitled sketch.
4. Julius M. Schottky, *Paganinis Leben und Treiben als Künstler und als Mensch* (Prague: J. G. Calve, 1830).
5. Francesco Bennati, "Notice psychologique sur Niccolò Paganini," *Revue de Paris*, May 1831.
6. A small instrument made by Hieronymus Amati ca. 1672.
7. Carlo Gervasoni first mentions such adolescent employment in Genoa.
8. Ignace Pleyel, the most important pupil of Haydn, had been living in Rome during the period 1776–83 and composed two violin concertos in the style of Haydn.
9. F.-J. Fétis, *Biographie universelle des musiciens*, 8 vols. (Brussels), 1833–44.
10. Schottky, *Paganinis Leben*.
11. Schottky, *Paganinis Leben*.
12. Schottky, *Paganinis Leben*.
13. Schottky, *Paganinis Leben*.
14. As his career prospered, Paganini owned many musical instruments. At the time of his death he had twenty-two violins, violas, cellos, and guitars—all priceless examples by Amati, Guadagnini, Guarneri, Roggeri, Ruggeri, Stradivari, and Tononi.
15. Arturo Codignola, *Paganini intimo* (Genoa, 1935).
16. Schottky, *Paganinis Leben*.
17. In 1982, the violin was used in concerts celebrating the two hundredth anniversary of Paganini's birth. Later that year it was exhibited for one day, under remarkable security measures, in the André Mertens Galleries for Musical Instruments at New York's Metropolitan Museum of Art.

Chapter Three: A Girl From Leipzig

1. Joan Chissell, *Clara Schumann: A Dedicated Spirit* (London: Hamish Hamilton, 1983), 9.
2. Nancy B. Reich, *Clara Schumann: The Artist and the Woman* (Ithaca: Cornell University Press, 1985), 42. All quotations of Clara Wieck that are not otherwise attributed are drawn from her diaries as excerpted in this source. The diaries themselves are kept in the archives of the Robert Schumann Haus in Zwickau, Germany.

3. Reich, *Clara Schumann*, 44.

4. Chissell, *Clara Schumann*, 22.

5. Robert Schumann, *Tagebücher (1827–1838)*, vol. 1, ed. Georg Eismann, (Leipzig: Deutscher Verlag für Musik, 1971), 364.

6. Chissell, *Clara Schumann*, 30.

7. Robert Haven Schauffler, *Florestan: The Life and Work of Robert Schumann* (New York: Dover, 1945), 95.

8. Reich, *Clara Schumann*, 71.

9. Chissell, *Clara Schumann*, 51.

10. Unsigned review, *Allgemeine Musikalische Zeitung* (Vienna), 7 March 1838.

11. Clara Wieck to Robert Schumann, Graz, Austria, 23 April 1838.

12. Berthold Litzmann, *Clara Schumann*, 3d ed., vol. 1 (Leipzig: Breitkopf, 1906), 229–30.

13. Clara and Robert Schumann, *Clara und Robert Schumann, Briefwechsel*, vol. 1, 1832–38, ed. Eva Weissweiler (Basel: Stroemfeld/Roter Stern, 1984), 272.

14. Clara and Robert Schumann, *Clara*, 1:230.

15. Wolfgang Boetticher, ed., *Robert Schumann in seinen Schriften und Briefen* (Berlin: Hahnefeld, 1942), 250.

16. Litzmann, *Clara Schumann*, 1:331.

17. Litzmann, *Clara Schumann,* 1:367.

Chapter Four: El Niño del Tost

1. H. L. Kirk, *Pablo Casals* (New York: Holt, Rinehart, and Winston, 1974), 51.

2. J. M. Corredor, *Conversations With Casals* (New York: Dutton, 1956), 15. All quotations of Pablo Casals that are not otherwise attributed are drawn from this source.

3. Pablo Casals, interview by Albert E. Kahn, *Observer Review* (London), 13 September 1970.

4. Kirk, *Pablo Casals*, 35.

5. Kirk, *Pablo Casals*, 40.

6. Corredor, *Conversations*, 35.

Chapter Five: A Family Portrait

1. Horace Britt in conversations with the author during the period 1953–71. All quotations of Horace Britt that are not otherwise attributed are drawn from this source.

2. The portrait by Rixens painted in 1886 hangs in the Art Museum of Valenciennes.

3. Inez Koutzen to the author, Mount Kisco, New York, 9 February 1975.

4. Roger and Cynthia Britt in conversation with the author, Woodstock, New York, August 1956.

5. Arthur Pougin, review, *Le Ménestrel* (Paris), 22 July 1894.

6. Unsigned review, *XIXe Siècle* (Paris), July 1895.

7. Arthur Pougin, review, *Le Ménestrel* (Paris), 21 July 1895.

8. G. Sauni, Minister of Fine Arts and Culture, to Horace Britt, Paris, 23 July 1895. Britt's medal is in the possession of his great nephew, cellist George Koutzen.

9. Unsigned review, *Le Matin* (Antwerp), 20 May 1896.

10. Unsigned review, *Le Méphisto* (Antwerp), 26 September 1896.

11. Unsigned review, *Le Matin* (Antwerp), 16 December 1896.

12. David Popper to Horace Britt, Budapest, 12 February 1897.

13. Unsigned review, *La France* (Paris), 20 March 1897.

14. Pablo de Sarasate to Jules Delsart, Paris, 1 July 1897.

15. Jules Delsart to Horace Britt, Paris, 27 June 1897.

16. Unsigned review, *Musical Standard* (London), 24 July 1897.

17. Unsigned review, *Le Nord* (Paris), 11 March 1898.

18. Alexandra Bibesco, Princesse de Brancovan, to Ernest Britt, Paris, 21 November 1898.

19. Queen Marie-Henriette's fan is now in the possession of Gaëtane Britt's granddaughter, Nadia Koutzen.

20. Inez Koutzen to the author, Mount Kisco, New York, 20 February 1975.

21. Unsigned review, *Le Soleil* (Paris), 6 May 1909.

22. Nadia Koutzen, "Reflections of a Child Prodigy" (Toms River, New Jersey, 1994, typescript). All quotations of Nadia Koutzen that are not otherwise attributed are drawn from this source.

23. Koutzen, "Reflections," 17.

24. Unsigned review, *Rochester Democrat and Chronicle*, 19 April 1939.

25. Samuel L. Laciar, review, *Evening Public Ledger* (Philadelphia), 5 November 1940.

Chapter Six: California Crossroads

1. Gregor Piatigorsky, *Cellist* (New York: Doubleday, 1965), 157. All quotations of Gregor Piatigorsky that are not otherwise attributed are drawn from this source.

2. David Ewen, *Men and Women Who Make Music* (New York: Little, Brown and Co., 1939), 103.

3. Unsigned article, *Ma'ariv* (Tel Aviv), 21 March 1950.

4. Boris Schwarz, *Great Masters of the Violin* (New York: Simon and Schuster, 1983), 433.

5. Herbert R. Axelrod, ed., *Heifetz* (Neptune City, New Jersey: Paganiniana

Publications, Inc., 1976), 131. All quotations of Jascha Heifetz that are not otherwise attributed are drawn from this source.

6. Hugo Rasch, review, *Allgemeine Musikzeitung* (Berlin) 39 (7 June 1912).

7. Unsigned review, *Signale für die musikalische Welt* (Berlin) 45 (6 November 1912).

8. Unsigned article, *The Saturday Evening Post*, 7 April 1928.

9. Schwarz, *Great Masters*, 434.

10. Unsigned review, *Musical America*, October 1917.

11. Seymour W. Itzkoff, *Emanuel Feuermann, Virtuoso* (University, Alabama: University of Alabama Press, 1979), 200. All quotations of Emanuel Feuermann that are not otherwise attributed are drawn from this source.

12. Itzkoff, *Emanuel Feuermann*, 213.

13. Itzkoff, *Emanuel Feuermann*, 49.

14. Itzkoff, *Emanuel Feuermann*, 60.

15. Emanuel Feuermann, "Cello Playing: A Contemporary Revolution," in *Who's Who in Music*, 1941, reprinted in *Newsletter of the Violoncello Society, Inc.*, Spring 1972.

16. Itzkoff, *Emanuel Feuermann*, 81.

17. Piatigorsky, *Cellist*, 26.

18. Jascha Bernstein, "Recollections of Grisha," *Newsletter of the Violoncello Society, Inc.*, March 1977.

19. This conversation with Lenin is recalled by Piatigorsky in *Cellist*, 48.

20. Margaret Campbell, *The Great Cellists* (North Pomfret, Vermont: Trafalgar Square Publishing, 1989), 171.

21. Arthur Rubinstein, *My Many Years* (New York: Alfred A. Knopf, 1980), 303.

22. Arthur Rubinstein, *My Young Years* (New York: Alfred A. Knopf, 1973), 7. All quotations of Arthur Rubinstein that are not otherwise attributed are drawn from this source.

23. Rubinstein, *My Young Years*, 40.

24. Rubinstein, *My Young Years*, 76, 79.

25. *Rubinstein Remembered*, a hundredth anniversary tribute in the PBS television series, *American Masters*, 1987, videocassette.

Chapter Seven: Midcentury Keyboard Masters

1. Sacheverell Sitwell, *Liszt* (London: Columbus Books, 1988), 98.

2. Otto Friedrich, *Glenn Gould: A Life and Variations* (Toronto: Lester and Orpen Dennys, 1989), 16. All quotations of Glenn Gould that are not otherwise attributed are drawn from this source.

3. Malcolm Troup, introduction to the symposium *Alberto Guerrero Remembered: The Next Generation* (Toronto, 25 October 1990), tape recording.

4. Joseph Roddy, "Apollonian," *The New Yorker*, 14 May 1960, 52.

5. Mary Willan Mason, "Alberto Guerrero," *Encyclopaedia of Music in Canada*, 2d ed. (Toronto: University of Toronto Press, 1992), 559.

6. *Alberto Guerrero Remembered*.

7. Edward W. Wodson, reviews, *The Evening Telegram* (Toronto), 13 December 1945, 9 May 1946.

8. Friedrich, *Glenn Gould*, 35.

9. Friedrich, *Glenn Gould*, 38.

10. Paul Hume, review, *The Washington Post* (Washington, DC), 3 January 1955.

11. John Briggs, review, *The New York Times*, 12 January 1955.

12. John Briggs, review, *Musical Courier* 153 (February 1955), 86.

13. Friedrich, *Glenn Gould*, 57–58.

14. Friedrich, *Glenn Gould*, 313.

15. Dean Elder, *Pianists at Play* (Evanston: The Instrumentalist Co., 1982), 151. All quotations of Martha Argerich that are not otherwise attributed are drawn from this source.

16. David Henry Feldman, *Nature's Gambit* (New York: Basic Books, Inc., 1986), 165.

17. Daniel Barenboim, *Daniel Barenboim: A Life in Music* (New York: Charles Scribner's Sons, 1991), 3. All quotations of Daniel Barenboim that are not otherwise attributed are drawn from this source.

18. Barenboim, *A Life in Music*, 4.

19. Carol Easton, *Jacqueline du Pré* (London: Hodder and Stoughton, 1989), 141.

20. Barenboim, *A Life in Music*, 48.

21. Easton, *Jacqueline du Pré*, 143.

22. Frederic Spotts, *Bayreuth: A History of the Wagner Festival* (New Haven and London: Yale University Press, 1994), 291, 302.

23. Dolores Fredrickson, "Van Cliburn Remembers His Remarkable Mother," *Clavier*, March 1996, 6.

24. Howard Reich, *Van Cliburn* (Nashville: Thomas Nelson Publishers, 1993), 10. All quotations of Van Cliburn that are not otherwise attributed are drawn from this source.

25. Reich, *Van Cliburn*, 6.

26. Fredrickson, "Van Cliburn Remembers," 8.

27. Reich, *Van Cliburn*, 16.

28. Reich, *Van Cliburn*, 17.

29. Reich, *Van Cliburn*, 21.

30. Jean Warner Stark, article in *American Music Teacher*, November 1961.

31. Reich, *Van Cliburn*, 31.

32. Reich, *Van Cliburn*, 44.

Chapter Eight: Discovery: Competitions and Management

1. Letters 440 and 441 in Emily Anderson, trans. and ed., *The Letters of Mozart and His Family*, 2d ed., vol. 3 (New York: The Macmillan Co., 1938), 1179–1182.

2. Mozart was also a Roman Catholic. In 1770, Pope Clement XIV had instructed Cardinal Pallavicini to confer the Order of the Golden Spur upon the boy "who since earliest youth had excelled in the sweetest sounding of the harpsichord."

3. Simon Collins, "Ruggiero Ricci," *The Strad*, March 1977, 909.

4. *Which Way to Carnegie Hall–2*, prod. Robert Chestermann, Telefilm Canada, Prometheus Productions, 1995, videocassette.

5. *39th Pablo Casals Festival*, prod. Bob Bower, Arts and Entertainment Network, Longstore, Inc., 1995, videocassette.

6. K. Robert Schwarz, "Living a Tale She Couldn't Make Up," *The New York Times*, 29 January 1995.

7. Schwarz, "Living a Tale."

8. Barbara Jepson, "A Prodigy Still, But Uneasily Older," *The New York Times*, 22 January 1995.

9. Howard Reich, *Van Cliburn* (Nashville: Thomas Nelson Publishers, 1993), 107.

10. Reich, *Van Cliburn*, 110.

11. Reich, *Van Cliburn*, 112.

12. Allen Young, review, *Denver Post*, November 1954.

13. Reich, *Van Cliburn*, 117.

14. Reich, *Van Cliburn*, 157.

Chapter Nine: Warsaw, 1935

1. Henry Temianka, *Facing the Music: An Irreverent Close-up of the Real Concert World* (New York: David McKay Co., Inc., 1973), 63.

2. M. J. Ronze-Neveu, *Ginette Neveu* (London: Rockliff, 1957), 31.

3. Ronze-Neveu, *Ginette Neveu*, 41.

4. Temianka, *Facing the Music*, 28.

5. Yakov Soroker, *David Oistrakh* (Jerusalem: Lexicon Publishing House, 1982), 24.

6. Soroker, *David Oistrakh*, 5. All quotations of David Oistrakh that are not otherwise attributed are drawn from this source.

7. Tully Potter, "David Oistrakh: Heart of the Matter," *The Strad*, October 1984, 408.

8. Soroker, *David Oistrakh*, 20.

9. David Oistrakh's "Letters from Moscow," quoted in Soroker, *David Oistrakh*, 20–23. See also Victor Yuzefovich, *David Oistrakh: Conversations With Igor Oistrakh* (Moscow, 1978).

10. Temianka, *Facing the Music*, 50.

11. Temianka, *Facing the Music*, 31.

12. C. F. Flesch, "The Last Sixteen Years," in Carl Flesch, *The Memoirs of Carl Flesch* (Paris: Bois de Boulogne, 1973), 360.

13. Robert Lewin, "Story of a Genius," *The Strad*, February 1971.

14. Lorand Fenyves, interview by the author, tape recording, The Banff Centre, August 1995.

15. Margaret Campbell, *The Great Violinists* (London: Granada Publishing, 1980), 267.

16. Lewin, "Story of a Genius," 501.

17. Carl Flesch to Josef Hassid, 6 June 1943, in Campbell, *The Great Violinists*, 268.

18. *Ida Haendel: Voyage of Music*, Program I, Richard C. Bocking Productions, Ltd., 1988, videocassette. All quotations of Ida Haendel that are not otherwise attributed are drawn from this source.

19. Campbell, *The Great Violinists*, 247.

20. *Ida Haendel: Voyage of Music*, Program I.

21. Simon Collins, "Ida Haendel," *The Strad*, May 1986, 31.

Chapter Ten: Virtuosos of the Twenties and Thirties

1. Aldo Parisot, interview by the author, tape recording, The Banff Centre, August 1995.

2. Boris Schwarz, *Great Masters of the Violin* (New York: Simon and Schuster, 1983), 539.

3. Karen Schnackenberg, "Classical, Etc.," *The International Musician*, April 1966, 19.

4. S. E. Rubin, "Who's One of the Three Best Cellists in the World?" *The New York Times*, 15 October 1972.

5. Naomi Graffman, "Bravo, Starker!" *Connoisseur*, November 1983.

6. Dennis Rooney, "Calm Mastery," *The Strad*, October 1988, 793.

7. Article in *Newsweek*, July 1973, 75.

8. Rooney, "Calm Mastery," 797.

9. Shirley Flemming, "The Case of a Child Prodigy Who Survived," *The New York Times*, 18 January 1976.

10. Boris Schwarz, *Great Masters of the Violin* (New York: Simon and Schuster, 1983), 534.

11. Renee B. Fisher, *Musical Prodigies: Masters at an Early Age* (New York: Association Press, 1973), 100.

12. Flemming, "The Case," 15.

13. Margaret Campbell, *The Great Violinists* (London: Granada Publishing Ltd., 1980), 236.

14. *Soldiers of Music: Rostropovich Returns to Russia*, prods. Susan Froemke, Peter Gelb, Albert Maysles, and Bob Eisenhardt, Sony Classical 46387, 1990, videocassette.

15. Claude Samuel, *Mstislav Rostropovich and Galina Vishnevskaya: Russia, Music, and Liberty* (Portland, Oregon: Amadeus Press, 1995), 37. All quotations of Mstislav Rostropovich that are not otherwise attributed are drawn from this source.

16. *Soldiers of Music*.

17. Mstislav Rostropovich, address before the Second American Cello Congress, Tempe, Arizona, 8 June 1984, typescript.

18. Robert Magidoff, *Yehudi Menuhin* (New York: Doubleday and Co., 1955), 95.

19. Yehudi Menuhin, *Unfinished Journey* (London: Macdonald and Jane's Publishers, Ltd., 1977), 22. All quotations of Yehudi Menuhin that are not otherwise attributed are taken from this source.

20. Evelyn Chadwick, "Schooled for Success," *The Strad*, April 1996, 364–365.

21. Unsigned Sun News Services article, *Sunday Express* (Edmonton), 1 November 1996.

22. In 1960, Dezsö Mahalek remarked to the author, "In 1928 when Sarah [Zara] was about ten, she won first prize in the solo class at the Winnipeg festival. She played Fauré's *Élégie* magnificently. The adjudicator Hugh Roberton said he had never heard such a performance."

23. Zara Nelsova, interview by the author, letters, and tape recording, New York and Los Angeles, September 1995.

Part Two: The Innovators

Chapter Eleven: Against All Odds

1. Andrés Segovia, *Segovia: An Autobiography of the Years 1893–1920* (New York: Macmillan Publishing Co., Inc., 1976), 3. All quotations of Andrés Segovia that are not otherwise attributed are drawn from this source.

2. *Andrés Segovia: The Song of the Guitar*, prod. Christopher Nupen, Allegro Films, London, 1976, videocassette.

3. *Farewell to the Master*, prod. Nola Safro, CBS television series 20/20, 1986, videocassette.

4. Frank Crane, "When Georges Barrère Played the Flute," quoted in Georges Barrère, *Georges Barrère* (New York, 1929), 34. See also Frank Crane, *Four Minute Essays* (New York: Wm. H. Wise and Co., 1928).

5. Patrick Gallois, interview by the author, tape recording, Paris, 12 December 1996.

6. Georges Barrère, *Georges Barrère* (New York, 1929), 1. All quotations of Georges Barrère that are not otherwise attributed are drawn from this source.

7. William Primrose, *Walk on the North Side: Memoirs of a Violist* (Provo: Brigham Young University Press, 1978), 45. All quotations of William Primrose that are not otherwise attributed are drawn from this source.
8. Isobel Moore Rolston, interview by the author, Banff, August 1996.
9. Primrose, *Walk on the North Side*, 59.
10. Evelyn Glennie, *Good Vibrations: An Autobiography* (London: Arrow Books, Ltd., 1991), 34. All quotations of Evelyn Glennie that are not otherwise attributed are drawn from this source.
11. *Breaking the Silence Barrier*, prod. Bill Einreinhofer, WNET television series *Innovations*, 1996, videocassette.

Chapter Twelve: Pocket Toscaninis

1. Unsigned article, *Life* magazine, 30 June 1947, 103.
2. Renee B. Fisher, *Musical Prodigies: Masters at an Early Age* (New York, Association Press, 1973), 87.
3. Michael T. Privitello, quoted in "A Note About Joey Alfidi by His Music Tutor," liner notes for *Command Performance*, Jubilee Records, Jay-Gee Co., Inc., GM 2-3000.
4. Review signed R. P., *The New York Times*, 19 November 1956.
5. Unsigned review, *Le Soir* (Brussels), 2 December 1960.
6. Louis Biancolli, review, *World-Telegram* (New York), 19 August 1939.
7. Mortimer H. Frank, "Conversations With Lorin Maazel," *Fanfare*, January/February 1985, 109.
8. Helena Matheopoulos, *Maestro: Encounters With Conductors of Today* (New York: Harper and Row, 1982), 304.
9. Frank, "Conversations," 109.

Chapter Thirteen: *The Rose Tree*, An Opera

1. Unsigned review, *West Chester Daily Local News*, 10 April 1920.
2. John Ardoin, "Samuel Barber at Capricorn," *Musical America*, March 1960, 5.
3. Barbara B. Heyman, *Samuel Barber: The Composer and His Music* (New York: Oxford University Press, 1992), 17.
4. Nathan Broder, *Samuel Barber* (New York: G. Schirmer, 1956), 12.
5. Heyman, *Samuel Barber*, 33.
6. Heyman, *Samuel Barber*, 35.
7. Samuel Barber to the author, Mount Kisco, New York, 16 October 1970.
8. Gian-Carlo Menotti, interview with Peter Dickinson, BBC broadcast, London, 23 January 1982.
9. Sidney Homer to Samuel Barber, New York City, 10 November 1931.
10. Francis Perkins, review, *New York Herald Tribune*, 25 March 1935.
11. BBC broadcast, London, 23 January 1982.

Chapter Fourteen: The Spirit of the Gypsy

1. Kató Havas, *The Violin and I* (London: Bosworth, 1968), 4.
2. *The Kató Havas Teaching Video* on the causes and cures of physical injuries in violin and viola playing. Lakeland Home Music, Watermillock, Cumbria, UK, 1991, videocassette.
3. Kató Havas, interviews by the author over a thirty-year period (1967–97), with reference to her written works: *The Violin and I* (London: Bosworth,1968); *A New Approach to Violin Playing* (London: Bosworth, 1961); *Stage Fright: Its Causes and Cures* (London: Bosworth, 1973); and *The Editorials of Kató Havas* (Waterloo: Castle Enterprises, 1995), a compilation of editorials originally published in the newsletters of KHANA.

Chapter Fifteen: Bass Is Beautiful

1. Unsigned article, *Time*, 22 February 1971, 14.
2. Simandl's *Neueste Methode des Kontrabass-Spiels*, an orthodox method written before 1912, was intended for orchestral bassists of the early twentieth century and does not address the evolving pedagogy of modern solo bass playing.
3. Gary Karr, interview by the author, tape recording, Victoria, British Columbia, September 1996. All quotations of Gary Karr that are not otherwise attributed are drawn from this source.

Chapter Sixteen: Born for the Cello

1. Raymond Ericson, review, *The New York Times*, 15 May 1965.
2. Colin Mason, review, *The Guardian* (London), 2 March 1961.
3. William Wordsworth, ed., *Jacqueline du Pré: Impressions* (London: Granada, 1983), 21–29.
4. Carol Easton, *Jacqueline du Pré* (London: Hodder and Stoughton, Ltd., 1989), 44.
5. Easton, *Jacqueline du Pré*, 57.
6. Wordsworth, ed., *Jacqueline du Pré: Impressions*, 38.
7. Easton, *Jacqueline du Pré*, 53.
8. Paul Tortelier, *Paul Tortelier: A Self-Portrait* (London: Heinemann, 1984), 213.
9. Easton, *Jacqueline du Pré*, 131.
10. Wordsworth, ed., *Jacqueline du Pré: Impressions*, 61.
11. Easton, *Jacqueline du Pré*, 20.
12. Wordsworth, ed., *Jacqueline du Pré: Impressions*, 136.
13. Yo-Yo Ma, interview with Charlie Rose, WNET Television, New York, November 1995, videocassette.
14. Samuel Applebaum, *The Way They Play* (Neptune, New Jersey: Paganiniana Publications, Inc., 1984), 265.

15. David Blum, "Ma Energetico," *The Strad*, January 1988, 21.
16. Blum, "Ma Energetico," 21.
17. David Blum, "A Process Larger Than Oneself," *The New Yorker*, 1 May 1989, 50. All quotations of Yo-Yo Ma that are not otherwise attributed are drawn from this source.
18. Edith Eisler, "Yo-Yo Ma: Music for the Soul," *Strings*, May/June 1992, 50.
19. Yo-Yo Ma, interview with Charlie Rose.
20. Anne Inglis, "In Pursuit of Excellence," *The Strad*, May 1984, 31.
21. Yo-Yo Ma, interview with Charlie Rose.

Epilogue: A Process of Prodigy

1. Leonard Bernstein quoted from liner notes for *Bejun*, Delos DE 3019, Mehta's first compact disc.
2. János Starker, *A Tribute to David Popper*, Delos DE 3065; János Starker, *J. S. Bach: Six Suites for Cello*, BMG/RCA 09026-61436-2.
3. Bejun Mehta, interviews by the author, tape recording, New York, 18 October to 23 December 1996.

Selected Bibliography

Anderson, Emily, trans. and ed. *The Letters of Mozart and His Family*. 2d ed. New York: The Macmillan Co., 1938.

Ardoin, John. "Samuel Barber at Capricorn." *Musical America* (March 1960).

Axelrod, Herbert R., ed. *Heifetz*. Neptune City, NJ: Paganiniana Publications, Inc., 1976.

Barenboim, Daniel. *Daniel Barenboim: A Life in Music*. New York: Charles Scribner's Sons, 1991.

Blum, David C. *Casals and the Art of Interpretation*. London: Heinemann, 1977.

————. "Ma Energetico." *The Strad* (January 1988).

————. "A Process Larger Than Oneself." *The New Yorker* (1 May 1989).

Broder, Nathan. *Samuel Barber*. New York: G. Schirmer, 1956.

Campbell, Margaret. *The Great Cellists*. North Pomfret, Vermont: Trafalgar Square Publishing, 1989.

————. *The Great Violinists*. London: Granada Publishing, Ltd., 1980.

Casals, Pablo. *Joys and Sorrows* [His own story as told to Albert E. Kahn]. New York: Simon and Schuster, 1970.

Chadwick, Evelyn. "Schooled for Success." *The Strad* (April 1996).

Chissell, Joan. *Clara Schumann: A Dedicated Spirit*. London: Hamish Hamilton, 1983.

Collins, Simon. "Ida Haendel." *The Strad* (May 1986).

————. "Isaac Stern." *The Strad* (August 1977).

————. "Ruggiero Ricci." *The Strad* (March 1977).

Corredor, J. M. *Conversations With Casals*. Trans. André Mangeot. New York: Dutton, 1956.

Cowling, Elizabeth. *The Cello*. New York, Scribner's Sons, 1975.

Daniel, Robin. *Conversations With Menuhin*. London: Futura Publications, Ltd., 1980.

David, Hans T., and Arthur Mendel, ed. *The Bach Reader*. New York: W. W. Norton and Co., 1966.

Deutsch, Otto Erich. *Mozart: A Documentary Biography*. 2d ed. Trans. Eric Blom, Peter Branscombe, and Jeremy Noble. Stanford: Stanford University Press, 1965.

Easton, Carol. *Jacqueline du Pré*. London: Hodder and Stoughton, 1989.

Elder, Dean. *Pianists at Play: Interviews, Master Lessons, and Technical Regimes*. Evanston: The Instrumentalist Co., 1982.

Ewen, David. *Men and Women Who Make Music*. New York: Little, Brown and Co., 1939.

Feldman, David Henry. *Nature's Gambit*. New York: Basic Books, Inc., 1986.

Fisher, Renee B. *Musical Prodigies: Masters at an Early Age*. New York: Association Press, 1973.

Flesch, C. F. "The Last Sixteen Years." In Carl Flesch. *The Memoirs of Carl Flesch*. Paris: Bois de Boulogne, 1973.

Frank, Mortimer H. "Conversations With Lorin Maazel." *Fanfare* (January/February 1985).

Fredrickson, Dolores. "Van Cliburn Remembers His Remarkable Mother." *Clavier* (March 1996).

Friedrich, Otto. *Glenn Gould: A Life and Variations*. Toronto: Lester and Orpen Dennys, 1989.

Glennie, Evelyn. *Good Vibrations: My Autobiography*. London: Arrow Books, Ltd., 1990.

Graffman, Naomi. "Bravo, Starker!" *Connoisseur* (November 1983).

Havas, Kató. *The Editorials of Kató Havas*. Waterloo: Castle Enterprises, 1995.

———. *A New Approach to Violin Playing*. London: Bosworth, 1961.

———. *Stage Fright: Its Causes and Cures*. London: Bosworth, 1973.

———. *The Violin and I*. London: Bosworth, 1968.

———. "What Is Artistic Freedom?" *Texas Quarterly* (Spring 1973).

Heyman, Barbara B. *Samuel Barber: The Composer and His Music*. New York: Oxford University Press, 1992.

Inglis, Anne. "In Pursuit of Excellence." *The Strad* (May 1984).

Itzkoff, Seymour W. *Emanuel Feuermann, Virtuoso*. University, Alabama: University of Alabama Press, 1979.

Kirk, H. L. *Pablo Casals*. New York: Holt, Rinehart, and Winston, 1974.

Klima, Slava, ed. *Memoirs of Charles Burney 1726–1769*. Lincoln, Nebraska: University of Nebraska Press, 1987.

Koutzen, Nadia. "Reflections of a Child Prodigy." Toms River, New Jersey, 1994. Typescript.

Lewin, Robert. "Story of a Genius." *The Strad* (February 1971).

Mach, Elyse, ed. *Great Contemporary Pianists Speak for Themselves*. New York: Dover, 1991.

Magidoff, Robert. *Yehudi Menuhin*. New York: Doubleday and Co., 1955.

Matheopoulos, Helena. *Maestro: Encounters With Conductors of Today*. New York: Harper and Row, 1982.

Menuhin, Yehudi. *Unfinished Journey*. London: MacDonald and Jane's, 1977.

Nichols, Roger. *Ravel Remembered*. London: Faber and Faber, 1987.

Ostwald, Peter. *Glenn Gould: The Ecstasy and Tragedy of Genius*. New York: W. W. Norton, 1997.

Piatigorsky, Gregor. *Cellist*. New York: Doubleday and Co., 1965.

Potter, Tully. "David Oistrakh: Heart of the Matter." *The Strad* (October 1984).

Primrose, William. *Walk on the North Side: Memoirs of a Violist*. Provo: Brigham Young University Press, 1978.

Reich, Howard. *Van Cliburn*. Nashville: Thomas Nelson Publishers, 1993.

Reich, Nancy B. *Clara Schumann: The Artist and the Woman*. Ithaca: Cornell University Press, 1985.

Ronze-Neveu, M. J. *Ginette Neveu*. London: Rockliff, 1957.

Rooney, Dennis. "Calm Mastery." *The Strad* (October 1988).

Rosenberg, Bernard, and Deena Rosenberg. "A Last Talk With Piatigorsky." *Newsletter of the Violoncello Society, Inc.* (March 1977).

Rubinstein, Arthur. *My Many Years*. New York: Alfred A. Knopf, 1980.

————. *My Young Years*. New York: Alfred A. Knopf, 1973.

Samuel, Claude. *Mstislav Rostropovich and Galina Vishnevskaya: Russia, Music, and Liberty*. Portland, Oregon: Amadeus Press, 1995.

Schauffler, Robert Haven. *Florestan: The Life and Work of Robert Schumann*. New York: Dover, 1945.

Schnackenberg, Karen. "Classical, Etc." *The International Musician* (April 1966).

Schwarz, Boris. *Great Masters of the Violin*. New York: Simon and Schuster, 1983.

Segovia, Andrés. *Segovia: An Autobiography of the Years 1893–1920*. New York: Macmillan Publishing Co., Inc., 1976.

Sitwell, Sacheverell. *Liszt*. London: Columbus Books, 1988.

Slenczynska, Ruth. *Forbidden Childhood*. New York: Doubleday and Company, 1957.

Soroker, Yakov. *David Oistrakh*. Jerusalem: Lexicon Publishing House, 1982.

Temianka, Henry. *Facing the Music: An Irreverent Close-up of the Real Concert World*. New York: David McKay Co., Inc., 1973.

Tortelier, Paul. *Paul Tortelier: A Self-Portrait*. London: Heinemann, 1984.

Weschler-Vered, Artur. *Jascha Heifetz*. New York: Schirmer Books, 1986.

Wordsworth William, ed. *Jacqueline du Pré: Impressions*. London: Granada Publishing Ltd., 1983.

Wyman, Carolyn. "Life With a Strad." *Yale Magazine* (December 1987).

Index